ISBN 978-1-331-71709-6
PIBN 10225434

1 MONTH OF FREE READING

at

www.ForgottenBooks.com

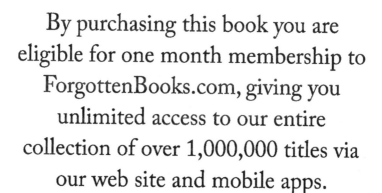

By purchasing this book you are eligible for one month membership to ForgottenBooks.com, giving you unlimited access to our entire collection of over 1,000,000 titles via our web site and mobile apps.

To claim your free month visit:
www.forgottenbooks.com/free225434

English
Français
Deutsche
Italiano
Español
Português

www.forgottenbooks.com

Mythology Photography **Fiction**
Fishing Christianity **Art** Cooking
Essays Buddhism Freemasonry
Medicine **Biology** Music **Ancient**
Egypt Evolution Carpentry Physics
Dance Geology **Mathematics** Fitness
Shakespeare **Folklore** Yoga Marketing
Confidence Immortality Biographies
Poetry **Psychology** Witchcraft
Electronics Chemistry History **Law**
Accounting **Philosophy** Anthropology
Alchemy Drama Quantum Mechanics
Atheism Sexual Health **Ancient History**
Entrepreneurship Languages Sport
Paleontology Needlework Islam
Metaphysics Investment Archaeology
Parenting Statistics Criminology
Motivational

THEOLOGICAL
TRANSLATION FUND LIBRARY.

VOL. XXIII.

EWALD'S
COMMENTARY ON THE PSALMS.

VOL. I.

COMMENTARY

ON

THE PSALMS.

BY THE LATE

DR. G. HEINRICH A. v. EWALD,

PROFESSOR OF ORIENTAL LANGUAGES IN THE UNIVERSITY OF GÖTTINGEN.

TRANSLATED BY THE REV. E. JOHNSON, M.A.

COMMENTARY ON THE POETICAL BOOKS OF THE OLD
TESTAMENT. DIVISION I.

VOL. I.

WILLIAMS AND NORGATE,

14, HENRIETTA STREET, COVENT GARDEN, LONDON;
AND 20, SOUTH FREDERICK STREET, EDINBURGH.

1880.

LONDON:
G NORMAN AND SON, PRINTERS, 29, MAIDEN LANE,
COVENT GARDEN.

TRANSLATOR'S NOTE.

————

THE present work consists of a translation of that portion of Ewald's "Poets of the Old Testament," which relates to the Psalms and the Lamentations (comprising the introductory matter to the Psalms from the first half, and the whole of the second half of Part I).

In following Ewald's exposition, we feel that we are under the guidance of a powerful and independent mind, which carries a vast erudition with ease, and never allows its originality to be suppressed. His treatment of the Psalms is characterized by intense poetic and religious sympathy, and by a keen and discriminating historical imagination. The Commentary can hardly be termed theological; it contains the results of the application of purely literary and historical methods to the study of Hebrew poetry. This constitutes the specific scientific value of the work; and it is perhaps the best course to reserve the theological and Messianic aspects for separate treatment and discussion, as being matters on which difference of opinion and controversy prevail. The great service of Ewald consists in laying firmly the scientific basis, in applying the general laws of literature, which include the laws of psychology, to the study of the Old Testament. Ewald's preface is interesting as containing some expression of his general views on this subject, with criticisms on the work of some of his eminent follow-labourers in this field. It is to be regretted that he should have permitted himself to have spoken with such dogmatism and severity of esteemed commentators like Delitzsch, Hengstenberg, and others. But Ewald, as is well known, is as conspicuous by the faults of his temper, *les défauts de ses qualités,* as by the power of his intellect and the extent of his scholarship. Happily, controversial references are excluded from the body of the work ; and we are left to follow undisturbed the course of his beautiful and spiritual exposition of these immortal songs. As to style, Ewald falls behind his matter ; his sentences are long and clumsy, his language often diffuse and redundant. The translator, while keeping close to the original, has endeavoured to aid the English reader by simplifying and breaking up to some extent the structure of his periods, and hopes to have produced a faithful and intelligible rendering.

The references by the simple number of the paragraph are to Ewald's Hebrew Grammar ; those by the Roman capital I. are to the first half of the first part of the *Dichter des Alten Bundes.*

E. JOHNSON.

September, 1880.

PREFACE.*

"In this second edition there is much that is made the subject of still closer inquiry and definition. Especially the historical elements, according to the principles already laid down in the first edition are further pursued,—more coherently arranged, and more completely exhibited. However, it is not very easy, nor indeed according to my taste, to say everything that might be said in favour of the opinions set forth or in opposition to the assumptions of others. It is well to explain satisfactorily the fundamental truths from an investigation of the facts before us, merely to indicate much that is collateral, and to leave many things to conjecture. Every superior writer has indeed before his eyes only the good, the experienced, and progressive among his readers. And if— along with the acuteness which I despise neither in others nor myself—I yet prize much more highly truthfulness, this quality is most valuable to me in the study of the Biblical books. To ascertain and firmly uphold their full undoubted truth is to me the one and only object of such writings. The pure and full truth will also, in the case of this peculiar Biblical book, not merely satisfy, but have the force to maintain itself by its own means; its beginning at least we will seize, its way we will not miss."

So ran the short preface which I wrote to the preceding edition on its completion. I hope that not a few readers at that time well understood the sense of these few words. But there began to appear, a few years later, a series of far larger works on the Psalter on the part of German scholars, which

---

* To the third edition of the *Psalms and Lamentations.*

is being continued to this latest time; and the question is not to be evaded here,—what attention have the authors of these works given to those brief words, but still more,—how have they treated our science in respect of the Psalms? In the first two editions of this work,—as could be obviously seen,—a science, in the stricter sense of the word, of the original relations and the true sense and value of the Psalms was in reality for the first time founded; and the above preface had, in a few clear strokes, pointed out the direction in which further labour may be most rightly and fruitfully carried on in this field. Further labour there might be in this field; this was already indicated in the above preface, as I have since shown, in fragmentary writings on several occasions.* To this my second labours of the year 1839 were still briefly confined, and they treated designedly of certain great features only, with such detail and care, that useful *addenda* in great number were possible. But what, now, has been the result of the large works which followed on this subject? Is science in the main advanced by them? Have they at least rightly apprehended the general beginnings of a more accurate science, which were there laid down, and not in some sort endeavoured to destroy them? We cannot here speak of isolated and small particulars; our question can in this place only touch general and great matters, which are concerned with this portion of the Bible. Alas! I can give no such answer to this question as I could wish to give.

The work, in four volumes of Hengstenberg, begun in 1842, was carried out with aims and objects which can neither be defended from a scientific nor from an ecclesiastical and Christian point of view: every friend of genuine science and every profound Christian could see that at once; and if many eyes preferred at that time to remain blind to the fact, as many

---

* In a larger conneXion in the *Beiträgen zur geschichte der ältesten auslegung und spracherklärung des A. Ts. I.* (Stuttgart, 1844), and in the *Jahrb. der Bibl. Wiss.*, v., 164 sqq., viii., 65 sqq , xi., 9 sq.

have now become open enough. But that the two large volumes of his half or whole imitator Delitzsch with their many-hued piety and their equally many-hued, and almost utterly perverse and vain science are in nowise better, I have elsewhere sufficiently shown.*

In quite other directions tend the general errors by which v. Lengerke's work (1847) and then that of Justus Olshausen have carried away; but in their pernicious character they are in nowise second to the former. He who has such confused notions of the height and depth of true religion, can as little correctly value the historical as the poetical element of the Psalms; and he who deals with Hebrew in the arbitrary manner of Olshausen, is not made for a happy expounder of these songs. The very freedom of judgment which he takes upon himself, and is able within Evangelical Christianity to assume, becomes the greatest misfortune to him. I have, however, elsewhere,† said enough of the later of these two works.

And what shall be said of Hupfeld's work in four volumes,—which, behind the most baseless pretensions, conceals so arrant an ignorance of language and history,—and with a tasteless, dry intelligence thinks to be able to deface the sense, the strain and artistic quality of Biblical poetry, and by self-created oblique doubts, and pale negations, to obliterate every better understanding that has been gained; and fears not to introduce vain, evil words and thoughts!‡ The Psalms, meanwhile, are happily a hundredfold better, and their explanation is at present much more secure than the expositor of to-day would make them.

Lastly, a new work of Hitzig's in three volumes has appeared: I can only wish that he had remained true to that spirit which

---

* In the *Jahrb. der Bibl. Wiss.*, x., pp. 194 sqq., xi., pp. 210 sqq.—On the new edition of the long obsolete work of De Wette, comp. *ibid.*, viii., pp. 162 sqq.

† *Ibid.* v., pp. 250 sqq.

‡ *Ibid.* vii., pp. 137 sqq., ix., pp. 164 sqq, *Gott. Gel. Anz.* 1862, pp. 176 sqq. Comp. with this what is said in vii., pp. 246 sqq., which he was bound to answer.

bade fair here in Göttingen, 1828-9, to develop in him, and
which—apart from a few defects, then already visible in the
higher consideration of the Bible—expressed itself in his first
works, exciting good hopes. But the Straussic desert-wind of
false freedom which subsequently arose only fructified those
defects in his mind; and some years back I expressed how
deeply I was distressed by the running-wild from all historical
consideration and explanation which suddenly appeared in his
work on the Psalms, of 1836; to which, however, at that
time I thought it well to publicly oppose nothing but my
silence in the preceding edition of this work, and perhaps
something in the sense of its above-repeated brief preface.
Nothing can be more untrue and perverse than the opinion
that there are generally in the Psalter Makkabæan songs; and
now even the greatest part of the Psalms is derived from that
source,—indeed songs from the last century before Christ, and
of the utterly degenerate Hasmonæan king Jannaeos! Perversity on this side cannot be greater, than upon the other in
Hengstenberg and Delitzsch; and the logical consequence
is dreary approximations, indeed tentative reconciliations of
these nevertheless irreconcilable opposites, as may have been
long observed. When experience showed what evil seed for all
true freedom, and sound advance in the fruitful explanation
and application of the Bible would have sprung up (but with
this was peculiarly connected the disturbance of the great
German shipwreck-year of 1848) I thought it necessary to
tear out the roots of the ever-widely spreading and perilous
error.* If he now in his new work seeks to re-set these roots
in a richer soil, as if they would sprout better there, we may
quite calmly wait to see whether this will be so, and I do not
think it necessary to speak further here on the subject. But
there are found in my old pupil,†—apart from these tough,

---

* In the *Jahrbb. der Bibl. Wiss.*, vi., pp. 20 sqq , viii., pp. 165 sqq., comp. ix.,
pp. 94 sq., 172.

† It has never occurred to me so to term my mere hearers; but it is somewhat
different with the others.

tenacious baseless prejudices,—many a better light, as he is, to his advantage, distinguished from the preceding three scholars in that he generally finds actual songs of David in the Psalter, and labours to bring them to light; although along with this such entirely groundless assumptions are forced forward, as that such are only to be looked for between Pss. iii.—xix., but among these, such as Pss. ix., x., are like-wise derivable from David. But what is one to say when one sees that such a procedure is now recommended to the German people as the only correct one, and any that springs from deeper knowledge and conscientiousness is slandered,—that all German science ever sinks more deeply on such a basis, and the spirits who boast of Evangelical freedom think they can do nothing better than in rivalry with their enlightened oppo-nents, promote this ever deeper decay.*

By all these works, then, the true task which lies before us at the present day in connexion with the Psalter is very little furthered. They contain rather (which is worst of all) in the main only retrogressions, and this in a field where such retro-gressions are quite inexcusable, while they exercise a per-nicious influence, and include in themselves the danger of a new destruction of all that is best which at the present day has been partly attained,—partly is yet to be striven for by true means on the open and levelled road. Of course there is con-cerned here only in a particular case that which holds good of the whole of present Biblical science; but the point at issue in this particular case is the following.

The Psalter has come down to us: we can neither change its contents nor the grand history from which it first pro-ceeded. But if it is to remain for us neither a dead superfluous book nor one mis-used for a thousand evil objects,—it is our duty to understand it and the whole living history from which it proceeded, as completely and as surely as is in anywise possible. Let us begin, then, with the certain understanding

---

* The theological reviews here meant I will absolutely not mention here.

of the particular: the sensible defects and great errors in the ordinary expositors begin here at the threshold. When every word, every clause, and every member of a song has been so understood that one can sincerely feel that the whole original sense from which the poet derived his song and shaped it with its full vitality and truth, has again become fresh and living in ourselves,—let the particulars be strictly compared : it will be found that notwithstanding all the extraordinary diversity of the many songs, many nevertheless stand so near to one another, that they may be ascribed to the same period or even to the same poet.

If these pieces of information be now vitalized by a true acquaintance with the whole great history of the people, and all these toils be unweariedly carried on, if it begin ever anew with most original independence, if throughout nothing but the pure truth be sought in this field of inquiry,—it will then be seen what noble fruit thence germinates, what rock-firm truths in the most different directions may be attained, and how the true worth of these songs may thus only be recognized and rightly prized. It will then be found that the Psalms are incomparably better than the various superficial expositors at the present day—according to their various follies—think them to be. There will be heard in them the wondrous voices which accompany almost step by step the development of all true religion through all centuries from David to Nehemiah. The history of the rise of our present Psalter will also be ascertained with satisfactory certainty. But he who seriously thus seeks to do his duty in the case of this Biblical book, as our time in the highest degree demands, —will, finally, feel no desire whatever to enter into much controversy with others ; and I here leave for the third time this work without any controversy with other commentators. Only the road in which one pursues one's inquiries, and would desire to allure other good energies to joint inquiry and further explanation, must be kept level, and clean ; and equally must it ever be clear what kind of endeavour at a given time is the most necessary and correct.

It is not at the present day the Hengstenbergs and Delitzschs, on whose great errors in the treatment of the Psalter and the whole Bible so much that is most important and indispensable turns; their whole aims belong to a past time, and it has long been easy to see how entirely unfruitful they remain, and must remain. But in the present day really palpable and profound errors proceed from the quarter of those who would offer something new and better; who demand and assume to themselves all freedom for this purpose, yet give themselves up, in science, to a thousand perverse impulses and interested feelings. That antiquity which the Puseys and Hengstenbergs pursue amongst us, just as the actual Popes and their worshippers do on the other side, is irreparably destroyed, and is visibly coming to the end which it deserves. If the new ideas which must make their way, and without the attainment of which all our present work will rush back into the most horrible chaos, have nevertheless to struggle sorely— they only must bear the immediate responsibility for this who do not carry on this struggle with clean hands,—and who while they exclaim loudly and constantly enough against the oppressions and persecutions which they may have had to endure,—are themselves so insincere that they will not comprehend how perverse their whole struggle is. If no country suffers under these evils, as is to be expected, like our own great and broad Germany, and if it suffers equally on all sides, in the North and the South, in the temporal and the spiritual sphere,—people and princes alike; will not those who boast of freedom finally apprehend what is true freedom? With this question I must here conclude. And if precisely this field of science be on many grounds one of the most difficult, the responsibility is the heavier of those who would cultivate it.

March, 1866.

CONTENTS OF VOL. I.

PAGE

GENERAL OBSERVATIONS ON THE BOOK OF PSALMS:

   I. ITS CONTENTS AND OBJECT 1

   II. ITS RISE 4

   III. THE INSCRIPTIONS OR ANNOTATIONS OF THE PSALMS 34

ON THE HISTORICAL EXPLANATIONS OF THE PSALMS . . 59

TRANSLATION AND EXPOSITION OF THE PSALMS AND
   LAMENTATIONS:

   I. SONGS OF DAVID AND OF HIS TIME . . . 64

   II. SONGS AFTER THE DIVISION OF THE DAVIDIC KINGDOM
     UNTIL ITS END:

     1. SCATTERED VOICES DOWN TO THE EIGHTH CENTURY 157

     2. NEW ELEVATION AT THE END OF THE EIGHTH CEN-
       TURY 216

     3. THE LAST TIMES OF THE KINGDOM . . . 238

The Psalms explained in the present volume will be found as follows :—

Psalm	i.	p. 318	Psalm	xxxix.	p. 200
..	ii.	,, 147	,,	xli.	,, 187
	v.	,, 250	,,	xlv.	,, 165
	vi.	,, 183	,,	xlvi.	,, 216
	vii.	,, 74	,,	xlviii.	,, 216
	viii.	,, 103	,,	l.	,, 310
	ix.	,, 320	,,	lii.	,, 250
	x.	,, 320	,,	liv.	,, 250
	xi.	,, 71	,,	lv.	,, 250
	xii.	,, 197	,,	lvi.—lviii.	,, 250
	xiii.	,, 183	,,	lix.	,, 290
	xv.	,, 84	,,	lx.	,, 112
	xviii.	,, 117	,,	lxi.	,, 250
..	xix.	,, 97	,,	lxii.	,, 200
	xx.	,, 158	,,	lxiii.	,, 250
	xxi.	,, 160	,,	lxiv.	,, 250
,,	xxiii.	,, 174	,,	lxv.	,, 232
,,	xxiv. 7-10.	,, 79	,,	lxvi. 13-20.	,, 187
,,	xxiv. 1-6.	,, 82	,,	lxxii.	,, 333
	xxvi.	,, 296	,,	lxxv.	,, 216
..	xxvii.	,, 174	,,	lxxvi.	,, 216
,,	xxviii.	,, 296	,,	lxxxviii.	,, 307
.	xxix.	., 91	,,	xc.	,, 208
	xxx.	,, 187	,,	ci.	,, 86
,	xxxi.	,, 302	,,	cx.	,, 107
,,	xxxvi.	,, 250	,,	cxl.—cxlii.	,, 240
,,	xxxvii.	,, 320	,,	cxliv. 12-15.	,, 154

GENERAL OBSERVATIONS ON THE BOOK OF PSALMS.*

I. ITS CONTENTS AND OBJECT.

THE Psalter is, in fact, the one collection of songs which has come down to us from the earlier Israelitish antiquity. The so-called "Psalms of Solomon"† contain only a small later collection of similar songs. One might accordingly be disposed to regard the Psalter as a miscellaneous collection, having no other object than to gather together scattered songs, perhaps the best of each kind. In truth, the book at first sight resembles a confused medley, as of accidental waifs and strays of song. But one does not comprehend why this should have been the case; since certainly David's songs would have been sought out before all others, and have been brought into a collection. Now, of the incontestably genuine songs of David contained in the books of Samuel, the 18th Psalm is alone found in this collection. It is inconceivable that all the rest should have been omitted from sheer ignorance. If we look further

---

* The productions, which appeared subsequently to the first edition of this volume, of *H*engstenberg and Delitzsch (*Symbolae ad Psalmos illustrandos isagogicae, Leipsic*, 1846, repeated in his *Commentary on the Psalms*) proceed on the assumptions of a spurious piety. That of Hupfeld, on the other hand, is characterized by peculiarly spurious and false scientific pretension. The above fall far behind the contents of that first edition of mine; and it is impossible to say which of the two views is the more erroneous and unsound.

† On these comp. the *Gesch. des V. Isr.*, iv., pp. 392 sq., and the *Jahrbb. der B. W*, xi., p. 215.

into the general contents of the songs here collected, a certain similarity appears amidst all diversity of details, both as respects the object and the tenor of the songs. All of them refer to the Divine,—in very different ways, indeed, but so as to be readily recognized,—as prayer, as thanksgiving, and praise, as simple thought and aspiration, as representations of Divine things and truth, as exhortations to godly works. Even where a king is addressed, Pss. xxi., lxxii., cx., the Divine, in its sublimity and dignity, is more prominent in thought than the human. Ps. xlv. certainly forms an exception, as not immediately starting from the Divine; yet it is a fine example of the manner in which the more purely human poetic art was penetrated by the same loftier spirit which inspired the Israelitish life and invention generally. Besides this, it is a very essential feature that this Divine object is regarded more in a general than a personal aspect, while very many songs remain without any personal reference. In others the peculiar reference which the poet had in his eye admits, without great difficulty, a wider application, and may be readily repeated by others with similar feeling under similar circumstances. It is clear that there are particular songs which avoid a personal sense; and although the prophetic but strongly personal song, 2 Sam. xxiii., might perhaps have been included in the collection as well as Ps. ci., or Isa. xxxviii., as well as Pss. xxxii., li.; and Jonah ii. not less readily than Ps. xlii.; yet, on both grounds, an elegy like 2 Sam. i. 19-29 could be in little agreement with the style of these songs.

Thus it might appear as if the object of this collection were merely that of gathering songs for the edification of the community of the true religion. But on closer observation it is seen to be one of a more restricted kind, and that in a twofold aspect. It is, in the first place, apparent that the songs referring to Sion and the holy city obtained the preference over others; so that the *Davidic* songs here predominate not merely because David was the greatest lyric poet, but also because he was the first and greatest poet whose songs glorified Sion as the holy mount. There is a manifest distance between these and the songs of the times before David or from other districts than Judah. For whatever may have been the original relations of Ps. xc. or Ps. xlv., nothing can be decided by these two songs alone. Secondly, it is equally unmistakable that all these songs were designed not merely for the edification of the individual, but above all for public use in the Temple at Jerusalem. We do not indeed know, and cannot maintain, that the whole of the songs and fragments here collected were at any time, without exception, or (as in the so-called Reformed Church) in their order publicly sung in the Temple. Moreover, the entire large collection presented in the book has manifestly, without a special object of this kind, rather grown historically out of more ancient collections of songs, as will be shown presently. But their employment in the Levitical Temple-service was, without doubt, at least a main object which at last governed the collection ; and owing to the fact that this musical service obtained its subsisting higher order in David and Solomon's time, songs still more ancient came to excluded. Hence the existence of this great collection is a weighty testimony to the power with which the ancient true religion grew from David's time, especially round about the Temple in Jerusalem.

The designed use of the collection is most clearly seen in its second half, especially from Ps. xc. onwards, where the Temple songs accumulate. Yet even the songs which have originally' no such public destination, particularly many in the first half, were, in the intention of the collector, certainly to be used by every individual in the community, as the source of holy thoughts and a help to pious contemplation. The oldest collectors had without question the further historical object in view of preserving what was most beautiful and enduring in this field of the more serious songs of antiquity, or—what was the same thing in their eyes—of collecting the Divine songs of

David and his friends. The inscriptions with statements of historical occasions, Pss. li.—lxiii., show that these collectors had also a correct feeling that many of the songs originally sprung from some particular reference and genuine historical occasion. Yet, on the other hand, this object was certainly limited at an early period by the other—that of collecting more general sacred songs, as is shown by the oldest name of such a collection, *Prayers* (therefore not songs generally) *of David*, lxxii. 2⁰. The historical object, as one more special, necessarily and increasingly receded before the more general one, of collecting sacred songs for the use of the community. And hence the entire present collection received from later Jews the name תְּהִלִּים, תלים, ὕμνοι—a name which, as it stands only in the Masoretic or external superscription, thereby alone betrays its late origin. Concerning this name we must presently speak further.

II. ITS RISE.

That the present large collection of songs was not the first and solitary one, but that others preceded it, is sufficiently evident in general. But to recognize this more closely and more certainly in detail is the real task before us; and although almost all external information and resources for this inquiry are wanting, yet the large collection in its actual condition offers a mass of means and of proofs, when once we know how to make genuine discoveries of the latter, and correctly to apply the former. The comparison of the songs with one another leads to inferences respecting the age, the series and order of all these songs in the mass; *e.g.*, we can easily see that increasingly towards the end of the collection lighter song-echoes of a later period follow, although too in the former series a few of this kind cannot be concealed.

Further, longér series of very similar songs frequently follow one another, uninterrupted by dissimilar ones, or only here and there so interrupted. Besides this internal comparison, we have as an extremely important means of investigation the mass of the *inscriptions* (*beischriften*) to be presently explained in detail. Under this *one* term we include *superscriptions,* which are the majority, *interscriptions,* and *subscriptions* of the individual Psalms. In these inscriptions,—their sense, their style, their existence or absence, a very large part of the oldest history of the collection is contained ; and whilst they give us the earliest traditions and opinions on the style and manner, design and arrangement, composers and occasions of the songs, they permit us to cast the deepest glances into the origin and rise of the whole great collection before us.

1. First of all, we recognize in this way the distribution of the present collection into three greater divisions, which must originally have been particular collections. That which now stands at the head must be considered the oldest, and that which stands at the end as the latest in point of time. These three particular collections are, according to present numera- tion—(1) Pss. i.—xli. ; (2) Pss. xlii.—lxxxix. ; (3) Pss. xc.—cl. All the various indications lead at last, when taken together, to this hypothesis.

If we consider—apart, in the first instance, from every other consideration—simply the common contents of each of these three parts, we find on a closer view that each, notwithstand- ing every variation, contains a mass of songs of a certain period and style peculiar to itself. In Pss. i.—xli. we find, along with much of later date, the true fulness of Davidic and generally of older songs—a fulness which to an equal degree recurs in none of the following parts, and which thus clearly designates this first part as the oldest basis of the entire present collection. The third part, Pss. xc.—cl., as certainly embraces, predominantly, the large mass of later and very late songs, though here and there a few more ancient, even Davidic songs appear to have been added supplementally. The part comprising Pss. xlii.—lxxxix. is distinguished by this peculiarity—that it gives in the main the songs of the middle period, mingled indeed with many later ones, but probably without a single specimen received in perfect purity from the most ancient time. Later songs run through all three parts; but are most sparse in the first, in the second begin to thicken, and predominate in the third. This relation, beautifully as it fits in with the order of our Psalter, does not flow from an empty assumption under the influence of which the perusal of the whole has been entered upon. It is the last deduction from accurate acquaintance with, and consideration of, all the details.

But further it may be remarked that each of these three parts must have passed through the hands of a special collector. This is seen—

(1.) From the inscriptions, which, on account of their great uniformity, are for the most part to be referred to the collectors, and not to chance hands that busied themselves with the work. There are superscriptions indeed in all these parts, but with important differences. The first part has superscriptions before every song; at least the two exceptions are insignificant, since Ps. x. belongs to Ps. ix., Pss. i. and ii. may probably have been placed before an already existing collection; and, though apparently quite late, Ps. xxxiii. may have been interpolated in such collection. The second part has also superscriptions throughout, with the single exception of Ps. lxxi., since Ps. xliii. belongs to Ps. xlii. Ps. lxxi. may be an appendix of later time to the series of songs named Davidic, li.—lxx.; or, as in style it belongs entirely to this series, it may at some time have been mistakenly combined with Ps. lxx., as is the case at present in several copies. The fact that in some copies Ps. xxxiii. is blended with Ps. xxxii. may be explained from the mere conjecture of certain copyists. Yet the style and contents of the superscriptions of this second part are slightly different, while they are elsewhere similar. In the first part the superscriptions state only rarely and sporadically an historical occasion, Pss. iii., vii., xviii., xxx., xxxiv; and these rest in the case of the really most ancient, *i.e.*, Davidic songs, on genuine tradition (comp. on this below). In the second part they give in one place, Pss. li.-lxiii., such historical notes almost in profusion; but these are, as will be made clear presently, of quite another derivation and stamp. The third part, on the other hand, has in· general very few superscriptions; these few are not homogeneous; and only those of Pss. ci., cviii.—cx., cxxxviii.—cxliii. bear a striking likeness to those of the first two parts. Similarly the סֶלָה explained on pp. 231-233 (*Dichter des A. B.*, i.) is found only in the first two parts, and in Pss. cxl.—cxliii., but occurs much more frequently in the second part than in the first. However, what is here most noteworthy is—

(2.) Even to the very language of the songs this stamp of the hand of either one of the three collectors, or at least (which on many grounds is the more probable) of one of the earliest copyists extends,—I allude to the remarkable interchange of the names of God. In the first and third of the parts the name *Jahvé* is found predominant, according to the custom in those ages. The name *Elôhim* is indeed found along with it, but almost exclusively used in the manner elsewhere usual.*

---

* In cases like Ps. iii. 3 ; vii. 10 ; ix. 18 ; x. 4, 13 ; xiv. 1, 2 (in ver. 5 the word is merely dependent on ver. 2). In xxxvi. 2, אלהים stands only for the sake of the more general signification, and thus, according to usage elsewhere, quite correctly suiting the sense. In deviation from this it stands only in Ps. v. 11 ; xxv. 22 ; xxxvi. 8 ; and besides these later songs, twice in a Davidic one, Ps. vii. 11, 12. Those later poets might have begun, according to the custom which crept in with the later writers, to use Elôhim for Jahvé ; and in Ps. vii. 11, 12 the correct יהוה is found at least in *one* copy. But, supposing the אלהים instead of יהוה had been written in all these five places only by a later hand, and under the influence of the same later faith, which is so distinctly expressed from Ps. xlii. to lxxxiii , and partly in Ps. lxxxiv.: the difference between Pss. i.—xli. and Pss. xlii.—lxxxix. remains too great to permit what has been maintained above to be set aside. I now observe only further, that I published this entire view concerning the interchange of the Divine names in the first edition of this volume,

That appeal cannot be made to Ps. cviii. will soon be made
clear. But in the second part the name *Elôhim,* on the other
hand, predominates from its very beginning, Ps. xlii., to
Ps. lxxxiii. throughout, so greatly, that *Jahvé* appears far more
rarely, and only as if here and there mistakenly written by an
altering hand.*

What is to be thought of so striking a phenomenon? That
it has nothing in common with the interchange of the same
Divine names in the Pentateuch admits of no doubt: the
poets of those earlier centuries used habitually the name
Jahvé. Are we now to suppose that the poets of this portion
made designedly an exception to this? and that all the very
various poets here united did the same? This would be in
itself inconceivable, even if it were not confuted by the fact,
that the same songs, when they appear in other parts, do not
bear this stamp: comp. Ps. liii. with Ps. xiv.; Ps. lxx. with
Ps. xl.; or, again, Ps. lxxi. with Ps. xxii.

Moreover, this rarer stamp ceases with Ps. lxxxiii., and
scarcely leaves one last trace in Ps. lxxxiv. (ver. 9); while,
nevertheless, Pss. lxxxiv.—lxxxix., with the exception of Ps.
lxxxvi., may—both with regard to the superscriptions and to
their whole style and manner—be readily conceived as forming
a whole with Pss. xlii.—lxxxiii. There remains only the

---

without knowing anything of Gesenius' explanations of אלהים in his Thesaurus,
which, moreover, are quite inapt.

* Pss. xlvi. 8, 12 ; xlvii. 3, 6; xlviii. 2, 9; lv. 17, 23; lvi. 11; lviii. 7; lix. 4, 6, 9;
lxiv. 11; lxviii. 17, 21; lxix. 7, 14, 17, 32, 34; lxx. 2, 5; lxxi. 1, 5, 16; lxxiii. 28;
lxxiv. 18; lxxv. 9; lxxvi. 12; lxxviii. 4, 21; lxxix. 5; lxxx. 5, 20; lxxxi 16;
lxxxiii. 17, 19; from which passages those can readily be abstracted where יהוה
is united with אדני, and where it was almost as difficult to alter as in l. 1;
lxxxi. 11. Again, the name אדני, very rare in the first and third parts (comp.
Ps. ii. 4, repeated xxxvii. 13; Pss. xc. 1; cx. 5; cxxx. 6) is strikingly frequent in
the second, xliv. 24; li. 17; liv. 6; lv. 10; lvii. 10; lix. 12; lxii. 13; lxvi. 18;
lxviii. 12, 18, 20, 23, 27, 33; lxxiii. 20; lxxvii. 3, 8; lxxviii. 65. This is less
decisive here, since אדני is in some places more frequent, as Ps. lxxxvi., Ps. cxxx.,
Ps. xxxv., and Ps. xxxviii. It is worthy of note that Ps. lxx. 6 gives אלהים
for the אדני, Ps. xl. 18, as if יהוה had originally stood there, as still in many
copies.

hypothesis that not so much the collector of this book of songs, Pss. xlii.—lxxxix. (for *he* would have surely remained consistent to the end) as one of the oldest copyists of the book introduced that interchange of the names of God according to his own pleasure,—perhaps under the influence of a similar belief to that which led the later Jews persistently to avoid the utterance of יהוה. This name יהוה is certainly found in the later books of the Old Testament; indeed, it predominates in the evidently later songs of the third part. But, on the other hand, it cannot be supposed that the use of this name was suddenly and universally avoided once for all. On the contrary, in the first instance, individual composers or writers might begin habitually to avoid the name, as, *e.g.*, Qohélet habitually and Nehemiah almost habitually (comp. i. 5 ; v. 13) writes Elôhim for Jahvé, while the Chronicler, again, allows himself greater freedom in the use of the name Jahvé.*
And thus the second part must have passed through the hands of a very ancient writer, who throughout wrote Elôhim in preference to Jahvé, yet here and there allowed the latter name to stand, and towards the end, in the appendix, Pss. lxxxiv.—lxxxix., which is on other grounds somewhat distinctive, again departed, from whatever cause, from his custom. From this remarkable phenomenon,—to mention this cursorily,—other not unimportant deductions may be drawn, *e.g.*, that Ps. lxxxvi. 14 is borrowed literally with the name Elôhim from liv. 4, 5 ; and Ps. cviii. from Pss. lvii. and lx., according to their present style. Therefore Pss. liv., lvii., lx. were not merely written earlier, but also had been already brought together by this same collector, when Ps. lxxxvi. came into the second, and Ps. cviii. into the third part.

(3.) Lastly, the *subscriptions* are here to be brought under consideration.

They are of two kinds :

a. Four, which in the intention of a last collector of the

---

* Comp. also what is said in the *Gesch. des V. Isr.*, i., p. 244, *note.*

entire present book might appear to designate, in the form of doxologies, the close of a longer section. They occur after Pss. xli., lxxii., lxxxix., cvi., and another similar to them was to be expected with the same reason after cl. But it is in itself necessary that we should here subject these fragments of song to a closer consideration. They proceed from the act of blessing. Blessing signifies in Hebrew originally what is equivalent to wishes or greetings of increase and prosperity.*

But if the relation is between man and God, so, according to the true religion, God alone in the stricter sense can be the blessing one. And the manner in which from the earliest times His blessing was asked by the priest in winged sayings for the assembled community we saw above (*Dichter des A. B.*, i., p. 35). But man may at times half despair even of the true God; and he can never be ashamed to rejoice in Him always more inwardly and deeply, always to welcome Him more freely, and so to approach Him cheerfully, as with ever fresh gratitude and with his own best greeting. And chiefly so when a peculiar impulse to this spontaneously presents itself. Such a motive is offered, amongst other occasions, on the retrospect of a happily completed work, when the spirit breathes more freely; and so on the conclusion of the composition or even toilsome copying of a lengthy writing; and the reader of it will, too, willingly join in such a word of blessing at the end. But in the ancient people Israel there existed too much sound feeling, especially in all matters of religion, to permit it to have become, as in the school of Islam hypocrisy, an ordinary and quasi-pious custom to conclude each book with such a phrase of blessing. We see only

---

* בֵּרֵךְ signifies as related to Arab. *blgh* and Sk. *vṛh* (vrk)—as was already remarked in the *Oesch. des V. Isr.*, i. p. 586 and elsewhere—a striving forth. glowing and becoming ripe, and בֶּרֶךְ, *knee*, is properly a bunch. From this word is first formed, entirely afresh, the strong active בֵּרֵךְ for cause to glow, wish prosperity, like our *greet* (grüssen) from *great* (gross.) The German *wachsen*, Eng. *wax*, is originally the same.

Books of Psalms thus conclude in the Old Testament, and
with them it is as if those loftier Divine tones which had
penetrated their whole structure from the beginning resounded
once more at the end; in the like poetic sublimity, but
with greater conciseness and freedom. If this be so,
we can readily understand that such a blessing addressed
to God (a Doxology) is, from the first, by no means intended
merely to designate the end of a particular section of
one Book of Psalms, and so to be uniformly repeated at the
end of all such sections; and that we must certainly not so
regard the four fragments of song at the end of Pss. xli.,
lxxii., lxxxix., cvi., we learn from their peculiar and great
diversities. For the saying in Ps. cvi. 48 :

Blessed be Jahvé , Israel's God,
   from everlasting to everlasting !
   and let all people say, " Assuredly ! "

does not belong peculiarly to this place. Rather does it sum up
—according to the elucidation given on p. 192 (*Dichter des
A. B.,* i.)—along with ver. 47, in the choir of priests, the
whole prolonged song to which in sense it well conforms; and
hence calls at the end upon the whole community to express
their concurrence aloud by Yea! Any individual indeed who
thus blesses God on his own account in the old priestly forms
of speech may further particularize his own just expressed wish
by a short Yea (Amen) at the end. Thus he may conclude, in
full self-assurance and with purest faith. Yet, as all these
sayings were certainly of priestly origin, so, too, this use of
Assuredly ! or *Yea !* is in the first instance a derived one. In
the three other cases where the saying has become a mere
poetic expression, the phrase *and let all people say* is correctly
omitted; and on the other hand the *Assuredly!* (or *Verily !*)
is doubled, in order to round off poetically the last line, which
had been otherwise too short. But the saying sounds at its
fullest and noblest only in Ps. lxxii. 18, 19 :

> *Blessed be Jahvé God, Israel's God,*
>   *who alone doeth wonders!*
> *and blessed be His awful name for ever,*
>   *be the whole earth full of his majesty!**
> *Verily and Verily!*

Here we truly feel the new poetic inspiration which now penetrated such ancient sacred words. The same condensed in Ps. lxxxix. 53:

> *Blessed be Jahvé for ever!*
> *Verily and verily!*

Again in Ps. xli. 14:

> *Blessed be Jahvé, Israel's God,*
>   *from everlasting to everlasting!*
> *Verily and Verily!*

Here it is far more like the above priestly utterance, and so far may pass for older.

Now, on the hypothesis that these utterances of blessing were first appended by the last collector of the entire present Book of Psalms to denote the end of the sections made by him, one cannot well comprehend why the utterance should have these three variations; and further, one would expect, inferentially, a similar utterance on the completion of the Book after Ps. cl. For the fact that this Ps. cl. itself sounds like a song purposely composed as a conclusion to one great collection of songs of praise to Jahvé, cannot here be taken into consideration; since the collector might have easily added a further short utterance of blessing for uniformity's sake. Again, such an utterance of blessing is by no means the same thing as a song of praise like Ps. cl. At all events, the absence of such utterances after Ps. cl. can the less induce us to see in the three blessings after Pss. xli., lxxii., lxxxix., merely the hand of the same last collector and publisher of the entire book. So far this phenomenon agrees with the foregoing. But again,

b. We find placed as a subscription of quite another

---

* The connexion of words according to *Lehrb.* § 281 *b.*

kind, after the blessing in Ps. lxxii., the sentence, entirely unpoetical, *The prayers of David, the Son of Jishai, are at an end.* This, indeed, confirms the fact that the blessing after Ps. lxxii. is actually intended to denote this end, but otherwise it stands in the present great Book of Psalms as extremely obscure and unintelligible. For in itself such an observation would be in place far earlier, as a subscription of the first part, Pss. i.—xli.; because in that section nearly all the songs are designated as Davidic, as was remarked above, p. 5. From Ps. xlii. to Ps. l., however, songs of other singers are found; and then the songs from Pss. li. to lxxii. are designated in their superscriptions as Davidic, with the exception only of Pss. lxvi. and lxvii., where, however, a few copies supply the designation; of Ps. lxxi., which in the copies appears to have been at one time generally united with Ps. lxx., as many still connect them; and of the last, Ps. lxxii., which is ascribed, exceptionally, to Solomon; so that all these exceptions are insignificant with reference to the main matter. The phenomenon is the more striking, because the series, Pss. lxxiii.—lxxxix., is, just as Ps. xlii., ascribed to other singers than David, with the single exception of Ps. lxxxvi., which, however, was noticed on p. 8, on other grounds, as foreign to this place. There is no way out of all these difficulties but by assuming that the songs Pss. xlii.—l. originally stood immediately before Ps. lxxiii., and were only transposed by a later hand; and, secondly, that the songs xlii.—lxxxix. sprung from a particular collection which was so arranged that the first half was to contain Davidic songs, and the second those of other singers. Thus may be explained (1) most readily why the end of the Davidic songs might be noted after Ps. lxxii.; the subscription has thus only the same sense which it has in other books (Job xxxi. 40; Jer. li. 64); it merely notes that now something quite different follows, and that a great section here occurs. But thus there follow (2) in original order correctly after one another Pss. xlii.—xlix., as songs of the sons of Qôrach, and Pss. l., lxxiii.—lxxx. as songs of Asaph; of which we are to speak further presently.

And with all this agrees (3) the fact that the blessings of these two sections, according to p. 12, point to the same hand, and to one which is quite different from that of the collector of Pss. i.—xli. Further proofs which tend uniformly to show that Pss. xlii.—lxxxix. composed in this sense a quite peculiar collection, will follow presently on the review of all the inscriptions.*

2. But further, closer investigation shows that each of these three collections pre-supposes, again, yet earlier collections and points back, in many ways, to older formations and changes.

(1.) This may most readily be seen and proved in the case of the third collection, because it, as the latest, has not undergone so many changes; and the quarry from which it was compiled is almost open to the light of day. Pss. xcii.—c. stand out at once for recognition as a peculiar small collection. They are so nearly related in contents, stamp, and language, that one is disposed to refer nearly all to one poet. Only Ps. xciv. is of somewhat different style and language; but all manifestly spring from the same period—a period in which the stock of the two first collections had long been in existence; for Ps. xcvi. is an echo of Ps. xxix.; and Ps. xcvii. 8 is repeated from xlviii. 12. Again, these songs are characterized by the fact that with the slight exceptions, xcii. 1, xcviii. 1, c. 1, they are without any annotations. In short, everything leads us to believe that these eight songs, in themselves separate from their surroundings, stood at first quite apart.

---

* Probably the same copyist who, as we saw on p. 7, altered the name of God, transposed the songs; and his hand may be recognized in the fact that, Pss. lix. 6; lxxx. 5, 8, 15, 20; lxxxiv. 9, he introduces the collocation אלהים צבאות, which appears nowhere else in the Old Testament. This indeed is explained from the like cases to those in *Lehrb.* § 290 e, but at the time could only pass for a great innovation. Further, the view above developed respecting Pss. xlii.—lxxxix. better agrees with all the facts than if one assumed, in order to explain the intermediate series, Ps. xlii.—l., that Pss. i.—l. and Pss. li.—lxxxix. were originally connected as two collections, each independent of the other, so arranged that first David's songs, Pss. i.—xli.; Pss. li.—lxxii., should come, and then those of his singers should follow. Whatever may be said for this hypothesis, and however more facile in a certain point of view, it nevertheless appears to me at present, looking at all other traces and indications, more forced and less elucidatory than the former.

That the fifteen songs, Pss. cxx.—cxxxiv., composed a special original collection may be conjectured from the words prefixed to each of these songs, and found nowhere else, שִׁיר הַמַּעֲלוֹת; and may be concluded still more certainly from the internal characteristics of the songs. For they are as closely related to one another in spirit and life, language and thought, as they are sharply distinguished from the adjacent ones ; in fact, from almost all others. Ps. cxxxii. only is of another kind, though probably from a period not much later. The above constantly repeated superscription is indeed somewhat obscure, since מעלות is ambiguous. According to the older usage we should translate *song of steps,* ᾠδὴ τῶν ἀναβαθμῶν, LXX. Yet it is not clear what tolerable sense could thus be obtained ; for we can hardly suppose a song to be sung on the steps of the Temple, according to the explanation of Jews in later times. But to suppose a prosodic explanation (according to J. D. Michaelis) is impossible, from the absence of a prosody and metrical system among the Hebrews in the sense of the Syrians or the Arabs. And some moderns have attempted a rhythmical explanation with as great arbitrariness as if these songs had not precisely the same rhythm which may be found in numberless other songs. Much more closely does the explanation, "Pilgrim's Song," according to the later signification of the word (Ezra vii. 9), correspond to the time in which this superscription arose; and with this the meaning of the songs for the most part concurs. For no one who reads them attentively will fail to recognize how freshly are reflected in them the sentiments of the first Israelites who were making a pilgrimage out of exile to the holy land, or were finally returning thither. The collection, then, might partly bear the name *Songs of the pilgrim-trains,* or of *those journeying to the ancient fatherland.* But in still closer agreement is the theory that these songs (with the exception of Ps. cxxxii.) proceed from a favourite poet, who lived about the first time of the new Jerusalem, but away from it, perhaps in Galilee ; and whose song-book was therefore soon used with pleasure by the pilgrim-trains, so that it was named after them. Ps. cxxxii. may then have been afterwards incorporated with it. Again, it may well be supposed that originally the entire collection was thus named, with a single superscription, שִׁירֵי הַמַּעֲלוֹת, Songs of the *pilgrim-trains,* or *festive journeys,** in the plural; but in the transference into the present larger collection, each individual song then obtained its superscription in the singular.

A third small collection may with great certainty be recognized in Pss. ciii.—cvii., cxi.—cxviii., cxxxv.—cxxxvi., cxlvi.—cl. For once, there is found in this series, from Ps. civ. onwards (which song is, however, manifestly only a side-piece to Ps. ciii.) the "Hallelujah," nowhere else found. It comes before and after the song in Pss. cvi., cxiii., cxv., cxxxv., cxlvi., cxlviii, cxlix., cl.; before it only, Pss. cxi., cxii., cxiii.; after it only, Pss. civ., cv., cxvi., cxvii., cxlvii. But why it is wanting here and there at the beginning or the end one does not perceive; and probably the present copies have here become very defective.

This much is now at once clear, that this short sentence, "Praise Jah!" possibly with the exception of Ps. cxvii. 2 (comp. above p. 142 *Dichter des A. B.,* i.) nowhere belongs in strict connexion to the song, since it generally stands outside the rhythm, and in certain places does not conform to the original stamp of a song, as Ps. cxvi. It is evidently a short standing formula, which probably from early times gradually became more current; and in these late times was generally favoured, and even elsewhere freely interwoven into the course of a song, as in Pss. cii. 18; cxv. 17; cl. 6. The LXX even regard it as a mere superscription like the לַמְנַצֵּחַ, and by no means to be blended with the song, as is clear from their arrangement of the words, Pss. cxlvi. 1; cxlvii. 1; cxlviii. 1. Accordingly, they never have it after a song, but at the beginning, more

---

* Comp. οἱ ἀναβαίνοντες. John xii. 20.

habitually and frequently than in the Hebrew text,—of Pss. cv.—cvii., cxi.—cxix., cxxxv., cxxxvi., cxlvi.—cl. One might even be led to adopt the theory that חללו יה had possibly been the general superscription of the collection, and afterwards transferred to each individual song, as a similar supposition was made in the case of the preceding collection. Yet this appears in the LXX more like mere conjecture and arbitrary alteration of the text. That the words might also serve as a concluding formula is shown by Rev. xix. 4; comp. 1 Chron. xvi. 36 with Ps. cvi. 48.*

We must then rather conceive that in a song to be sung in the public assembly, and mainly of cheerful import,† the Hallelujah as a standing word must denote the more vigorous beginning, and again the more vigorous close. Further, we deduce the conclusion that it was accompanied‡ not by the

---

* In places like Pss. cxv. 18 ; cxvi. 19, it might certainly be supposed that the Hallelujah belonged rather to the beginning of the following song ; and after Ps. cvi. this hypothesis would be thoroughly necessary if the blessing, ver. 48, was intended to denote nothing but the end of a collection. But that the latter assumption is incorrect was noted on p. 11 sq.; and the main point is that such a short exclamation is readily conceivable as well before as after the song in the public gathering, according to p. 190 sq. (*Dichter des A. B.*)

† Certainly the formula appears at first sight to bear a full meaning only along with such contents. However, Ps. cvi. must rather be termed a penitential song. On the use of the word in the ancient Church, see Augusti's *Handbuch der Christl. Archäol.*, ii., pp. 91-94.

‡ This short cry may certainly be of primeval origin, dating even from Moses's time, so that its application in the Scripture in these songs only is new. In fact, the constant use of the *Jah*, shortened from *Jahvé* and *Jáhu* in this phrase, is thus most readily explained. This curtailment is here simply the stronger pause in which the powerful acclamation sounded forth. Through the use of this constant sacred phrase the short expression *Jah* was afterwards probably brought into use elsewhere, at least practically,—originally likewise only in pause, Ex. xv. 2 ; xvii. 16. Elsewhere, too (setting aside the later artificially-formed phrases בְּיָהּ יִשְׁמוֹ, Ps. lxviii. 5 ; Isa. xxvi. 4, which is drawn from Ex. Xv. 2), it is only found in pause, namely, Pss. lxxvii. 12 ; lxxxix. 9 ; xciv. 7, 12 ; cxviii. 5, 14, 17, 19 ; cxxx. 3 (also cxxii. 4), where again it is only revived by later writers after Ex. xv. 2 ; and in the song of king Hizqia, p. 161, where it is merely repeated in the second clause. In this manner the whole usage of *Jah*, standing alone, is explained. When the LXX express הַלְלוּ יָהּ by ἀλληλουΐα, either the more Aramaic expression has crept in, or more probably it is a pausal expression ;

ordinary Temple-music, but, according to p. 217,* by the higher priests with their trumpets; but the whole congregation, according to p. 190 sq., was expected loudly to join in with their voices.

Now, these twenty songs have further that which is in common in their contents. They are the proper Temple-songs for thanksgiving, prayer, and feast-days, designed for the use of the second Temple and of the whole congregation (Tob. xiii. 18), since Ps. cxvi. might be readily applied to a more general use. Since other songs might just as well be designated by Hallelujah, *e.g.*, Ps. c. or lxxxi. as well as cxvii., we observe on twofold grounds that a special collection is here before us of songs which moreover belong to the latest poetry, and up to Ps. ciii. 1 have throughout no further annotation. These three small collections, then, the last collector of Pss. xci.—cl. found existing. Possibly also he found Ps. cxix., which in length is almost equivalent to such an entire collection, and which the LXX infelicitously attached to the Hallelujah songs. But besides this, we can very certainly see that he had a far more complete copy of the same collection of songs before him which now remains as Pss. xlii.—lxxxix. This weighty fact is inferred (1) from the peculiar style of the annotations, Ps. ci., Pss. cviii.—cx. and cxxxviii.—cxlv., as will have to be established presently; and (2) from the fact that Ps. cviii. is nothing but a new collection of two great fragments of Ps. lvii. and Ps. lx. Whether the explanation be that these two songs were already thus abbreviated in the copy of this collection which was before our last collector, or (which is less probable) that he himself so abbreviated them, the result is that, in style and contents, these songs, Pss. cviii.—cx., cxxxviii—cxlv., bear the greatest resemblance to those of the one half of that collection, Pss. li.—lxxii.

All this being pre-supposed, the procedure of the last collector can here be readily recognized. He formed his collection

---

for the two words were not closely joined together, as in the Masora, but were slowly and solemnly separated.   * *Dichter des A. B.*, i.

out of these large fragments, and further added a few more single songs, which he might find dispersed in other series. He manifestly preferred to collect such songs as were best suited to the second Temple; and these few made the small collection, Pss. xcii.—c., and the Hallelujah-songs the two bases of his collection. For many reasons he appropriately concluded with the last Hallelujah-songs, placed the *songs of pilgrim-trains* with the long devotional Ps. cxix. in the middle; surrounded this centre with songs from that Davidic book of songs from which elsewhere, Pss. li.—lxxii., and many more, have been retained; placed, from other sources, at the head of the first collection, in Pss. xc., xci., two of the most important songs which open the whole new collection with such surpassing splendour; and at the head of the Hallelujah-psalms in like manner the two Pss. ci., cii., which appeared to him equally important, and of which he might have found the former in the Davidic book of songs mentioned; and added before the last series of the Davidic songs Ps. cxxxvii., which had been elsewhere retained. In entire isolation, *i.e.*, without a customary superscription, and without standing in a larger collection of similar songs, appear of the whole collection only Pss. xci., cii., cxxxvii., with the exception of Ps. cxix. By the side of these Ps. xc. presents itself as quite peculiar. The whole then may be briefly brought into one view in the following table:—

Pss. xc. xci.	xcii.—c.	ci.		
cii.				ciii.—cvii.
		cviii.—cx.		cxi.—cxviii.
cxix.			cxx.—cxxxiv.	cxxxv. cxxxvi.
cxxxvii.		cxxxviii.—cxlv.		cxlvi.—cl.

Such a last hand may have also added here and there the few other superscriptions of a scattered and peculiar character: xcii. 1; xcviii. 1; c. 1; ciii. 1; cxxii. 1; cxxiv. 1; cxxvii. 1;

2 *

cxxxi.; cxxxiii. 1.   In this way the growth of this entire collection of sixty-one songs in the *strata* of which it is built up may be fully traced, and may be in principle readily ascertained.

(2.) It is more difficult, in the case of the middle collection, Pss. xlii.—lxxxix., to point out the traces of earlier arrangement and gradual improvement, because the longer their transition from hand to hand, the more they lose their original form. But on closer comparison a few facts may be ascertained.   For if we place the two halves of this collection side by side in the way shown in pp. 243-50*; and if we further note the true relations or differences, and also the age of the songs here collected, it becomes tolerably clear *how* this mass grew, little by little, to its present form.   For we still see in it the older and the later portions together in small accumulations, or these related *cumuli* may, with a little circumspection, be readily re-discovered.   To make this provisionally apparent, we give the following conspectus:—

1. Pss. li.—lxxii.	2. Pss. xlii.—l., lxxiii.—lxxxix.
lxii., lv. lxv., lvi.—lvii. lix. (lxxii.) lii. . . liv. . . lviii., lxi. . . . . lxiii.	xlv., xlvi. . . . . xlix. . . . . lxxv., lxxvi. xlii., xliii. . . . . lxxxiv., lxxxviii.
li., lxix.—lxxi. liii.	lxxxii.
lxvi.—lxviii. lx.	xlvii. lxxxvii. lxxxv. xliv., lxxiii., lxxiv., lxxvii.—lxxxi.
	lxxxiii., lxxxix.
	lxxxvi.

---

* *Dichter des A. B.,* i.

In the second half are Pss. xlvi., xlviii., lxxv., lxxvi., which certainly stood originally together, forming along with the somewhat older Ps. xlv. and with Ps. xlix. the oldest basis of the collection. They spring from the eighth century or the Assyrian period; and the earliest of the first half, Ps. lxii., cv., further, lxv., and the two songs of *one* poet, lvi., lvii., are to be placed also about the same period. Ps. lix. (and Ps. lxxii.), the three by one *poet*, lii., liv., lviii., and the two again by one poet, lxi., lxiii., are probably from the course of the seventh century. To them correspond in the second half Ps. l., the songs further of *one* poet, Ps. xlii., xliii., lxxxiv., then Ps. lxxxviii., and perhaps also Ps. lxxxii. Belonging to the times immediately after the destruction of Jerusalem come then Pss. li., lxix.—lxxi.

The beginning and basis of this entire collection thus fall in the eighth century. Then a new collection must have been arranged; and all the songs on the one side, Pss. li., lii., liv.— lix.,lxi.—lxv., and on the other, Pss. xlii., xliii., xlv.—l., lxxv., lxxvi., lxxxii., lxxxiv., lxxxviii., might already have been put together at the beginning of the Babylonian exile. In that which concerns the half of the collection, named after Davidic singers, we can prove this by the special circumstance that the poet of the Lamentations must have known them. For although too great stress must not be laid on the very remarkable resemblance of Lam. iii. 6, 7 to Ps. lxxxviii. 6, 7, 9 by itself, it is the more certain that the expression, Lam. ii. 15, points back designedly to the two passages placed indeed in this collection near to one another, but in other respects very different, Ps. xlviii. 3, l. 1; whence it follows with certainty that the poet of the Lamentations read these songs precisely in the same order.

The remaining songs may have been composed during the further course of the Babylonian exile and afterwards, and have been inserted here by a later collector; and these very latest insertions stand for the most part still in a mass together, Pss. lxvi.—lxviii. (which must be regarded, in accordance with

p. 198,*as *four* original songs), Pss. lxxiii., lxxiv., lxxvii.—lxxxi., &c. And the fact must not be overlooked that the greater number of these later songs in both collections have been placed almost wholly at the end, and have there remained.

But, finally, the following is here very noticeable : only after these earlier and later materials were thus strongly mixed in these collections, a still later hand may have added the super-scriptions and other annotations, which are very complete in this part, according to the most important contents; because these Pss. xlii.—lxxxix. have remained unaltered throughout the entire present great collection. This leads to important deductions respecting the age and nature of these annotations. This collector then perhaps placed also Ps. lxxii., as a Song of Solomon's, at the end of the Davidic songs, because he regarded this position as the best. On the other hand, Ps. lxxxvi. was inserted still later, as partly its superscription and position, and partly the internal indications explained on p. 8, show. The nature of this song generally also favours this assumption.

It is certainly not too bold and unadvised to return upon such traces; for we do not in this way venture beyond that which is certainly ascertainable, and lies open to our view, nor do we invent empty hypotheses. At the same time we do not overlook and neglect facts that actually lie at hand.

(3.) It is accordingly to be expected that the first and oldest of the three existing collections should present the most various characters, as having gone through the longest changes; and that it should be the least easy to penetrate its earlier forms. If we review, however, these songs with regard to their probable age, setting aside for the moment Pss. i., ii., xxxiii., they fall under the following three divisions :—

Oldest : iii., iv., vii., viii., xi. (xv.), xviii.—xx., xxiv., xxix., xxxii.—ii.

---

* *Dichter des A. B.*, i.

Older : vi., xii., xiii., xxi., xxiii., xxvii., xxx., xxxix., xli.

Later : i.—v., ix., x., xvi., xvii., xxii., xxv., xxvi., xxviii., xxxi., xxxiv.—xxxviii., xc.

Latest : xiv.—xxxiii.

And a few weighty conclusions may be drawn. For plainly the cycle of genuine Davidic songs which is quite peculiar to this collection stands out in relief as the oldest substance of the present collection. Nothing from Pss. xlii.—lxxxix can be placed by the side of them, and Pss. xc.—cl. only make a few additions to them. These songs stand still predominantly at the head of the present collection, and where they have, in a superscription, a statement of the historical occasion, this is approved as a genuine ancient tradition. With this cycle is immediately-connected a number of songs not so ancient, but still of somewhat ancient songs, which may have been connected with the former at a time anterior to the exile, and in which we still plainly see here and there marks of coherence, as vi., xiii., and xxx., xxiii. and xxvii., especially also xxxix. and xli. They contain no statements whatever of their historical occasion. But, lastly, a considerable mass of later songs must have been added from the time shortly before, during, and shortly after the exile—songs by which Ps. xxvii. was first separated from xxiii., and which betray their origin by the fact that they are placed more towards the end. The connected portions in them are mostly near together : xvi. and xvii., xxvi. and xxviii., xxxv., xxxviii., xl., xiv. Amongst these latter songs none so late is found as in the second existing collection, Pss. xliv., lx.; and the similar super-scriptions and intermediate notes have then doubtless, as usual, been added, though not so uniformly and numerously as in the second collection. But the first two songs, which are without any annotations, appear quite as if they had been externally prefixed to an already existing collection, although certainly not in the latest period. Ps. i. is evidently designed to be such an introduction to the whole collection; and Ps. ii. was probably an ancient song which one of the collectors and editors was unwilling should perish. Very similarly stand, as was remarked above, in the latest collection Pss. xc., xci., before Pss. xcii.—c., Pss. ci., cii., before Pss. ciii.—cl. Not until the latest period can Ps. xxxiii. have been inserted—a song which resembles in all respects those most frequent in the third collection and has remained without superscription.

We have now discovered the original collections of each of the three existing collections. Yet it is plain that these original collections were of very different primary form, and belonged to times of very opposite character. The object was in each case to preserve the most beautiful songs of the period, so that no song could be repeated in the same collection. But it is not less certain that each collection has from such beginning onwards run through its peculiar history of enlargements and other changes, independently of the others. For we see a few songs taken up into two of the existing collections, which could hardly have been done had such collections been at that time already united. Ps. liii. has found its way as Ps. xiv. into the first collection. Ps. lxx. could not have stood along with Ps. xc. in *one* collection, nor Ps. cviiii. along with Pss. lvii. and lx. These cases show that the three collections subsisted at a very late period in their peculiar character, and were in course of being augmented. But it is equally certain, on all the grounds above adduced, that they originated in the same serial succession in which they at present stand; that thus, finally, a hand which united the third with the two preceding put forth the whole as it now lies before us. And certainly, both the particular smaller collections out of which the third grew, and the two earlier ones, had already obtained public esteem when a last collector united the whole.

3. Behind the present Psalter, then, there is concealed an extensive history of the fortunes of lyric songs among the Hebrews,—a history which indeed could be viewed much more

clearly and fully were not this Psalter itself almost the only source of knowledge. A mass of older and later, smaller and larger collections of songs must have preceded those in existence; and many of these earlier collections must, in whole or in part, have undergone, through centuries, the most manifold changes and passed through many forms before they were here brought together; and it is certain that many a noble song, especially from earlier times, must have vanished without a trace, if it found finally no reception here. If we further bear in mind that the same song in different copies and editions must frequently have passed through the greatest changes, as, *e.g.*, Ps. xviii. compared with 2 Sam. xxii., Ps. liii. compared with xiv., Ps. lxx. compared with xl. show; further, that earlier songs treated by later poets or readers in manifold fashions are partly repeated, freshly worked up, or freshly put together, as Ps. cxliv. 1-11, Ps. cviii., and many other clear cases teach us; and, as in xix. 2-7, lx. 8-11, cxliv. 12-14, x. 1-10 only the remains of older complete songs are preserved; we see still more plainly how many and in part very different books, copies, and collections preceded the present collection; and how thoroughly justified we are in looking, in this field of inquiry, beyond that which offers itself to our first glance. Thus all leads to the result that we possess in the present Psalter, those flowers of the lyrical poetry of the Hebrews most suitable for public edification and instruction— so far as their contents belonged to this head—out of all centuries from David down to the latest times. The great mass of the songs, however, as was inevitable, gradually accumulated in later times; while the few which have been preserved out of the remoter antiquity are the most beautiful and of the most abiding interest. The material which had been brought down the stream of time unexhausted from the Davidic source, and the immediately following centuries, has finally drifted into this book, in company with a mass of later additions and admixtures.

Meanwhile, we are able to sketch out, from the traces scattered here and elsewhere, a fairly complete and coherent

history of the whole collection of such songs. The songs of
David alone form the mighty original stream of all these
collections. They were certainly collected immediately after
the death of the great kingly singer;* but at that time
without discrimination and without reference to public use.
But many of them became early immortalized as the finest
expression of the profoundest piety in the hearts of living men.
Many of them may have increasingly displaced in the Temple
at Jerusalem the older priestly songs which were used in the
earlier centuries after Moses. But however many of them
may have become universal favourites, side by side with them
poetic art was ever putting forth fresh blossoms. Especially
did every new period of highly awakened activity send forth a
fresh and mighty stream of beautiful songs. Again, for the
Temple-sacrifices and feast-days of every kind fresh songs
were always being produced, as we can still plainly enough
perceive, from numerous examples. As in the ancient people
of Israel, in consequence of its peculiar religion, no kind of
songs could come into more splendid flower than that which
we may designate by a short word, the *song of God*
(*Gottcslied*), and as moreover David had given the most
creative specimens of this kind; the mass of such songs
was even more strongly on the increase after his great
precedent, and even of the better class of them there
was always something like an inexhaustible supply. From
this supply proceeded the collections from which finally sprung
our Psalter. There were collections of Divine songs, as there
were, according to pp. 236, 237,† also collections of other kinds
of songs. Through long periods, not merely were proper
Temple songs incorporated with them, but Divine songs of a
more general sense, and with this reference as a guide, songs
of other kinds were excluded. But with this object was
readily connected that of collocating other songs for edification

---

* Comp. the *Gesch. des V. Isr.*, iii., p. 360 (2nd edit.)
† *Dichter des A. B*, i.

in general, even although they contain no address to God.
The collections were repeatedly sifted, with this object in view;
even although, exceptionally, in one of them, such a song—
highly distinctive in other respects, and morally faultless,—as
Ps. xlv., was allowed to remain. Regard was paid also to the
readily intelligible, generally pleasing character of the contents;
and a song like Ps. xxviii. was adopted in spite of its somewhat incomplete artistic form; but not that of king Hizqia,
explained on pp. 161 sq.,* which is extremely artistic, but somewhat heavy. Davidic songs were long made the basis of such
collections, and others related in sense and spirit were connected with them; but gradually collections of another kind
were put forth. And since these collections had the object of
edification simply in view, the mere names of the poets were
not of so much importance† to the most ancient feeling, and
thus the names of the poets of the songs adopted in these
collections gradually disappeared; with the exception of that
poet who had laid the foundation of this whole species of
poetry and of these collections, and who might suffice by
himself alone instead of all others. Moreover, each separate
collection was subject to the thousand accidents already suggested, before it found its resting-place in the present Psalter.
With respect, however, to details, so far as we can survey them
at the present day:

(1.) The first collection of this kind may have been formed in
the middle of the tenth century. It is still the firmest foundation of those songs retained in Pss. i.—xli., with the exact historical notes affixed to Pss. iii., vii., xviii. It went on, however,
from that point, it is certain, through repeated new editions,
with additions and omissions; amongst which we can recognize with peculiar clearness one from the eighth century, when
songs like vi., xii., xiii., xx., xxi., xxiii., xxvii., xxx., xxxix.,
xli., must in part have been brought together out of earlier

---

* *Dichter des A. B.*, i.   † See on this further remarks presently.

collections. For, according to relationship of sense, the Pss. xx. and xxi., in other respects very different, still stand in juxtaposition. Another is from the seventh century, by a Deuteronomic editor.* Himself a poet, he placed the didactic song, Ps. i., at the head, as if in recollection of the particular sense in which these songs were to be read, and he probably also placed Ps. ii. from an old collection in this place. Ps. xiv. must have been inserted still later; and at the latest period Ps. xxxiii., which was left without a superscription.

(2.) There are plainly recognizable traces of a similar collection in Pss. li.—lxxii. But this is richer in later songs, and, on the other hand, it contains in its actual present condition no song of David preserved in its purity. Such a song is only found incorporated in the later Ps. lx. It might thus be supposed that the oldest songs of this entire collection were not earlier than the age after David and Solomon. But since we must conclude, from sure indications, that the author of the last collection, Pss. xc.—cl., was acquainted with this collection, and adopted from it the pieces above noticed, we draw the conclusion that it was originally much more comprehensive, and included, besides, songs from David and his time (Pss. ci., cx.) Thus this collection also might, on such grounds, pass for Davidic. Ps. lxxii. was added to it in like manner by a last collector, as in the preceding Ps. ii. was at a later period placed at the beginning.

That there were, however, at a comparatively early date, collateral collections of quite a different description is shown by Pss. xlii.—l., lxxiii., lxxxix., which originally, as shown on p. 13, belonged to *one* collection. For if lxxxvi. be excepted, which was manifestly interpolated in this place from preceding collections, it is plain that we have here a collection which, according to its annotations, was intended from the beginning to contain no Davidic material. Further, in regard to the adoption

---

* The significance of this is explained in the *Gesch. des V. Isr.*, p. 227 (3rd edit.)

of many later songs by a last editor, it resembles the preceding collections, and its first arrangement, in like manner, cannot be earlier than the eighth century. We shall touch presently on the manner in which it was at first divided, and on the fact that it was originally much fuller; but it has already been shown, pp. 4 sq., that a last editor more closely united it with the preceding collections as well as with its other half; and it was at a later period that it was brought into its somewhat altered present form before it obtained its permanent position along with those now inseparably connected with it, by the agency of the collector of the entire present Psalter.

(3.) With the earliest times of the new Jerusalem there arose fresh collections of entirely new songs, as was shown on pp. 14 sq. But about those junctures in which all literary treasures of the earlier times, especially so far as they concerned the sanctuary at Jerusalem, were sought out with a new zeal, and repeated in new editions, and put forth in enlarged forms,* the older collections of songs before described were again published anew. This entire old and new literature must at that time have been full of life-stirrings. Collections of songs of all kinds were accordingly of great numerical extent, some perhaps of moderate excellence. But it was precisely those immediately referable to the Temple and Jerusalem which were the least collected. A new collector then resolved to arrange the above-described last great collection, Pss. xc.—cl. As meanwhile he had no design to displace the earlier collections already preserved, it must soon have been felt that the best course now was to unite the two earlier preserved ones with this latter more closely in *one* grand whole; and at that time there was sufficient accurate insight to give the first place to the relatively earliest and most important among these, Pss. i.—xli. The work at that time did not amount to a careful collection of all possible songs of a cognate sense, which might

---

* As I have shown with sufficient definiteness in the case of the *Prophets of the Old Testament,* and also in the case of other collected writings of the Old Testament.

have been discovered scattered about in writings. And thus several remained outside the great collection, which would have been generally appropriate to it; as the song of Jonah, explained on pp. 155 sq.,* or the song of victory, 1 Sam. ii., explained on pp. 158 sq., which moreover, as proceeding from a king of the kingdom of the Ten Tribes, was, in earlier times, probably designedly left out of the series of such Davidic collections of songs. Such particular series show us how many collections of songs of other kinds once existed in Israel. But as yet the individual parts of these three collections were still left unsifted. No attempt was made to adjust the inequalities among them; *e.g.*, Ps. liii. was left quietly alongside of Ps. xiv., Ps. cviii. by the side of Pss. lvii., lx., although they are the same songs. These three collections manifestly held their ground, each for itself, as publicly preserved: they were left side by side as they existed at that time, and importance was attached simply to their union.

We now know with sufficient certainty that this great book, having thus originated, obtained, under the general name *Davidic* (τὰ τοῦ Δαβίδ) by Nehemiah's co-operation, that peculiar consideration at the Temple which it ever afterwards maintained.† The final more fixed order of all the conditions of the new Jerusalem, and pre-eminently the *rénaissance* of the Temple-music, to which the Chronicles bear witness, is manifestly connected with this circumstance.

From all this, however, it may with great certainty be inferred that the number of 150 Psalms now in use is not original. In general, it is difficult to conceive of a numbering of these songs in earlier times. On the contrary, it is obvious that at an early date a few songs were incorrectly brought together in certain copies: as Pss. xxiv., xxvi., closely

---

* *Dichter des A. B.*, i.

† Compare the *Gesch. des V. Isr.*, vii., pp. 425-29 sq. That the Psalter was not completed at a later date, and that it included no so-called Makkabæic psalms, I have in each case more definitely proved, and shall return to the point in the new edition of the second volume

observed, break up each of them into two different songs; others were separated near to the time of their origin, as Pss. ix· and x. in the Masoretic text, Pss. xlii. and xliii. in the LXX, and in many copies of the Masoretic text. But when men began to count all the songs of the completed present great collection, many evidently endeavoured, with a certain preference, to complete exactly the round number of 150. At least there is an agreement here between the Masoretic text and the LXX in the Cod. Alex., along with deviations in other respects.* The Masoretic text separates (in most copies) Pss. ix. and x., which are rightly connected in the LXX; but the LXX connect also Pss. cxiv. and cxv., quite contrary to the original sense, and on the other hand (1) separate cxvi. 1-9, from cxvi. 10-19, which destroys a fine connexion; (2) cxlvii. 1-11, from cxlvii. 12-20, which is at least conceivable and may be tolerated.

The first certain trace of the completion of the present Psalter is to be found in the Chronicles. The narrator refers to the time of David and Asaf, 1 Chron. xvi. 7-36, a Temple-song, which is derived from the latest constituents of the present collection of Psalms. For if we attentively compare vv. 8-22 with Ps. cv. 1-15, vv. 23-33 with Ps. xcvi. 2-13, and vv. 34-36 with Ps. cvi. 1, 47, 48, no doubt will remain that various materials which stand in every point of view in their place and in the most proper connexion in the Psalter are in the Chronicles loosely put together, in apparently a more arbitrary fashion, to form a new whole. And with this theory the fact agrees, that the text of the words in Chronicles is seen to be much less original and correct; in fact, in its latter part,

---

* But that the number of the Psalms, probably even to 150, is very ancient, we gather plainly enough from the superscription of the Apocryphal Psalm, to be more closely considered presently. This is found in all copies of the LXX, and was therefore certainly introduced by the translator himself into the Greek Psalter. Again, according to Hippolytos, 150 Psalms had long been the general reckoning (comp. his words in Lagarde's *Analecta Syr.*, pp. 83, 29, and his *Hippolyti quæ feruntur omnia græce* (1858), p. 189).

altered, transposed, and abbreviated.*　Moreover, the Chronicler can only have transposed those songs which were certainly of most frequent use in his time in the Temple, for the reason that already the entire present Psalter, including such anonymous songs as xcvi., cv., cvi., was referred, without careful discrimination, to David.　In like manner 1 Chron. xvi. 41 shows the existence of the latest collection of Psalms.　But Chronicles was not written earlier nor later than at the end of the Persian dominion, or, at latest, at the beginning of the Grecian.

The next clue after this is the translation of the LXX, who follow in the Psalter a copy which departs from the Masoretic text only in less important and thorough-going particulars. But in the matter of the annotations, this latest part, (speaking generally) of the whole,—it misunderstands or arbitrarily alters many of them.　Hence it follows that between it and the completion of the present book a considerable interval must have elapsed.　But the LXX append a song, in which a very late writer puts in the mouth of David a Goliath song, which runs as follows :—

1.

Little was I amongst my brethren,
　youngest in my father's house ;
I tended the sheep of my father,
　my hands formed an instrument,
　my fingers tuned a harp.

2.

Yet whoso to the Lord confesses his need,†
　He is Lord, and *He* hears ;

---

* This also yields proof that by the τὰ τοῦ Δαβίδ, 2 Macc. ii. 13, not merely the oldest collection, Pss. i.—xli., or the Psalms as far as lxxxix., are to be understood, which indeed is of itself utterly improbable.　Comp. on what is maintained above, the *Jahrbb. der Bibl. Wiss.*, vi., pp. 22 sq.

† The words as they here stand are entirely without sense, if we do not decide to assume that after καὶ τις ἀναγγελεῖ τῷ κυρίῳ μοῦ, a word like צָרָתִו has dropped out.　For τῷ κυρίῳ μοῦ, which is unsuitable to the sense, it is probable

and *He* sent His Angel,
> and took me from my father's sheep,
> and anointed me with His oil of anointing.

3.

My fair and my great brothers—
> in them had the Lord no pleasure.
I went against that foreigner,
> and he cursed me before his idols;
> but I, drawing his own sword, beheaded him,
> and took the dishonour from Israel's sons.

This is certainly a small song composed quite in accordance with the old laws of art, with three strophés of five lines each, of which the last only, quite in accordance with pp. 169—170,* becomes one of six lines. The song was certainly written in Hebrew, as we can see distinctly enough from the stamp of the Greek. But this "Psalm, written by David with his own hand, and found outside the number" (*i.e.*, not found among the 150), as it is very sincerely designated in the superscription, was unquestionably borrowed from the translator of a later life-description of David, in which the history was treated with great arbitrariness; and where David, according to a completely groundless notion, but quite aptly, in the sense of later times, was praised as the inventor of the harp. What a distance, in all respects, between this empty song of pure invention and those of the genuine Psalter! And yet the translator found it existing—a plain proof that between his time and that of the conclusion of the Psalter which had entered the Canon there lay a wide interval. It was not, again, until a later time that Jewish readers arrived at the conception that the blessing above mentioned, pp. 11-12—Ps. cvi. 48—might, just as the three standing after Pss. xli., lxxii., lxxxix., designate the end of a section, and held the more tenaciously

---

that merely לַאדֹנָי stood, according to p. 245. The *Cod. Sin.* inserts πάντον before εἰσακούει without improving the sense.

* *Dichter des A. B.*, i.

to this entirely erroneous notion, because the Psalter thus, like
the Pentateuch, appeared to fall into five books. In this sense
the Massôra afterwards proposed by its additions to distinguish
five books of Psalms. But although this opinion may have
been predominant in the schools in the second century after
Christ,* it is nevertheless entirely erroneous.

III. THE INSCRIPTIONS OR ANNOTATIONS OF THE PSALMS.

To the understanding of these brief words, which may readily
appear utterly obscure,—or at least to make an assured step
towards the understanding of them,—we have already made good
preparation in what has gone before. Our business is now to
give a short but distinct summary of all that refers to them.
For with such fragmentary words it is apt to be the case that
they remain yet more obscure than is necessary, so long as
they are regarded rather in their individual relation; whilst
a more accurate review of the whole discovers a certain
resemblance and regularity among them; and thus we no
longer remain so entirely helpless or in such arbitrary conjectures with reference to particular details.

Now we must here note, first of all, that such annotations
must once have been widely diffused outside the present
Psalter. We perceive this from the perfectly similar annotations in the song of king Hizqia, Isa. xxxviii., from Habakk.
iii., and from the "Psalter of Solomon." And likewise
we may take preliminary note of the fact that even the
arrangement and order of the annotations, according to all
evidence, is not accidental, but points back to a peculiar art
and knowledge concerning their sense.

If we look immediately at the contents,—

1. An important part of them refers to the musical setting

---

* As we see from Hippolytos (*Græce ed.* Lagarde, pp. 187, 193.)

of the songs. These have been so adequately explained above,
pp. 209 sq.,* that it is sufficient here to draw from all that was
said the weighty conclusion that the few words not only stand
in close connexion with one another, but also certainly
explained fully for the experts, who possessed the key to these
formulæ, the musical character of a song. Again, it has been
already shown above that, except סֶלָה, which may stand at the
end of a song as at the end of any verse, all these observations
in the Psalter always stand at the beginning. This may now
be laid down as a closer definition, that לַמְנַצֵּחַ thus always
subordinates to itself the statement of the tune; but with this
appurtenance always takes its place at the beginning, in the
superscriptions, whilst the four designations elucidated on
pp. 228-30* of the mere rendering of a song follow in the
third place. Ps. xlvi. forms the solitary exception from that
order, where the name of the poet is inserted; however,
this may be merely an old copyist's error. But it follows with
certainty from the second law that the words לִבְנֵי קֹרַח
שִׁיר מִזְמוֹר, which, in Ps. lxxxviii. 1, stand before לַמנצח
with its appurtenance, did not originally belong to that place,
which in this instance is seen to be true on other grounds soon
to be explained. But since each of the four designations of a
musical song explained on pp. 228-230 gives, notwithstanding
all brevity, a perfectly clear sense by itself, it is not surprising
(1) that each may stand alone, and hence first; and (2) that
the two other designations may also be repeated at the end of
a song. At all events, there prevailed a greater freedom of
this kind in other instances than the collections of Psalms, as
we may shortly call them.†

If we give further attention to the different songs to which

---

* *Dichter des A. B.*, i.

† As is seen in a twofold way in Hab. chap. iii. : (1) inasmuch as בִּנְגִינוֹתַי
לַמְנַצֵּחַ, ver. 19, stands at the end, and (2) inasmuch as in the superscription,
ver. 1, instead of the brief שִׁגָּיוֹן at the beginning (as in Ps. vii. 1), עַל שִׁגְיֹנוֹת
as a more diffuse designation is placed at the end; this, however, is only because
the piece, in conformity with the plan of the whole writing, was to be briefly
designated from the first, according to its contents.

these musical notes are attached, it might indeed appear as if we must entirely give up the task of deciding why in some songs merely למנצח or למנ בנגינת *without* statement of the tune appears, and in a few others even the mere סֶלָה. But of equal importance for us remains the difference of the presence or omission of such notes generally—already touched upon on pp. 4 sq. For this much is of itself clear, that they—in so far as the Psalter contains songs destined to be sung, in the use of the whole community—might properly be added to all songs, perhaps with the exception of Ps. cxix. and a few others, which rather serve for the edification of the individual reader. But, in fact, we find that only those of the second of the three great collections above defined, in the present Psalter, contained these notes with the greatest uniformity. Between Pss. xlii.—lxxxix. the following only constituted an exception :—Ps. lxiii., which may be accidental, since the song obviously belongs to the same class as Ps. lxi. ; Pss. lxxiii., lxxiv., lxxviii., lxxix., which, according to pp. 20 sq. are among the latest of this collection, and where the omission of the musical notes is not so accidental ; and finally, Pss. lxxii. and lxxxvi., in the case of which the quite peculiar relations exist which are elucidated on pp. 8, 22.

In the first collection, Pss. i.—xli., the notes are found in some frequency, yet far more rarely than in the middle part; they are quite wanting in Pss. xv., xvi., xvii., xxiii., xxv.—xxx., xxxiii.—xxxv., xxxvii., xxxviii., several of which have other slight annotations. In the last collection, Pss. xc.—cl., they appear only as rare exceptions ; in Pss. cix., cxxxix., cxl., cxliii., and the masses of later songs here accumulated are entirely without them ; but the former themselves belonged, according to pp. 7 sq., originally to the second collection.

Subsequently, certain songs, or rather books of songs, were specially and with preference so treated ; and the older songs were, relatively, more frequently so treated than the later ones. But before the two first collections in the present Psalter obtained, as it were, their greater repose, many a note of this kind may possibly have dropped out, owing to the less restricted freedom still used by the copyists; and the Sélah may also have been misplaced in several passages. But where after the למנצח the designation of the tune is wanting, perhaps the nearest of all is intended, and merely for that reason is not named. At all events, we may thus explain why in the case of so many songs it is not designated at all.

2. It must, however, have been customary at a very early date to designate a song quite briefly according to its particular kind with a word of denomination; and that there were many particular names of this kind, and that the songs might be constantly with brevity thus distinguished, is precisely one of the many tokens of the high early development of all poetic and musical art in the people of Israel. These briefest and yet significant superscriptions are hence unusually frequent on the whole, and are found in many songs, even without more definite musical treatment, i.e., not furnished with the למנצח and the statement of the tune, and the Sélah. Considered more in detail, these short names are of two very different kinds:

(1.) The often-mentioned designations of the musical rendering of a song, elucidated further on pp. 228-230: מזמר, שִׁגָּיוֹן, מִכְתָּם, מַשְׂכִּיל. The use of them was here the more frequent, as the Temple-music appears to have been arranged simply with the view of giving the finer distinctions of musical rendering thereby denoted. At all events, none of the four are now found elsewhere than as attached to songs for the Temple use. But for this very reason the too general name (see p. 30*) שִׁיר hymn, is avoided on the superscriptions of these songs. This word is actually found only in Ps. xlvi., where, however, it is either to be more strictly connected with the preceding designation of the tune, and is to be translated, *to be sung to the tune of* . . . , as a similar expression is found (p. 227*) in Ps. lxxxviii. 1; or a מִזְמֹר has been dropped

---

* *Dichter des A. B.*, i.

from it, for this (p. 30*) is often connected with it in the second collection.†—Quite different from these names are,

(2.) Those which define the contents or, in a certain sense, even the use of a song. These, however, occur far more rarely, and were manifestly much less held to be necessary; and as an old name of the kind, only the *love-song* in Ps. xlv., elucidated on p. 146,* is certain, speaking generally. Only two somewhat later poets have themselves named a song תְּפִלָּה, *prayer,*—the prophet Habakkuk, chap. iii., and the poet of Ps. cii., of whose song we are to speak further presently. But particular songs of those already collected seemed to the readers or collectors to be peculiarly well adapted for prayer; and thus particular psalms were probably so distinguished in the superscriptions,—chiefly Ps. xc., and also Pss. xvii., lxxxvi., cxlii. In a wider sense, indeed, all songs, as they were to be read in such collections, may have been used by individuals as prayers. It is sufficiently worthy of note that a collector or new editor (see p. 12) thus designated the whole collection, Pss. li.—lxxii., as *prayers*. But at the period when this editor certainly lived —namely, that following the destruction of the Temple, and in the midst of the great dispersion—such songs might, indeed, in the mass, be always best used in the first instance as prayers; seeing that they powerfully contributed to preserve the true religion amongst individuals of the dispersion. By the name תְּהִלָּה, *praise*, or *song* of *praise*, p. 35,* the one Ps. cxlv. is first designated, although many similar ones might have been thus named. Other names, however, besides these, do not belong, speaking generally, to this place.

How entirely different are these two kinds of names of songs may meanwhile be gathered from the fact that two may meet in the same superscription, provided only that each is of an opposite kind. We see this in Pss. xlv., cxlii., and Hab.

---

* *Dichter des A. B.*, i.

† The LXX have merely ψαλμός, as if they had read directly מזמר; yet this hypothesis is unnecessary.

chap. iii. The fact carries its own explanation with it, according to what has been above stated, but is here worthy of particular remark because the preceding four names are still in many ways misunderstood. With any one of these short names that of the poet or singer may readily be united, as in Ps. iii., iv., and elsewhere frequently in the Psalter; Isa. xxxviii. 9; Hab. iii. 1. This is as constantly done quite shortly by means of ־לְ (see *Lehrb.* § 292 *a*). Only in the very ancient song, Ps. vii., the designation of the poet occurs in a longer and, as it seems, more original mode of expression. And from this constant brevity of manner we also perceive how fully developed were all kinds of learned writing among the people from ancient times. The name of a song as that of the poet may stand alone in a superscription; but these cases are rarer, and accordingly require in every instance closer consideration; for such a difference may point to the different hands which were busy with the annotations.

In general the manner in which these names of songs are used, and in which side by side with them those of the composers are stated, is, again, very different in the three main divisions or collections of the present Psalter; and in several points of view it may repay our trouble to give heed to such apparently unimportant matters, since they are closely related to others of greater importance.

In the first collection these statements are of the simplest and shortest description, and yet, when both occur, they are most accurate and measured. In several songs, indeed, merely the name of the poet is stated, which is noteworthy where it frequently occurs, namely, in Pss. xxv.—xxvii., xxxiv.—xxxvii., the same songs to which the musical notes are wanting, with the exception of Ps. xxxvi., where למנצח for once stands, and in the isolated instances, Pss. xi., xiv. But where the other statement is added, it consists of a single fixed word which finds its orderly position before the mention of the poet, and only stands after it in Pss. xxiii., xxxii., and xl. This single word is as a rule מִזְמֹר. As similar to this, the

three other musical names are interchanged with it, each
only once: שִׁגָּיוֹן, Ps. vii.; מִכְתָּם, Ps. xvi.; מַשְׂכִּיל,
Ps. xxxii.; תְּפִלָּה is only found in Ps. xvii. From this constant simple custom of the writer of these superscriptions, it
follows with great certainty that the words to be presently
further discussed, שִׁיר חֲנֻכַּת הַבַּיִת, Ps. xxx., must have
been inserted between מִזְמוֹר and לְדָוִד by a later hand, as
also their contents render very probable. Further, it is the
first collection alone which twice distinctly terms David the
servant of Jahvé, Pss. xviii., xxxvi.

In the middle collection the poet merely is indeed very
seldom named, Pss. lxi., lxix., lxx., lxxxi. On the other
hand, twice in the midst of the series of related songs the
mention of the poet's name is wanting, Pss. lxvi., lxvii. in
these instances probably for the sake of brevity. For that
these very two songs belong to the post-exilian period cannot,
considering the arrangement of the rest of the collection and
of its superscriptions, be fairly questioned. But the name of
the poet is here very frequently prefixed, Pss. xliv.—xlvii.,
xlix., lvi.—lix., lxviii., lxxvii., lxxx., lxxxiv., lxxxv., lxxxvii.
(comp. in like manner in the last collection Pss. ci., cix., cx.,
cxxxix., cxliv.). The names מַשְׂכִּיל and מִכְתָּם are more
frequent than in the first collection (see above, p. 229).* Along
with מִזְמוֹר is here found, even frequently, the more general
שִׁיר, either before or after it, Pss. lxvi., lxvii. (likewise
Ps. xcii.), but never between the poet's name and מִזְמוֹר, and
so in the three possible positions, Pss. xlviii., lxxxiii., lxxxviii.
(likewise cviii.); Pss. lxv., lxxv., lxxvi.; Pss. lxviii., lxxxvii.
Hence it is clear that this שִׁיר, according to the sense of
these superscriptions, was never added except as an external
elucidation to the older מִזְמוֹר לְדָוִד, as if it proceeded from
a particular editor or copyist.† On Ps. xlvi., where it stands

---

* *Dichter des A. B.*, i.
† The LXX where שִׁיר stands with מִזְמוֹר, instead of using μελῳδία,
give ῳδή along with ψαλμός, which yields no sense, in spite of the fact that

alone, see above, p. 35. This entire use of שיר is foreign to
the first collection. But the inference from all the preceding
is very worthy of consideration, that in Ps. lxxxviii. 1 two
quite different superscriptions must have been blended,
although only in an external manner, since the first, running
as far as למנצח, can be readily separated. It is, however,
inconceivable that the same song had the one or the other
at pleasure because of the different significations of מזמור
and משכיל. We can only assume that after the first, the
whole song belonging to it has been lost, which will be
further substantiated presently. On the other hand, that
Pss. lxxii. and lxxxvi., as stated on p. 28, came into this
place is shown by the peculiar style of their superscriptions
even in this point of view.

In the last collection these two-sided statements, when they
are found, occur in precisely the same way as in the middle
collection, which is explained only by the remarks on p. 18.
The שיר is also thus found, Ps. cviii. If now these are
excepted, as borrowed from the one half of the earlier second
collection, Pss. ci., cviii.—cx. cxxxviii.—cxlv., superscriptions
of this kind are in general very rare and scattered,—namely,
מזמר without the name of a poet, Ps. xcviii., and מזמור שיר,
Ps. xcii.; but the name of the poet alone in Ps. ciii. and in
the Pilgrim songs, cxxii., cxxiv., cxxxi., cxxxiii. Neither the
one nor the other is found in any of the other songs.

3. But it is now necessary to speak particularly concerning
the poets named in the superscriptions. They are designated,
as elsewhere in such cases, by the preposition לְ; and
looking, in the first instance, merely to these statements, the
following are named :—

(1.) David. He is named as poet in all pieces of the first
collection, with the few exceptions explained on pp. 6, 23 ;

Hippolytos (*Opp. Gr.*, p. 191) busies himself to find a very lofty meaning in it
by means of allegory. On the distinction between νάβλα and κιθάρα or λύρα,
on the other hand, he speaks with greater intelligence, p. 191.

further, in the half of the second collection, Ps. li.—lxxi., with very few, and in this case quite unimportant exceptions, above elucidated ; but beyond this only at distant intervals, Pss. lxxxvi.; ci.; ciii. ; cviii.—cx.; cxxii.; cxxiv.; cxxxi.; cxxxiii.; cxxxviii.—cxlv.; thus altogether seventy-two times (xxxvii., xviii., xvii.). He bears besides, in Pss. xviii., xxxvi., the very high name of honour, according to the sense of the Old Testament, of the *servant of Jahvé.*

(2.) Davidic singers appear exclusively in those songs which form, according to p. 13, the second half of the middle collection. In particular, various singers among them are named :

(*a.*) The *sons of Qôrach,* Pss. xlii.—xlix., further as in a supplement, Pss. lxxxiv., lxxxv., lxxxvii., and in the first of the two superscriptions, in Ps. lxxxviii. They are, according to Numb. xxvi. 58; 1 Chron. vi. 7, 22; ix. 19; xii. 6 (xxvi. 1), one of the oldest Levitical houses, out of the distant præ-Davidic period, related to the still older house of Qehâth the son of Levi. In David's time, one of this house, *Haemân the Ezrachite* the son of Joel, had peculiarly distinguished himself as a singer, and had led many of his relatives to the arts of the Muses, 1 Chron. vi. 18-23 ; so that henceforward the Qôrachites became a proverbial word for "singers," 2 Chron. xx. 19. From this circumstance may be explained how Ps. lxxxviii. in the first superscription might be ascribed to the Qôrachites in general, in the second to Haemân, in particular did not the other reasons mentioned above, p. 35, show that the two superscriptions are not entirely coincident with one another. It remains, however certain, that since Hämân belongs to the sons of Qôrach his name is to be *attached to* the two psalms following in the same series, which is otherwise designated by the names of the sons of Qôrach.

(*b.*) *Asaf,* Pss. l., lxxiii.—lxxxiii. This name appears among the three most renowned singers of David, and superintendents of his music as a whole, Hämân, Asaf, Aethan ; frequently again as the most eminent or at least the most renowned: comp. 1 Chron. xvi. 5 with the more copious representation in xv. 17-21, and with the somewhat different account in xxv. 1 sq.; xxvi. 1. Indeed, in the historical writers of the Old Testament, from the post-exilian period, he is the only one who is associated unhesitatingly with David, as singer and poet, and almost given an equal position with him, 2 Chron. xxix. 30; Neh. xii. 46. In the books of Ezra and Nehemiah and Chronicles, the *sons of Asaph* are also named in a similar way to that in which the sons of Qôrach are named in these superscriptions of the Psalms.

(c.) *Aethan the Ezrachite* is named only in Ps. lxxxix.: he appears as the third of the three great music-masters of David, 1 Chron. vi. 29-32; xv. 17, and in the other places just named. Unfortunately, however, we can say very little else concerning all these three great masters of music and song of David's. It admits of no doubt that they as men of uncommon gifts, in David's and Solomon's times, brought song and music amongst those who, from their status, were chiefly bound to cultivate it—the Levites, to a development earlier unknown, and became the creators of a grand artistic music. But this might well be the only genuine historical fact that can be stated concerning them. Further, it is certainly by no accident that *three* great singers are always named as the leaders of all. This must refer to a fixed order of music, because in 1 Chron. vi. 18-32 the relative position of these three was legally defined; and because we meet the above-noted (pp. 228-230*) musical distinction so closely marked that we cannot here overlook it.

In other places instead of Aethan appears Jeduthun, for reasons unknown to us, as if that were only another name from another period for the same position, 1 Chron. xxv. 1; 2 Chron. xxxv. 15; Neh. xi. 17: comp. 1 Chron. ix. 16; xvi. 38, 41, 42. Jeduthun is, however (p. 224*), known to us from other sources as a creative master in music. And whilst

---

ᵏ *Dichter des A. B.,* i.

each of the three, Hämân, Asaf, and Aethan, 1 Chron. vi.,
appears to be descended from one of the three, all-embracing
chief families of Levi, Qehâth, Gerschom, and Merari, we must
rather believe, on a closer comparison of 1 Kings v. 11 and
Pss. lxxxviii., lxxxix., with 1 Chron. ii. 6,* that Hämân and
Aethan were originally like David of the stock of Judah, and
were adopted gradually, *honoris causâ,* as men distinguished by
high wisdom and art, as teachers of music and founders of
imperishable Levitical schools of singers into the tribe of
Levi, as we read in the post-exilian books.†

(3.) Besides these seventy-two songs which are derived from
David, and twenty-three from Davidic singers, the Hebrew
superscriptions further set down two only to Solomon, Pss.
lxxii. and cxxvii., and,

(4.) The solitary Ps. xc. to " Moses the man of God." Thus
altogether about a third of the songs of the present Psalter
are left without any statement of a composer; at least this
is so in the Hebrew text.

But here immediately a mass of considerations and reflections, not to be set aside, press upon the attention of the
historical student. For if all songs are thus assigned to
their poets, and, with the slight exception of the above three,
must proceed only from David and his singers; how comes it
to pass that the Psalter gives the names of no poets at all out
of the many other periods and centuries? The fact that until
the single exception of Ps. xc. no pre-Davidic poets are
named is explained of itself, since David is the earliest master
of Sion's song; but can it be that from the Davidic time onward
sacred song in Israel was silenced? If this in the light of more
accurate history is impossible, because it contradicts other

---

* Haeman is indeed expressly named merely in Ps. lxxxviii., not 1 Kings v. 11,
an Ezrachite; but he might have been so here also, since the language is here
obviously abbreviated, and such pieces of information as 1 Chron. ii. 6 would pass
before the historian's mind.

† Comp. on this further the *Oesch. des V. Isr.,* iii., pp. 354 sq., *note,* in the
2nd edition. The name Aethân is perhaps only an oral abbreviation of
Jedûthôn or Jadithôn.

clear testimonies like Isa. xxxviii., Jonah ii., how are we to understand the fact that the Psalter mentions no later poets at all in the superscriptions? Was it then arranged in its present form already in David's time? But this would not explain why a third of the songs, and obviously in greatest part the latest, contained no names. But if the inner style and peculiarity of all songs ascribed to David or to one of his singers be investigated, it is obvious even on a slight degree of attention, much more to a penetrating study, that the external similarity of very many of such songs is so great that it is purely impossible, in the strict historical sense, to refer them all to the same poet. Compare, *e.g.*, only the twelve ascribed to Asaf, and there is immediately seen to be between Pss. lxxv., lxxvi, and those surrounding these two, the greatest difference in all matters which might pass as tokens of derivation from the same poet. How much more does this apply in the case of the many ascribed to David! The distance, *e.g.*, between Pss. iii., iv. and Ps. v., between Pss. vii., viii. and Pss. ix., x. is infinite. If, on the other hand, we trace out the actual internal resemblances of the songs with regard to poets or periods, we soon discover how almost everything assumes another aspect; in fact, how, now and again, that which is actually related is separated widely from its connexion by means of the superscription, *e.g.*, Ps. lxxxii. (Asaf) from Pss. xiv., lviii. (David). But most difficult is the task, lastly, when in the particular case of any song it is desired actually to refer every word and every verse and thought to the composer named in the superscription, to give a consistent account of the whole. The problem, *e.g.*, is clearly to set before the mind how David, if he is actually the poet of Pss. iii., iv., vii., viii. (as close investigation certainly shows), can also have composed Ps. v. and Pss. ix., x. It is precisely the expositor who is thorough and sincere, who will here above all meet with the greatest difficulties, indeed impossibilities; and will either gain his knowledge of everything in the midst of the extremest confusion and uncertainty, or will be bound to adopt some other mode of thought in order to avoid remaining in complete obscurity.

Moreover, we learn only by means of the superscriptions—irrespective of Ps. xviii., comp. 2 Sam. xxii.—to what poet and singers these songs are ascribed; but that the superscriptions do not proceed, nor profess to proceed, from the poets themselves, has already become manifest to us from the close examination of them—at least in general. They do not come (setting aside the cases presently to be remarked upon) from the poets themselves, but from collectors, editors, and old readers, whose different hands can be readily distinguished in them, and who by no means desired to be regarded as of the same authority with the old poets. Therefore, no greater weight can be attached to them than they claim. If David is designated in the superscriptions of Ps. xviii., xxxvi., by the editor of an ancient collection of David's songs, as "servant of Jahvé," we learn from the very fact that he did not pretend to be David himself; and if David in a later collection (Ps. cxliv. 1) is named as the poet, although in the same song, ver. 10, laudatory mention is made of him as this "servant of Jahvé," we can place the brief note in the inscription no higher than the mind and purpose of the poet himself. We are thus by this means only warned in principle with reference to the superscriptions, not to forget the contents, nature, and history of the songs, or the very sense of the poet himself; but rather in this point of view again to bear in mind the manner, as above set forth, in which the present collection of songs arose. It is possible that several of these inscriptions contain a genuine historical tradition about the composer. But this must be derived, in each particular case, from the song itself; and we may nowhere avoid the trouble of seeking for the agreement of the internal and external testimonies. The conclusion from all exactest investigations of this kind is, to express it briefly in this place, that certainly a considerable mass of songs, and those the finest and most important, proceed from David, or at least from his time. The greater mass is derivable from later times and from very different poets and periods. The more frequently and profoundly we subject the whole to investigation, the more firmly is this conclusion arrived at; and it is a conclusion which by no means holds good merely in general (for in that case it would be very uncertain), but it may be established on certain grounds and indications, in the particular details of each song.

But if it be now inquired how, under such original conditions, such statements of the authorship·could be introduced into the superscriptions; we must in the first instance recall the general mode in which such books arose and were formed in ancient literatures. Of this—so far as it refers to the poetic literature of the Old Testament—we have already spoken, p. 233 sq.,* compared with p. 4 sq.

Further information is obtained for the most part by the closer examination of the three collections of which the Psalter consists. For in this point of view, again, these three parts are distinguished, as above defined, by the most significant tokens. The *first* collection, Pss. i.—xli., actually includes the greatest part of the most ancient songs, and very many in it spring from David or from his time. Again, there is no difficulty whatever in conceiving that the statements concerning David as poet here in the case of many songs springs from ancient and sound tradition,—*e.g.*, from such historical works on David as those of which we possess a type in the books of Samuel. In the case of Pss. iii., vii., xviii., this obtains, by means of another token, a peculiarly great probability, as will be presently explained. In this collection we have, then, a genuine Davidic foundation, and if the last hand which presided over these forty-one songs, ordering and bringing the superscriptions into their present form, did in fact designate also several later songs as Davidic; we can readily comprehend how several centuries after David a collection, whose basis is Davidic, might pass, without closer distinction, as generally Davidic.

---

* *Dichter des A. B.,* i.

It is quite otherwise with the *second* collection, Pss. xlii.—
lxxxix., whose superscriptions, according to p. 12 sq., indicate
in the one half songs of David, and in the second those of
Davidic singers.   This has no equally ancient and broad foundation; and if it never contained more than fifty-eight songs,
the most careful investigation could not succeed in placing
a single one of these songs in the form in which they here
appear in Davidic times.   But we have already laid too good a
ground in various preceding observations to allow us to remain
in entire uncertainty here.   For so far as we can now trace back
the history of this great collection of the present fifty-eight
songs, in accordance with various indications, the following is
the state of the case with reference to the statements of the
superscriptions concerning the poets and singers.   Alongside
of that first book of Davidic songs, there was another which
likewise was composed of genuine Divine songs of David and
of his time (according to p. 28), but in which were added,
especially in its later editions, many more of a later period.
Thus the basis of this collection also was Davidic, and those
added from a later time appeared, in spirit and in language, to
be so similar to the older ones, that this, like the preceding
collection, was on the whole regarded as Davidic.*   By the
side of and about contemporaneously with it a collection of
Divine songs was formed upon quite another basis; collocating
songs concerning which it was well known that they were
throughout un-Davidic.   The names of the poets, even where
they were possibly still known, were here purposely omitted,
and the more so because these songs were to subserve a higher
object.   They were, accordingly, never published as Davidic,
but passed, nevertheless, as fully worthy even of the Levitical
Temple-use, and were thus gladly distributed among the
three schools of Levitical singers and their ancient sacred

---

* Comp. as an example out of the treasury of Arabian poetic art the *Divân
of Ali*, and the treatise on it in the *Zeitschr. für die Kunde des Morgenl.*, ii.,
pp. 192-200.

heads, into three sections as songs of the sons of Qôrach, which might also be named after Häman, their head, songs of Asaf, and songs of Aethan.* This collection was originally much larger than it at present appears in Pss. xlii.—l., lxxiii.— lxxxix. For if the first two-thirds, songs of the sons of Qôrach and of Asaf, extend to Ps. lxxxviii., the third must certainly have originally contained much more than merely Ps. lxxxix. But we have seen a closer indication, pp. 41 sq., in the doubled superscription of .Ps. lxxxviii., of the fact that the number was certainly at one time larger. Again: their first order is now somewhat broken. It certainly was in the beginning (1) songs of the sons of Qôrach, Pss. xlii.—xlix., lxxxiv., lxxxv., lxxxvii., lxxxviii.; (2) songs of Asaf, Pss. l., lxxiii.—lxxxiii., and it is worth consideration that we possess of the former and of the latter precisely twelve, or at all events (if the reckoning be otherwise) an almost exactly equal number of songs; and (3) songs of Aethan, Ps. lxxxix.; whence it may be inferred that this song could not have originally thus stood alone. Thus there were Davidic books of songs and Levitical ones quite different from them. Here it is self-intelligible that the names of David and of the Levitical singers were at first only as the consecrated vessels for the reception of songs of both kinds, and served only as general inscriptions of the individual books or sections. When a new collector united the Davidic and the tripartite Levitical collection, he introduced the superscriptions with the names of the poets and singers in all the songs. In a similar way, in the oldest Davidic collection, Pss. i.—xli., it was new editors

---

* Nothing more resembles this than the manner in which the primæval songs of the Rig-Veda were distributed among the great Brahmanic priestly tribes, and even referred in detail to eminent heads of those tribes as ancient holy men. Comp. Max Müller's *History of Ancient Sanskrit Literature*, pp. 463 ff. Thus, in these names of books, both among the Hebrews and the Indians, the memory of the most ancient schools of priests and companies of singers has been most firmly retained.

who for the first time introduced these superscriptions throughout.

That these superscriptions arose in some such way is also clear, from the quite general reference of each of the twelve songs named on p. 42 *to the sons of Qôrach*, as if the super-scriber, even in the case of the individual song, desired to give no definite name of the particular singer. That he shunned the mention of it from another cause is not apparent.* But why this song was ascribed to the Qôrachites, and that to Asaf or Aethan, it is now more difficult to say. It is, however, to be observed that if we conceive the songs of the Qôrachites, Ps. xlii.—xlix., lxxxiv.—lxxxviii., as again put together; and further (p. 42) recollect that Häman and the Qôrachites are properly the same; then Häman (or the Qôrachites), Asaf, and Aethan, in the book of Davidic singers, follow one another in the same consecrated order as in 1 Chron. vi. 18-32.—But were there a similar collection of Salômonic songs, it would be easy to explain how out of such a Ps. ii. at the head of the older collection, Ps. lxxii. might come at the end of the later Davidic collection ; and that Ps. xc. (similarly to Deut. xxxii.) is borrowed from a collection—which sprung up in a similar way, but was only in extensive use among the ten tribes—of Mosaic songs, will be further elucidated in Vol. II.

In the *third* collection, Pss. xc.—cl., the statement of David's authorship appears, in a few songs above mentioned as being of a peculiar character, Pss. ci., cviii.—cx., cxxxviii.—cxlv., as if borrowed with these songs themselves from the former more complete second collection of Davidic songs. But Ps. xc. might be derived by the collector from Moses, and therefore placed at the head, because he found it in an older book of Mosaic songs, as has been before suggested. Elsewhere the

---

* But it is not permissible to explain — לְ otherwise, in cases where the like difficulties arise.

name of David appears only rarely and sporadically, Pss. ciii., cxxii., cxxiv., cxxxi., cxxxiii., as if from a first conjecture concerning the poet, which is here and there fixed where editors thought most readily to find David. Similarly, Ps. cxxvii. is quite singularly ascribed to Solomon, merely as it seems for the reason that a reader explained the house which Jahvé builds, ver. 1, of the Temple. For we arrive with these last entirely sporadic and here and there, as it were, invective references of songs to David or to Solomon,—manifestly at the last period of the entire development of these collections and new editions of song-books for higher uses. In the manner in which these sporadic inscriptions appear in the latest portions of the Psalter, they only show how gradually mere conjecture forced its way increasingly into this field of inquiry, and how genuine historical recollection of times so primæval was lost by degrees. Under such conditions, however, there is no reason why conjecture should stand merely here or there. It is always insinuating itself to an increasing extent ; and once in its course breaks away in another direction than the usual one. Thus the LXX ascribe a few more Psalms to David,* while on the other hand they refer others in a striking manner to well-known prophets ;† and this may be the first beginning of properly learned conjecture. In ordinary life it was, how- ever, the custom in Palestine in the last centuries before

---

* Namely, Pss xxxiii., lxvii , lxxi., xci , xciii.—xcix , civ , cxxxvii. The whole series, Pss. xci.—xcix , which in the Hebrew text is very bald, does not stand so bare in the LXX, as generally the LXX give to each Psalm a superscription, a note- worthy innovation ! Ps. ii , which was without superscription, was in old copies of the LXX, as still in some Hebrew copies, attached to Ps. i., as is seen from Acts xiii. 33. On the other hand, and this is much more important for us, they omit the name of David in the series, Pss. cxx.—cxxxiv., apparently because their Hebrew copy had not these additions, as may well be believed in this case.

† Pss. cxxxvii., cxxxviii., cxlv. (cxlvi.)—cxlviii , comp. lxxi.; Jéremjá, Haggái, and Zakharjá are here named, the last two even together, But the manner of citation is essentially different, and the sense different—the more so because some- times David's name is also found. Again, they translate Ps lxxii. otherwise. All this points to the hands of different translators, or even of mere conjecturists.

Christ, to refer the whole Psalter, without more exact discrimination, to David.*

The Chronicler, indeed, Neh. xii. 46, places David and Asaf
together as general examples of great ancient poets,† and a
name like τὰ τοῦ Δαβίδ, for the entire large Psalter, might
be intended briefly to designate, in the place where it first
appears (p. 30), the whole book merely by the most renowned
of its poets' names. But it is well known what gross misunderstanding was gradually attached to this designation, and
how later learned men among Christians and Jews, in part down
to our own time, have drawn the strangest conjectures from it.

But it is sufficient at the present day to have a concise
historical knowledge of such matters.

4. The state of the case is similar with reference to the
statements concerning the *historical occasion*, which is much
more rarely forthcoming, and in every case only with Davidic
songs. A genuine tradition may lie at the bottom of these,
but the greater part rest on the conjecture of later readers;
and here again the three collections in the same way give the
basis of the distinction.

In the *first* collection the superscriptions to Pss. iii., vii.,
xviii., give incontestably true historical traditions concerning
the occasion of the songs, and they completely concur
with the contents; further, the information with Ps. vii.
is drawn from historical books which have been lost to us.
Only Ps. xviii. recurs in 2 Sam. xxii. We see moreover,
from Isa. xxxviii. 9, that it was very usual in historical books
to mark the occasion of a song with standing brief expressions.‡
—Again, the fact that the above three Psalms stand together
in the early part of the first collection is not unimportant.
For it is only in Ps. xxxiv. that such a superscription appears

---

* See above, p. 30, Acts xiii. 22-36, &c.

† For if the הַלֵּל דָוִיד with him, 2 Chron. vii. 6, comp. xxiii. 18,
Ezra iii. 10, must be, without question, only a short expression for the present
Psalter, in other quite corresponding passages as 2 Chron. xxix. 30, at least he
places Asaf together with David.

‡ With — בְּ and infinitive following, *when he* . . .

in another manner—namely, in the manner which we first see predominating in the

Second collection. This contains a mass of such historical explanations, but they are apparently borrowed by the same hand from the present books of Samuel, and show only the attempt of a later editor to refer to David's life such songs as were held to be Davidic. The single exception to this is perhaps formed by the superscription of Ps. lx.: "when he quarrelled with the rivers of Arâm (Mesopotamia) and quarrelled with Ssôba-Arâm, and Joab turned from him and (thereupon) in the salt-valley of Edôm slew to the number of twelve thousand." For in the first place this information sounds so independent of 2 Sam. viii. 13, 14, comp. x. 16, 1 Chron. xviii., as if the superscriber had here quite other ancient sources before his eyes. Again: הִצָּה, "quarrel" is a rare and ancient word. Further, this song certainly contains, as is shown in Vol. II, an old genuine Davidic element, so that the superscription may thus be as ancient as in Pss. iii., vii., xviii. Lastly, there is here a significant departure from the choice of superscriptions in this collection elsewhere. For whilst here an occasion is stated from the later history of David, almost all other songs have his older history in view, and seek, when it is possible, any conceivable occasion from the first Book of Samuel. These other are the following: (1) Ps. li.: "when the prophet Nathan came to him, after he had gone to Bathsheba," 2 Sam. xii. This would be expected earlier with the older song, Ps. xxxii., which without doubt refers to such a case. (2) Ps. lii.: "when the Edômite Doeg came and announced to Saul, and said: David has come into the house of Abimelekh!" from 1 Sam. xxii. 6 ff. According to this, the tyrant addressed in this song would be Doeg, which appears like pure conjecture. (3) Ps. liv.: "when the Zifæans came and said to Saul: is not David concealed among us?" from 1 Sam. xxiii. 19, as though the Zifæans were as dangerous as the violent men depicted in the song.   (4) Ps. lvi. : " when the Philistines kept him captive in Gath, according to 1 Sam. xxi. 11-16, where indeed not the same words, but still a similar sense is found.   (5) Ps. lvii. : " when he fled from Saul into the cave," according to 1 Sam. xxii., probably because the song alludes to a flight in the first verse.   (6) Ps. lix. : " when Saul sent (people) and they watched the house to slay him," from 1 Sam. xix. 11, because the beleaguering of a city is spoken of in vv. 7, 15.—(7) Ps. lxiii. : " when he was in the desert of Juda," according to 1 Sam. xxii., because in ver. 2 there seemed to be a reference to a desert.

Quite answering to the style of these seven superscriptions are further :—(8) in the *last* collection, Ps. cxlii. : " when he was in the cave, a prayer;" again in accordance with 1 Sam. xxii., because the song treats of persecutors, and of the shutting-in of one pursued.   (9) In the first collection, Ps. xxxiv. : " when he dissembled (*i.e.,* played the madman) before Abimelekh, and he drove him away and he went," from 1 Sam. xxi. 14—xxii. 1, because the song gives thanks for a deliverance.   The copyist appears here only to state the name of Abimelekh, well known from Genesis, for a Philistine king, instead of Akhisch, so that it is hardly necessary to think of diverse sources of information.   That the editor of the last collection borrowed Ps. cxlii. from the second Davidic collection of songs is certain of itself, according to all the preceding.   Perhaps Ps. xxxiv. was likewise at last introduced from it into the oldest collection.

But now, in this instance again, we cannot see why the conjecture of later readers should hold its ground in the case of these nine songs ; and in fact we see in the LXX how still later readers went further in this direction; indeed in part extended their conjectures in quite other directions.   Pss. xxvii., xciii., xcvi., cxliii., cxliv., they sought to place at a remoter distance from David's life ; but they refer Pss. lxxvi., lxxx. to Assyrian history, and in this they hit upon the entirely correct explanation, at least in the case of Ps. lxxvi.

In a certain sense the superscription "Song of Pilgrim trains" has, as was explained above, p. 15, a purely historical significance; but must be separated from all others, as unique in its kind.

5. Lastly, in the case of a few songs, further short observations on the *design and use* of them are given. That is (1) לְלַמֵּד, *to teach*, Ps. lx., seems certainly intended to be understood as 2 Sam. i. 18; comp. above, p. 234;* since according to another token just explained,.at least the basis of this song is genuinely Davidic. (2) לְהַזְכִּיר Pss. xxxviii., lxx., probably signifies, according to Isa. lxvi. 3, *to be used as offerings of incense*, since אַזְכָּרָה is an offering of incense, but a suppliant song spoken in the Temple is like the offering of incense which ascends as a sweet savour to heaven,† Ps. cxli. 2; Rev. viii. 4. Such suppliant songs were then also to be used in the Temple along with the offerings of incense. The counterpart to this is לְתוֹדָה, Ps. c., to be used as a *thank-offering*, and as a *thank-song*.‡ (3) The words "song of the dedication of a house," which, according to p. 40, were introduced at a late period into the superscription of Ps. xxx., probably do not denote that this song was sung at the dedication of the house of *David*, as the LXX take them, or that the Psalm was to be sung at the dedication of any house; for it is self-intelligible that the Hebrews in such cases sung (Deut. xx. 5) merry popular songs, while this cheerful song has no reference at all to such an occasion; and, according to the whole spirit of the Psalter, so commonplace a popular reference would hardly have found place in the superscription. Probably this thank-song had been sung at the dedication of the second

---

* *Dichter des A. B*, i.

† Although אַזְכָּרָה is translated by the LXX, and following them, in Sir. 416, by μνημόσυνον, it has originally a much more definite sense: comp. the *Alterthümer*. p. 51.

‡ That לְעַנּוֹת in Ps. lxxxviii. is to be understood otherwise has been already suggested, p. 227; if it were taken as "for singing," it would yield no suitable sense: since every song serves of itself for singing, and Ps. lxxxviii. has nothing whatever peculiar about it.

Temple (although the song itself may be older), and it was hence so named, because it was appointed to be sung at every yearly memorial celebration of this day.*   More definitely the superscription runs, Ps. xcii. : "a song for the sabbath-day," to be sung on the sabbath, although the song appears to have been originally of a more general sense, and this definition was not given to it until later.   The LXX go much further in this very direction, as these new superscriptions—in part harder to be understood—show : Pss. xxiv., xxix., xxxi., xxxviii., xlviii., lxvi., xciii., xciv.†   Such superscriptions, too, are always very instructive both in the Hebrew and in the Greek text, so far as they contain historical traces of the application of songs in those ancient times.

On the *subscriptions* of the present divisions of the Psalter we have spoken on pp. 9 sq.   That the name *prayers* for the entire book which once (p. 12) assumed the predominance did not in the end prevail, may be readily explained after the first two collections were united with the third.   The entire large book was now destined, in the first instance, for the Temple-song ; it was therefore briefly denominated "Songs of Praise," תְּהִלִּים,‡ although in the LXX, after the frequent מִזְמֹר

---

* It will be readily understood that this day was yearly solemnized for a long period.   The festival may, however, have become gradually extinct, and then (*Gesch. des V. Isr.*, iv., pp. 406 sq) revived in the Maccabean period from quite new causes.

† Thus Ps. xxiv. was to be sung on *Sunday*, τῆς μιᾶς σαββάτου, Ps. xlviii. on *Monday*, δευτέρα σαββάτου, Ps. xciv. on *Tuesday*, τετράδι σαββάτου, and Ps. xcv. on *Friday*, εἰς τὴν ἡμέραν τοῦ προ σαββάτου.   Here only two days of the week are wanting ; but Ps. xxix. was also designed for the last day of the Feast of Tabernacles, ἐξοδίου σκηνῆς.   The ἐκστάσεως in Ps. xxxi. is noteworthy as merely taken from the words ἐν τῃ ἐκστάσει μοῦ, ver. 23, but can hardly signify anything other than ἀναστάσεως, Ps. lxvi., *on awakening* (a prayer); and in like manner the εἰς ἀνάμνησιν περὶ σαββάτου in Ps. xxxvii. probably denotes simply a song for Sabbath edification.   These annotations recall to some extent the manner in which the Greek and Syrian churches have divided the Psalter : comp. the extracts from Syrian copies and impressions in Franz Dietrich's " Comm. de Psalterii usu Publico et divisione in ecclesia Syriaca," *Marb.* 1862.

‡ Correctly formed like the תֻּכֻּלִּין, which likewise first appears in the Rabbinical writings, according to *Lehrb.*, § 177 c.   The further abbreviation, תִלִּים, θελειμ, is found in Origen and Hippolytus.

(p. 30*) the general designation ψαλμοί came into use; and this short name of the entire book, which was fixed only in a quite external superscription, was fully adequate even in this brevity. Only because editors gradually busied themselves (p. 1) also with Solomon's Psalms, the word "David's" was probably added after the other short designation (p. 52).

It is now easy to draw more general conclusions respecting the nature and origin of all annotations. Among all those annotations there is not a single one which we could be induced to derive from the poet himself. We do not certainly maintain by this that a poet might never in those times append with his own hand to his song an observation of the kind. But in this case the same hand must, by any safe token, be recognized; and this actually occurs once in the late song, Ps. cii., whose superscription is of quite another kind, and, according to all indications, affixed by the poet. Also in Hab. iii. 1 it occurs; but Habaqqûq is here named in a quite peculiar manner only as himself a prophet. In all other songs it can never be proved that the poet himself added such observations. On the contrary, all signs are against it. Generally speaking, it is not to be expected in the higher antiquity of poets who either did not write at all—or, at all events, certainly sang more than they wrote—that they should have deemed such observations necessary. Particularly it cannot be proved that the poets in the people of Israel attached their names immediately to the Divine songs. It was only the prophets who must always mention their names;† and the didactic poets who resemble them (Prov. xxx. 1) readily adopted this custom.

Hence, however, it follows, not that all annotations, without distinction, must on this account spring from the latest time. In fact, they increase in the course of time with the literature itself, as has been plainly recognized above by so many indications; and we see by the LXX how they still increase

---

* *Dichter des A. B*, i.   † Comp. the *Gesch. des V. Isr.*, i., p 86.

after the close of the Palestinian Canon. But the beginning
of them may reach into much earlier times: and the result is
that we obtain a measure of certainty concerning the relative
age and the value of annotations so various in kind.

For the oldest portion, several historical statements concerning the poet, the occasion and tradition of a song, may be
retained; for such were frequently found in the oldest historical
books. To this head belong the words from Pss. iii., vii., xviii.,
comp. 2 Sam. xxii., also Ps. lx. 1, 2 and Ps. ci., just as 2 Sam.
i. 17, 18, Isa. xxxviii. 9. These are to be definitely recognized
as remains of primæval genuine traditions; it is all but manifest
of itself that there were more of the kind, which, *e.g.*, did not
remain without influence upon the collection Pss. i.—xli.

The simplest designations of the kinds of songs, מִזְמֹר,
שִׁגָּיֹון, מִכְתָּם, מַשְׂכִּיל, as they, *e.g.*, stand in the first collection,
and Isa. xxxviii. 9, may also be relatively ancient, and have
been written long before the Babylonian exile. The same
holds good of the *Séla.*

The other musical notes may preserve many old genuine
recollections. They appear, however, in their entire present
form, to have been added, at the earliest, during the first
times of the new Jerusalem; and with this agrees the fact
that the use of the words נֶצַח, and מְנַצֵּחַ, p. 216 sq.,* recurs
according to present indications, for the first time in post-
exilian books.

In general, the great mass of the annotations was added by
degrees from the seventh and sixth centuries, not by one
hand, but by several in different times; the last were certainly
not added until about the middle of the Persian rule.
Further, the Psalter must, during these centuries of the
Persian rule, have been subject to considerable additions
and changes. The date of these to a year and day we are
not now in a position to state, but, according to certain
indications—for the consequence and effects we can clearly

---

* *Dichter des A. B*, i.

observe—they must actually have taken place. At present, viewed from afar, such a period as that of the first centuries after the destruction of Jerusalem may appear a barren obscure space without movement or change. We can no longer distinguish particular events in it by order of time to a year and a day; yet although on the whole it was a troubled time, it is certain that literary matters had a vital movement in it, and the period lasted long enough to inspire important changes in them. It is, however, our business to pursue as far as possible our inquiry into those matters which became unnecessarily obscure during those long intervening times. We have above shown that it is still possible to gain acquaintance if not with all, yet with the greatest and most important particulars.

ON THE HISTORICAL EXPLANATION OF THE PSALMS.*

If, then, many songs remained without any historical note concerning composers and occasions, and if, where such superscriptions are found, further investigation is first indispensably requisite; the historical explanation is thereby rendered very difficult for us moderns. It comes to this, that these songs, in the nature of their collection (p. 1 sq.), have nowhere very particular personal contents. In none of them, *e.g.*, is a human proper name found, except the well-known names of the sublime primæval fathers of the people, of countries, peoples, and towns. That it might be quite otherwise in other songs is shown by Judges v., 2 Sam. i. Even such deeper historical colouring as in Pss. lxviii. 26 ; lxxxiii. 7-9, is relatively rare : so carefully do the collectors of favourite

---

* Comp. of an earlier date *Berl Jahrb f. w. Kr.*, 1831, March, Nos. 45, 46. A beginning towards the historical explanation of the Psalms was attempted by the Antiochene-Syrian school : comp. the notes in the *Catal. Codicum Syr. Musei Brit.*, pp. 9, 10 ff, and in Badger's *Nestorians*, ii , p. 366.

songs avoid too strong a reference to particular individual histories. Only in Ps. xviii. 51 is David once named, in an ancient song; in one of later date, Ps. cxliv. 10.

It might thus be readily supposed that the historical explanation of these songs was in general either unnecessary—it being sufficient to explain the thoughts—or that it was impossible or unadvisable; and yet nothing is more certain than that it is neither superfluous nor entirely impossible.

For if we have in the Psalter merely songs which from the beginning had been designed for general use, we could indeed readily dispense with the history of their origin. Even in that case it would throughout be no matter of indifference for the history of religion and of the people Israel, whether a song sprung up in this or in that century. But on closer examination we can see without difficulty that a very large and important part of these songs, as particular impressions, proceeded purely from the peculiar history of the time; and such songs can only again completely revive for us in every word and every strophé, provided we understand the time and the conditions from which they sprung. It was in the midst of the great movement of the time, in the struggle of the higher spirit which was at work in Israel with the hostile world, that the deepest thoughts came to light which seek in these songs a manifold revelation. The object, again, of the superscriptions, in so far as the occasion of the songs is stated in several —let these statements have originated as they will—shows us that antiquity on the whole had still a correct feeling for their historical significance and would not be content with empty generalities in the explanation. The course of exegesis has also long shown how every expositor, whether he seriously desired it or not, had recourse to interpretations of the songs from the history.

If now it is impossible to dispense with the historical explanation, it is necessary on the other hand not to be led astray by arbitrary fancies and empty presumptions. It is precisely here, in the unmistakable difficulties of the facts, that errors and mistakes of every kind lie at hand, and are so dangerous. The brief review of the exegesis of the Psalter teaches, in this point of view, that confident assumptions, happy or otherwise, rather than those founded in history, were foisted on those songs; and the utmost attempts were made to elucidate many or all from the life of David. When this mode of procedure was seen to be untenable, unhappy doubts of historical truth set in so strongly in later times,—because closer examination did not immediately substitute something better,—that this whole field of inquiry fell into confusion, and it was scarcely understood whether a song was to be derived from the Davidic time or that of the exile. But it is impossible again to linger in such grievous uncertainty, whether the loss at the end be not much more sensible than all which it may be thought we have gained by doubt. To open the way to a firmer historical view is thus our present task. To pursue this with success we must first learn correctly to apply the proper means of investigation.

The Psalms do not stand alone in the collective literature of the Old Testament. It is the most accurate acquaintance with all the other parts of the Old Testament, in all their historical and grammatical relations, which will throw a bright light on the songs, short as they mostly are. Hitherto there has been a great neglect of this vital inter-connexion of all small portions of the Psalter with the remaining, for the most part, much clearer portions of the Old Testament, in an historical point of view. Yet so far we may be prepared from the first, in accordance with the rest of the Old Testament, to identify by certain signs the Davidic, Jesajanic, Jerémjánic, exilian and post-exilian periods; and on such first researches in the Psalter to be not entirely without resource for acquiring some certain information.

Then the Psalter itself—what manifoldness of songs, hard to be overlooked, and what variety, do we discover in it on a deeper penetration! Here is again a peculiar, widely extended, and diversified field, which above all we must strive to know most carefully and accurately in all its particularities. But if we have obtained in detail safe and comprehensive notions, then on a free glance over the mass, at first sight very confused, the related and the non-related matters separate into smaller, firmer, and brighter series; what is dispersed is again collected, on the principle of resemblance or difference, again into its groups; and an original clearness of the remoter or nearer connexion between the songs, often so strangely arranged, begins to be manifest. To follow up these with equal firmness and penetration, prudence and certainty, in all tokens and traces, in language, thoughts, and historical expressions, is a chief means for recovering the historical element of the songs in the sense of the poets themselves; and for assigning, where possible, each song to the place which belongs to it in the historical sequence. In this way the one is presently eluci-dated from the other, and a certainty previously unhoped for is built up. There are thus found numerous groups of more or less closely connected songs; and should a song actually (as is well possible) stand somewhat alone, the fact can be securely ascertained only in this way.

Finally, it is shown above, and it finds further particular confirmation, that also in the position and arrangement of the songs there lie significant indices for the history of the songs, so soon as we understand how to discover them in the right way.

All these means of investigation are now together to be so applied that every proposition which appears to result from the process may always find its warranty from the exact explanation of particulars; and where all means which can be applied, without putting any strain upon the words, harmonize, we have reached a certainty which becomes a secure basis for further inquiries.

It is true that in this slow and sure way it will not be possible immediately to assign every song to its time and composer with all certainty. All the above means do not occasionally suffice, in the want of ample historical information, for the precise definition of the day and year of a song. Still less can we in many cases, even when the period of a song can be identified with a degree of certainty, recover the name of the poet. It is impossible here to pretend to know everything. On the contrary, we succeed only in the first instance in finding in some songs from different times so many solid and immovable bases and grounds for further investigations. The songs which lie more in isolation, and more difficult to recognize, will then increasingly be open to exacter knowledge, so far as we can get at them with all the present possible resources at our disposal. On the age of a song in general a strong doubt can now hardly exist.

The utility of such historical knowledge, now securely being built up, is in all ways great. We shall thus begin to understand again every song for the first time in its complete nature. We shall with high joy observe how the voices of the exalted song of the religion of Jahvé resound through a long series of many centuries, never entirely dumb and sleeping. This is precisely a main advantage that we now clearly see,— that the Psalter includes in itself the blossoms of Divine song not from one or two periods, but rather from all the exalted times of Israel from David onwards ; whereby the Psalter first appears in its proper position relative to the other books of the Old Testament. The lyric song with its warmth and depth is, as it were, the heart of the Old Testament religion. To appreciate the emotions and pulsations of the heart and to follow them through all times cannot be without the most important consequences for our whole conception of the Old Testament. Finally, we can then also clearly review the changing fortunes of song in the course of those centuries, and amidst riches so great, at once with confidence distinguish the more original, weighty and permanent elements ; and thus we obtain, by giving up certain prejudices and errors of our predecessors, not merely new truths in exchange, but in fact a much greater good than all that we have apparently lost.

With such objects in view we have unquestionably the right to treat the explanation of the individual Psalms in another order than is customary; and the purely historical arrangement would be incontestably the best for learned consideration. Meanwhile, since in the case of several songs not much more than their general period can be defined; a material order may properly encroach upon the ruling order of time. Yet the more purely and completely the historical sense of any song gradually, by means of continued painstaking, comes into relief, the more must recourse to such a material order be superseded.*

I.

SONGS OF DAVID AND OF HIS TIME.

There is a series of Psalms, of peculiarly powerful genius, and unique in the elevation of their sentiment, which, according to the coincidence of all indications, can spring from no other and no less a poet than David himself. If we look for a moment away from these songs and from the whole Psalter, it cannot be doubtful, from the other sources, what manner of man David was in his innermost being as man and as poet. His was a spirit readily aroused and kindled by every important occasion and every great appearance, but ever proudly conscious of its unassailable elevation and power, its innocence and its right. From youth upwards he was borne up and strengthened by the still more lively consciousness of Jahvé the God of Israel as his mighty Leader and Defender,

---

* I now leave, 1865, this entire historical elucidation unaltered, just as it was put forth in 1839. How little since that time my successors have regarded the truth, and the fresh mischiefs that have thence sprung up, I shall be compelled to notice more fully in the following volume.

his only Giver of Victory and Exalter. In all circumstances and experiences of life he bowed his human pride before the Divine destiny, and resigned himself full of clear confidence and pure trust to the Divine gracious leading. Thus through all troubles and changes of life he grew from step to step, in genuine knowledge, in rock-like firmness of faith. As ruler and king he remained the same, a man of unfeigned sincerity and child-like submission, quickly returning from every kingly error and crime with irresistible force of true repentance to the ˙eternally true, and remaining to his extreme age ever a blest and blessed man. Such does David appear in the light of the feeble remains of historical recollection concerning him. That this extremely susceptible, deeply emotional spirit, of original creative power, early possessed the gift of expressing every true and deep impression in poetic form, and maintained and exercised it undisturbed to old age, we know not less certainly from the information in the historical books than from the genuine examples and monuments of his poetry collectively preserved in these. We see plainly from these that the poet was equally great with the man. For it will ever be true that the most elevated man may also be the greatest lyrical poet of his people.

If thus, in a collection of about 150 Psalms, which later tradition collectively ascribes to David, there are contained actually Davidic songs ; it cannot be too difficult to distinguish them by their spirit and contents. A part of this sublimity and of this consciousness, of these fortunes and experiences, so unique in the whole ancient people, must be clearly recognizable in every song, in every sentence. On continued acute examination, all these songs of like kind and cognate spirit must be definitely separated from all others, without the uncertainty remaining considerable which may readily appear on first inquiries and conjectures.

The result of all my often-repeated investigations is that Pss. iii., iv., vii., viii., xi. (xv.), xviii., xix., xxiv. 1-6, xxiv.

7-10, xxix., xxxii., ci., of which Ps. xviii. also recurs in 2 Sam. xxii., actually bear on them this genuine stamp of their derivation from David himself, and point, in unmistakable features, to that greatest poet. For in the first place, if they are read side by side, we find in all the same style and colour, as will be presently further shown in detail. Everywhere we meet with the same lofty and unique spirit, and we observe that *one* poet must have been the composer of the whole. But further, those true tokens of Davidic origin shine with equal clearness through all. The manner in which this poet feels his inward elevation, כָּבוֹד, iii. 4, iv. 3, vii. 6, xviii. 44-49, comp. 2 Sam. xxiii. 1,—as he is sensible, through the Divine grace, of being lifted up and strongly distinguished above all men, iv. 4, xviii. 21-31, comp. 2 Sam. vi. 21,—is perfectly unique as a phenomenon. No other poet could feel and express himself in his kingly dignity as he does in ci. 1-8, xviii. 44-46, 2 Sam. xxiii. ; raise himself as in iv. 3-6, in the consciousness of that unassailable elevation, with all-prostrating, involuntarily prophetic power and directive authority against his persecutors; and along with this ever bear the true weal of the people of Jahvé in his heart, as in iii. 9, xxix. 11, comp. 2 Sam. vi. 18, vii. 29 ; whilst words of harsher sound, like iii. 8, xviii. 35-43, xxiv. 8, comp. 2 Sam. xxiii. 6, 7, betray the alike fortunate and strenuous warrior and restorer of order. Moreover, think of that sun-like clearness of heroic confidence in Jahvé, scarcely once disturbed in the greatest distress by a short groan (iii. 2, 3, iv. 7), that strenuous feeling of right, that childlike openness and directness of mind, those unsought deep glances into the Divine and human ! And everywhere the outburst of originality and genuine creative power ! All this is found in mutual connexion only once, in its full peculiarity, and in the whole Old Testament is nowhere else to be found but in this great poet. In the case of a few other songs, *e.g.*, Pss. xxiii., xxvii., lxii., lxiv., cxxxviii., it might be a matter of doubt, at the first glance, whether they did not belong to the same

series, as incontestably Davidic songs served as a pattern to
many later poets. But in every instance, on a closer view, the
same conditions, the like sublimity and splendour of the spirit,
will not be found in them.

Other grounds and indications do not oppose this conclusion,
but only serve more and more to confirm it.

The language of these songs is obviously ancient and
entirely original. We even meet with words, connexions,
and significations which elsewhere early disappear, as תָּנָה,
Ps. viii. 2, קַו, Ps. xix. 5, מַבּוּל, Ps. xxix. 10, elsewhere only
in Gen. vi.—x., and there more as a proper name of the Flood
of legendary history; צֹנֶה only in Ps. viii. 8 for צֹאן (see
Lehrb. § 176 b); הָדְרַת קֹדֶשׁ, xixx. 2; and in the contemporaneous cx. 3, later repeated with the whole mode of
expression, xcvi. 9; the *phrase*, "when wilt thou come to
me?" ci. 2; favourite expressions like מַיִם רַבִּים, xxix. 3,
xxxii. 6, xviii. 17, frequently repeated in later writers;
יִשְׁרֵי לֵב, "the straight in heart," vii. 11, xi. 2, xxxii. 11,
comp. xi. 7, frequently repeated later, xxxvi. 11, lxiv. 11,
xciv. 15, xcvii. 11 : comp. cxix. 7; and as no other poet the
word בְּלִיַּעַל, which appears to be taken out of common life,
so frequently used by this poet (xviii. 5, ci. 3, 2 Sam. xxiii. 6,
comp. elsewhere only Ps. xli. 9, in the citation of another's
language). Hardly is another poet so fond of the כָּבוֹד for
the word's sake, both in reference to oneself, iii. 4, iv. 3, vii. 6,
and in reference to Jahvé, xix. 2 ff., xxiv. 7, xxix. 1, 3, 9. If
songs of other poets from the earliest centuries are compared with these, we shall be bound to admit the distinction
and the peculiar colour of all these songs; while not until
about two centuries after David, living poets regarded, as if
designedly, these old songs as the highest models, and repeated
much verbally from them. Just so we meet here with a mass
of quite peculiar figures and proverbs, for the most part not
found elsewhere, as iv. 8, vii. 8, xi. 2, xviii. 5, 6, 11, xix. 6, 7,
xxxii. 9. But most frequently do warlike expressions of all
kinds recur ; so that we observe how the great hero, versed in

battle and victory and all the arts of war, entirely breathes and lives amidst such thoughts and scenes. He speaks of Jahvé as his *shield*, מָגֵן, iii. 4, vii. 11, xviii. 3, 31, 36, comp. 2 Sam. i. 21; as his *rock*, xviii. 3, 4, 32, 47, 2 Sam. xxiii. 3. No older poet has spoken in this way, as the songs, which are also warlike, Ex. xv., Judg. v., show; whilst in later poets these same majestic figures are re-echoed, but in softer sounds.

Still more sensibly do the thoughts themselves, with the whole style of the poetry, show here original power and life. The grandest is creatively formed with light-winged art; a higher thought compresses others. Only in Ps. xviii., for particular reasons, which may apply to it as an intentionally long hymn of victory, is the language prolix. How truly this mass of songs was the old germ of didactic poetry, and the treasury of grand thoughts, which the people in later times increasingly adopted and wrought up, we may observe in the whole further spiritual development of the people. This will be presently shown in detail by many examples, although it is a difficult matter to exhaust this subject.—On the other hand, we nowhere meet in these songs with thoughts or even modes of expression which point to a post-Davidic time. For that David, after he had by him in Sion the ark of the covenant, could speak of the *holy mount*, iii.5, xxiv. 3; that by the הֵיכָל or great and splendid edifice, *palace* of Jahvé, xi. 4, xviii. 7, xxix. 9, is not to be understood, according to the clear connexion of these passages, the Temple of Solomon, but absolutely the heavenly palace, heaven itself, requires no further proof. (It would be a strange supposition that the Hebrews were in David's time ignorant even of the word and notion of a היכל, *greater house*, or palace.)

The position of these songs in the present Psalter, and their historical superscriptions, greatly favour the opinion of their high antiquity, and their derivation from David, as has been shown in Vol. I.* This external proof admirably supports the

---

* *Dichter des A. B.*

internal evidence. A similar external proof is the recurrence of Ps. xviii. in 2 Sam. xxii., of which we will speak further presently. For every one who understands the general course of the ancient literature of the people Israel, it would remain an inexplicable enigma, if no song at all of the greatest singer of Israel had been retained in the Psalter. And certainly we should be mistaken in supposing that David merely sang the comparatively few songs which now remain in the Old Testament. He, that fertile singer, who, according to the brief intimations of the historical books, described every important occurrence of his life in song, would compose far more songs; and the mouth of "the sweet singer of Israel" (2 Sam. xxiii. 1) was, according to all plain indications, far more frequently full of inspired song. But those songs in the Psalter which we at the present day can recover, and verify as unquestionably proceeding from him, are the more certainly his. And certainly these twelve songs in the Psalter, united with the remaining three in 2 Sam., are not merely the flower and crown of all Old Testament songs, as well as the proper basis of all the Psalms; but they completely suffice for the recognition of the great poet and king himself in his innermost life and in all his greatness. Still more clearly than in the historical remains of recollection concerning him we peruse in his own songs the great heart of David, and perceive with no small satisfaction that his ancient high poetic renown is not baseless; and that he justly names himself, in the clear anticipation of his eternal poetic glory, at the head of his last song, 2 Sam. xxiii. 1, the sweet singer of Israel.

But we possess, further, some songs which must proceed, if not from the great lyric poet of Israel himself, yet from poets of his time. The song, Ps. cx., is unquestionably of his time, and refers to his history. Ps. ii. is connected, at least most nearly, with his time. These songs bear the greatest possible resemblance to those of David, both in language, in thought, and in their whole tenor, and thus in no slight degree confirm the same conclusion.

We will, however, make further the provisional and probable admission that, besides these songs, important fragments of Davidic poetry, adopted into later songs, may by these means have been preserved. And this is actually proved (as was already incidentally observed in the first edition) by the closer examination of several passages. xix. 2-7 is properly only the beginning of a Davidic song which a later poet has used. The following pieces are, according to all indications, woven into the substance of later songs:—lx. 8-11, lxviii. 14-19, cxliv. 12-14, in a song where indeed vv. 1-7 are also borrowed from Ps. xviii.; pieces in style and colour, spirit and life, so closely resembling the songs of David himself, or at all events of his time, that they may with safety be ascribed to the same poet. And although, of these fragments, in translation and explanation we do better to leave the lines lxviii. 14-19 in the place where the later poet has interwoven them with his song, we prefer to take the others as immediately belonging to this position.

Lastly, the following is a further important proof of the genuine derivation of these songs from David,—that, along with all their internal similarity, they reveal on the other hand such extraordinarily various situations and great changes of life in the poet, such as we could only expect from David's strange vicissitudes of fortune. Small as may be the number of the preserved songs of David, we nevertheless perceive in those which originated not like Pss. viii., xix., xxix., merely from the calm contemplation of universal truths, but from the commotions of the outward life itself, some of the most important experiences and turning-points in his life, and cannot without some result and profit compare therewith the historical traditions.

This leads us to details; and we must now venture the

attempt, so far as practicable, to collocate the individual songs
in their relation to David's life-career.   In fact, in the case of
most, no important doubt can arise to which of the sections
of that life they generally belong.

1. Psalm xi.

Even in the midst of great life dangers the poet declares, in
opposition to the anxieties and dastardly counsels of faint-
hearted men, the firmest and purest confidence in the majesty
and justice of Jahvé, who knows and judges all earthly beings
alike, against whose penetrating glance the most stealthy
cunning of the wicked man is powerless,—a fine and sharply
drawn contrast of human and Divine procedure!   All is the
rapid powerful outgush of *one* great impression.   After the
poet, from the very first, vexed by the dastardly counsel,
briefly explaining his confidence, has collectively set before
himself the words and reasons of the faint-hearted ones, vv. 1-3,
his higher consciousness urges him the more strongly to
express clearly and sharply the confidence of the pious man
with its reasons, and thereby to console himself, and to raise
himself up, vv. 4-6 ; until he concludes with a brief firm glance
into the dark future, ver. 7.   The reasons for disgraceful flight
appear weighty enough to the faint-hearted ; on the one hand
the present well-laid designs of craft; the imminent danger
(ver. 2) ; then, generally, the complete dissolution of order in
the state, which, making everything insecure, seems to counsel
flight to the upright man (ver. 3).   But all such anxieties
cannot deprive the poet of his higher tranquillity, nor tempt
his firm and upright mind to dastardly flight, as he here says
from the very first, ver. 1, with the most powerful brevity, and
then from the second strophe onwards, recurring to the same
point, in a more amplified expression.   Unquestionably uttered
by David in the first serious dangers of his life under Saul.
But the historical information is here least adequate, and
remains, until David becomes king, very incomplete.

The brief song falls, in conformity with the development of its fundamental thought, into two strophes, each of three verses. But these, in the restlessly fluctuating language, are extended to seven verses. A very short third strophe with only *one* verse concludes the whole, with the greater calmness of effect.

1.

1   To Jahvé I cleave! how can ye say of my soul:
       "flee to your mountain, birds!"
    "For lo! the wicked bend the bow,
      fit upon the string their arrow,
  to shoot in the darkness against the upright in heart."
    "When the foundations are overturned,
The righteous man—what shall he do?"

2.

Jahvé is in His holy palace,
    Jahvé—in heaven is His throne;
His eyes behold—His eyelids try—the sons of men.
5   Jahvé tries the righteous man;
but the wicked and lover of cruelty His soul doth hate;
    causeth to rain upon wicked men coals of fire with
      brimstone
a glowing blast is the portion of their cup.

3.

For righteous is Jahvé, loving all that is right;
    he who is upright, shall His countenance behold.

Ver. 1. חסיתי, in like manner at the beginning, vii. 2, xviii. 3. On תאמרו ל, comp. iii. 3, iv. 7, xxvii. 8.—*Flees:* is a proverb which indeed is only found here, but it is quite clear that it was a pitiful cry of lost men, as of birds threatened by huntsmen, exhorting them to save themselves by hasty flight. צפור as a noun of multitude with the *plur.*, *Lehrb.*, § 176 *b*, so that the K'tîb is correct. The figure of the hunter thus

correctly continues, ver. 2.—Ver. 3, comp. on the figure,
lxxxii. 5; lxxv. 4. כִּי as a particle of time, *when*, usually comes
immediately after the verb, but here and Job xxxviii. 41 it
stands in a singular manner before a circumstantial proposition
(comp. § 337 c) with the *imperfect* in the signification of the
present. In the main sentence then follows the *perfect*, גָּעַל
as after a conditional clause; and here we note as a somewhat rare phenomenon that it remains after the interrogative
word מַה, comp. § 326 b.—Ver. 6. The Massor. accentuation
is here omitted. Since the word פַּחִים as *nets*, derived from
פַּח, here gives no sense, and an expression like פִּיחִים from
פִּיח, *soot*, would likewise be of no assistance, it is better to
read instead with transposition of the י and in the closest
relation to the following word, פַּחֲמֵי אֵשׁ, *coals of fire*, formed
just like גַּחֲלֵי אֵשׁ, Ps. xviii. 13. Although פֶּחָם according
to Prov. xxvi. 21, in itself denotes the *coals* as *black*, but גֶּחָל
as glowing, it may notwithstanding, in the connexion of
language, very well denote these also, B. Jes. xliv. 12, and is
joined with אֵשׁ quite in the same way as in the *Aeth.*, 4 Ezr.
xiii. 13; xiv. 41. And although it usually, as a noun of multitude, does not appear in the plural number, § 176 b, yet it can
assume it in the same way as the גֶּחָל formed quite similarly.
The whole verse, however, manifestly only obtains its true
sense through this understanding of the words. The first
member thus yields the figure, so frequent in the Old Testament, of a rain and fire of brimstone falling from heaven, as at
Sodom on one occasion; the second, the figure of a poisonous
simoon, as if to be imbibed or inhaled in the cup of poison—
which does not come down like the other, straight from heaven.
On יַמְטֵר, see § 343 b.—Ver. 7. יָשָׁר with the plural in the
predicate, according to § 319 a. The last and highest hope is
here expressed at the end: that the upright shall at last behold
the pure light, however long the darkness may have lasted;
shall certainly in the end feel themselves thrilled and exhila-
rated inwardly by a Divine beam; comp. iv. 7; xvii. 15. The

צְדָקוֹת are, according to § 176 c, the expressions of righteousness or the virtues of man.   On פָּנֵימוֹ, see § 247 d.

2. PSALM VII.

Here we see the same David already become great and
mighty in dangers and battles, as leader of a band of his own
amidst the changing fortunes of whole peoples (ver. 9) and
conscious of his higher dignity (ver. 6), but not yet as king.
[All evidence concurs in favour of finding in the superscription
an old and certain tradition, according to which David sung
this song because of a Benjaminite Kûsh.] The latter, as a
Benjaminite, probably a partizan of Saul's, had, according to
vv. 4, 5, only sought the friendship of David in order, when
the opportunity came, the more keenly to injure him—an
occurrence quite in keeping with the character of those times,
one of the thousand dangers of David under Saul, although
all our present historical books tell us nothing of this particular
case.   The song itself shows us David in his first most violent
excitement and revulsion of feeling concerning the faithless
treachery of the false friend.   Although from the first seeking
to collect himself in confidence towards Jahvé, he is yet
overmastered by the thought of the profound unworthiness
and basest villainy of the traitor, as well as of the greatness
of the danger that has thereby arisen.   A storm of most
various thoughts, fears, hopes, breaks in changing language
forth from the inward commotion of the poet's mind.   Justly
is the song named in the superscription a Dithyramb (שִׁגָּיוֹן).
But the more intensely the pure strong soul of the poet in the
midst of extreme danger feels the inward vileness of the
faithless deed, the more freely he, in the consciousness of his
own incapacity for such wickedness, can call upon God to
punish him in the severest manner, if he should ever do the
like : the more strongly and boldly does he demand and expect
Divine judgment for the punishment of that wicked one, as of
all ; and the more confidently does he confront the disclosure

of the immediate designs of the crafty deceiver. Thus the language falls, having passed from the more composed beginning soon to the highest excitement,—gradually down to greater rest, until at last all feelings are silent in the *one* thought of rest and hope in God. Thus at first the poet, on his cry for help, is soon so overpowered by the representation of the greatness of the villainy committed, that he calls upon God anew—instead of to save him—to punish him in the most sensible manner, if he should do as the enemy. Here his feeling and his language become even more unrestful and stormy the more clearly he represents to himself the villainy committed, vv. 2, 3, 4-6. But the more zealously he wishes that such villainy might receive retribution in his own person (were it necessary), the more boldly, after a pause, does he cry to God to punish the wrong actually done. And since private persons were not concerned, but the fates of whole tribes and peoples, he appeals for an universal judgment to be held upon the earth. This freer glance of prophetic outlook into the eternal Divine operation and into all the future, wonderfully calms the storm of the poet's bosom, and softens his language, vv. 7-12; so that at last, again recalling what is immediately before him, he foresees as certain that the foe will renew his treachery, but also in loftier calm, looks beyond to the speedy destruction in which his craft and malice will end, while the faithful evermore rejoices in God, vv. 13-18.

The proper and peculiar art of this song lies in the fact that the poet understands how to bring to a proper and perfect level, and to smooth down all the storm of his bosom and the fluctuations of his thoughts in the remembrance of God, and so in the expression and flow of his language, by means of a loftier mood of calmness, which becomes victorious. Thus it falls into three somewhat extended proportionate strophes, each of six verses, the first two of thirteen, the last of twelve verse-members. In each the first two verses are strongly separated from the last four. Between the first and second lies the highest excitement; the first rising to the acmé of unrest, the second sinking down from that point. At the end of the second, rest and largeness of view are already won. But the third gives further the application of this to immediate circumstances. More briefly: in the first part the force of complaint predominates; in the second rest returns through the contemplation of the eternal Divine righteousness. In the third we have the joyous and tranquil glance, thence arising, towards the immediate danger. Thus this song is a splendid example of the manner in which, even in extreme danger and unrest, higher contemplations yield true hope and rest, pacifying the storm of the passions.

1.

1   Jahvé, my God! to Thee I cleave:
        from all my persecutors, help, deliver me!
    that he tear not like a lion my soul,
        rending asunder without saviour!
    Jahvé, my God! if I do *this*,
        if iniquity is in my hands;
5. if I my friend with evil recompense

·   ·   ·   ·   ·   ·

·   ·   ·   ·   ·   ·

    I delivered him who oppressed me without cause—
    then let the enemy pursue, take my soul,
        and tread to the ground my life,
    and my greatness let him pin to the dust!*

2.

Up, Jahvé, with Thy wrath,
    lift Thyself up with the punishment of my oppressors!
stir Thyself for me, appointing judgment!
    and let the community of the peoples surround thee,
and above them do Thou return to the height!—

---

* The Séla is in this impression so denoted.

Jahvé judges the peoples : give sentence concerning me,
    O Jahvé !
  according to right, according to innocence let it be
    done to me !
But let the evil of the wicked pass away, so that thou   10
    . strengthen the righteous man,
  Thou trier of heart and reins, O righteous God !
My shield stands with God,
  who helps the upright in heart ;
God is a judge of the righteous,
  yet a God who is angry every day.

3.

It may be He will again wet His sword ;
  the bow he already bends and directs,
prepares death weapons for himself,
  makes His arrows burning.
But lo ! he will hatch vanity,
  pregnant with mischief, he will bring forth deceit ;   15
a grave he digged, hollowed it deep
  and fell into the abyss which he makes !
His mischief will turn upon his head,
  upon his crown his cruelty rush down !
O praise I Jahvé according to His righteousness,
  and sing Jahvé's, the All-highest's Name !

xix., ver. 3. The transition here into the *sing.*, shows, as
frequently, that the poet now, in the representation of the main
danger, thinks more closely of the enemy at that time especially in
pursuit of him, or of the leader of his enemies : comp. vv. 13-17.
But he who threatens the poet with danger to his life is also
that most faithless friend, whose treason has just been ascertained ; and the feeling of the baseness of this treason seizes so
violently on the poet that he immediately, vv. 4-6, imprecates
on himself the extremest punishment from God, if he should do
the like. נאת, ver. 4, more closely explained by ver. 5, and the

perf. vv. 4 and 5, is only explained in this connexion by
§ 355 *b*. But, in fact, he *cannot* so act. The faithless friend
alone has broken the covenant ; then against him be the
penalty ! ver. 7 ff.—The second half of ver. 5 expresses plainly
the opposition—how that the poet is not merely incapable of
requiting good with evil ; but, on the contrary, has shown
kindness and saved the life of the enemy who wars upon him
without cause. This is eminently appropriate to David's
famous magnanimity, 1 Sam. xxiv. 16, and thereby the sense
is truly completed. The ‍ should here of itself express the
contrast ; but this in the present connexion is too impossible.
Much more probably two whole clauses have here been lost,
somewhat as follows :

אם גמלתי שלמי רע
וְשִׂנְאָה אֲשַׁלֵּם אוֹהֲבִי
אִם לֹא פִעַלְתִּיו טוֹב תַּחַת רָע
ואחלצה

that is :

> *if I do ill to my ally,*
> *and with hostility reward my friend,*
> *if I requited not his evil with good,*
> *and delivered . . . .*

The over-sudden transition is thus softened ; but the best
confirmation of this hypothesis is furnished by the circumstance that in this way each of the three strophes would
uniformly consist of six verses.—Ver. 7 : *with* thine anger,
bringing thine anger, or, as the following clause explains, the
punishment of thine enemies (§ 176 *b*).—On the perfect צוית,
comp. lxxi. 3, and § 341 *b*. The imagination of the poet
reviews here the whole grand process—how the judge appoints
judgment, around him all peoples throng to receive justice,
and He, when the process is finished, high above the great
host, again soars up to heaven (*to the height,* xviii. 17), so, in
vanishing, showing clearly to all that He is the highest judge :
comp. Judges xiii. 20 ; Isa. iii. 13.—Ver. 10 : בוחן for ובחן

according to the LXX Pesch.; the same transposition of the
ו is found lv. 20; Ezek. xiii. 7; 2 Sam. xiv. 14 (*Gesch.*
iii., p. 237).—Ver. 11 : עָלָיו it lies *upon* him, to protect me,
lxii. 8.—Ver. 13 : אִם לֹא, as an oath, as elsewhere; *certainly* He will, &c. The dependent proposition begins plainly
with the sharp הִנֵּה ver. 15.* The לּוֹ, ver. 14, is without
emphasis, inserted after ו, § 307 *b*. From vv. 13-17 the
same subject only. On vv. 13, 14, comp. quite simply xi. 2.
The poet certainly anticipates that the enemy would soon
afresh in craft purpose to slay him. With ver. 17, as very
similar, agrees 1 Sam. xxv. 39.

The next songs which can be discovered in David's life are
the two dirge-songs which were not adopted into the Psalter,
see Vol. I, pp. 149 sq., and p. 141.† From the grand time when
David, anointed to be king over all Israel, took his seat in conquered Jerusalem, and there also appointed to the ark of the
covenant its abode, we have, however, in the Psalter immediately the song—

3. PSALM XXIV. 7-10.

This is plainly the festive song wherewith the ark of the
covenant was brought to Sion, and there obtained its firm seat,
2 Sam. vi. It is fully characterized by the cheerful mirth and
innocence, the figurative simplicity and high nature-poetry, of
the Davidic time. Whilst one half of the priests are stationed
at the gate to receive the sacred ark and bring it to its place in
the city, it is brought ever nearer to the gate by the other half.
The alternate song which thus becomes possible (i., p. 49)†
is built on the thought on the one side of Jerusalem, on the

---

* It is not necessary to show in detail how on all original grounds it is entirely
incorrect and unworthy to explain *if he* (the enemy) *turns not, i e.*, does not
improve, *He will*, that is, God, *wet his sword*, &c. Anything so grossly sensuous
and lowering, as if the true God were only a Jew, the Bible nowhere expresses of
Him. The apparently very similar places which might here be appealed to, are
not similar.

† *Dichter des A B*, i.

other of the sanctuary of this only God. In the following manner :—

Into the ancient venerable city a new king must now pass, and he the highest and mightiest conceivable—Jahvé himself, throned on His ark of the covenant; for this king, whose equal never entered this city, the grey gates, venerable in their antiquity, are too small and petty (for the height of the gates must answer to the dignity of the entering lord of the house), so that sometimes gates of extraordinary height were built;* let them then lift themselves up and renew themselves! so cry to them from afar those who accompany the new king. But each new demand excites at first merely astonishment, and the authority of the old king rises against it. Therefore the grey gates do not immediately obey; but the inquiry sounds back first from them: Who the new king is? And then he is more exactly described in his glory, and anew resounds the demand upon the gates; new responsive inquiry, new answer, with still more exact designation of the highest attribute of the new ruler, so that the doors at last silently obey, whilst at the same time the thronging train arrives, and as the ark of the covenant enters, the old gates rise to new dignity and height.

Thus this little song serves with true appropriateness for the novelty of this solemn train; and imperceptibly the exalted God of Israel in all His dignity is also praised as the mighty God of war, to whose rule Sion must be subject. David may, without difficulty, be considered the poet.

1.

Lift, gates, your heads;
   lift yourselves, gates of eld,
  that the glorious king may enter in !
    " Who is then the glorious king ?"
   Jahve, the mighty and hero,
    Jahvé, the hero of war !

---

* Comp. Prov. xvii. 19; *Jour. As.*, 1856, ii., p. 479; Munzinger's *Ostafrikanische Studien*, p. 328, 5, 6.

2.

Lift, gates, your heads ;
  lift them, gates of eld,
that the glorious king may enter in l
  " Who is, then, the glorious king ?"
Jahvé of hosts ;
  He is the glorious king !

The most significant point in the alternation of these two strophés is manifestly that the one designation *Jahvé of Hosts* in the second must be much weightier than all the three in the first. Great is Jahvé already as the *Mighty One and Hero,* or more definitely as the *Hero of War,* as He once approved Himself, Ex. xv. 3, and now again in the latest time ; but incomparably higher is he still as *Jahvé of Hosts,* so that as soon as this name, short as it is, resounds, all bow before him. Thus we feel that at that time this Divine Name passed for the newest, most adequate, and, as it were, most magical, seeming, by the sense of its singular juxtaposition, to point to a mysterious Infinite. How this is to be historically understood, is further explained in the *Gesch. des V. Isr.,* iii., p. 87 of the third edition.

Since, now, under David and Solomon a great frequentation of the new sacred place in this new and higher time certainly very early set in, poetry might hold it appropriate, in ex-plaining the dignity of the place and protecting the truth, to teach that only the pure man was worthy of the holy place, and only he in visiting it, would obtain salvation and blessing, Ps. xxiv. 1-6, Ps. xv. Here, therefore, short, but very clear and powerful pictures of the true Israel are sketched, and we can thence briefly see what demands that time made on each man among the people. Thus these songs, designed for the instruction of the whole people, probably sung by alternate choirs of priests before the sanctuary, have a very great historical significance. They also afford the first example in

this place of an application of poetic art to teaching. Most
expressive and rich in contents, also the oldest, and breathing
entirely the same spirit as the song, presently to be explained,
Ps. ci., is of the two

4. PSALM XXIV. 1—6.

After preparation has been made by a brief lofty description
of Jahvé as Creator and Sustainer of the whole earth and of
all men, for the thought of the nature and dignity of this
Supreme God, vv. 1—2, it is asked, Who is worthy to tread
His holy place ? ver. 3. And there sounds back the suitable
reply that only *he* in whom there has been a preparation of
goodness, and who thus for the higher strength seeks God, can
bear from the sanctuary increasing strength and salvation as
his reward. Thus peculiarly the whole community of Jahvé
should be disposed, and be blessed, vv. 4—6. Two strophés
in calmest language, each of three verses, and 6—7 verse-
members.   How ancient is this song appears from the fact,
that in context and form it echoes Isa. xxxiii. 14—16.

1.

1   Jahvé's is the earth and its fulness,
               all land and they who therein dwell;
          for *He* has founded it on seas,
               and on streams He now holds it fast.—
          Who will ascend Jahvé's mountain ?
               who stand at His holy place ?

2.

          " He who is of pure hands, of clean heart,
               lifts not his pleasure to vanity,
          and swears not for deceit :
5.   he will receive blessing from Jahvé,
          and righteousness from the God of his salvation.
          Such are they who seek him,
               who seek thy countenance, Jakob's God !"

According to ancient opinion, the earth, as it is plainly
described in ver. 2, is a plane surface, rising out of the water,
surrounded by the stream of Ocean ; for the water seems
everywhere deeper, and even under the earth springs and
rivers appear to confirm this. The looser therefore this ground
the more wonderful appeared the holding of the firm land,
supported by mountains like deepest pillars, cxxxvi. 6, Prov.
viii. 27, 29; Gen. i. 2, 9, 10.—Ver. 4. נַפְשׁוֹ the reading,
after xxvii., Prov. xix. 18. According to the Q'rî the sense
would be : he who pronounces not to evil (impiously)—Ex.
xx. 7—my soul, *i.e.*, me, swears not falsely by me ; but neither
does Jahvé here speak, nor is that explanation in itself easy ;
for in that case we expect שְׁמִי for the here unsuitable נפשי.
—Ver. 5. *Right* often thus is found beside *Salvation, Righteousness* along with *blessing,* as consequence and recompense
proceeding from God for goodness. For the pure original
right is indeed, in general, eternal in God, and maintained by
Him. But not until the individual man approaches him and
virtually seizes upon it, does it become for him right—fruitful
and active right—a right which is thus identical with *salvation*
and blessing, and is frequently interchanged in expression
with these. Comp. xxiii. 3, xxii. 32, especially cxxxii. 9
with ver. 16. Conversely, עָוֹן unrighteousness, sin = perdition,
suffering, xxxi. 11. Before יעקב ver. 6, אֱלֹהֵי is to be
inserted from the LXX, Pesch., and a few copies. The turn
of the language to address is at the close very appropriate.
But precisely because it is new, the name of God cannot well
be wanting, whilst "Jakob" as a name of the people would
stand here at the last altogether too isolated. It must have
been understood emphatically of the true "Jakob," or the
ideal Israel. But for this there is here no ground at all ;
and the higher sense would be in nowise suggested and
intelligible.

But here, plainly, the song is entirely at an end ; it has an
external conclusion, and, moreover, it is internally completed.

vv. 7—10 must form an entirely different song, and have also an entirely different meaning and object. In the second song Sion must first receive the ark of the covenant and become a holy city. In the first it is already the ordained holy place. The second must be older by some years. The first is a purely didactic song, and Jahvé appears as the God of all men; the second a song of victory and Jahvé a God of war. The beauty of the question, ver. 8, would be entirely lost, if Jahvé were already named. Every transition and every bond of union in words and thought is wanting; in opposition to which each song shows for itself a full clearness and completeness. In common both are distinguished merely by a high antiquity, and both refer to Sion. Theirs is therefore no original connexion.

5. Psalm xv.

Is also ancient, yet somewhat more recent than the previous song, and more like an early copy of it. Here the further exposition of a part of the preceding only is new; the description of the Pure man, which appeared to a poet to be all too short and general in the preceding song, ver. 4, and which is here further portrayed in detail with great impressiveness. But to the above object diligence is here only applied; and it is incontestably no accident that it is a series of exactly *ten* propositions to which here the whole life of the pious man is referred.* The fine introduction and completion of the preceding song is wanting here, in regard to material. For the rest, the language is not held here as in the preceding song, merely of those who come to visit the sanctuary. It is also the stated dwellers in Jerusalem of whom the poet speaks. They carelessly suppose that as dwellers near the holy place they shall ever dwell in security and happiness. Unquestionably this belief was the peculiar means of peopling the holy

---

* Comp. the *Gesch. des V. Isr.*, ii., p. 239 of the third edition

city, and that increasingly. But the more powerfully does the poet here speak against the superstition which was so readily connected with that belief; comp. Isa. xxxiii. 14-16, Ps. l.

> Jahvé! who shall sojourn at thy tent? 1
> who dwell upon Thy holy mountain?
> He who walks sincerely, who practises right,
> Who in heart speaks truth,
> harbours not slander on his tongue,
> doeth not ill to another,
> raises not reproach against his neighbour;
> To whom vileness seems contemptible,
> but who honours the fearers of Jahvé;
> who has sworn to his hurt and changes it not;
> who gives not his money to usury, 5
> nor takes bribes against innocence:—
> who does *this*, shall never waver!

From the *dwelling*, ver. 1, it might readily be imagined that strangers ordinarily remained a longer time at the sanctuary, *e.g.*, for a week, or took in the city a stated dwelling always standing open to them; the like of which is now done at Mekka, comp. Burckhardt, "Arabic Proverbs," n. 480 on *djawr* = גּוּר. But in fact the song has in view rather the constant inhabitants of Jerusalem, as is especially clear from the conclusion, ver. 5 c.—Ver. 3 to the last clause of ver. 5 is the relative clause, begun at ver. 2, continued from the participle through all verbal moods, as they are suitable, according to § 350 b. Ver. 4, נִבְזֶה better suits the thought, taken as neuter (Isa. lviii. 13, and especially similar, Ps. xxxvi. 5) than as masculine. The poet seems to suggest this also by putting in the opposition, where the person may also be very well spoken of, the plural. But if it were proposed to take the words in this way, *who thinks himself contemptibly un-worthy*, something quite incorrect would thereby be expressed, not God, but men forming the opposition. The words, too, according to 1 Sam. xv. 17, 2 Sam. vi. 22, would rather run שָׁפָל וְקָטֹן בְּעֵינָיו · That לְהָרַע cannot be so much as לְהֵעָדֹהּ ver. 3, is plain from grammar and usage, the Massora rightly treats it as infinitive Hiph. The phrase is thus formed precisely as נִשְׁבַּע לְבַטֵּא with the active infinitive *he swears*, so that he speaks imprudently = *imprudently*, Levit. v. 4; and the sense would be: *he swears* so that he does evil, hurts, = *to hurt*, of course his own (it might be supposed, that לֹו was wanting before וְלֹא yet the phrase appears to have been intelligible without this לֹו). The description would then be entirely suitable in this connexion: who does not alter (violate) his oath because he learns by and bye that he has taken an oath to his own hurt, but esteems the oath more sacred than his advantage. On the *not taking interest*, ver. 5, comp. the *Alterthümer*, pp. 207 sq. The conclusion: "he will never waver," corresponds directly, advancing a step in the thought, to the question at the beginning. For the full sense is: he will not merely be worthy to dwell at the sanctuary, but also rewarded and strengthened with eternal blessing, will never vacillate, will be maintained by a higher power. But the first half of this proposition is readily understood of itself by the second, which is loftier and more expressive.

6. PSALM CI.

would now in order of time immediately follow Ps. xxiv. 7-10. The poet, as a king of mighty authority, may readily be discovered to be David; for David's higher genius is throughout expressed. Sion has already become the seat of David and the house of Jahvé, ver. 8; but as yet all things are not ordered and made, even in the new administration of David. The new state has to be more firmly developed, especially the surroundings of the king, on the character of which, according to the fashion of the old kingdom so much depends, have to be selected and sifted. David himself is still standing on the ' steps of a general decisive period, not strong and armed

enough in the inner man for the difficult, the progressive task
of his future life. Yet even in this first period of the rule in
Jerusalem, in the splendour of victory, and of the newly-
obtained crown over all Israel, in a time also when lesser
princes were so readily blinded and overcome by the treacherous
brilliance of prosperity, or had given way before their difficult
task, David feels himself all the more urged to enlighten and
strengthen his own heart in the constant praise of Jahvé, and
His virtues, and in unwearied longing endeavour after Him.
He desires to apprehend the true principles for the conduct of
a government equally strong and just; and therefore to hold
far from his heart every evil intention, and in like manner from
his court every common thing,—every flatterer, slanderer, and
wicked man. But already the new sanctity of this city now
chosen as the seat of Jahvé, demands, that least of all should
unholiness be suffered in it. He who begins his rule with
such intentions, as they here gush forth in guileless simplicity,
is bound to end it happily. Nothing opens to us so clearly all
the nobleness and the powerful light of David's soul than this
short song. For the song is like a brief involuntary outburst
of clear, long-cherished sensibility, without further artificial
desire entirely to exhaust the thought. And as in the heart of
David there is but this *one* great sentiment, this *one* endeavour
completely fills his mind, and is expressed here in *one*
burst; so the whole song forms an indivisible whole, breaking
only into two quite similar restful strophés, each of four verses,
and eight mostly long verse-members; correctly, however,
with such progress, that in the second the poet looks more
freely about and beyond himself into the world. The predominance of the long verse-members is the more suitable
because the whole is presented as a self-contemplation.

1.

Mercy and Right let me sing,   1
   to Thee, O Jahvé, play !

let me observe the guileless way,—when wilt Thou come
to me ?—
walk in my house in guilelessness of heart !
Will not before my eyes set wickedness ;
Work of the False do I hate, it shall not cleave
to me !
crooked heart shall depart from me,
Evil will I not know !

2.

5   Who secretly slanders his neighbour, him will I
destroy ;
who is of proud eyes, of swelling heart—him endure I
not :
on the faithful of the land I look, that they may dwell
with me ;
who walks in the guileless way—*he* shall serve me.
There shall not dwell in my house he who works deceit ;
who speaks lies—shall not stand before my eyes :
watchfully will I destroy all the wicked of the land,
in order out of Jahvé's city,—to root out all evil-
doers !

The poet begins with the thought of the Divine virtues of
grace and justice, since the king, who before all other men,
should exhibit them in his life, after the Divine example,
cannot sufficiently reflect upon these and praise them. But
thus the song is at the same time an ascription of praise to
Jahvé. The poet has indeed often already reflected upon these
virtues, often already aspired to Jahvé, and to an even, blessed
life, entirely laid hold of and led by Jahvé. That his earlier
endeavour was not fruitless, is shown by the very manner of
this song. But not yet is the goal reached ; anew he exhorts
himself to new intensified carefulness and fidelity, heping that
at last,—what he so deeply longs for,—Jahvé will entirely and
abidingly come to him and dwell in him. The doleful question

and prayer מָתַי, etc., thus contains, although only compressed in the flight of the language, a main thought. And it is readily understood that the coming of God is here not an external one, or one visible by an external token. Neither the narrative of 2 Sam. vi. 9, nor the yet earlier modes of speech, Gen. xx. 3, Ex. xx. 24, must be brought into comparison. From ver. 3 onwards the strongly-moved language becomes softer, whilst the poet depicts what he feels and calmly wishes as his firm resolution. If סֵטִים could be taken as an *abstraction*, the inf. עֲשֹׂה would most readily suit: *to do falsenesses* (properly departures from the true) *I hate*. But Hos. v. 2 (where שׁחטה = שׁחת, ix. 9) is opposed to this; and the *sing.* יִדְבָּק speaks more in favour of the actual doing being here the subject. *Doing of the false*, i.e., so to do as false men do, hence מַעֲשֵׂה was not necessary, but, on the contrary, עֲשֹׂה may then be formed according to § 150 b. סֵט must be adjective equally with זֵד, לֵץ, גֵּר; quite otherwise יָרֵשׁ with י, which comes from רִישׁ (which is here stated with more exactness than in § 146 e). Ver. 4 quite as xviii. 23 ff.; ver. 7 רְמִיָּה quite as xxxii. 2. Ver. 5, רחב *wide*, extending itself, swelling heart, when external pride and haughtiness, that of the eyes, penetrates also the innermost man in covetousness and self-seeking. Prov. xxi. 4, xxviii. 25. Ver. 8 לַבְּקָרִים every morning, *i.e.*, always with the greatest zeal, early beginning each day with fresh energies, as the similar lxxiii. 14. In the repeated mention of the *house*, vv. 3, 6, 7, we readily observe that only as great a king as David could thus speak,—he from whose new habitation in Jerusalem rule went literally forth over the wide kingdom, and who, like no later king, could call all Jerusalem *his*, and look upon it as *his home*, without over-looking the fact that it was at the same time the city of a still Higher One.*

---

* No one, *e.g.*, will here think of King Ḥizqia, who accurately knows him and his time, or even only his song, i. pp. 161 sq. (*Dichter des A. B.*)

Here is, perhaps, the most suitable place to insert the three nature-songs which originated so independently of the external history that we are absolutely unable to offer conjectures respecting the definite period of their origin.—Such *nature songs* are indeed rare.   They are, in that beauty and freedom in which they here appear, peculiar to the age of the highest bloom of lyric poetry.   Later, when the force of the Israelitish spirit even more narrowly confined itself to other objects, and at last even the poetic impulse became dormant, there resound at most a few weak echoes, Ps. civ.   Again, they did not spring from a learned acquaintance with nature, but only from particular movements of higher excitement or contemplation, when either an extraordinary natural phenomenon, thrusting itself upon notice with fearful violence, awakens a poet to deeper contemplation (Ps. xxix); or, conversely, a poet finds confirmed by the consideration of Nature, the truths that have welled up in his mind from other suggestions (Pss. viii., xix.). Hence it is at most but particular sides of Nature at first, a few great marvellous phenomena which seize upon the singer's mind, and the contemplation is opened, not in long pictorial representations, but in brief suggestive traits and hints.   The object and impulse of the poet is not to describe nature, but full of Divine thoughts and open to nature, he apprehends and depicts her as she moves before him full of God and revealing God to him.   But, considered more closely, there lies in this very circumstance a great superiority in these few songs; for here is nature-poetry, neither anxiously laboured and forced, nor artificial and petty; but the impression which the grandeur, splendour, and order of nature involuntarily produces upon a pure poet's heart, here finds its bright mirror; and because an Israelitish poet especially in presence of nature can never forget the living God, there shines out of all these poems the genuine connexion of poetic thoughts on God and nature, whilst to the poet even nature becomes for the first time inspired with life and capable of being understood

through its Lord. In this way, such songs, little as they may
have this in view, are yet always at the same time songs of
praise to Jahvé. In this style, and in the quite peculiar
sublimity of poetry, all three songs resemble one another.
They may be termed the old Hebrew nature-songs, and the
mutual likeness is so complete that their derivation from the
same poet becomes thereby obvious.

(7.) PSALM XXIX.

The poet must have recently experienced a violent tempest,
so that the feeling of it still vibrates through him, and the
picture of it still stands most vividly before his soul. Let us
represent to ourselves the rare, but when it does occur, the
more fearful spectacle of a Southern, especially a Palestinian
tempest, as it seems in a few moments, with loudest crashing,
to bring the whole creation into uproar, destroys the high and
the low, breaking the highest trees on the mountains, con-
vulsing the lower wastes. It is a piece of good fortune if it
passes the cities quietly by. Nothing, in fact, has the power
to bring the omnipotence of the heavenly God so near to the
feeling of the ancient Hebrews, nothing so strongly to show
him the relation between heaven and earth, and the operation
of the former upon the latter.* Particularly, the most forcible
Divine judgment is frequently thought of under the representation of such a tempest, Isa. xxx. 27-30.

The poet, indeed, now conceives in this song of that storm,
the sublime scene of which thus trembles in his soul, as a
Divine judgment; but at the same time this feeling is in him
glorified to a still higher picture in the free glance upward to
heaven, whence the storm comes, and down to earth, which is
smitten by it. This most violent natural experience appears
to him to set forth, beyond aught else, clearly and sensibly,
the living connexion itself between heaven and earth. First,

---

* Comp. in David himself further, Ps. xviii. 7 sq.

because God Himself, the Invisible, He who sojourns unap-
proachably as in the furthest heights, He so often in vain
longed for by His people, now actually as it were brings
Himself again near to the earth and to His own, and makes
Himself as strongly as possible sensible to them.* Secondly,
because the tempest is raised, as if quietly and unobservedly,
in the most inaccessible, remotest heights of heaven, then,
with a mighty crash, suddenly rushes through the world, and
leaves its traces behind in the very depths of the earth, so
that all things without exception in the world, from the
extremest height to the lowest deep, once again experience
the power of God. But in what entirely different ways do
the different parts of this world experience it! And to depict
this with all brevity as picturesquely as possible, is a main
object of the song.. There, in the mysterious heaven, where
the storm seems to gather unobserved, and whence thunders,
like Divine words of power, resound and terrify the whole earth,
is this like all the Divine manifestations and actions prepared.
It may also be beheld more nearly, more purely in its origin
and objects from the first, as it were, by the higher spirits who
surround the throne of God. But yonder there is nought but
joy and jubilation over such a voluntary new revelation of the
Highest. On the earth, on the other hand, and in the world,
the manifold variety of creatures are dumb and resistent. Here
His mighty thunder prevails, and whilst the clouds bear *Him*,
the mountains and forests and all that lives here below must
tremble and break before Him,—man also, even his own
people, must pass away before Him, if it were not they who
could rejoice again at this His coming, even in such an uproar
of the whole world,—rejoice in the fructifying traces of His
presence. Thus even in this most fearful manifestation they
may rather revere a token only of the omnipotence and of the
omnipotent nearness of their Lord, who, even as He is able to

---

* Comp. the *Gesch. des V. Isr.*, ii., pp. 534 sq. More feebly and obscurely the
same feeling pervades also Indian songs, as is seen from the later *Méghadûta*.

dominate the tempestuous storm, yea, anew to fructify the land by its means, so also amidst all the storms of the peoples, can ever anew strengthen His people. Thus human fear is resolved, by the contemplation of the Omnipotence that trembles through the world, into joy, and into that rock-like confidence in the true God which distinguish the earlier times of Israel, and especially those of David. No song marks this more simply and more beautifully than the present one.*

But seldom does the earth experience such a day. As an earthly king, on certain days, holds judgment and exercises authority, surrounded and done homage to by the great men of his kingdoms, so does this rare day of the tempest appear such a solemn day of assembly and judgment of the highest king, where He, receiving the praises of angels as the only Mighty One, from His throne directs and governs the thunder below. But His people upon earth do not merely endure in silent homage this judgment. They at least feel that it is fructifying and blessing in its discharge, and in the management of these fearful masses of storm and water own the mighty Lord of their community, who in the end ever leaves blessing behind Him. Thus this fearful day appears rather as a new day of revelation and glorification of the eternal Jahvé in heaven and upon earth. And the poet now being desirous, under such an apprehension of the meaning of the event, to bring before the mind and immortalize the rare occurrence, from the beginning to the end, as if anew, in the manner in which he has experienced it, and as it now stands before his soul : he projects (I. a. p. 193)† his representation as if in a victorious song, in three members, of ancient style. (1.) In a prelude, vv. 1, 2, he appeals to the angels who stand around the throne of Jahvé, as in the solemn moment before the

---

* How weak, in contrast, is the similar conception in the Tscheikessen ! (Bodenstedt's 1001 Tag., ii., p. 73 f.)

† Dichter des A. B.

opening of a great drama, worthily to render homage to the
highest Lord, in the immediately following, still more solemn
moment, in which He will reveal Himself as the only Mighty
One.   (2.) Immediately, without delay, open all the revelations
of the Divine Power, like so many majestic commands and
victorious operations upon the trembling earth, whilst in
heaven at the same time the praise which has been excited on
the part of the angels who surround the Divine throne and
behold the revelation of Jahvé's might, unbrokenly resounds,
vv. 3—9.   (3.) Men also from the effect learn anew the true
mode of the Divine power and activity, vv. 10, 11.   The most
detailed of these three parts is, and justly so, the middle one;
the description of the tempest, to which vv. 1, 2 are related
only as introduction, vv. 10, 11, as consequence.   All the
sublimity of the storm, its rise, its wide development, its
career is here signified in three mutually correspondent
strophés (each of five verse-members).   As the tempest seems
to sink down from the higher heaven, ever more profoundly to
the mountains and plains, the poet here paints it in three
stages, first in the upper air apparently over the sea of clouds,
vv. 3, 4, then suddenly seizing the mountains, vv. 5—7,
finally spreading itself out in the plains, vv. 8, 9, thus stirring
up and vibrating through everything in the whole land, from
the rigid mighty mountains, and their heaven-high cedars,
down to the beasts and small trees of the desert and plain, and
from the North, where are the high mountain-ranges, down to
the lower South.   Then the thunder to the feeling of the
ancients, is the most important part of the storm, seeming to
be the commanding voice, the terrifying exclamation of Jahvé.
Hence the poet begins with the thunder, and derives all from
it.   And the continuous echo of the thunder resounds also in
the mind of the poet.   In each of the three short strophés the
קוֹל יַהְוֶה *the voice*, or rather the *sound* or *clangour of Jahvé*,
must recur several times, at least twice.   But it always stands
quite forward in the sentence, as if the language permitted the

thunder, ever suddenly falling on the ear, anew to re-echo;
and with this, in manifest design, seven times—3, 2, 2—
according to the three strophés. Finally, the whole depicts—
both the harsh and fearful, and again the easy and swift
skipping movement of the storm, its gradual progress, and at
intervals sudden extension, and again sudden feebleness and
languor,—with creative power of representation.*

1.

Give to Jahvé, ye sons of God, 1
    give to Jahvé honour and praise!
give to Jahvé the honour of His Name,
    do homage to Jahvé in holy attire!

2.

Hark Jahvé is on the waters,
    the God of glory thundered,
        Jahvé on many waters;
hark Jahvé is in strength,
    hark Jahvé is in pomp!
Hark Jahvé, how he breaks cedars, 5
    where Jahvé so breaks in pieces Lebanon's cedars,
and makes them dance like calves,
    Lebanon and Shirjon like young buffaloes;
hark Jahvé, how he sprinkles coals of fire!

Hark Jahvé trembles through the desert,
    Jahvé trembles through the Qadêsh desert;
hark Jahvé maketh hinds to be in throes
    and bares of leaves the forests:
whilst in His palace—all speak "honour!"

3.

Jahvé ruled the great flood: 10
    so Jahvé rules as everlasting king!

---

* See on the whole further the *Jahrbb. der Bibl. wiss.* viii., pp. 69-73.

Jahvé will give to His people strength,
Jahvé will bless His people with salvation !

The בְּנֵי אֵלִים, ver. 1, cannot be so interpreted, that אֵלִים should be supposed absolutely used instead of אֱלֹהִים *God,* for this never occurs ; but the plural is in the compound name twice expressed, first in the first member, where it very readily finds place, especially according to the signification of בֵּן ; secondly, again in the second.　Elsewhere in similar cases it is expressed either in the first or the second member, § 270*c.*—All the sentences, vv. 3 ff., are perfectly clear so soon as the קוֹל is correctly understood according to § 286 sq.　On ver. 3, comp. xviii. 12-14.　Here, however, the clouds in heaven are seen suddenly to gather with increasing strength, as the *many waters, c,* beside the simple *a* shows.　Ver. 4 depicts the joy in seeing *Him* as a victorious hero, as if in sublime toil.—Ver. 6 must refer to an apparent or actual earthquake (the like are often mentioned in conjunction with violent storms, comp. Matthias of Eclessa, "Armenian Hist.," p. 288, Dul.)　The rigid mountains Lebanon and Anti-Lebanon (Shirjon) skip like young animals leaping up in alarm.　The suffix in וירקידם must hence refer to the mountains already present to the imagination of the poet, and presently more plainly named.　The storm has here reached the highest stage.　The thunder seems to divide perpetual flames, since the flashes of lightning appear as serpentine or forked flames, and it is difficult for natural feeling to decide whether they, in quickest succession, depend on the thunder or the reverse.　At all events, the divided flame appears to be connected with the broken sound of the thunder and the word.—Ver. 8.　Qadêsh opposed to Egypt.　How the hinds, terrified thereby, more quickly bring forth, Imrialkais, "Moall." v. 76.　The הֵיכָל, ver. 9, is unquestionably the heavenly, for the poet returns to 1, 2.—Ver. 10. ישב as "rule" rightly with brevity connected with — לְ as the dative, and וישב expresses the consequence or conclusion.　מַבּוּל cannot here be used in the limited sense of the tradition, Gen. vi. 17, but has here its full original signification, as this too alone suits the connexion of the sense of the entire song. Comp. the *Jahrbb. der Bibl. Wiss.*, viii., pp. 2, 3.

8. PSALM XIX.

If the preceding Psalm is suggested by the heaven in stormy movement, the present points to the perfectly calm and clear sky, as it usually shines with all its splendour in Palestine. To the view of the senses the glory and order of the restful firmament appears so great, so glittering, unchangeable as eternity, the same in its clearness and manifestness, that the heaven, as one of the Divine works, becomes for every man who is not utterly insensible, the most eloquent witness and most speaking herald of the glory of its Master and Creator in all His works. Thus powerfully does He demand that conclusions be drawn from the seen to the unseen, from particulars to the universal. And the *way in which* this is to be done is further explained in close connexion, in the assurance that the splendour and order of heaven is eternally the same, each day and each night; and therefore this praise and this instruction of heaven abides ever with men, as if they were communicated with and informed from one day to another, from one night to another, in unbroken succession, ver. 3.—This is the underlying thought of the poem, from vv. 2-7. And since the song proceeds from the quite tranquil heaven, and in its contemplation alone the happy soul is lost, this underlying thought comes out in its restful truth with perfect consistency from the first, ver. 2. But now the questions press upon the attention—when, where and how the heaven is this herald of the glory of God. And the progress of the thought answers these questions in the first instance to this effect—that each fresh day and each fresh night are in their constant succession as the traditioners or teachers of this eternal doctrine of heaven. For the heaven announces a very clear word, one perceptible over the whole earth, concerning God, although it is properly dumb, vv. 4, 5 *a b*. But while the effect of everything is at first only to heighten the enigma, and to strain expectation to the highest degree towards its solution, the latter may now follow the more suddenly and the more clearly. For is there not this marvel in the heaven by day—the ball of the sun, each day uniformly beginning and completing its wide course, as if with new spirit and fresh strength, penetrating all things with its heat? And does not this marvel of the daily sky, as it is here intimated with complete conformity to the most primæval and simplest feelings, vv. 5 *c*-7, indicate most powerfully even to reluctant minds, the Creator,—so that it may be said the heaven praises in this way with sufficient clearness the Divine glory?

Beautiful and full of feeling in conception and execution as these verses are, it is nevertheless impossible that the poet closed the song with them. For what is begun in ver. 3 is absolutely un-completed, and after ver. 7 we miss the description of the way in which the *night*—mentioned in ver. 3 as equally important—teaches the glory of God. If, however, we reflect, and see from Ps. viii. that the night teaches this glory with equal power, although in another way,—we must then say that some of the most beautiful words have been lost after ver. 7. But their sense and colour may, to some extent, be recovered from Ps. viii. 4. The same conclusion is yielded by the structure of the strophés, since a first strophé is manifestly completed from vv. 2-5 in nine verse-members, the second, therefore, vv. 6, 7, is now only half preserved. This ancient song then, has come down to us only as a torso.

We find, indeed, in vv. 8-15, words which yield a plain conclusion, but it is not the less certainly clear that this cannot have been the original conclusion. In the first place, the contents are against this. The law and the religion of Jahvé are here three times most gloriously praised as in themselves pure, correct, faultless, secure, and eternal, and hence also

teaching truth and reviving the soul, vv. 8-11. But the more
the poet feels this from his own consciousness, the greater is
the anxiety lest he should neglect to fulfil the whole law, and
thereby incur the loss of its blessings. Hence the prayer to
Jahvé to forgive him his unknown errors; also to protect him
from the dominion of light-minded, impious men, that he may
not be led astray by their persuasion or compulsion, vv. 12-15.
Thus could men for the first time pray since the seventh and
sixth centuries, when the written law was in all particulars more
strictly observed; but the internal parties, through this very
circumstance, are more sharply opposed to each other. Again,
the less forcible language, the colour of the style, the art of
the verse, point to a later age; for we have, indeed, here also
two strophés, each with four verses, but the long-membered
verse alone predominates. Then there is no transition at all
from the first piece to the second, neither in the thoughts nor in
the words. All inward community and relationship is wanting,
and the chasm between ver. 7 and ver. 8 is not merely rugged
and harsh, but without any bridge, any possible connexion.
Yet as the first fragment is without ending, the second is
without satisfactory beginning; for ver. 8 begins too frigidly
for a prayer. Hence the conjecture only remains to us, that a
later poet fastened this conclusion to the above ancient
fragment, in order to place side by side the revelation in
Nature and that in Scripture. Either he found the ancient
fragment in this state without its original conclusion, or, what
is more probable, the old conclusion no longer satisfied him,
since in his time the Scriptural revelation had attained high
importance, and it seemed to him fitting to touch also upon
this.*

1.

The heaven tells God's glory,   2
   His handiwork the firmament praiseth,

---

* Comp. on the whole further the *Jahrbb. der Elbl. Wiss.*, viii., pp. 73, 77.

Day to day teaches the story,
    night to night reveals the tidings,
without tale, without words,
    without its voice being heard,
5   resounded through the whole earth its noise,
    and to the boundary of the earth's round, its language,
where a tent in it the Sun-man hath.

2.

And he steps like a bridegroom from his chamber,
    bounds like a hero to run his path;
hath from heaven's end his rising,
    and his circuit unto its ends;
whilst nothing is concealed from its heat.

    *   *   *   *

3.

Jahvé's law is perfect, refreshing,
    Jahvé's revelation is faithful, instructing ignorance;
Jahvés commands are honest, heart-rejoicing,
    Jahvé's precept is pure, enlightening the eyes;
10   the fear of Jahvé is pure, eternally abiding;
    Jahvé's sentences are truth, righteous together,
they, which are more precious than gold and many
      treasures,
    and sweet before honey and before honey-comb.

4.

Thy servant also feels himself enlightened by them:
    to keep them brings great reward!
Errors who marks?
    from unconscious ones, O clear me!—
Also from presumption spare Thy servant,—that it
      dominate me not!
    then shall I be innocent and free from great iniquity.

1 5   May my mouth's words be well-pleasing to Thee, **and**
         what my heart thinks before Thee,
      Jahvé, my rock and my redeemer !

הַגִּיד, ver. 2, frequently in poets so, in the best sense " praise."
—Ver. 4 might in itself be also thus explained : *no saying* is it
(the above mentioned, ver. 3), and *no words whose voice* would
be *unheard ;* on the contrary, ver. 5, *through the whole earth
their sound has become loud.*   But this would give only a somewhat feeble observation, and the dance of the two members,
ver. 4, would so far cease, as their negations would not
correspond.   Other instances, comp. § 341 *d*.   This sense
indeed might be supposed : *no language* among the tongue of
the peoples, *and no speech is there where* (according to § 332 *a*)
its voice is not heard.   But to speak of the different languages
of the peoples does not belong to this connexion ; and in any
case the finest meaning is that where the so significant אָמֶר,
repeated from ver. 3, receives indeed a quite new reference, in
such a way that the thought thereby powerfully advances,—but
no new meaning.

   The קָו יָצָא might indeed be understood according to
Jer. xxxi. 39, but with this neither בְּ in this phrase, nor the
following מִלֵּיהֶם, nor the entire connexion, would agree.
Most of the ancients have here correctly a word like φθόγγος,
LXX, ἦχος, Sym. ; but the question is, how to find it
etymologically.   קוה is properly " stretch," like τείνω, *tendo*,
hence קָו, " cord," from drawing firmly together ; in Pi.
hold on, stay.   But equally well is קַו transferred to the voice
— its *intension*, straining, *tone*, — as τόνος denotes both
cord and tone, τοναία, a loud voice ; *kawah, kawaky*, cry out,
Qam. p. 1938.   קוֹל is itself remotely related therewith.   Comp.
also the *Jahrbb. der Bibl. Wiss.*, viii., p. 75.   The thrice used
suffix ‌ם can refer absolutely to nothing but to the main word
השמים, ver. 2, and to this points back also the following בָּהֶם.
For the poet, very pertinently, since he must once introduce

the sun, connects immediately with the mention of it the just-
named end of the earth, where the sun or the sun-god, according to the old tradition, slumbers for the night in his bed of
rest, in order on the morrow the more freshly and boundingly
(for the sun appears actually to leap at his first uprise) to begin
his wide course, as if this ever self-refreshing youth stepped
out of the darkness of every night, bold and self-conscious as a
bridegroom from the dark chamber. Instead of שָׂם (*he
placed*, which must refer to God) שָׂם taken relatively suits the
connexion better,—*where, i.e.,* on which end of the earth
Helios has a tent in them, the heavens; for this tent stands
indeed at the end of the earth, but reaches at the same time
even into heaven, as the ends of the earth and heaven were
generally thought of as meeting and colliding. The *sun*
becomes here in quite a new manner a man and hero, because
the poetic sense of the figure requires it, § 174 *c*: so pliant in
this ancient way is language in the application of sex, in like
manner as among the Indians, who always regard the rain as
masculine, while, at least the Vêdic language may also use it as
feminine. (comp. A. Weber's *Naxatra*, ii., p. 364 sq., *Indische
Studien*, v., pp. 270 sqq.)

Vv. 8-11. A very artistic laudation of the written religion
(יִרְאַת) of Jahvé; first, according to its inner nature; second,
according to its corresponding effects; hence always two
different epithets, rightly without copula. Yet only in three
strophés or three laudations is the whole completed, the
thought being twice renewed, but for the last time, vv. 10-11,
extending itself the furthest, and setting apart the description
of the effects in a new verse. Each of these three laudations,
vv. 8, 9, 10-11, consists again of two smaller propositions,
subjects and descriptions. *Eyes enlightening,* ver. 9, might be:
cheering him whose eyes would become troubled by grief,
xiii. 4; Ezr. ix. 8. It would then correspond to the first
clause of this as of the preceding verse. But where the
language is of doctrine and laws, *eyes enlightening* is manifestly

understood directly of the spiritual eyes, whereby indeed also here the likeness of the sense in both verses is first completed. The hesitations to which the pious man is subject, as to whether he can keep so high and so recompensing a law, are of a twofold kind; (1) inwardly, the fear of his own errors, ver. 13, which indeed at that time lay the nearer at hand, the more comprehensive was the mass of the commandments of the Pentateuch, now ever more definitely laid down; (2) externally, the fear of presumption, ver. 14. To hold oneself entirely free from the seduction or the compulsion of presumptuous men, of great men inclined to heathenism (פֶּשַׁע רַב) was actually at that time not so easy. Hence the later psalmists pray so often (liv. 5, cxli. 4) for strength, perceiving that only in remaining free from this temptation they can avoid great guilt, and that unconscious offences are more readily pardonable than this conscious inclination to heathenism. And this fear increased as the new Jerusalem was actually under the dominion of the Gentiles, comp. Ps. cxxv. 3, and the *Jahrbb. der Bibl. Wiss.*, v., p. 168. The words of appeal, ver. 15c, are taken from Ps. xviii. 3, and may prove that the later poet found these songs already in the same series.

9. PSALM VIII.

This short song is most completely pervaded by the tranquil contemplation of nature and of man. Grand indeed are the wonders of the heaven as witnesses of divine operation, and the previous song celebrated them in detail. But at bottom still more wonderful is the creation and the nature of man, low and weak inhabitant of earth as he is, when viewed in contrast to heaven and its creations; yet nevertheless by his participation in the divine spirit on the other hand so highly placed, and so gloriously endowed for the rule of all inferior things, and for the knowledge and praise of God. Thus in man the strongest contrasts meet. But whilst this weak, guilty creature stands in a spiritual relation so immediately near to

God, and is by Him so wondrously exalted, God has glorified
Himself in him in the most wondrous manner.   Because
human beings are on the face of the whole earth, His glory
likewise as Lord and Creator is great through the whole
earth ; and one may say that the true greatness of Jahvé's
glory is first shown by the fact that He, whose splendour and
might are extended over the heaven, has also so gloriously
revealed Himself, upon the whole earth, in every place where
men are found and know Him,—in the order and beauty of
earthly things, and especially in man himself!   This same man
may indeed, because he is so highly placed (endowed with
spiritual freedom) even misunderstand and abuse the greatness
and the goodness of Jahvé, exalting himself against the
Divine order, and accusing God of his own aberration and of
his own misery (these senseless ones the ancient language
terms " wicked enemies of God "). .But this is not nature and
order; it is degeneration and exception, as is shown by the
still undisturbed and pure nature of man, of the child in his
uncorrupted inner serenity, his full joyousness,—his unconscious feeling for the right and the true,—whether his
inward joy and bliss is first expressed in his babble, or in
unrestrained questions and answers.   It is here that the
deepest oppositions begin.   The weakest and most defenceless
of all creatures, yet in himself the most blessed, and involuntarily expressing thus his inward happiness !   But so must it
be if God has thus poured out His whole glory upon man.
Ever must in this way the unconscious, involuntary praise of
the Creator from the mouth of children be mightier than
degenerate lamentations and wild cries to Him.   Out of the
former pure nature eternally speaks, and she alone can instruct
and give content.   The renown of Jahvé thus remains at all
times and in all places great and exalted.

Such thoughts are expressed by the poet with equal force
and brevity.   Vv. 2-3 contain at once, with all precision, and
hence with all possible brevity, the whole truth.   But after a

short pause follows the inward, more exact adducement of proof, vv. 4-9, with which the poet returns to the primary thought of the beginning, ver. 10. But if we follow up the brief suggestion, we find the spiritual view of man,—a flash cast into the darkness of creation; moreover having this advantage over Gen. i. 26, that we here see no narration and tradition concerning the spiritual truth, but the bubbling of it from the first source.

1.

Jahvé, our Lord!   2
> how exalted is thy glory through all the earth,
> thou whose splendour is raised above the heaven!

From the mouth of sucklings and children
> hast thou founded a defence—because of Thine adversaries,
> to silence foe and thirster for revenge!

2.

When I behold thy heavens, work of thy fingers,
> moon and stars, which were formed by Thee

what is man, that thou rememberest him,   5
> son of man, that thou esteemest him,

abasedst him not much before God,
> and with splendour and honour crownedst him;

causest him to have dominion over the works of Thy hands,
> layedst all at his feet,

small cattle and oxen, all,
> even the great beasts of the field,

birds of heaven and fishes of the sea,
> that which passes through the paths of the seas!

3.

Jahvé, our Lord!   10
> how exalted is Thy glory through all the earth!

To understand the תִּנָה ver. 2 c, we must, above all, not overlook the fact that the poet by this last sentence has to express much the same thing that is further described in ver. 4; for in ver. 4 he intentionally resumes the here subordinate and not completed thought. Moreover, in this verse this much is clear from the context, that the second clause can say nothing further than that the glory or rather the splendour of Jahvé is also extended over heaven. Hence it is best to take the word as תָּנָה, or as verb in the perf., and descriptive of הוֹדְךָ, as the LXX have ἐπήρθη. תָּנָה is certainly not found elsewhere, yet we cannot doubt that it signifies "stretch out," "reach," prop. *dehnen* (Ger.), *tend* (*tan* in Indo-Germ.). Comp. תַּנִּין, *tanan*, "withdraw," *tuna*, "dwell," prop. spread out, *tîn*, Aeth., "broad." The *t* is most essential; for even *mad*, *nat*, are related.—Ver. 3. עֹז, at the first glance seems, as in xxix. 1, possibly to signify *praise*, as the LXX took it as αἶνος,—suitable also here in speaking of a glory and praise as it were firm for eternal ages, immovably *founded*. So *bany*, *build*, of deeds of glory, *Ham*. p. 296, 4 v. and 419 vl. But, in fact, the mode of expression in this connexion would be too short and incomplete, even heterogeneous and unintelligent. Rather do all the thoughts and figures turn on hostility and war. Against enemies, the more malignant and obstinate they are, one the more needs a firm defence, and just such an one has God Himself founded, in opposition to his enemies, out of the weak mouth of children! What contrast! Yonder the wild, insolent, destruction-loving foe,—here the weakest creature, and yet his merry babbling mouth provides a defence of the Creator against all the calumnies of that foe! One feels that here, too, a warrior speaks in the language of his craft.—But, again, in vv. 5, 6, the language, if more flowing, yet condenses an uncommon amount of thought into the shortest space. God ever remembers man, and searches him out, because the latter can never get free from the thought of Him, according to the inex-

haustible mystery of the connexion between the human and
Divine spirit as it subsists since the creation. What a wonder,
then, that this weak human being is thereby, notwithstanding
his weakness, in every moment so near to God Himself, and
God to Him! that God has thus subjected him to Himself,
but placed him as a ruler over all other living things!
Thus does the affectionate man ever think of his friend,
ever seeks him, asks for him, and never merely leaves him
to himself! And thus the poet comes from this nature, the
nearest and most certain of all, ver. 5, to the more remote, the
primæval nature of man, which is always the same, vv. 6-9.
—Ver. 6 is thus merely a continuation of ver. 5. as similarly
Job vii. 17, 18.—That the sun is wanting, ver. 4, is not
because the poet must have composed in the night; but since
the representation of the day and of the daily heaven is the
nearest, the second clause only recurs to that of the mighty
heaven, whose splendour certainly is quite peculiarly pertinent
in this place. Similarly, Job xxv. 5.

There follow now the songs from the time of the great wars of
David against the allied heathen peoples. And here we may
most suitably explain in the first place:

10. PSALM CX.,

a song, spoken to a king, in all respects like a Divine utterance (oracle), as he, certainly after sacrifice and prayer in the
temple (comp. below, Pss. xx., xxi.), was about to set out for
war against mighty foes.*

Since also the language of the short song is not opposed to
it, we may certainly regard David as the king referred to, for
king and kingdom here appear in the highest degree of
nobility and glory. As the kingdom was glorified under

---

* The literal application of the superscription being presupposed, the song
would be David's, and he would thus address another in it. The conclusion
would in this case be valid which is drawn in Matt. xxii. 41, 42. But *I* have
already spoken further on this matter in my work on *The Three First Gospels.*

David, experience showed how a human king may agree and be compatible with the heavenly, an external state with the theocracy, in the fairest way. There existed no contention between temporal and spiritual rule, and the king was at the same time priest, 2 Sam. vi., 1 Kings viii., comp. Zach. vi. 13. The primæval unity of royalty and priesthood, as the story relates it, with reference to Melchizédeq, Gen. xiv. 18-24, appeared again restored in the greater national family. But if the king stands on this high stage, the higher priestly sanctity and inviolability is also bound up with his person. And thus the present oracle promises, advancing to higher things, that the king, led by Jahvé, will with the greater power have victory over his enemies, and the more securely obtain higher strength even in the time of need; inasmuch as he, according to Jahvé's will, is and shall remain consecrated priestly king. He shall stand therefore higher and nearer to Jahvé than ordinary kings, and none may do him causeless injury without at the same time having to fear Jahvé's anger. The two primary thoughts come out with genuine prophetic brevity and sharpness,—first, how Jahvé promises to lead this king to battle, and at his side to overcome his foes, ver. 1; and then how it must be so, because Jahvé has destined him for ever to be the holy priest-king, as is said in the beginning of a second strophé, ver. 4, manifestly as the mere echo of a more ancient Divine oracle.* After each of these two sayings there follows, in more tranquil language,—the poet rather than the prophet coming forward,—the application and illustration of the thought, the encouragement of the king, and the depiction of the manner in which such a divine strength is preserved in the heat of battle from the beginning to the end, as the poet's sacred fancy beholds it,—in a few grand, briefly-sketched

---

* We must not overlook the point that the words, ver. 4, do not, as those in ver. 1, give an entirely new oracle, but only point back to an earlier, as to one ever standing entirely firm. By this too the period of this song is more exactly defined.

pictures, vv. 2-3, 5-6; until, in a weaker resonance to the oracle, fancy at last, ver. 7, glances at the extreme end of the conflict, and,—even in the following pursuit of the flying foe,—the unwearied strength and fresh vigour of the king, ever capable of new exploits.

In spite of the seeming want of connexion of the propositions, a higher unity nevertheless is diffused over the whole. And along with genuine lyric brevity and compression, there is no confusion of the thoughts and images. The oracle serves generally rather merely to indicate than to follow out details. Here it is indeed clothed,—in the age of the greatest lyric poet of Israel, and as if after his example,—in the guise of a song, but maintains the fugitive brevity proper to it, and the mere pictorial suggestiveness. Thus there come into relief at the head of each of the two small strophés (of three verses and seven clauses) the purest contents of the oracle, and with full power. After this very powerful beginning the language in each seems to subside, with figures further suggestive of the whole subject. Whilst the flight of prophetic vision overlooks the whole course of the conflict and victory of the king in its particular stages, it goes forward, ver. 5, precisely from the point where the representation at the end of the first strophé, ver. 3, came to a pause; adding in a last up-spring, ver. 7, a new image from the farthest distance.

1.

To my lord speaks Jahvé: "Set thee at my right hand, 1
    till I lay the foes as a stool for thy feet."—
The staff of might will Jahvé send thee out of Sion:
    rule in the midst of thy foes!
Thy people is willing for sacrifice on thy muster-day;
    in holy attire, out of the morning's bosom,
    thou hast the dew of thy youth!

2.

Sworn hath Jahvé, and will not rue it:

" thou art for ever priest,
   after the manner of Melchisédeq !"—
5   The Lord at thy right hand
       dashes in pieces kings on the day of His wrath ;
       will judge among the heathen—full of corpses is it,—
       dashes in pieces the head upon the wide land.

3.

From the brook by the way will he drink :
   therefore lift up his head.

Ver. 1.   The figure is throughout consistent.   Not the king
alone, without Jahvé, is to march to battle, but Jahvé will
march for and with him.   Jahvé accordingly requires him to
sit at His right hand, until the foes give way before the
victorious chariot.   Comp. Judges v. 13, 23 ; Ps. xliv. 10 ;
2 Sam. v. 24.   This indeed is said as a deduction from the
general truth that the true king is a σύνθρονος θεοῦ.   But
it would be perverse to mistake the closer application and the
complete picture in this place.   Ver. 2.   *The sceptre of thy
power,* the sceptre by which thou canst mightily fight and
conquer, will (if perhaps in the midst of the stir, thou thinkest
thou hast it not) Jahvé will send thee out of Sion.   The
Divine warranty shall not fail thee.   So, with naught but
courage in thy heart, *shalt thou* then *rule* (§ 347 a).   Thus the
poet, in more quiet illustration of the thought, drops the first
figure from ver. 1 ; for bodily Jahvé does not march out from
the holy place, especially since the ark of the covenant was no
longer carried out of Sion into war.   But at the new beginning,
ver. 5, the first figure recurs.   Ver. 3 now further explains
how much devolves upon the people, if what is expressed in
ver. 2 is to be fulfilled.   As the dew in countless drops appears
from the bosom of the early morning, so will thy young men
on the morning of battle come to meet thee suddenly in countless brave bands (2 Sam. xvii. 12 ; Mich. v. 6).   Thou needest
not to be anxious whether they will be there, and whether in

full numbers. And as the fresh dew revives all that it touches, so will thy young men, holily attired (Isa. xiii. 3) for the holy war, meet thee, reviving thy courage. Both figures, which find their connexion in the notion of the dew, are thus immediately united with wondrous brevity. But most brief of all and most pointed is here the first word *thy people is willing for sacrifice* (§ 296 *b*), is itself like a number of free-will offerings,—offering themselves of their own accord on the day of battle like a sacrifice to God, in order to further the Divine work. The notion of the sacrifice already coming in with נְדָבוֹת, the language passes quickly, with the more ease, into the figure of the sacrificial attire. Ver. 4. *Thou* king, thou who wert long leader of armies and king, thou *art* from this moment forward *priest*, just as the king Melchizédeq was at the same time priest. The solemn transference of the priestly dignity to one who, as is self-obvious, was already king, is accordingly here the new element. Vv. 5, 6. The poet now returns,—according to this second prophetic saying, whence it still more follows how mightily Jahvé will support this king, —in a somewhat different way repeating the figure of the right hand, ver. 1,—immediately to the illustration of particulars. And since in vv. 2, 3, the mere power which will serve the king was rather designated, so, on the other hand, he here sketches pictures of the issue,—of the battle and the complete victory. The fancy of the poet contemplates a wide field of battle, full of corpses, the victory therefore gained, whilst Jahvé as if invisible at his side, beats down, in the capacity of judge, the heads of the allied kings. But first the hasty pursuit of the defeated crowns the victory; and often the victor wearies on the last way, losing all fruits of his exertion. But this king will never weary and fail; and should he, pursuing the flying foe, be on the point of fainting in the heat and haste of the conflict, he will find in the morning a brook, as if bubbling for his sake, to give him refreshing drink (comp. an example in 2 Sam. xxiii. 15 and sqq.), and so strengthened, pursue his way with undiminished courage. Hence the subject matter itself shows that in ver. 7, along with the new thought and figure, the king appears as a new subject; and now, in the wane of the song, he is only spoken of in the third person.

In this manner, not seldom does a single short sentence re-sound, following upon an oracle, whilst the glance, as if now weary, once more kindles into life towards the distant view (comp. *Jahrbb. der Bibl. Wiss.*, viii., p. 36 sq.). Only thus is the transition in this sentence, ver. 7, from the second to the third person explained. Compare for many other instances, the *Jahrbb. der Bibl. Wiss.*, xi., p. 212 f., and *Gött. Gel. Anz.*, 1862, pp. 768-772. Should any one, because of the *for ever*, ver. 4, mistake the whole sense of the poet, let him consider that the expression indicates nothing but a time undefined—in the sense of every time of the speaker; therefore a time the end of which the poet of that time neither sees nor wishes for. Especially the rule of a good king is always desired as eternal, comp. xxi. 5; xlv. 3, 7; lxi. 7; 1 Kings, i. 31; Prov. xxix. 14; Ps. xli. 13.

One of David's own songs from the midst of the deepest dangers of this most bitter war, is certainly preserved in

11. Psalm LX.

Not indeed in the form in which this song at present appears. It will presently be further shown, that in its present form it finds its place amongst the latest. But in the midst of it, the words, ver. 8, to זנחתנו, ver. 12, are proved, on closer investigation, to be quite foreign to the later poet, and here introduced by him out of an old song of David himself, because their contents seemed to him very well to suit his song. Since we have thus here nothing but a large fragment of a Davidic song, it is somewhat more difficult to ascertain its occasion and its contents. Yet plainly the peculiar kernel of it has been saved, and by this we are left in no doubt as to the emergency in which David was at the time. The possession of the entire holy land was at that time more precarious than ever. All the foes surrounding its borders thought to be able soon to conquer it, and already spoke of dividing it among themselves. According to ver. 11, even the subject Edom in the far south had risen against David, whilst he in the far north lay in the open field in arms against the Aramæans. Under these circumstances, he cried from the depth to God. The earth seemed to him to lie in ruins, and it seemed to him doubtful how he could despatch even an army only into Edom, in this unexpected revolt. But a favourable oracle, which he had received in answer to his inquiry in the camp, determines him as speedily to the highest joy in God, and turning to his firm, rock-like confidence in God, ever habitual to him, he sings this song, the principal part of which was probably the free communication of the priestly oracle, vv. 8-10, with a few short preliminary and appended words, as they may be in some sort imagined in David's style, in conformity with Pss. iii. and iv. Of this epilogue, the words, ver. 11 to the beginning of ver. 12, have been retained. It is more difficult to decide, whether some words from the prelude, at all events here and there, came to be inserted in the present first strophé, vv. 3-7.

Further, the correct view of the above ancient fragments of the present song, and especially of their historical importance, receives a further support in the superscription preserved in vv. 1, 2; in so far, that is, as the latter in two of its portions (p. 54 sq., I. p. 234) refers to the earliest period of the collection of Davidic songs. It is further shown, in the *Gesch. des V. Isr.*, how completely this historical occasion, still indicated by it, is consistent with actual history, and how certain it is, that it must have been written at a very early date.

1.

O God, thou hast rejected us, broken through us,   3
  been wrath : O restore us again !

Thou hast shaken the earth, cleft it;
   heal its breaches, for it totters!
5   Hast caused Thy people to behold hard things,
   hast made us drunk with wine of reeling,
given to Thy fearers a banner,
   that it may be unfurled before the bow:
that Thy beloved may be set free,
   help, strong right hand, and listen to us!

2.

God spake in His sanctuary, causes me to rejoice:
   " I will divide Sichem,
   and measure out Sukkot's vale;
mine is Gilead and mine Manasse,
   and Efráim is the protection of my head,
   Juda my ruler's staff;
Moab—my wash-pot is it,
10   upon Edom cast I my shoe;
   because of me, cry out, Peléschet !"

3.

Who will lead me hence to the strong city?
   who conducts me hence to Edóm?
wilt not Thou, O God, Who hast rejected us,
   and goest not forth, O God, in our armies?
give us help from our oppressors,
   since vain is the help of men!
through God we shall gain the victory,
   and He will thrust down our oppressors!

The first main division, vv. 3-7, contains three times both complaint and prayer, corresponding to one another. In accordance with this and with lxxxv. 15, lxxx. 4, the תשובב in ver. 3 is to be taken. The mediate connexion with ? has come in owing to the figurative remoter signification of the verb. Ver. 4, in accordance with Isa. i. 5, 6. Ver. 6 says, in the play on words: Thou hast indeed given to those who fear Thee a *banner* because they took the field on behalf of the true religion, but only to *ban* them [or *flag*, that they may *flag*]— properly, that they may make their escape—before the bow, not to conquer thereby, but to be conquered. קֹשֶׁט is a corrupt later reading for קשׁת, bow, *keshet*, Syr.; the Massoretes seem, indeed, by the expression קֹשֶׁט and by the accentuation to follow quite another explanation (to rise for the cause of truth, from בֵּן, not from נוס) but opposed to the connexion. On יְמִינְךָ ver. 7, which is here translated with freedom only, comp. § 281 c. *In His sanctuary*, ver. 8, because the ark of the covenant was carried with the host into the field. But in adding, *causes me to rejoice*, he thereby also sufficiently indicates that he had not himself received this oracle. If Jahvé wills to divide Sikhem and Sukkot (as ancient holy cities on this and that side of the Jordan, Gen. xlviii. 22, xxxiii. 17, mentioned instead of the whole of Canaan), no one hostile to himself can divide it, and therefore, *e.g.*, not the Aramæans or the Philistines who now aim at conquering it and dividing it amongst themselves. On the contrary, He retains as arms and attire, of which he boasts as warrior-hero, the strength of Israel, the tribes of Gilead and Manasse,—as helmet the ancient, venerable leading tribe (as it were, head-tribe) of Efráim, the tribe still at this time so serviceable for strong defence,—and as sceptre, finally, Juda, the royal tribe (Gen. xlix. 10); Moab and Edom too are in the vicinity, serving Him as useful tools; but Moab is, by the side of the above tribes, only as the wash-basin (in opposition to the crown, an inferior, contemptible utensil, comp. Wilken, *Hist. Gaznevidarum*, or *Chr. Pers.*, p. 142, 7), in which the king, resting from the toils of the day, washes* (in blood?), and Edom as the ground whereon He at the same time casts His shoe, that He may rest. But the country on

---

* Still more exactly is this figure, apparently so strong and yet, according to the royal custom of the time, very familiar, elucidated in the *Gesch. des V. Isr.*, iii., p. 386, 3rd edit. Comp. the *Jahrbb.*, v., p. 172.

which one freely casts one's shoe and there leaves it, one takes
possession of as a subject and servile land, the shoe being the
sign of the standing of this person over the land, and so of its
possession by him. Comp. Ruth iv. 7. *Founding of the City
of Pataliputra,* edited by H. Brockhaus (Leipsic, 1835),
pp. 1 sqq. Moab and Edom being thus subject, will Philistia
(of which David, from the far North where he now stands,
rightly thinks in the last instance) rise? On the contrary,
because of me, because of my victory and my energy, *cry aloud,*
bewail *Philistia!* thou wilt soon know me as a conqueror,
Isa. xv. 4. The *reflexive* would then be used, merely because
Philistia comprehends all the individual Philistines, and
התרועע could not express a voluntary jubilation in this place,
as in lxv. 14, but the sense would be: already subject, Moab
and Edom will be unable to rejoice, how much less Philistia!
Meanwhile, the earliest reader whom we know has understood
the התרועע as θριαμβεύειν as if this had been its ordinary
meaning (as θρίαμβος, *triumphus,* Vol. I. p. 230 takes its name
from the cry of victory), but has somewhat altered the reading:
over Philistia I rejoice as subject to me, Ps. cviii. 10; and if
we point הִתְרוֹעָעִי, this might perhaps mean *over Philistia is
my triumph!* (§ 156 a). But this would ill suit the tenor of the
language in the two previous verse-members. Rather does
that stronger sense form only the just transition from *b* to *c.*
The "let me rejoice!" ver. 8, belongs in any case not to the
oracle itself, wherein it would be otiose, possibly inconvenient,
but expresses provisionally the joy of the poet at so joyous an
oracle. For the ancient poet proceeds immediately, in accord
with the oracle, in the *sing.,* ver. 11: *who will lead me to a strong
city?* (מָצוֹר is well explained by מִבְצָר Ps. cviii. 11). The reason
is that David had at that time to encamp in the open field, and in
this camp much was to be feared. Further, who *leads me*
(comp. on the *perf.* on xi. 3) *unto* the distant *Edom,* which has
just revolted, to chastise it? Wilt *not* Thou, Thou *who,*
according to such an oracle, wilt again give me victory? But

from ver. 12, the later re-touching again occurs, which may be recognized in the whole song by the fact that in it the first person plural is used, whilst the ancient poet spoke of himself only in the singular. Instead of David, the whole of Israel now speaks and supplicates.

The great victor song which David sung after obtaining a complete victory over all the allied heathen peoples is certainly

12. PSALM XVIII.

For this is a grand, a splendid song of victory, which contains no momentary brief effusions of the mood of joy. It is composed with great art, in lofty, calm, and clear copious details throughout, and certainly with a view to some special occasion of festivity. In this way may be also explained the tenor of the song, which is general, the poet rejoicing not so much over a particular deliverance just experienced, as over a multitude of various dangers and hostilities out of which he has emerged, as from the highest and last stage of a life in many ways disturbed and troubled, yet never cast down, ever renewing its struggle. He praises Jahvé as his mighty and faithful and gracious Deliverer, who has subjected to him all his enemies, near and afar off, who has raised him, His faithful beloved one, to the head of the peoples, and will also further eternally bless his race. The whole song discloses the exalted love which is tried by temptation and sufferings, whereby the poet has ever clung to Jahvé, and in the power of which he overcame all hostility, and now is conscious, in a more advanced age, of strength and might for evermore; but, more closely considered, it is, moreover, a very definite epoch in the life of David, in which alone he could speak and sing as he here does. This epoch may be conjectured from the fact that we have here a grand song of victory in which there is no reference to domestic foes (after civil wars there should never be triumph, at least David was sufficiently great and noble never to indulge in this), but only over foreign, *i.e.*, heathen enemies,

vv. 32-46. But along with the lofty representation of his
most recent deliverance, with which the song, after the general
introduction, begins, vv. 5-19, David simply sketches a single
comprehensive picture of all the manifold deepest dangers
which he had passed through during the last great year of
war, in this most violent struggle with all heathen peoples,
and in the midst of which he seemed to the world and even to
himself a ruined man.

The song of victory begins only with the calmest reflection,
whilst the flow of the language gradually rises, and frequently,
in further explanation, again mildly subsides. ˙ In the solemn
introduction, vv. 2-7, slowly and gradually rising to a height,
at the conclusion, vv. 47-51, with loftier calm and certainty,
the leading thought comes out in purity and brevity. In the
middle, vv. 5-46, it is pursued and confirmed, being completed
in three grand strophés; for while the poet would celebrate *how*
he was delivered by Jahvé's grace there passes immediately
before his mind, in historic review, all the greatness and fearfulness of the most recent danger from which he now, with
joy and pride, sees himself delivered. The greater the danger
the more wondrous the deliverance, the loftier the reminiscence
and depiction of the Divine salvation. If the poet was a king
of the community of the true religion actually worthy of the
highest Divine favour, and there hinged upon his life and his
preservation a portion of the history of the kingdom of God
upon earth,—the power of the whole earth and the threatening
of death could avail naught against him; yea, it must appear
as if Jahvé, in anger at the opposition of the world, had come
from heaven in storm and tempest to draw him with irresistible power as from the gates of the deep hell; and so the
language here rises quickly to an extremely vivid picture of
extreme danger and of signal deliverance, through the appearance of Divine judgment, vv. 5-20. Yet the inner truth of
this particular history lies in the suggestion that such deliverance and glorification of the man by Jahvé became possible

only through the fulfilment in this particular matter of the eternal laws of the living covenant of a man with the only true God. The ever faithful and pure man can alone experience it, only the true spiritual God (of Israel) can give it. Accordingly, the poet now brings out, on the one side, the human relation, and exhibits the pure and holy life of his mind with childlike openness, and with the consciousness that man generally can obtain salvation in no other way; with this the language falls into calmest, most measured description, vv. 21-31. On the other side, the poet feels that the true spiritual God can only give salvation to the man so united with Him, and so at last the song again gradually rises higher, representing Jahvé as One who alone gives strength and true victory, who also could alone exalt so highly and strengthen the poet, vv. 32-46. For God, in the true Theocracy in which the poet had the blessing to be born, is known more clearly, and therefore also more mightily and more inspiringly than outside its pale. In this manner the song then of itself returns to the full thanksgiving with which it began. Thus the three middle great divisions, which form the proper substance of the song, are connected with one another and with the brief introduction and conclusion, easily and with gentle transitions. The entire development of the leading thought cannot be completed in all its members, and up to its true climax, more clearly and nobly than is done in this sublimest artistic song of victory.

But this long song is pervaded still further by art, which symmetrically distributes its contents into three great divisions. The prevailing measure of a strophé in it is a series of five verses. The first and the third of the three main divisions is thus each distributed into three strophés, the middle one into two; but the last strophé of each of these three main divisions is enlarged to six verses. To these eight (3, 2, 3) strophés one similar is added at the beginning as prelude, and one at the end as an epilogue, and thus the whole song consists of exactly ten similar strophés. So far the art of the whole may be completely recovered from the resources at hand. We cannot, however, recognize a perfect similarity of the verse-members within such strophé, by the use of these expedients. Long verse-members are nowhere seen.

The superscription, " David sang this song to Jahvé when He had delivered him out of the power of all his enemies, and out of the hand of Saul," fixes indeed the occasion of the song in too general a manner. We may not overlook the fact that Saul is here named only as the most dangerous, not as the last foe. But even thus the original reference of the song would be too far extended, and in words like vv. 18, 49, an allusion to Saul would in vain be sought. The great and detailed picture which the poet sketches of his deliverance, vv. 5—21, need not be taken too narrowly of a particular case. It is too large and too comprehensive for this. Rather does the reminiscence of all dangers and deliverances of the last year collect itself in the poet's mind in order here to serve for this one Divine picture. Yet this description at the beginning of the long song is very different from the words vv. 32—49, where the poet quite leaves that picture, and more freely looks back upon the whole of his past life. But in this the super-scription contains a sound recollection of David's authorship. In fact, not the least difficulty appears in deriving the song from David, who has moreover, in ver. 51, an appropriate place, named himself, in the thorough simplicity of ancient feeling. The character of David, his habit of mind, and his lofty consciousness, his experiences, unique as they were in all the world, are here all finally expressed with clearness. That the poet was a king, exalted by his peculiar capacity under Jahvé's help, to be the head of the peoples, is not merely plain from ver. 51, but already from ver. 44. But no later king could boast of such things. Even the fact that at the end the poet names himself in noble pride, and in full consciousness anticipates the continuance of the Divine blessing even to late posterity, speaks for David as the poet; for the last words of

David show the same high confidence, 2 Sam. xxiii., comp.
vii. 19. The details are indeed strikingly prolonged, and here
and there the language appears to be too languid and attenuated.
But the song probably belongs to the later age of David, when
the fire of lyric poetry has now a milder gleam; and in this
case it would be a song of the highest calm and of the most
blessed peace, in which the description of its own accord
falls into greater copiousness of details. On the other hand,
the language in other places acquires boldness and elevation,
and hardly is there elsewhere so grand an execution of truly
poetic pictures as is found here, vv. 5—21. The individual
words have a quite Davidic stamp.

To all this may be added as a very weighty external
testimony to the high antiquity and the Davidic origin of this
song, its recurrence in 2 Sam. xxii., with the same historical
superscription. For (1) all the other songs which are inserted
in the Books of Samuel as springing from David, are certainly
genuine Davidic songs. Therefore, on this account, the probability is in favour of this song also having been known, .
according to safe tradition, as Davidic to the comparatively
ancient composer of these books. (2.) The comparison of
the diverse readings of the song in the two books leads to
important inferences. The copy in the Psalms is certainly
later; this may be concluded, apart from the history of the
literature of the two books, from the much greater number of
vocal letters, see vv. 5, 6, 19, 47; 6, 16, 31, 35, 38, 48; 23;
on the other hand, vv. 14, 30. Notwithstanding this, the copy
in the Psalms must have proceeded not from Samuel, but from
another very good and ancient source; because the song in
many important passages recalls it, more faithfully, more
originally, with less corruption than the very fugitive copy in
Samuel, for the most part erroneously defective, but which sometimes makes spurious additions, frequently obliterates what is
more ancient. Comp. especially vv. 2, 11, 13, 14, 23, 24, 33, 34, 36,
38, 39, 42, 46, 47. In some other passages the text in Samuel is

more faithfully preserved, see especially vv. 3, 5, 8, 16, 41, 43, 44,
45. Since now the good and original text is so strongly divided
between the two, both must in different ways and at different
times have been borrowed from a more ancient source. Or
rather, the original copy had very early broken up into a mass
of derived ones, and in these, through the freedom of the
oldest copyists, had become more and more various, until at
length one copy of these was adopted in Samuel, another later
in the Psalm.* It further follows from this, that the song
which early underwent such variation must be very old, and
as one much known and read, must have been much copied.
Both considerations point to a Davidic origin.

1.

2   Dearly beloved I hold thee, O Jahvé my strength!
       Jahvé, Thou my rock and my battlement,
           my Deliverer Thou and my Redeemer;
       Thou my God and rock on whom I trust,
           shield and horn of my salvation;
       my fortress and refuge, Thou my helper,
           Thou who succourest me from hurt!
       worthy of praise, I cry, is Jahvé,
           and from my foes I become free.

2.

5   Waves had surrounded me,
           streams of destruction affrighted me;
       bands of hell had surrounded me,
           death's nets fallen upon me :—
       in my affliction I cry to Jahvé,
           complain aloud to my God;

---

* The older view, that the deviations in the Psalms and Samuel proceeded from
the hand of the poet, is not more erroneous than that of Gramberg (in Winer's
Exeget. Stud. I, pp. 1-25) that the "recension" in the Psalms is more ancient and
genuine, and that that in Samuel is borrowed from it; which I confuted in
Jen. Lit. Zeit., 1829, *Erl. Bl.*, and later C. v. Lengerke, in his *Comm. crit. de duplici
Ps. xviii. exemplo.* Regim. 1833.

He from His palace hears me cry,
  my complaint pierces his ears;
and the earth trembles and totters,
  and heaven's pillars shake,
    wavered—because He glowed!
there went up smoke in his nostrils,
  fire devoured out of his mouth,
    coals were kindled from Him.

3.

And the heaven He bowed, came down,   10
  —cloudy darkness under his feet;—
advanced on the cherub and flew,
  took flight on the wings of the wind;
makes the darkness his screen,
  round about him in his pavilion;
  —darkest waters, thickest clouds!
Before the brightness in front of Him,—passed away
    his dark clouds
  —hail and coals of fire!
and from heaven thunders Jahvé,
  and the Highest sounds aloud;
  —hail and coals of fire!

4.

He sent His arrows and—scatters them,   15
  slinging lightnings, and—scares them.
Then appeared they, the beds of the sea,
  and the earth's foundations were bare:
—before Thy threatening, Jahvé,
  before the blast of the wind of Thy nostrils!
reaching forth from the height He takes me,
  draws me out of many waters;
sets me free from my cruel enemy,
  my haters, since they were too strong for me.

They indeed fall upon me on the day of my distress;
    yet Jahvé did become my support,
20   led me out into the open,
    sets me free—because He loves me.

5.

Jahvé doeth to me according to my righteousness,
    according to the purity of my hands He rewards me.
For I kept Jahvé's ways,
    departed not wickedly from my God:
for before me stand all His judgments,
    His commandment I removed not from me;
so also was I honest towards Him,
    kept myself from my iniquity;
and so Jahvé rewarded me according to my righteousness,
25   according to the purity of my hands, clear before Him.

6.

Towards good men Thou showest Thyself good,
    upright towards the upright man;
towards pure men Thou showest Thyself pure,
    towards the perverted as perverse.
But *Thou* doest help afflicted people,
    and abasest proud eyes;
but *Thou* causest my light to shine
    —Jahvé, my God, enlightens my darkness!
30   For through Thee I shatter hosts,
    and through my God I overleap walls;
that God whose way is upright,
    Jahvé's word is refined,
      a shield is He to all who trust in Him!

7.

For who is God but Jahvé,
    who a rock except our God?

that God, who has girded me with strength,
    caused me to bound on my way unharmed,
Who made my feet like hinds' feet,
    and causeth me to stand upon my heights;
Who hath inured my hands to war,   35
    that my arms bend the iron bow,
Thou who gavest me the shield of Thy salvation,
    Thy right hand sustains me,
        Thy humility exalts me!

8.

Thou makest wide my steps under me,
    and my ankle-bones do not tremble;
I pursue and overtake my enemies,
    return not until they are destroyed,
and crushed that they cannot stand,
    fall under my feet!—
Thus Thou girdest me with strength for the war,   40
    bendest my adversaries under me;
turnest to me the backs of my foes,
    my haters—I bring them to naught.

9.

Though they cry—without deliverer,
    unto Jahvé—He listened not to them;
that I may grind them like dust of the earth,
    tread them as dirt of the streets!—
Thou rescuest me from the people's broils,
    preservest me to be the head of the nations,
        people, unknown, serve me;
at the hearing of the ear they obey me,   45
    sons also of the strange land do me homage.
The sons of the strange land vanish away,
    Tremble in affright from out of their castles.

10.

Live Jahvé, be my rock blessed,
    and exalted the God of my salvation !
that God, who gave me vengeance
    and subjected nations to me;
Thou who savest me from my foes,
    yea, exaltest me in the presence of mine adversaries,
       freest me from the man of violence !—
Therefore praise I Thee, Jahvé, among the nations,
    make music to Thy Name !
50   to Him, to the lofty Helper of His king,
    to Him, who shows favour to His Anointed,
to David and His seed for ever !

1. Vv. 2-4, the sublime introduction, itself at the outset a full, ardent ascription of praise to Jahvé. I love Thee, my mighty protector in power and deed, who fitly, as even now, called upon in the presence of my enemies, ever does and did help me. To this entirely restful beginning ver. 2 is so peculiarly appropriate that we cannot see why it should be wanting in Samuel, except through a copyist's mistake. רחם is, besides, a rare word ; and the omission was easier than the addition. On the other hand, ver. 3 has certainly been preserved in its entirety in Samuel; for the משׂגבי stands in the Psalm quite abruptly and confusedly, so that it must have been considered spurious, or the mere remainder of an originally longer series of words: but Sam. gives the fully appropriate supplement. Instead of לִי which in Ps. cxliv. 2, and Sam. stands after מְפַלְטִי, a preferable reading is וְגוֹאֲלִי, as the poet of Ps. xix. 15 must have had it before his eyes. In this way theré is formed an appropriate division; the praise of Jahvé, here unfolding itself in the right place, is resolved into three larger members, and each again into two halves, of which the earlier depicts the strength of Jahvé which awakens confidence,—the second the application, or the

actual end and consequence, the deliverance. Each small and large member is thus completed, and the whole in a perfectly satisfactory manner. The מְהֻמָּם here at the beginning, well coincides with the conclusion, ver. 49.

2. Vv. 5-21. The utterly lost and unhappy one thinks of himself as if cast down a deep precipice, or as sinking irre-deemably in deep water floods, comp. xxxi. 2 ; xxxii. 6 ; xl. 3 ; lxix. 2, 3. He who now knows himself to be near to death, may suppose himself to have been cast into the deepest bottom of the sea, to the point where the lower world begins, as if he were already in the smoking streams which lead to the lower world (Jon. ii. 4, 6, 7 ; Job, xxvi. 5, 6) or according to another rarer figure, as if he were already in the nets of death that ever waylays mankind. (Hence the Indian mythology repre-sents Jamas with a rope, comp. *Savitri-Upâkhjânam* v. 8, and the German *sage* tells of Hell's fetters which wind around the neck of the dying ; comp. also *Hamâsa*, p. 111, 8 v., and G. Müller's *Amerikanische Urreligion* p. 98). But though the faithful one lie on the very verge of hell, it is never too hard nor too far off to move him, if it please God. Even the depths of the sea and the gates of the lower world must feel Jahvé's power, and stand open to His word (Job. xxvi. 5, 6). Hence the beautiful representation—how whilst the prayer of the poet throbs from the lowest depths to the listening Jahvé in the highest heaven, suddenly from the utmost height to the extremest depth through the whole resistent world the delivering word of Jahvé hastens, and Jahvé as with mighty hand draws the faithful one up out of death. But always with this another figure is blended. If the poet lay then below as on the verge of death, it was peculiarly the hostile world, it was (as presently in vv. 18 sqq. is more calmly stated) his cruel enemies who had brought him thither. But if the wrong was on their side, the Divine anger must be enkindled against them ; and if their rage against him was so violent, a Divine anger must be kindled, which as if burning above in the

secrecy of the remotest heaven, came over the earth like a
thunder-storm, and overcoming all resistance of the world,
became like a tempest laying bare the foundation of the sea,
in order again to draw forth and to deliver from the extreme
depth him that lay there as one lost. But nothing shows so
vividly, and with such fearful power of impression the connexion of the heaven and the earth,—as Jahvé like one in
wrath, bows the heaven over the earth,—and the earth even to
the lower world trembles before His word,—than the Palestinian storm, as it is occasionally seen, uniting the tempest and
the earthquake ; Ps. xxix. Pictures of such manifestations of
Divine activity in great moments of the earth are indeed not
rare elsewhere (lxviii. 9 ; Judges v. 4 ; Am. ix. 5 ; Mic. i. 3 ;
Hab. iii). But nowhere is the figure so fully carried out as
here. From the beginning to the end the figure is retained,
in three great divisions. First of all, there appears, with the
rising and kindling of the Divine anger, a distant quaking and
bluster, while amidst storm and trembling on the earth, a
glowing thunder-cloud forms in the higher heaven, already
announcing itself by distant flashes, as it were the bursting
fire of anger no longer to be restrained, vv. 7-9. Then the
violent hurricane, as in a rapid storm, comes ever nearer, it
soon stands like a black mass of cloud, in threatening aspect
over the earth ; and Jahvé seems, bowing the heaven, in
this dark guise to be drawing fearfully near, vv. 10-12,—
until out of the heavy black clouds riven by His word, as
by a bright flash, lightnings, thunder and hail burst forth
unceasingly,—Divine weapons, by which He scares all
resistance, and divides the flood which kept the faithful im-
prisoned, vv. 13-15. Thus finally, the bottom of the sea being
laid bare by tempest and violent storm, and the gates of death
being opened, Jahvé draws forth the lost one with a strong
hand, mightily protecting him from all his foes, vv. 16-18. And
now the language, the grand picture being completed, passes
more calmly into the simple imagery, vv. 19-21. This entire

portion of the song, the most vivid and artistic, thus falls into
three smaller divisions, and each of these again into two
similar halves : cause and beginning of the Divine deliverance,
vv. 5-9 ; details ever more exact and complete, vv. 10-14 ;
completion, vv. 15-20, and the figure of the sinking in the
depths, with which the whole begins, vv. 5, 6, is thus designedly
at end again taken up and completed, vv. 16, 17. But
precisely because the single figure of the water, including all
the rest in itself, remains unchanged from the beginning to
the end,—we must unquestionably read, instead of הבלי, ver. 5,
which has found its way into the text from ver. 6, מִשְׁבְּרֵי
according to Samuel, since only this is here suitable. But also
for מֶוֶת, which appears early enough in ver. 6, is rather מַיִם to
be held the original reading, as the phrase is found in xciii. 4,
and abbreviated in cases like xlii. 8.—Ver. 7. That היכל
denotes here not the temple at Jerusalem, but the heavenly
palace, is quite plain from the sequel. לפניו appears earlier
than באזניו, which Samuel has, a later addition ; for one
of the two is certainly not original. On the other hand, תבא
is wanting in Samuel, inaptly. Ver. 8. For חרים, Samuel
has certainly the more original השמים ; *the foundations of the
heaven* (comp. the counterpart, ver. 6) are the extreme
mountain-tops as bearers and pillars of the heaven, according
to a representation rare among the Hebrews, but plainly
appearing also in Job xxvi. 11. Thus *all* the earth and heaven
fell into commotion as in an earthquake.—Vv. 10-12. A fine
delineation of the quickly-gathering, violent storm. *He bowed
the heaven,* which with the burden of dark clouds, seems ever
to sink deeper, and to touch the smoking mountains, as is
further explained later, Ps. cxliv. 5. But Jahvé seems to be
concealed in the dark mass of clouds, borne by the Kerûb
as by the storm, threatening to approach the earth. The
clause וַעֲרָפֶל is a static clause (§ 341 *a*).—Ver. 12 contains
unquestionably (against the confused reading of Samuel) two
members, each falling into two halves. With fine cadence the

9

ever more blackly gathering storm is described, until it reaches
"darkest waters, densest clouds," comp. § 313 c.—Ver. 13.
Very noteworthy is the description of the manner in which the
darkest water discharges itself. As it is discharged, there
appears suddenly a bright flash, tearing asunder the gloom of
the heavy clouds. It is as if the gleam of light which always
immediately encompasses Jahvé (Hab. iii. 4), breaking forth
with His word, divided the gloom asunder. Hence with
brevity, *before the brightness before Him, i.e.,* which immediately
surrounded Him, *passed away his dark clouds,* while He
scattered them, and breaking forth revealed Himself. Very
aptly is then figured by the repeated exclamation : *hail and
coals of fire !*—how unceasingly during the near-resounding
thunder the Divine weapons are hurled down (Samuel certainly
very incorrectly omits the last part of ver. 14). Hail is very
rare in Palestine, but if it falls, ordinarily the more fearful and
destructive, comp. Job. xxxviii. 22, 23, Jos. x. 11. מִן־שָׁמַיִם,
Sam. is better. Thus He sends, ver. 15, lightnings as His
arrows, to divide asunder *them* the threatening floods, or
without figure, the enemies ; for that the suffix ver. 15 refers
immediately to water is clear from the following explanation,
ver. 16, and from the beginning, ver. 5, to which the poet now
recurs. רָב must be the verb = רָבָה, רָמָה, the LXX in Samuel
correctly ἤστραψεν, comp. the correct explanation, cxliv. 6.—
Ver. 16. For מַיִם Samuel, has the better reading יָם, comp.
Ex. xiv. 21.—Ver. 17 שָׁלַח, *stretch,* where in the connexion
the language is plainly of taking and seizing,—may readily
stand without the nearer object "hand," as even in prose,
2 Sam. vi. 6.

3. Vv. 21-31. Not without reason did the poet conclude the
long first main part, v. 20 b, with the brief new expression—let
God save him *because He favours him,* loves him. By this means
the full transition is suddenly prepared, to the detailed description from the one side of the human reason for that deliverance,
in order thereby to recur to the praise of God from this moral

side. The poet feels, that only because he has never striven in thought or deed to depart from Jahvé, could he on the other hand be favoured and delivered by Him. This, first briefly expressed in vv. 20, 21, is then argued out in vv. 22-25, in order in a second strophé, vv. 26-31, that he may return from the general truths which here are fundamental, vv. 26-28, the more purely to his own moral experience, full of gratitude to God, vv. 29-31. But if the peculiar feeling of the poet rests here upon the general eternal relation of reciprocity between God and man, according to which God ever deals with man as man with God, vv. 26, 27; and if even the faithful man has often to suffer, as indeed the poet above narrated of himself,— nevertheless, humility and patience, and the consciousness of that inward purity, yield true hope and strength, ver. 28. The poet feels with joy that he has overcome all dangers, not by himself, by proud self-seeking endeavours, but in the midst of perpetual anguish and distress, patience and endurance, through Jahvé alone, vv. 29-31. We see the poet clearly understands the true mode of inward preparation and sanctification. But it is from no vain pride that he refuses to conceal his own inward nobleness—although later uninstructed readers might very readily misunderstand such expressions,—but from child-like innocent transparency and inspired feeling. We must not overlook the manner in which the non-departure from Divine commands, ver. 22, is explained by the direction of the disposition, ver. 23, comp. xvi. 8. The various reading of Samuel in the second clause, ver. 23, is hence less suitable.

Vv. 26, 27 appear to speak very harshly and crudely of God, but in truth not incorrectly. For it is a necessary truth, that man is conscious of God in his breast after the manner in which he conceives and defines Him,—and this reciprocal relation is moreover required externally by eternal justice. As then he who conducts himself piously, uprightly, purely, feels in himself and experiences without himself that God is the like: so upon the perverted man, thinking and acting perversely, this per-

9 *

versity has necessarily a reactive operation. Within and
without himself he loses more and more the Divine light, and
finally, forsaken of true counsel and true happiness, must
think to know God as a perverted, malicious, ungracious being.
So is it in the midst of life ; more exact inquiries on the extent
and limitation of these feelings do not belong to this place.
Ver. 28. עַם must, on account of the general saying, be our
"people," comp. ver. 44. A reference to Israel lies neither in
the word in itself, nor would it be in anywise suitable here.
In the second clause the reading — here too allusive — of
Samuel probably arose merely from the false reading of עינים
as עיניר, the last stroke of the ם being effaced.—Ver. 30.
The punctators have אָרֻץ, because they derive it from רוּץ
"run." The uniformity of the members is not however to be
so strictly taken; and to the thickly thronging band, אָרֹץ
from רץ "break through," better suits. This part issues,
ver. 31, in a brief celebration of Jahvé's praise, that is, which is
the immediate suggestion in this place, of His moral trust-
worthiness and purity.

4. Vv. 32-46. On the other side it is equally true that the poet,
only in covenant with *this* God, the eternal and true God, could
experience such salvation. *He* only gave him the true strength,
and arms *for the* fight, vv. 32-36 ; the true strength *in the* fight,
vv. 37-41, and so the great victory, vv. 42-46. But what strength
and what all-overcoming courage and what nobleness this very
God may give, he has recognized in his own experience, and he
can sufficiently render thanks for out of his own long life. The
figures of the raging war and of the constant victory over all,
even distant foreign peoples, pass away here, in the presence
of these recollections. But the poet finely begins, ver. 36, to
celebrate the Divine powers of salvation alone as the forces
and arms wherewith Jahvé has equipped him and destined him
to be victor. How much of bodily strength and bodily apti-
tude, how many arms the warrior needs ! as David here brings
out, quite similarly to the song of praise, 2 Sam. i. 21-23. But

he knows that only the Divine strength could so furnish and
equip him, that the best *shield* was His *salvation*, the best
support His *righteousness*, and the best exaltation in misfortune
His gracious condescension (humility), as is said at the close of
the strophé, ver. 36, in the briefest and aptest manner. And
similar is it with the forces as man employs them *in the midst*
of the battle, as David in the second strophé, vv. 32-35, in
further retrospect of all the experiences of his earlier warrior-
life sketches the most picturesque description of them.
Hence, passing on to the recollection of the long series of the
victories he had gained, he cannot here refrain from the new
thought of how also his enemies in distress cried to heaven for
help, but in vain—for the mere cry for help cannot yet bring
deliverance—vv. 42, 43.

In this way a counterpart to the previous grand delineation,
vv. 5-21, appropriate to the whole connexion of the song,
arises. But the more does he recur, as to the last conclusion,
to the thankful description of the great victory which has now
been obtained, vv. 44-45. And since the whole song properly
aims only at thanksgiving and praise to Jahvé, this must again
be prominent with the greater force towards the end of the
long words. Thus the language here soon passes unobserved
into address to Jahvé, from whose grace the poet derives all
his greatness.—Ver. 32 reminds us strongly of Deut. xxxii.
4 sqq., but where the original is retained, is not long doubtful.
Comp. also 2 Sam. vii. 22. For וַיִּתֵּן, ver. 33, Samuel has
probably the more original reading, וַיַּתֵּר; הִתִּיר, "let free"
might then be taken absolutely for "leave," "let be," but
וַיַּתְרֵנִי is then a still better reading, since תָּמִים stands in any
case here in the natural sense, like Prov. i. 12. On the other
hand Samuel introduces in this and the following clause the
third person, which does not suit this whole strophé, nay would
insert a general proposition about the upright man not
belonging to this connexion.—Ver. 34. Speed of foot indis-

pensable in attack as well as flight. *On my heights,* on those
which I have ascended, have occupied, *he causes me to stand,*
it being impossible for an enemy to pursue and hunt me down.
The possession of Palestine depends on the possession of the
heights. Here is the original to Hab. iii. 19.—Ver. 35. How
monstrously heavy were frequently the bows, and how labo-
rious it was to bend them (נִחַת properly press down the bow
with the foot, otherwise *tread*) we best learn from many stories
in epic description, as in the Odyssey and in the Ramajana.*—
But the true arms and means of defence—ver. 36 adds—are
the divine, the shield of his salvation, his right hand for the
holding of the falling one, His condescension and kindness
(xlv. 5) wherewith he comes down from His elevation in order
to exalt the helpless. The reading ענתך Sam., which must
have then been pronounced עֲנָתְךָ, arose through hasty
omission or erroneous reading of the ו.—Ver. 38, אשיגם
against Samuel is defended by vii. 6, Ex. xv. 9, as by the
good connexion.—Ver. 41. A very short expression: *Thou
settest* (makest) *my enemies to the back,* backwards, *i.e.,* causest
them to turn their backs to me, to flee, xxi. 13, Ex. xxiii. 27.
Ver. 42. יְשַׁעוּ Samuel, arose again through the cursory omission
of the ו in ישועו; this is sufficiently defended by the context
and by ver. 7. On the contrary, in ver. 43 " before the wind" (as
dust flies before the wind) might be held an irrelevant addition
in the Psalm, since here the shattering, not the scattering is
the main thing. Comp. ver. 39 whither the language recurs,
quite otherwise places like Isa. xli. 2, 15, 25. Again, subsequently, Samuel would have better read אֲדִקֵּם for אֲרִיקֵם
I empty them out, spout them out. But if all the various
readings of both books be taken together, and the sense is
more sharply examined, it is most probable that the words
originally ran somewhat as follows:

---

* Comp. also Her. iii., 21. Ibn.—Batuta in the *Journ. As.,* 1823, i., p. 228.
Nibel., xvi., 961. *Berl. Akad. Abhl.,* 1851, p. 278.

תְּהֵמֵם כְּמֹץ עַל פְּנֵי רוּחַ
וּכְקַשׁ יָבֵשׁ תְּרִיקֵם
וְאֶשְׁחָקֵם כַּעֲפַר אָרֶץ
כְּטִיט חוּצוֹת אֲרִקָעֵם

Thou drivest them hence as chaff *before wind*,
  as dry straw Thou spoutest them out
  that I may bruise them as earth-dust,
  trample them as dirt of the streets.

Though this strophé thus becomes longer by a verse, yet the whole is perfectly appropriate. Ver. 44. Sam. has much more expressively, and suitably to the whole song, תשמרני for the bald תשימני.—Ver. 45. "By the hearing of the ear," *i.e.*, already from afar; for the sound makes its way further than the hand. Similarly, but in another application, Job xlii. 5.— Lastly, in ver. 46, a forcible brief figure, setting forth how little resistance the enemy can make. They *melt away*, exhausted in the severe battle, Ex. xviii. 18, and *tremble out of their strong castles*, the fortresses, begging for grace and protection. Mic. vii. 17 well explains this. הרג is *harakh*, Arab., to be narrow, distressed (Sur. vii. 1) *flee*. On the other hand the reading חגר must have been compared with *chagar*, Syr. *limp*.

5. Vv. 47-51. Conclusion in joyous praise of Jahvé, the Deliverer, all the previous figures being here once more compressed in brief touches. Comp. 2 Sam. vii. 26. The חי *live!* in the like connexion is antiquely simple, § 223 *b*.—אף ver. 49 is indeed very rare in more ancient songs, and is only frequent in certain later ones. That it might however be found in David's time is shown by Judges v. 29. Ver. 50 I consider to be the original of a saying which so often occurs in later times. Later poets thus sung in the expectation that the religion of Jahvé must be extended ever more widely and without fear and dread among the Gentiles also, in the midst of whom they in part lived. But if David thus sung, with not quite the same experience and expectation, he had never-

theless conquered through Jahvé the Gentiles, and could not
delay to proclaim Jahvé's praise before the whole world wherein
he ruled.   David and Solomon's lofty age is thus characterized for the first time by a striving to bring the Gentiles also
to the religion of Jahvé ; an endeavour which soon came to an
end, was only prophetically maintained; but finally, in consequence of the exile, again appears with new zeal and new
light, in a more powerful and comprehensive form.

Meanwhile, he who stands in the highest position, and has
been the longest prosperous, may the more readily be led
astray by sudden temptation, and the more deeply fall; David,
already long king in Jerusalem, did not even remain untouched
by the great danger.   How severe and bitter is such a fall,
and after what deadly struggles salvation may again arise ; and
again, how glorious is the finally attained victory of a spirit
like David's, is shown in the following quite peculiar song: ·

13. PSALM XXXII.

The poet has successfully maintained a sore inward struggle,
and now stands on the threshold of a new time.   He had
sinned greatly, led astray by passion.   Sin has its logical consequences, and the evil conscience its obduracy.   But while
the poet thus at first sought to continue to live in the mood of
mind in which he had sinned, and to defend himself, the
inward and outward consequences of his sins, unrest, grief,
misery,—became ever more consuming and deadly.   In the
most burning sorrow he groaned forth a prayer to God for
help, without however finding relief and refreshment.   At last,
when he was now exposed to the extreme danger of entire
perdition,—inwardly changed, weary of deceptions, having come
to a nearer consciousness of the greatness of his guilt and to
true repentance,—he again found rest and serenity in the
clearness and the peace of God.

Again he vividly heard in his soul the voice and the counsel
of God, and with higher confidence glanced towards the

future. At this stage, whither we here see him arrived, he experiences the blessing which springs from sincerity before God, and the folly of seeking to resist, like irrational beasts, the higher (Divine) reason. And all this so extremely and powerfully, that he feels himself compelled to communicate this his own experience to all the world, and to exhort all to avoid spiritual self-deception. This song has then, because springing from such a state of feeling, a decided tendency towards general representation and exhortation,—the personal experience of the poet appearing only as elucidation and deduction. The more general teaching coming forward from the very first, becomes towards the end, as it passes into exhortations, alone predominant. And thus the whole falls into four strophés. First comes out calmly the blessed truth, the basis of the whole song, that only the man who practises no deception before God may expect salvation, vv. 1-2. This indeed the poet, as the second strophé says, vv. 3-5, has most powerfully experienced in his own person. To this personal experience there is joined on the one side the intense wish that every pious man may at the right time apply in prayer to God. Thus the poet, though once in a condition of deadly peril, yet now with joyous assurance feels that he returned at the right time to a right mind, so that he may now eternally experience the protection and counsel of God, vv. 6-8. On the other side is the exhortation to all not foolishly to resist God, since the sinner has many sorrows, whilst the righteous man rejoices in God and ever may rejoice, vv. 9-11.

The song is plainly ancient, original throughout, the token of a powerful mind. Hardly can the inward misery of a torn heart, together with the higher serenity of the again reconciled and sanctified one, be more intensely expressively and powerfully described than here. The more severe the struggle was in this heart, the more glorious the victory, the more clearly and joyously now streams from him the earnest word. Since too the stamp of the language is Davidic, it cannot be doubted that the song was sung after the event narrated in 2 Sam. xii. The fact that neither Nathan nor any other prophet is here named as the instrument of awakening David, would be a very slight objection, since David would never have experienced remorse had not the power of the prophetic word inwardly seized him, and sharpened anew the feeling of truth in him which had been merely repressed. Again, we must in any case assume that the poet, not during the change itself, but at some later time, after he had completely regained inner rest and serenity, in the higher survey of all the past, and of the whole order of Divine grace, thus speaks; and in this song concludes as it were the whole tragedy which had passed in his inner life. By this circumstance especially this Psalm is greatly distinguished from that indited in the midst of his conversion, before he fully regained rest, li. The first echoes of vv. 1-2 we find in Prov. xxviii. 13.

The three verses of each strophé are extended to seven verse-members. On the shorter first one, comp. I, pp. 168 sqq.

1.

1　　Blessed he whose misdeed is forgiven,
　　　　whose sin is pardoned!
　　Blessed the man to whom Jahvé imputes not guilt,
　　　　and in whose spirit there is no deceit!—

2.

　　When I was silent, my bones mouldered,
　　　　whilst I continually groaned;
　　for heavily did thine hand oppress me day and night;
　　　　my sap was changed into summer's dryness.　*
5　　My sin I declared to Thee, not concealing guilt,
　　　　said, " I confess to Jahvé my faults :"
　　and Thou removedst the guilt of my sin !　*

3.

Therefore let every godly man pray to Thee at the right
    time :
    They will, in flood of many waters,
    not reach to him !
Thou art a shelter to me, wilt guard me from trouble,
    ever surround me with jubilations of deliverance !   *

" will teach, thee, point out the way thou shouldst go ;
    will lift mine eyes on thee !"

4.

Be not like horse or mule without insight !
    bit and bridle must close his jaws,
    that approaches thee unfriendly.
many sorrows has the wicked man :   10
    but he who trusts in Jahvé, him does He surround with
    grace.
Rejoice in Jahvé, and be merry, ye righteous !
Shout for joy all ye upright in heart !

Ver. 4. Whilst the poet felt himself externally bowed down
by sore sufferings as from the hand of the chastising Jahvé
(Job. ii. 5 ; xiii. 21), his inner part was at the same time
burnt up and withered by the most glowing anguish, as if his
body with sap and blood had been changed into the driest
summer ground : comp. cii. 4 ; xxii. 16 ; lxix. 4.—Ver. 5.
Note here the poetic change of the imperfect and perfect in
the two substantial parts of this sentence, *I confess—thou hast
forgiven,* wherein the sense is : *so soon as I confessed*—thou
hadst *already forgiven.*   So closely and necessary do both
hang together, and so truly does God's act anticipate his.   In
the intermediate words, כסיתי‎, אמרתי‎, the unusually selected
present is resolved into the ordinary tone of narration : comp.
§ 357 *b.*   The Divine pardon is not here further pursued ; but
its consequences and its nature are further touched upon,
vv. 1, 2, 7, 8.—Ver. 6. That יתפלל‎ is to be taken as jussive

is shown, apart from the connexion of the whole song, by the assuring רִק, subsequently occurring. *Only,* if he, as I wish, prays at the right time, will, though certainly in a great deluge, which threatens to carry everything away, the waves not reach him. Finally, then, will he stand, though in the most threatening danger. A main part of the emphasis lies on לְעֵת מְצֹא, *at the time of the reaching* (מצא, reach, reach to, Num. xi. 22); *i.e.,* at the time when the goal, the object can still be reached, therefore at the suitable right time, like the Lat. *aptas* from Sansk. *âp* reach ἱκανός, LXX rightly according to the sense ἐν καιρῷ εὐθέτῳ.—This hope has also entered the poet's heart. He hears again, and more vividly than before, the Divine voice within him, and it is to him as if Jahvé's counsel and leading would never forsake him, ver. 8. In fact, a beautiful revelation of simply strong, truly enlightened faith : comp. Isa. xxx. 20, 21. אִיעָצָה cannot mean in this connexion " I will counsel;"* but יעץ = יצע, *wadda,* Arab., properly fasten, ground, hence figuratively counsel, so far as this is a supporting, holding ; and remains here in the sensuous signification, as the LXX rightly ἐπιστηριῶ, and as it is explained in common speech by the better known אָשִׂימָה, Gen. xliv. 21 ; Isa. xxiv. 6 ; xl. 4.—Ver. 9. The עֲדִיו is here harsh. Either עֶדְיוֹ is derivable from עֲדִי, "attire of the body, especially of the head,"—the reading of the Massora and the explanation of the Targum ; with bit and bridle, his trappings, is he to be tied (to be bound) who approaches thee not. Thus bit and bridle may indeed form a glittering equipment of the horse, as an obstinate, self-willed man may outwardly show off to the last degree in his pride and scorn : but is this attire a noble and a worthy one ? Meanwhile the bringing into relief of this very thought of attire lies remote

---

* It is incomprehensible how it should still be sought to defend this groundless meaning. But a Latin or Greek school-word like *constructio praegnans* seems, in the eyes of so many German scholars of the present day, always quite sufficient to cover everything they do not wish to see.

to the whole context. The figure must be simpler, and the בלם " fasten," demands a more exact definition of the trait in the picture thereby given. But the עֶדְיוֹ, according to ciii. 5, might be derived from quite another root, as if it meant *his temper is to be fettered*. But this word does not mean generally, or in a bad sense, *temper*, but only *appetite of eating*. Most appropriate is certainly the explanation, after the LXX, by " jaws," so that עֲדָיִו would be read, and עַד as = *khad*, Arab., or the cheek itself would be named from *eating* (like *mandibulum*), so that the root of both words would be the same, and the reading עֶדְיוֹ might be retained in the same signification. If the first member of the second half reads thus : with bit and bridle are his cheeks to be tied (*i.e.*, his resistance to be fettered), in the second supplementary member " of that which unfriendly approaches thee," the transition into the address to God may be more readily tolerated ; for the whole second half of the verse thus very markedly drops the hortatory address to man, passing over in the same figure to the representation of the truth in itself, as ver. 10 then immediately adds the many sorrows which the foolish man, just because he strives against reason, and allows himself to be forced against his will, suffers. קְרוֹב in *constr. st.* (§ 289 *b*) describes with אֶל the friendly loving approval and devotion which should exist between man and God: comp. Zeph. iii. 2, and elsewhere, for the sense Isa. xxxvii. 20; Hos. iv. 15; Prov. xxvi. 3.—סוֹבֵב, ver. 10, just as in ver. 7 (§ 283 *b*).

The changeless rest and assurance that David attained in his later age, is shown in the following two songs :—

14-15. Psalms iii. iv.

Ps. iii. belongs, with the following, plainly to the same poet, and also probably to the same time, only that Ps. iv. appears to be somewhat later ; and it cannot be doubted that they, as the superscription to Ps. iii. says, fall in the period of the flight from Absalom. The elevation, the stamp, the style of David are unmistakable. But as one who had now long stood on the summit of human power, now long enjoyed the highest favour with God; the higher calm towards the end of a much disturbed, but ever growingly blessed life, is brought out in all his words. And with infinite frequency already (comp. iii. 5, iv. 4) had the poet poured forth his feelings in songs, strengthened himself in confidence towards God. New occasion for this is given by the most recent ever increasing danger, and the thereby increased spiritlessness of friends. But the old trust in God readily overcomes anew in brief and mighty prayer all sense of distress. Thus these songs appear as new brief outbursts of a poet long used to song and prayer. And since David may, especially in the time of Absalom, have sung very many songs, it would be thence explained why in these two little songs Absalom is not expressly mentioned, even if it were not admitted that Absalom was but a tool in the hands of David's enemies, and if we did not readily perceive that David in that tender feeling with which he clung to Absalom (2 Sam. xviii. 5-22) would wish nothing evil against his son. But in the circumstance that the poet, however fate may turn, before every thing desires blessing on the head of Israel, iii. 9, we recognize very clearly the noble spirit of David in that flight, which might exorcise the gathering, threatening storm, and roll off from the people the burden of the approaching civil war: almost, as he explained at the end of the prayer, willing rather to sacrifice himself and his hope, so that it might but further the welfare of the people. The one short word throws a bright light upon the depth of his noble soul.

More closely, the occasion to Ps. iii. must be sought in the elevation and strengthening which an unexpectedly quiet night gives the poet (vv. 6, 7). The calmer mood of a cheerful morning is here expressed, whilst the distress which returns, vv. 2, 3, must immediately give way before the memory of the long tried (vv. 4, 5), and even now in the last night again experienced Divine strengthening, vv. 6, 7; so that at last higher boldness as well as tranquil resignation in fulness returns, vv. 8, 9. Accordingly, four brief strophés; but so that the two middle ones are more closely connected together.

1.

Jahvé! how many are my oppressors become! 1
  many lift themselves against me,
many say of my soul:
  " no salvation has he in God." *

2.

Yet thou, O Jahvé, art a shield around me,
  my pride and lifter-up of my head!
loud I cry to Jahvé, 5
  and He heard me from the holy mountain. *

3.

I laid me down and slept:
  awoke, because Jahvé supports me;
I fear not before many thousand people,
  who have encamped against me round about.

4.

Up then, Jahvé, help me my God!
  Thou didst verily strike the cheeks of all my foes,
    the teeth of the wicked Thou didst break to pieces!
Jahvé's is the victory!—
  Upon Thy people thy blessing! *

Ver. 3. The words of desponding men, that the ancient truster in God, now near to perishing, must have lost his health in God, are, as is readily understood, not heard aloud by the poet; yet the poet knows that they thus think of the health of his life; comp. iv. 7. So we must manifestly in ver. 3 think of lukewarm friends. Ver. 5 must depict a habit of the poet's, whereby he is repeatedly sure of his hope in God; so often as I

cry or cried to God, I felt that I was heard from Sion. The ark
of the covenant had therefore long been in Sion.—Ver. 6. The
proof from that one last might; because of the new thought
אני stands forward with emphasis.—Ver. 8. Picture of a wild,
unruly beast. But such wild raging enemies the poet had
earlier in great numbers : therefore plainly again of the many
battles of David.

Ps. iv. is according to ver. 9 an evening song, and most probably sung on the evening of the same day on the morning of which
the previous song had sounded. In the short interval the
danger had become more urgent. But freshly then had arrived
the report of continuous passionate slanders and invectives
wherewith many pursued the noble fugitive, as we know to be
the fact from the history of the Absalomian time, 2 Sam. xxv.
Comp. iii. 3. The louder, however, the slanders become and
the more the poet is forced to reply to their contents, the
clearer speedily becomes to him their entire baselessness.
Instead of being bowed down by the truth and injury of the
slanders, his noble and clear consciousness with the more
strength and boldness, and what he would on another occasion
not so clearly have confessed to himself, not so boldly have
expressed--stands now suddenly in a clear picture before his
soul, and escapes from his lips in righteous indignation at the
baseless slanders. It is the certainty of higher strength and
distinction through the God whom he truly honours. If every
truly great and noble man feels most powerfully his inward
strength and elevation in the very crisis of danger, and when
threatened by baseness, it is not surprising if David, becoming
momentarily conscious of all his elevation, turns immediately to
denounce in noble wrath his distant slanderers, who are nevertheless clearly present in all their pitifulness to his spirit. He
reminds them in serious castigatory language of the truth ; and
since they have accused of sin to God Himself the noble man,
the beloved of God, dragging him into the dust,—to God who
wondrously protects IIis beloved,—he counsels them in quiet

and repentance again to seek God's grace; as if David desired, although irritated and injured to the highest degree, not personal revenge, but merely reverence and awe before the human and Divine majesty which are present in the covenant. The outburst of this feeling is the predominant and impelling force in this song, because it was in that time new. After a short cry to God, ver. 2, the poet is induced by his noble feeling, irritated at the baseness of the slanders, to use most threatening language against the slanderers. He by no means first prays God to secure him against slander, but is so full of the feeling of the unworthiness of such liars, that, in higher flight and prophetic certainty, he immediately uses denunciation against them, vv. 3-6. At last, vv. 7-9, returns, in calmer collectedness, and with a glance upon what is nearer at hand, a feebler echo of the previous song, but already with the higher peace gained by repeated prayer. And so the wish: that to remove the ever continuing despondency of his friends, soon may a beam of Divine salvation come! But *in himself* the poet feels fear nor gloom no longer. A higher Divine serenity already dwells in him, and in restful confidence he looks upon this night and all the future. Thus three unequal strophés (comp. I. p. 171, *Dichter des A. B.*).

1.

Hear me when I cry, God of my right,   2
    Thou who didst give me space in distress;
be gracious to me and hear my prayer !

2.

Ye sons of man ! how long shaming my glory
    will ye love vanity
    will ye seek lies ?*
Know then, Jahvé has distinguished the man true to him
    Jahvé hears when I cry to him !
quake and—sin not !
    consider it on your couch and—be silent !

give the due sacrifices,
   and turn in hope to Jahvé!

3.

There are many who say : " Would that we might see
   good !"
lift the light of thy glance upon us, O Jahvé !
Thou hast given a joy into my heart
   higher than when one has much corn and must.
In peace I lay me down and rest at once !
   for Thou, Jahvé, alone—
   wilt cause me to dwell safely !

Ver. 2. Since in the first strophé something more than the
mere cry, at least the ground of the poet's hope must plainly
appear, because the poet, relying upon that, turns forthwith to
his slanderers : בצר חרח must be taken as a relative sentence,
as a continuation of אלהי צדקי.   Ver. 3 לכלמה כבודי forms an
interpolated proposition, placed dependently (in the accusative)
in remarkably brief phrase : that my glory becomes a shame
—shaming my glory. Comp. § 341 b.   Ver. 6. The sacrifice is here that for sin already committed ; they are to
sin no more, ver. 5, and turning in believing confidence to
God they are to atone for their former deed. The mode of
speech, ver. 7b, occurs here manifestly to the king in sudden
reminiscence of the primæval priestly form, Num. vi. 20.
Ver. 8. The suffix הֵם is to be taken as in the verb the third
person plural, without definite object before the mind, xlix. 9 ;
lxv. 10. § 294 b.   The opposition in the sense is this : the
inner serenity and Divine joy, as the poet now feels them, is
also, in the absence of all external enjoyments and splendours,
much higher than the greatest superfluity and the most noisy
outward joy, as, e.g., there was at the harvest festival after a
rich harvest. For we must not overlook the fact that the oldest
kings practically occupied themselves, by taking an actual part

in husbandry and harvest. Comp. 2 Sam. xiii. 23, Isa. ix. 2.
But certainly David had at that time no great superfluity,
2 Sam. xvii. 27-29 ; and simply because he might hear around
him at that time every morning and every evening unusually
great lamentation over the want of such absolute necessaries of
life in the camp, his thoughts turn to this picture which is here
remote from the other contents of the song. From this underlying thought the poet immediately says further, ver. 9, that he
will lie down in tranquil confidence, because Jahvé *alone* is
consolation and hope enough for him, and without Jahvé all
men's protection will not help him. יַחְדָּו, putting two things
together as coincident in point of time (to lie down, and
immediately that one is laid down, to sleep peacefully), cxli. 10,
Isa. xlii. 14.

In the connexion חָסִיד לוֹ ver. 4, may be seen a peculiar
token of the higher antiquity of this song and of its derivation
from David. Later poets, even that king in 1 Sam. ii. 9, say
instead of *he who is devoted to Him* in pious love, more shortly
חֲסִידוֹ, *His devoted one.* Comp. the *Jahrbb. der Bibl. Wiss.*,
vii., p. 139.

Besides the above,—of songs which we can with historical
certainty ascribe to David, his last words only have been
preserved, comp. I. pp. 143 sqq. We subjoin, however, in this
place as the most convenient,

16. PSALM II.

Here we listen to a king speaking, who solemnly anointed a
short time before in Sion, is full of serious and true feeling
concerning his high destiny and strength in Jahvé. Subjected
peoples are now threatening revolt and rebellion—as far as we
see from no other cause than because they now see, under
the fresh and untried rule of the young king, a favourable
opportunity for shaking off the apparently heavy yoke of .the
religion of Jahvé and of the royal house at Jerusalem. It is
true that the religion of the dominant people, even if it has no

recourse to compulsion, has always great influence on subjected peoples (comp. only *e.g.* Ps. xviii. 44-50). The subjected heathen peoples also had a great zeal for the re-conquest of their freedom, because they could in that case the more freely fall back into their heathenism. In opposition to them stands the young king, inspired and strengthened by a prophetic encouragement at his anointing as well as by his own consciousness. He is aware that he has a fellowship with Jahvé as His son and earthly representative, and with this truly kingly feeling he surveys the whole scene with calmness. The danger so little affrights him, he rather advances towards it with a lofty clearness of vision and repose of soul. Far exalted above it, he is in the mind to appeal to the thoughtless rebels with a word of serious warning and well-meant menace. The discontented at bottom merely find the dominion of the religion and law of Jahvé oppressive, and desire to return to the old rudeness and licentiousness; and would only fall away at an opportune moment from the king of Sion, because he has founded and maintained the rule of Jahvé over them. But this attempt must most certainly be from the beginning vain in the Divine eyes, provided the king be actually the true king of Jahvé, and that he stand in true covenant with Him. Or, the rebels may suppose that with the new king conditions are changed. If so, he must feel and must tell them that he is Jahvé's true king, that through Jahvé he is strong to subdue all opposition—how much more these insurgents to whom the wise and kindly monarch would counsel a renunciation of their vain attempt, before evil consequences are seen. This song is a noble outburst of these truly great reflections, these sublime sentiments. In detail, too, it is very complete and artistic. The first astonishment and reflection on the true views of the insurgents, vv. 1-3, must be immediately followed by the sharp contrast or the expression of the firm assurance of the futility of such an attempt, and how, if continued, it can only produce serious Divine repulsion and punishment, vv. 4-6. But after the thought of the poet has been kindled to the highest degree by the sharp decision of the pure contrasts, and has also become clarified, his mind then begins more calmly to reconcile these oppositions by explaining the true condition of things, overlooked by the insurgents, vv. 7-9 ; and in conclusion, by hearty counsel for the future, vv. 10-11. There are thus four strophés, the one flowing out of the other. But the language in the two first advances to an ever higher excitement and tension ; in the two latter, from the point of highest tension, runs a calmer course, and falls to a satisfying conclusion. This is the type of a. perfect song, blending in itself rest and unrest, contemplation and sensibility in the finest manner.

This beautiful song must necessarily proceed from the most splendid period of the kingdom, when the purest harmony prevailed between the aims of the theocracy and that of the kingdom, and the king, as the Anointed of Jahvé, felt himself infinitely strong and inspired. This flourishing period of the kingdom is nearly confined to the time of David and the earlier time of Solomon. To this the mention of so many subject-peoples in the song also points ; for at that time Jerusalem was the centre of a great kingdom, embracing many peoples. But David cannot well be the poet. The colour of the style is different ; the flow of the language easier and more symmetrical, the form more polished. In fact, in point of elegance this song surpasses all of David and other poets. Moreover, David was not anointed in Jerusalem, vv. 6-7. See 2 Sam. v. And the reminiscence of the whole earlier life of David before his anointing nowhere gleams through this song. We cannot sufficiently take note of the fact that the speaker here, the Anointed, can appeal, after the inner consciousness of his strength, which is to be approved, to nothing external and historical, but the solemn anointing and the oracle then spoken. Thus, without historical preparation and trial, yet at once strong and wise at his anointing, Solomon only appears.

It is in itself readily explicable and credible that at the death of David, and before Solomon's strength was ascertained, the conquered peoples rose. Although historical books give no account of this, the simple cause may be that those attempts were quite abortive. This may be gathered from the representation of the power of the young king in this song. Moreover, the existing historical accounts of Solomon are very concise. Therefore, we may here assume a song certainly proceeding from Solomon, like which he sang many, according to 1 Kings v. 12. Assuredly, this is worthy of Solomon's fairest time. Indeed, we may think to hear in this Psalm many of David's sublime and royal conceptions continued. Comp. further the *Gesch. des V. Isr.*, iii., pp. 293 sqq. of 3rd edit.

Each of the four strophés has three verses, seven verse-members; only the second six merely, perhaps because a member has fallen out at the end of it.

1.

1   Why did peoples join together
        and nations meditate vanity,
    the kings of the earth rise up
        and princes have taken counsel together
        against Jahvé and His Anointed :
    " let us break asunder their fetters
        and cast their bonds from us !" ?

2.

    He that is throned in heaven laughs,
        the Lord scorns them ;
    then will he speak to them in wrath,
5   and terrify them in His fury :
    " and *I* have nevertheless anointed my king
        on Sion my holy mountain !"

3.

    Let me tell of the covenant ;
        Jahvé spake to me : " my son art thou,

I have this day begotten thee !

Demand of me, and I will give the peoples for thine
    inheritance
    and for Thy possession the bounds of the earth ;
thou shalt break them asunder with an iron rod,
    like potter's vessels dash them to pieces !''

4.

And now—ye kings, be wise,   10
    take warning, judges of the earth !
reverence Jahvé in fear,
    and quake in trembling !
take counsel, that He be not wrath and ye perish ;
    for soon doth His wrath kindle :
Salvation to all who trust in Him !

Vv. 1-3 form *one* sentence. But from all the descriptions
here used, it is clear that at that time designs and conspiracies
of all kinds existed, but it had not yet come to brawling and
open war against one king among the heathen. The translation
ἐφρύαξαν, *they brawled,* of the LXX, for רָגְשׁוּ ver. 1, cannot
therefore be correct. The correct signification of the word is
rather given by the entirely corresponding passages, Ps. lv. 15,
lxiv. 3. Comp. the *Jahrbb der Bibl. Wiss,* v. p. 165, and
below on Ps. lv. 15. Vv. 4-6. Now, indeed, Jahvé smiles as it
were in all calmness at the vain enterprise ; but *then,* if the
foolish work should be carried out,* He will surprise them
with punishment, making Himself felt by them in wrath, and
as addressing them : Ye do thus, ye dare to begin an idle war,
although I have solemnly recognized and consecrated my king,
and will therefore protect him ? But in the rapid, wrathful

The אַךְ and the conneXion of the speech is so constantly and readily misunderstood, that it may be well to note at least a quite similar throne-speech in the
Shâhnâme i ., p. 214, 4*f*. Mohl.

address the first member, easily to be supplied, is wanting;
and the speaker begins immediately with an additional proposition ואני pointing to something earlier, and here self-
intelligible. Just so, Isa. iii. 14; and as all in the song
appears beautifully rounded off, the two first strophés appropriately conclude with the lively open language of the opposed
parties, as the true thoughts of each. But on the other hand,
the poet is led by the recollection of that solemn moment of
anointing, and by the now urgent wish for the reconciliation of
the opposing parties, to the further detailed description of the
prophetic oracle spoken at the anointing—probably by Nathan,
2 Sam. vii., 1 Kings i. It re-echoes in the poet's soul as a
deep truth, and its meaning dispels the confusions of the
present time. For if the king actually new-born from the
hour of his consecration, entirely feels and lives in Jahvé, there
must verily be permitted to him in this covenant the dominion
over all that he in this Divine sense seeks. How much more
must he be strong against such weak and idle attempts as were
at that time in hand. All particular confusions and embroil-
ments, even those in the present, are in the clear glance of the
poet readily solved by the fundamental truth, explained by the
prophet and living in himself. We need not suppose that the
prophet actually said all this to him, or nothing but this. For
in the poet himself the truth now lives, and he can freely speak
from its inspiration. Here the sharpness and exactness is
astonishing with which he comes from the highest primary
truth, ver. 7 to the nearer, ver. 8, and to the present case,
ver. 9—shortly but not too quickly returning to the object.
As regards that fundamental truth itself, its proper sub-
stantiation and explanation did not belong to this place; but
the contents are very finely set forth with the deepest feeling
of the poet, ver. 7. *I* (אני has the emphasis) Jahvé, and no
other, have begotten thee *to day*, even now, at the same time
with the anointing and the oracle, my son shalt thou from
henceforth be, and deem thyself. If every human being must

thus through Jahvé, *i.e.*, spiritually in his maturer age be born anew; yet this new birth has still higher significance in the case of the consecrated and anointed king, in proportion as the king must stand higher than the rest. Before all others the king must, from the sacred moment of his external consecration onwards, become also inwardly a new man. And as he retains all external power, so must he feel himself inwardly to be the son of God, and devote himself to God, as no other can do. This is the idea of the true king, and in this hope he is consecrated. The king who here speaks does not merely feel this in himself; it became public and manifest at the anointing, was prophetically spoken and ratified. Hence the poet here calls it a חֹק, *i.e.*, an *ordinance* clearly announced to the people by the prophet or other interpreter of the Divine will, adopted by the king and by the people, thus mutually consecrated and legalized. Elsewhere it is called a *covenant*, 2 Sam. v. 3; 1 Sam. x. 25. The inner sense of this covenant is clear in the mind of the poet; and thereby he is strong and bold.

The נַשְּׁקוּ בַר, ver. 12, understood as "kiss the son," *i.e.*, do homage to the Anointed of the Lord, will not, more closely considered, be here suitable. It appears indeed to agree well with vv. 2, 7; and it might be conjectured that the king would be suitably mentioned once again at the end. But against this is the connexion of all the words, vv. 10-12, where nothing further is said of the king; further, the high tenor of the whole, according to which the poet throughout only conceives and brings into prominence the Divine, regards the rising in this sense properly as a rising against Jahvé, and mentions himself only when it is necessary. That here at the end where all again rises higher and the poet himself becomes a prophetic counsellor in the mind of Jahvé, the mention of the lower relations, of the homage and the king should be even better omitted entirely, appears no false expectation. "Son" again would be in this connexion expressed too briefly and cursorily, in fact, quite

unintelligibly; since it is only in the New Testament, that
ὁ υἱός in places like John v. 19; viii. 36; Heb. i. 1, can be
used so shortly and sharply, and even in these places it is
always sufficiently clear in meaning from the context. But the
Aramaic בַּר for בֵּן is found generally only in the peculiar
passage, Prov. xxxi. 2, and there only in the mouth of a woman.
But our poet says, according to ver. 7, like all other Hebrew
poets, בֵּן. The Pesch. which is induced by similarity of
sound to translate נשקו ברא "kiss the son," hence appears
here to prefer the δράξασθε παιδαίας of the LXX, בַּר "the
louder," would be poetical for counsel, louder warning *nâsdjah*.
נשק expresses, however, properly a fastening on one another,
or suffering to hang (then kiss), and so from the new active
(in Piel) it may very well describe a taking hold of, serging.
The Targ., similarly, and probably independently of the LXX,
קבילו אולפנא.

What *service* of Jahvé in this connexion among the heathen
it may suffice to think of, is clear from Isa. xviii. 7; Ps. lxviii.
30-34, and other passages of the kind.

We here subjoin further

17. PSALM CXLIV. 12-15,

a piece which indeed so far stands in its present place correctly,
as it is elaborated by a later poet from an older song, but afterwards was incorrectly united with Ps. cxliv. 1-11. From the
later poet comes plainly only the conclusion, ver. 15, and closely
connected with this according to the present connexion of the
sense, the word אֲשֶׁר at the head, ver. 12. Suppose these
wrappings removed, which the later poet first placed upon all
the remaining words, and we have here an extremely remarkable fragment of a manifestly ancient song. In this, some poet
had described the splendid prosperity and happy peace in
which at that time the people of Israel lived. As such times
of an enduring happy peace and general prosperity in Israel
were rare, this free poetic representation of it stands in the

Psalter as a piece of a peculiar character, and shows us how readily the ancient people under the protection of its religion, which furthered real human welfare, lived in happy contentment, provided only that the conditions were those for the development of all the good that lies in a long and honourable peace. But such a time for this people only set in under Solomon's rule. And since the sketch of the occupations of the people and the childlike as well as powerful language of the fragment points us back into early times, there is no reason for doubting that it is really of Solomon's time. But again, the fine picture only here presented of the wall-pillars beautifully hewn in the manner of temple and palace architecture, ver. 12 *b*, points us to the first half of the Solomonic period, when the higher architecture in Israel was domestic, and much occupied men's minds.

The poem itself from which this fragment of so singular a kind has been preserved, was perhaps no Temple song, perhaps also of considerable extent rather than so brief as it might appear at first sight. But the later poet who lived in the still distressful times of the new Jerusalem, gave to the fragment such a setting that the whole has now *this* sense: we, a people of whose peaceful, joyous happiness an ancient poet sketched this splendid picture,—we may not despair beneath the protection of the true God! Thus taken, the short piece might be well adopted into a collection of Temple songs, as plainly the later poet had this in view. No other judgment can be passed upon the small song-fragment. The verse is of long members with the ancient poet, quite otherwise with the late one, ver. 15.

> We whose sons are as young trees—growing high in
> their youth,   12
>   whose daughters as wall-pillars—hewn after a palace-
>   pattern.
> the granaries full, dispensing corn on corn,   13

the sheep in thousands, ten thousands on our pastures,

14   the cattle teeming, always without abortion,

    *   *   *   *   *

and no compulsion of war, no complaining clamour
in our markets;

15   O hail to the people with whom it is thus,
O hail to the people whose God is Jahvé !

The comparison of the young men to freely shooting *seed-lings* (young trees in nurseries), and the slender growth of the daughters to fine corner and wall-pillars, adorning the inner hall like Karyatides is finely consistent. The comparison of the tall daughters with such pillars is indeed not rare in other poets (comp. the *domoyah*, *Hamása*, p. 184, v. 2; 'Antara in the *Journ. As.* 1840, ii., p. 517; Plaut. *Poen.* iii. 54). But the peculiarity here is the indication of such pattern-pillars, as they were at that time to be seen in Palestine, especially doubtless in Solomon's palaces. The words, vv. 13, 14, are partially obscure to us in the present day because the verse structure appears to be here destroyed, and some verses have probably entirely fallen out. Manifestly, ver. 13 *b* and ver. 14 *a* form *one* verse together, which speaks of the rich condition of the cattle; but then the last member to ver. 13 *a* and the first to ver. 14 *b* must have fallen out. Since the people at that time manifestly sought its chief prosperity in agriculture and grazing, מִזַּן אֶל־זַן, *from kind to kind* may be understood of the different sorts of corn. Similarly, the יוֹצֵאת after Amos v. 3, may best be understood of a community which *goes forth* with its best sons to war, even compelled by a kind of feudal service or our present conscription—which if against the will of the community may give rise to loud complaints. If, then, the words אֵין פֶּרֶץ had merely remained from the close of a first verse-member, they might mean *without* hostile irruption, as if it were the happiness of the people neither to be destroyed by hostile invasion nor to be compelled by conscription to personal service in the war. But if this phrase was closely connected with the preceding מסבלים, then פרץ must, as if in jesting word-play, with its counterpart פלט and מלט Job. xxi. 10 (xxxix. 3) ; B. Isa. xxxiv. 15, lxvi. 7, designate abortion as a *rent*, whereby the fruit falls before its time, falls out of its costly repository, and perishes.

II.

SONGS AFTER THE DIVISION OF THE DAVIDIC KINGDOM UNTIL ITS END.

1. Scattered voices down to the eighth century.

From the two first centuries of this long period a few songs, as all closer examination shows, have been preserved in the Psalter. The fulness of songs from the Assyrian period has manifestly crowded out all the earlier songs to such an extent that only the Davidic have been preserved in somewhat greater number and coherence.

These next songs after the Davidic period are to be recognized, among other signs, by this their single and dispersed occurrence. These are a few, very isolated monuments of a time in which in general the poets had more peculiarity and independence, and the collective life of the people had not yet reached the later uniformity and definiteness.

We cannot but expect that precisely in these times the Davidic colour, the height of joyous feeling and of confidence in his songs, should remain unimpaired in many songs— whether it be in collisions with the Gentiles or in inner struggles and perplexities, but most of all in the royal songs themselves, to which also the song explained in I, pp. 158 sqq. —of a king of the kingdom of the Ten Tribes, 1 Sam. ii. 1-10, belongs. We begin here suitably with

18. Psalm xx.

A king is setting out for war against the heathen; and as he previously prays in the sanctuary with sacrifices and vows, the assembled community wish him success and victory, in joyous spirits and clear confidence in Jahvé's spiritual help, already anticipating the victory as certain. Ver. 7 then is plainly a strong pause and important turn, and the transition from the plural into the singular is not to be overlooked. From the review of the whole it becomes clear that first of all vv. 2-6 are sung by the whole community, then after the sacrifice has been offered and the prayers of the king, the priest-prophet strikes in, as if announcing the pleasure of God in the sacrifice, and giving encouragement, vv. 7-9. Finally, the whole community concludes with a short prayer, ver. 10: comp. on the art of the song further, I., pp. 193 sq.—Thoughts and description are here distinguished by grand simplicity. No other Temple song expresses with such ease, beauty, and power the reason of the truth of the firm confidence in Jahvé as vv. 8, 9. By these indications and those of the language the song might be of Davidic time. But a high personality and a grand past does not appear in the king here designated, so that we may rather think of another, but in any case, very early king of Sion.* At all events, the poet is certainly another person than the king, for whom here blessing is desired. The song is also in a liturgical point of view very important as a fine monument of more ancient times.

(The people).

2   May Jahvé hear thee in the day of distress,
        may the God of Jacob's name defend thee!
    send thy help from the sanctuary,
        and support thee from out of Sion;

---

* It has been further shown (*Gesch. des V. Isr.*, iii., pp. 479 sq. (2nd edit.) that we may most correctly assume king Asa to be referred to.

remember all thy gifts;

    thy fat offering may He accept;*

grant thee thy heart's wish,   5

    all thy counsel may He cause to succeed !

O let us rejoice because of thy salvation,

    exalt the name of our God;

Jahvé will fulfil all thy prayers !

(The Priest).

Now I know that Jahvé helps His Anointed,

    will hear him from the holy heaven

    with the might of the help of His right hand !

Those boast of chariots, these of horses,

    but we of the name of Jahvé our God;

They bow down and fall,

    but we stand and continue.

(The people).

O Jahvé, help the king !   10

    May He hear us on the day that we supplicate !

Ver. 4. יְדַשְּׁן from דָּשֵׁן *turn to ashes* would refer to cases like 1 Cor. xviii. 38, Lev. ix. 24, which however are more founded in narrations than in prayer. Better from דָּשֵׁן *fat* : to taste or eat something as fat, *i.e.*, willingly accept a rich food, as the Arabic translator, induced by a correct feeling gives *astdsm*, comp. *astmra, Hariri*, I. p. 14, 6. Ver. 6. Now already they might rejoice in the victory and praise Jahvé as conqueror, previously certain that Jahvé will make the king victorious. דָּגַל related to גדל is *exalted* (דֶּגֶל the *exalted* sign, banner) hence *praise*, sing, boast, like all words of similar signification connected with בְּ of the object. In ver. 8 it is explained by הַזְכִּיר, The LXX correctly μεγαλυνθησόμεθα. Ver. 7. *Now*, since the people *prays*, thus courageous and bold in Jahvé, and since the king's sacrifice and prayer is assumed to be accepted, now *I know that* God helps; and that spiritually from out of heaven. Though the enemies may boast of external strength, and brave it with war-horse and war-chariot, we, although without this external protection, feel inwardly strong through Jahvé, unbent, invincible. Comp. Judges i. 19, iv. 3, 13; Josh. xvii. 16, on the other hand 1 Kings xi. 26-29; Isa. ii. 7. Ver. 10 would be translated according to the accents:

> . O Jahvé, help!
> the King hear us now as we supplicate!

as though *the King* were identical with Jahvé. But absolutely Jahvé can never be so called; and the verse-structure would be grievously injured. The language may rather pass in the second member into the calmer third person, because this verse stands quite alone at the end, its members are thus more readily sundered at the close of the address. Comp. also on Ps. cx. 7, above, p. 112.

19. Psalm XXI.

stands manifestly still in the present series of songs, designedly after Ps. xx., because in contents, as well as in structure and art, it is very similar to it. For the first and longest part, vv. 2-8, is plainly to be sung by the community in prayer on the king's behalf in the sanctuary, then the priest is to strike in with his higher word, vv. 9-13, and finally the congregation again return with brief wishes to their commencing prayer, v. 14. The structure of this alternate song is then entirely the same as in Ps. xx. And although here the sacrifice is not made so verbally prominent as there, yet these alternate songs in like manner are certainly to be sung on the occasion of a solemn festival in the sanctuary, and here too the priest was to reply with his lofty address to the accepted offering of the community. But in other respects an important distinction opens between these two songs, both in regard to the immediate occasion of this alternate song, and to the tenor of the language, and the age,—in fact to the popular kingdom of the two kings.

The community which here surrounds the king who is present in heathendom, is not one which raises shouts in hopes of victory to the kings as they set out for the field of battle,— as is the case in Ps. xx. and similarly in Ps. cx. (see above, pp. 107 sqq.). The sacrificial festival which has here been made is rather the birthday of the king. This is sufficiently plain. Long has the latter happily ruled, and this happiness too befalls him, that he is able to solemnize his birthday once more with thanksgiving to God in the Temple, ver. 5. His people have gathered about him on the occasion, to thank God with sacrifices on this joyous day, and to pray to God on behalf of his further welfare. But certainly about those times the territory of the king must have been threatened by many foes from without. And although the king now lay not, because of the winter season, in the field, and did not intend forthwith to set out for the war,—the priest in his oracle, following the accepted sacrifice, vv. 9-13, has regard alone to these enemies who threaten from without, and promises the king, with lofty words, the Divine victory over them.

If this was the immediate occasion of the solemnity, we can understand how the form of the language becomes somewhat different from that in the previous alternate song. There the people ranged themselves around their king as he was setting forth for the war. The community accordingly addresses him while he sacrifices, and first the priest then speaks on behalf of all the higher word of faith, with which the community at the close concurs. Here, on the other hand, the community assembles, in order spontaneously to celebrate the solemnity of the royal birthday, and prays on his behalf to God,—whilst the priest, responding to the sacrifice of prayer brought by the community on his behalf, directs the gracious oracle to the

11

king in person, and the community at the end turns again to God in thanksgiving.

The language and thoughts of this song are, however, one can feel, very different from those of the preceding song, and far less ancient than in it. The flight of the song is also, as compared with the former, very subdued. And if we ask who the king was, about whose festival all is concerned, we find not the slightest indication pointing to a king of David's house, or to the sanctuary in Jerusalem, as conversely in the previous song all points to such an one. This king may then be fairly assumed to be one of the kingdom of the Ten Tribes, as we shall presently find such an one in Ps. xlv.

As in Ps. xlv., it appears that the king ruled more through the free choice of the people than by strict hereditary right, so here the same fact may be gathered from the words, vv. 4, 6. And in this way, too, what is unusual in style and matter may be most readily explained. King Jeroboam II. is the most readily suggested, who although on the whole a prince of happy and powerful reign, was nevertheless greatly entangled in foreign wars, and who, at the time this song was composed for the solemnity of his birthday,* might be well advanced in years. Again, towards the end of his unusually long reign, the foreign sky may have again become clouded around the kingdom of the Ten Tribes, as its history subsequent to his death shows.

(The Community.)

2   Jahvé ! the king rejoices in thy might,
            in Thy salvation—how highly glad is he !
      His heart's longing hast thou given to him,
            his lips' wishes not refused :

---

* Of birthday festivals in Israel there is no mention elsewhere in the Old Testament. They were, according to all traces, originally rather Egyptian, have their fullest meaning in Egyptian religion, and probably came thence earlier to the kings of the kingdom of the Ten Tribes than to those of Juda.

thou anticipatest him with best blessings,
    placest a golden crown upon his head;
he begged life from thee, thou gavest it him,   5
    duration of days, abiding, eternal.

great is his power through thy help,
    splendour and pomp thou placest upon him,
Yea, wilt make him an everlasting blessing,
    gladden him before thee with delight;
because the king trusts in Jahvé,
    he will not waver, through the favour of the Highest.

(The Priest.)

Thy hand will reach to all thine enemies!
    thy right hand will reach thine haters,
wilt make them, when thou appearest, as a furnace;   10
    —Jahvé bring them to nought in his wrath—fire
        consume them!—
wilt destroy their fruit from the earth
    and their seed from among men.

Though they allege evil against thee,
    devise mischief—they shall not prevail;
for Thou wilt strike them back,
    with thy sinews aiming at their countenance.

(The Community.)

Rise, Jahvé, in Thy might!
    sing we and play to Thy power!

The prayer of the community, vv. 2.-8, plainly falls into two
small strophés, vv. 2-5 and 6-8, as the high word of the
priest, vv. 9-13, in like manner into two still smaller, vv. 9-11
and 12, 13, which may however be readily condensed into *one*
somewhat longer. Both strophés of the prayer begin with the
same leading thought; but the beginning of the second, ver. 6,
briefly again states the entire contents of the first, so as to pass

11 *

over, vv. 7, 8, to the hope for the future, whilst the first suitably
concludes with the allusion to the birthday solemnity. All
these words of the community, vv. 2-8, are only fully understood when we remember that the king himself is meanwhile
present in the sanctuary sacrificing and praying. Then too we
best understand the high words of hope, ver. 7, where the first
member is spoken after the likeness of the words in Gen.
xii. 2, and the last gives hope that Jahvé will give the king
continually the pleasure of dwelling in the neighbourhood for
the protection of the sanctuary,—as he now in holy joy (Isa.
ix. 2) stands sacrificing and praying *before it.* In a further
application the hope is also therein contained of his return in
joy and power to the sanctuary, and so again witness the consciousness of the delight of God (comp. xxviii. 4, 5). Thus a
preparation is made for the following expressions of the priest,
vv. 9-13, of desire and prediction. This high utterance of
the priest-prophet, vv. 9-13, sounds as if spoken out of most
warlike times to a most warlike king; and even its strong
pictures are not too strong for those times. Ver 10 : *thou wilt
make them as fire-ovens,* so that they quite disappear in the
fire, as once the heaven-destroyed Sodom appeared from afar
like a great furnace, Gen. xix. 28 ; and that לְעֵת פָּנֶיךָ *against
the time of thy countenance,* so soon as thy countenance appears,
as the mere glance of God's wrath annihilates the sinner,
xxxiv. 17. This is certainly very loftily spoken of the human
king,—still, in the assumption that he, in highest courage
inured to war and battle, is the true man of God,—and through
Jahvé, if it must be so, dreaded, powerful, and in a moment
destroying evil by his appearance. But the poet himself feels
in what bold figures he has spoken ; hence forthwith the
intermediate sentence, ver. 10 *b,* as in explanation, while the
agency of Jahvé himself is introduced. Ver. 12. כִּי is best
understood as admitting the possibility, § 362 *b,* when it may
nevertheless be also connected with the *perfect,* when the sense
permits it ; *ut struxerint, though they may have laid up.* Thus

בל יוכלו is plain as the apodosis, and the whole connexion of these two verses is better.*

We subjoin here, because of several resemblances,

20. Psalm xlv.

In this song, power and justice, the first essentials in kings, are praised. The king is described as highly blessed by God; but along with this, aspects of the royal happiness are touched upon, which the royal psalms in the Psalter never elsewhere mention,—the delight and the splendour of the inner palace,— especially a new queen, as also the personal beauty of the king, ver. 3. These aspects are pre-eminently depicted, and in the greatest detail, the praise of the king beginning and ending with them. We must suppose then that a joyful occurrence in the honour of the king was the immediate occasion of this song. This becomes certain from a review of the whole; and according to vv. 9-17, it is undoubted that the song was sung whilst a new queen with her train was led in splendid pomp into the palace. Thus the song is a nuptial ode, if we choose so to call it. But this, to take a passing view of the matter, takes nothing from its dignity, if the poetic art is found to gather into its sphere, and glorify all noble life-relations; and therefore the sole question is as to the way in which the poet employs the opportunity offered to him, and seizes on the new and weighty relation. None will seriously maintain that the event in question is a wholly impure vessel into which no pure thought may be cast. But here we are bound to recognize, that this poet apprehends the subject with sufficient dignity. He looks upon this last joyous event not in itself, but in the light of a free review of the whole life and higher destiny of the king. It becomes clear to him in his poetic conversation, that the last piece of happiness is only a fresh result of the Divine blessings that are richly streaming

---

* The correct view of this song was given in the *Jahrbb. der Bibl. Wiss.* v., p. 169.

down upon the king, and worthily received by him. This same
king has by nature high physical beauty and perfection.
Antiquity looked upon such physical beauty as most essential
in the persons of kings.   He is as mighty in the field as just
in administration.   Must not one so singularly endowed and
blessed obtain also in his house fresh blessings from God?
As he reflects on this grand connexion of facts, and is elevated
by the influence of the present solemnity, the poet feels
inspired to sing the praise of the great king on the festive day.
The peculiar object of his poesy is to set forth how the
divinely blest, ever praiseworthy king, is not unprepared and
unworthy, but receives the last happiness in accordance with
Divine appointment.

As the spirit of the poet mixed with these thoughts, he
strives purposely to depict the king with an eloquence worthy
of all his greatness.   The song actually shows no little art,
delicacy, and tenderness ; and these features are all the more to
be prized in connexion with such a subject.   Nothing deserves
more admiration than the tact of the poet in dealing with the
associations of such a festival.   Quite imperceptibly he leads
up to them from quite other points of view, and allows himself
to be thus led up.   The song proceeds, in accordance with these
primary materials, in three strophés,—each successive one being
always more complete, more eloquent, and only the last touches
the proper occasion.   The first, after a solemn prelude, touches
briefly on the physical advantages of the king, vv. 2, 3.   The
second marks with more vividness the twofold supreme virtue
of the ruler,—strength in war, and righteousness, vv. 4-8.
The third brings us to the palace, passing over with light
touches the object then nearest and to be most fully described,
with a short conclusion, embracing the whole, vv. 9-17, 18.
But along with this there prevails in this song, as one of
peculiar joy (I., pp. 152 sqq.), the quite peculiar art of the
climacteric construction of the strophés, which is carried out
in our poet with the highest perfection in such a manner that

five verse-members obtain as the unity, and hence as the simple compass of the first strophés, and this unity is twice gradually duplicated. But with an art so high another is connected by which the smaller strophés thus arising are rounded off, sensibly enough, into three progressive ones. Each concludes (I., p. 199) with a species of *return-verse,* in which a chorus surrounding the poet is intended to break in, and that always as if quite involuntarily, in the mere course of thought. Thus each concludes with a thought-result (עַל כֵּן " therefore"), but this only in such a way that in the two first we are pointed to what was at that time the highest thing to be said in the third. Thus each suggests the lofty and imperishable character of the blessing and of the praise, vv. 3, 7, 18. For the living king all the wishes that are felt for him are to be wished *for ever,* according to the ancient custom, noted on p. 112. Thus, moreover, these sounds have the king-like word *for ever* in each of the three strophés—in the first and third as the last concluding word of the return-verse, loudly echoing, vv. 3, 18, in the intermediate one somewhat before the return-verse in a suitable place, ver. 7. But the eternity concerns in this way, only with the greater beauty, the blessing, ver. 3, the kingdom, ver. 7, and—this is the very appropriate conclusion of the whole song,—the after-glory of the king, introduced by this very song, ver. 18. So artistic is the finish of this song, in whatever direction we look.

It follows from all this, that the song is certainly somewhat diverse from the others in the Psalter. An art so designedly devoted to a king is nowhere else seen in it. Not God, but rather the king, is here the object and the end of the praise. And in this praise things not simply Divine are included. Poetic art thus subserves in this instance, as in the Song of Songs, not an immediate purpose of holiness. And the question may arise, in what sense was the song adopted by the compiler of the Psalms? Was it retained from an older miscellaneous collection, perhaps by an oversight? or was it at the time it was here adopted, explained allegorically, that is Messianically? Heb. i. 8, 9 shows that at an early date particular passages (vv. 7, 8) from this song were referred to the Messiah, although the New Testament is far removed from the grovelling error of later expositors, to wit, that because particular words may bear a Messianic sense, the whole song in all its words and thoughts must be Messianic. But such questions about the meanings of later readers do not touch the meaning of the song, which from its singular character cannot be misunderstood. And if the song is unique in the Psalter and more like secular poetry, yet it is in itself by no means unworthy and impure, and so little opposed to the Divine life that it deduces in fact everything from the Divine blessing. It is in a certain point of view always instructive to see how a relation that is in appearance merely secular is ennobled by the poet. The loftier spirit of Hebrew poetry and religion cannot be quite foreign to the lower relations. He who looks upon the Old Testament from a freer point of view, be he theologian or merely *littérateur*, will on no account dispense with so rare a fragment of Hebrew antiquity. Incontestably the lower throws a light back upon the higher.

The poet is, according to his expression, ver. 11 (daughter!) a man of age and experience, otherwise entirely unknown. It is equally difficult to decide who the king is with historic exactness. Neither is the queen more definitely described, nor the king. What is said of him in vv. 4-8 is according to the customs of those times too general to enable us to gather much from it. This much only is clear from vv. 10, 11, 14, that the new queen was a king's daughter and sprung from a foreign land, but not from Tyre, since homage is to come to her thence as a dependent or closely allied kingdom, ver. 13. The language of the song points to an age not so early as the Davidic or Solomonic. It is lofty, at times bold, elegant throughout, it is wanting inwardly in the true fire. We feel much more frequently the unusual art of the composition than its original life and power. On the other hand the king is certainly a Hebrew. For the opposite, *e.g.* for the supposition that he is a Persian, there is no evidence; and the fact that merely Tyre is named as the rich city which will bring her homage, points necessarily to a Canaanitish king. It might be supposed that the king was rather an Israelitish than a Judaic one, because the northern kingdom stood in much closer relations to Tyre than the southern, and in fact it is usual to pursue this thought further only in the end to abide by it as the only correct one. While there is not the least indication of Jerusalem and a Davidic king, the king in this song, ver. 8, is rather designated as one in an elective kingdom where he is only the first among equals. The kingdom of the Ten Tribes remained substantially an elective kingdom. Again, the air of an almost luxurious and effeminate and royal splendour which we here breathe, points to the northern kingdom; more of this was almost always to be found there rather than in Juda. In the previous song we discovered a royal song from this region; and we may the more readily expect one here. But in this case we may most readily think of Jeroboam as the king of the song; who was early a very warlike prince, but in his youth, to which the song certainly belongs, did not rule, as later monarchs, over a wide territory. To him whose predecessors were kings is most appropriate the suggestions of glorious augury, ver. 17. The unusual language and art of the poem, again, lead to the kingdom of the Ten Tribes, and is not too ancient and unusual for the age of Jeroboam II.*

---

* This view of the king was put forth in 1847 in the *Gesch. d. V. Isr.* vol. iii., and it better agrees with all the indications than Hitzig's (*Begriff der Kritik*, pp. 28 sqq.) which refers the psalm to the marriage of Ahab with Jezebel; an hypothesis much more tolerable than that which assumes the king to be a Persian. Another conjecture would be that the king was a Tyrian, the bride a maiden of Israel. But the allusion to Tyre, ver. 13, would then be much too weak, apart from the improbability of the case in itself.

1.

1   My heart bubbles up with a fair word ;
    I think, my poem avails the king ;
       be my tongue a ready writer's style !—
Fair, fair art thou in thy form before the sons of men ;
    a flowing grace is on thy lips ;
therefore God also blesseth thee for ever!

2.

On thy thigh gird on thy hero's sword,
    thine ornament and thy pomp !
5   and putting on thy pomp, go forth
      for truth and for humility, straight on !
      that thy right hand may teach thee wonders !—
Sharply pierce thy arrows—the peoples fall under thee—
    into the heart of the king's enemies !
Thy throne is of God, for ever and ever,
    the rod of rectitude is thy kingdom's sceptre ;
thou lovest right and hatest wickedness ;
    therefore doth God anoint thee, thy God,
    with oil of joy before thine equals !

3a.

Myrrh and aloes, cassia are all thy garments ;
    from ivory palaces music on stringed instruments
      rejoiceth thee !
10   the king's daughters are amongst thy dear ones ;
    there stands the queen on thy right hand
    in gold of Ofir !—
O listen, daughter, see and incline thine ear,
    forgetting thy people and father's house ;
and let the king desire thy beauty,
    since he is thy lord, and do him homage ;
and Tyrus' daughter will flatter thee with gifts,
    the richest people !—

3*b*.

All splendid the king's daughter enters,
 of gold embroidery her apparel;
in variegated attire brought to the king   15
 maidens, her favourites, behind her,
 brought to thee!—
So they come, in joy and jubilation,
 brought hither into the king's palace.
Sons shall replace the fathers for thee:
 wilt make them princes in the whole land,—
that I may glorify thy name for all times!
  therefore shall peoples praise thee
   ever and aye!

1. The introduction, ver. 2, is truly beautiful, and reveals a profound poetic heart. At first the thought powerfully but irregularly gushes up in his inward feeling, and its beauty and charm can already be felt. But it is only by reflection and art, —here modified by the consideration that the song is to be a royal one,—which enables the beautiful conception to be readily expressed. In very truth, it is not in vain the poet here promises eloquent matter. *Lip* in Hebrew so often denotes *language*, that in ver 3 *b* we might merely think of the charm of the the king's address. But nothing here suggests this narrow reference. Rather is it, ver. 3, only the general portraiture of the physical advantages of the king on which the poet's address here rests. Such advantages,—generally desirable as primary qualifications for a king,—are on this day to be brought into peculiar prominence, since the king is on the way to his wedding. Thus these words point from the very first to the grand ending of the song; and the return-verse which immediately occurs alludes still more closely to it. But there follows—

2. Vv. 4-8, adding something first that is of still greater importance. To explain the colouring of the first words,

ver. 4, in this sudden transition, it might even be supposed
that with the nuptial day, a day for girding on his sword had
been connected for this young king,—like another coronation
day (Cantic. iii. 11). So our Friedrich I. once solemnized such a
festival of sword-girding for his two sons with the participation
of the whole Christian Europe of the time. Yet it is enough
to assume that the poet here desired to depict the twofold virtue
of the ruler, power in war as in peace by means of justice. And
since the young king has hitherto had less opportunity to
approve himself as a warrior, the poet might on that account
merely demand of him, if it must be so, that he will take up
arms for the defence of spiritual possessions,—certain that so
soon as he does so, victory will not evade his heroic courage.
He may, going forth only in warlike attire, boldly trust in the
strength of his right hand, which in the moment of the battle
will help him to do great wonders, undreamed of by himself,
unexpected by the enemy, so that while whole peoples fall
beneath his victorious advance, his sharp weapons strike
straight to the heart of the hostile princes. Then the second
half is appropriately connected with this. Since the king
exercises the highest inner virtue—namely, righteousness—
his throne must be externally firm, his kingdom must be a
kingdom of God, and new joy thence blossom for the king.
The וַהֲדָרְךָ, ver. 5, is resumptive, after the preceding
thought, lingering on the splendour of the royal arms, and
thereby somewhat interrupted. For the simple proposition is :
having thine armour on, march forth, that thy right hand may
teach thee wonders (§ 347 a). צלח is, however, to be taken in a
physical sense, don, put on; thus *salah* = *sçaleach*, "arm," comp.
further the *Jahrbb. der Bibl. Wiss.*, x., pp. 200 sq. There is much
that is strange generally in this song of a poet of whom we
appear to possess not a single verse elsewhere. Just so, immediately after, ver. 5 and ver. 9, the asyndeton in the third word
in a climacteric address, comp. § 344 a. On אֱלֹהִים, ver. 7,
comp. § 296 b. In ver. 8 it is most clearly explained by the

expressive conjunction, "God, thy God," who is wholly thine own. The same short connexion of subject and predicate recurs, ver. 9 : myrrh and aloes, cassia are thy garments, so full of these perfumes. The "ever, aye" is also in this song always merely an accompaniment, never itself a predicate, as the idiom, Ps. lii. 2, is of quite another kind. The LXX erroneously, as an address : O God !—The return-verse of the second strophé points, especially by the mention of *joy*, directly to this festival of joy now to be celebrated ; and alludes in this way as that one which follows the first strophé, to the proper and peculiar object of the whole solemnity which now imme- diately follows. The *perf.* מָשַׁח is accordingly to be referred not merely to the past, and may, both here and ver. 3, be best rendered by our *present.*

3. Vv. 9-17. In the beginning of the last strophé it is as if something quite new suddenly opened, as if a new fragrance came in overwhelming power over the poet, as he must again proceed. What do I smell ? what do I hear ? Here, among sweet scents and music, a high festival of joy must be about to be celebrated. Ver. 9. But whilst the inner room of the king is thus opened, the poet seizes the opportunity generally to praise the splendour of the inner palace or harem, until he is suddenly arrested by the sight of the royal ladies, and amongst them, on a nearer view, by that of the queen-bride. He thus with artistic adroitness comes to the new queen, exalted above all other women (שֵׁגָל), vv. 9, 10. Here he, as having arrived at the main object of his song, cannot do other, as the dignified friend and singer, than utter his weighty word in encouragement and exhortation of the foreign and timid daughter of the king, vv. 11-13. Meanwhile the nuptial train, the bride accompanied by her companions, has arrived quite close to the palace ; and the poet concludes with the picture of this splendid train, and the wishes here suitable for the king, vv. 14-17. So well is all here again set forth in the wider space, and the address running through the whole song to the

king is here—in the sight of so many new persons, vv. 11-15—
broken off to some extent in the middle, but only to be
immediately resumed at the right place. It is not to be
overlooked that וְיִתְאָו, ver. 12, is a pure passive; "let
the king desire thy beauty," oppose not his longing for
thee. So,—concludes the poet this intermediate address,
ver. 13,—would acts of homage of the most splendid kind
stream in upon the new queen. For custom demands that all
towns and lands friendly to the more powerful kingdom shall
offer splendid presents on the accession of a new king or
queen. The nearest and richest state of which this might at
that time be expected, was Tyre, which probably needed to
remain on good understanding and peace with Israel. To the
expression "Daughter of Tyre" corresponds very briefly the
answering expression in the second member, "the richest
people" (§ 313 c), quite as in ver. 4 the הודך והד to the
הרבך. The פְּנִימָה (derived by intermediate members from
פְּנֵי, לְפְנֵי) is the most important word in the new beginning,
ver. 14. It means "into," therefore "enters into" the
palace, as is further described in ver. 16. Levit. x. 18.* In
לִרְקָמוֹת ver. 15 לְ describes the way and manner; in variegated, *i.e.*, adverbially, clothed in variegated costume (§ 217 d).
Plainly by this description the end of the preceding verse
is resumed.—Ver. 18. The "therefore" is now no clumsy
transition; and it cannot be said the poet was bound simply
by the chosen artistic division of the strophés to conclude with
this strophé. But it is especially to be observed that the first
member, ver. 18, according to the sense, belongs closely to
ver. 17 (§ 347 b).

21-22. PSALMS XXVII., XXIII.,

are two very peculiar songs, which bear the greatest resemblance to one another (comp. especially xxvii. 4, 5, and xxiii. 6),

---

* Comp. § 220 a; connected therewith is לְפְנִים מִן within *M.* Megilla, i., 11. *M.*
Soferim, ii., 11.

and both uuquestionably are of the same poet, who does not
elsewhere appear in the Psalter. Ps. xxiii. appears to be somewhat later. The joyous serenity and strength in Jahvé which
both breathe forth, the self-announcement of the poet as a
warlike leader of the people, the beautiful picture of the
shepherd, xxiii. 1—all this would readily suggest the *quondam*
shepherd David, and both songs would in that case necessarily
express two moods of the Absalomic time. But there is very
much ˙opposed to this view.. The stamp, despite some
resemblance, is not quite the Davidic. All is softer and
milder, not so overpowering and striking, not so original and
so overflowing in strength. We feel that this poet, great as
hero, stands somewhat nevertheless below David, in life and
art. Among other features, the למען שמי xxiii. 3, afterwards
often repeated, is new, and the rare word שֹׁרְרָי xxvii. 11. The
Solomonic temple must have long been standing, xxvii. 4,
xxiii. 6. Against David's authorship the evidence of 2 Sam.
vii. and xv. 24 ff. is too clear. David might indeed expect
help from the holy mountain of Jahvé, iii. 5, but could not yet
speak of the earthly temple. The poet is thus another leader
who possibly had to carry on tedious wars on the boundaries
of the land, whose name and particular fortunes appear
hitherto without historical basis. But he probably lived in
early times, since the sense and style of the songs remind us
still so strongly of the height of the Davidic time, and the
words of this poet are recalled by many other poets.

In Ps. xxviii. we see the poet in the midst of misery, at a
distance from the safe and sweet sphere of the sanctuary,
threatened by a severe war, and without hepe of an easy
return to the sanctuary. (But the deepest distress urges him
only the more strongly to seek in Jahvé) as he had done in his
previous life, and peculiarly now, all true strength. He has
been long accustomed to a most vital sense of his strength and
hope in God, and by firm faith to overcome fear and despair.
He thus feels himself from the first so exalted by a mood of

Divine inspiration that his song bubbles over with the mighty stream of the feeling of high courage, and nothing is present to his mind but the thought of his real strength in Jahvé which fears nothing external. He only wofully deplores the absence of the pleasure which the immediate neighbourhood of the Temple gives; but through his strength in God he hopes soon again to enjoy this highest pleasure of life after the conquest of his enemies, vv. 1-6. Then, as after a last and most profound reflection, finally, vv. 13, 14, a short retrospect follows, a recollection of self in the world, after the absorption of prayer; a recovery for new activity in the world, in the recollection, firm and rock-like, of how salvation is for him in firm faith. And lo! already he has thus again strengthened himself in faith and feels himself by means of prayer quite restful and resigned!—The song thus falls into three short strophés of three verses and seven verse-members each; but the verse-members are for the most part lengthened, as so readily occurs where the poet gives himself up to contemplation: comp. above Ps. ci. Only the last strophé is shorter.

In the midst of this song we see (vv. 7-12) interpolated a song with abrupt ending, of quite another kind in contents, art, and period. Here there calls not out a great and strong hero of war at a distance from Jerusalem for help: the suppliant is, according to vv. 10-12, one driven about without home, but it is only the internal divisions and hostilities in the people which have thrown him into distress. And we hear in this place, according to the language, one of the many persecuted ones of the seventh century, whose voices we shall presently hear in greater number. The thoughts of the poet are indeed of such depth and such childlike piety, that they would be quite worthy of the preceding poet; and for this very reason they may have been here inserted by a collector. But their expression is quite different: even the construction of the verse is different. The song, too, appears to be contained only in one strophé and a half. The original conclusion is wanting, since **vv. 13, 14,** carry us back in every word and breath to the older poet.

1.

Jahvé is my light and salvation : whom do I fear ?　　　1
　　Jahvé is my life's defence : before whom do I quake ?
if evil-doers approach me, to tear my flesh asunder :
　　who oppress and persecute *me*—
　　they stumble themselves and fall !
though a host beleaguer me—fearless is my heart ;
　　if war rises against **me**—then I have confidence !

2.

One thing have I sought of Jahvé—that I wish :
　　in Jahvé's house to dwell all the days of my life,
　　　that I may joyously behold Jahvé's grace, refresh myself
　　　　at His Temple !
for He hides me in His tabernacle—in the day of　　5
　　distress ;
protects me in the covering of His tent, lifting **me** upon
　　rocks !—
So shall my head triumph over my foes round about,
　　that in His tent I may offer sacrifices of joy, may sing
　　　and play to Jahvé !

1.

Hear, Jahvé, my loud crying,
　　be gracious and listen to me l
Of Thee my heart thinks : " seek my countenance !"
　　Thy countenance, O Jahvé, I seek !
Hide not thy countenance from me,
　　cast not away in scorn Thy servant !
Thou wert my help : reject me not,
　　forsake me not, God of my salvation !
Though father and mother have forsaken me :　　10
　　Jahvé will take me up.

2.

Teach me, O Jahvé, Thy way,
    and lead me on an even path,
    because of those who lie in wait for me !
give me not up to the greed of my oppressors,
    since against me stand lying witnesses and they who
      breathe cruelty.

      *   *   *   *

3.

O believed I not, to taste Jahvé's goodness
    in the land of the living !—
Hope in Jahvé, be strong, and let thy heart take courage !
    and hope in Jahvé !

Ver. 2. The connexion אֹיְבַי לִי produces, by the doubled expression of the pronoun, merely a strong opposition to the following pronoun, as in other cases, § 311 *b*.—Ver. 8. Of Thee speaks to me my heart as Thou criest to all men : *seek me !* and this heart-impulse I follow. A fine expression of true deep feeling.—Ver. 9. The עזרתי היית must, in correspondence with the following אלהי ישע, spoken out of the earlier experience of the poet, contain here a ground of hope in the prayer.—Ver. 11. *Because of those who lie in wait against him,* peculiarly, the poet desires that, strengthened by God, he might walk upon an even way,—that is, that he may not give his enemies, who lurk watchfully about all his steps, the slightest occasion to see him stumble and fall. Otherwise they would certainly conclude from the results that the poet was actually, as they accuse him of being, guilty and an object of Divine punishment. The like frequently in later Psalms : that the rude persecutors and light-minded slanderers *may not rejoice,* attaining then their evil object, v. 9. Actual sin, however, the poet feels, would cast him into misfortune, and subject him to shame in the eyes of the world. Therefore he supplicates, in a time of perplexity and difficulty, for strength.

שׁוֹרְרִי is a word quite peculiar to certain songs of these times, recurring lvi. 3, liv. 7, lix. 11, v. 9. That it was only a different expression for צֹרְרִי, *my oppressors,* is improbable, on the ground that this word and the similar צָרַי are found not merely in our older poet, xxxiii. 5, xxvii. 12, but the related צָרָה, צַר, also in the same, liv. 9, lix. 17. A mere change of sound is therefore improbable. The שׁוּר also signifies a *lurking,* Hos. xiii. 7 ; but the sense of *malignant liers-in-wait* very well suits other passages (comp. lvi. 7, and עֲקֵבַי, xlix. 6). It may then be justly assumed that the word is abbreviated from מְשׁרֵר (§ 160 *b*) ; and as alongside of עֹלֵל, *child,* עוּל was gradually formed, so שׁוּר, xcii. 12. Similarly Aquila: ἐφοδεύειν.—Ver. 15. O how unhappy,—thus does the poet at last most vividly feel, would he be, if he had not faith. But he has faith, and therefore encourages himself finally, ver. 14, in patience and fixed hope under all events. Comp. cxvi. 10 and § 358 *a,* according to which it is unnecessary and more than bad to suspect or strike out the לוּלֵא, with old readers.

In Ps. xxiii. we see the poet, not indeed freed from straits, and returned as conqueror to the sanctuary, the beloved spot of delight and rest, but as already having experienced an unexpected happiness as the first proof of Divine assistance. Of what kind this help was cannot be historically more closely defined. This much is clear from ver. 5, that it was, in the midst of felt want, a streaming overflow of life-necessaries whereby the poet found himself and his warriors strengthened and protected whilst his enemies believed him to be already annihilated. The occurrence in David's history, 2 Sam. xvii. 27-29, may always serve as an example. Slight as the piece of good fortune may have been in itself, it is significant for the poet in his situation and state of mind. Conscious, through the unhoped-for occurrence, once more of Jahvé as his wondrously kind deliverer and loving leader, feeling this with new vividness,—a loftier confidence, a joyous serenity again

springs up in his bosom, a beam of blessed hope that under
the faithful guidance of Jahvé, to whom he is wholly devoted,
he will in like manner overcome all future dangers, rapidly
thrill through him.   A brief and noble song streams from
this pure joy in Jahvé as the loving and watchful guide of his
life.   There is but *one* feeling in his calm and equal mind,
gushing forth in only two short strophés of similar kind to
those of the preceding song,—the poet only looking, as it
were, somewhat further about him in the second strophé.
The figure of the shepherd is continued almost throughout,
because it expresses most fitly the ever anxious loving guidance
of the Higher One, to which the lower willingly and trustfully
resigns himself.   Comp. Isa. xl. 11; John x.

1.

1   Jahvé is my shepherd : I want not.
       on green pastures he lays me down,
            to water of refreshment he leads me ;
       quickens my soul,
            leads me in pastures of salvation—
       for His name's sake !

2.

       Even when I pass through gloomy valley, I fear not
            evil, because Thou art with me :
       Thy rod and Thy staff—*they* console me !
5   Thou settest out for me my table in spite of my
            oppressors ;
            hast anointed my head with oil, my cup is overflow.
       Only happiness and mercy shall follow me, life-long,
            that I may dwell in Jahvé's house for long days.

Ver. 3. On צֶדֶק, *right, salvation*, see above, on xxiv. 5. With
this word the poet leaves the figure hitherto retained of the
shepherd, giving it up, because it is merely figure, and hastens
to the higher conclusion. Hence immediately follows : *for His
name's sake, i.e.,* not for mine, because I have deserved it, but

that He may be really known and experienced by me and all men as *the* Good one,—as He is named and praised, and so to the furtherance of His good kingdom. Through each new deliverance, moreover, His name will be ever more known and more praised, lxxix. 9.—Ver. 4. If the poet was at that time or shortly before in a valley עָכוֹר, *i.e.*, *dark, gloomy*, such as lie in desert spots, *e.g.*, Hos. ii. 17, Isa. lxv. 10 ; and if we recall how powerfully the cheerfulness or wildness and straitness of the spot influenced generally in those times the feelings of men,—all is clear.—Ver. 5. This is indeed not to be explained in a low and slavish sense, as if the poet, singing thus, with anointed head, had sat down to table, &c. But certainly it is no empty and general figure for any possible happiness, it points to something more definite, the immediate occasion of this song. And why should not an unexpected overflow of necessaries, coming at the time of greatest need, in a wild and dark spot, produce still greater devotion and joy in one already devoted to God?—Ver. 6. The וְשַׁבְתִּי would be derived immediately from שׁוּב, so that שׁוּב בְּ־ would shortly stand for שׁוּב וּבֹא בְּ־ as vii.17. But it is more simply suitable to the connexion and to the passage xxvii. 4, if we may assume that it stands for וְיָשַׁבְתִּי ; and though we absolutely cannot say that שַׁב ever stands in itself for the perf. of יָשַׁב, yet the collocation with the *Vav conseq.* may here condition a greater abbreviation of the word from the beginning, § 234 *e.*

But in general these earlier centuries fall to a lower key, and lose increasingly the pure untroubled strength and elevation of Davidic life. Outwardly rendered secure, there arise among the people the most tedious internal struggles. The genuine religion would extend its power completely, but old and new perversions and prejudices of every kind throw themselves in opposition to it, and the faithful have often to suffer severely. But grief and distress are the more deeply felt, in proportion as a happier past is present to the recollection of the people.

In *one* case there was imminent danger, even for the otherwise firmly trustful spirit, of falling into entire despair: the
sufferings of a sickness that threatened premature death.   The
paralysis of all activity, the fearful prospect of sinking into the
gloomy lower world, devoid of light and joy—the scorn of the
frivolous, awakened by the threatening disaster, who deem
deadly sickness, because of its sufferings, as equivalent to
desertion by God, and just punishment (comp. the Book of
Job)—the readily insinuated belief of the sufferer himself in
this notion: all this may harass the man in the most painful
manner and reduce him to despair.   He is not conscious of
such great and deadly sins; rather does he feel within him the
desire and the power, by grand and noble deeds and worthy
words, long in the sunny upper world to praise the goodness of
God and further His kingdom.   So long as life in itself is
esteemed the indispensable and highest good, no other danger
can beget such despair as that of losing it in youth, before the
satiety of weary old age.   Hence no explanation of songs
proceeding from such circumstances can be more erroneous
than that which takes the description of deadly sickness in a
figurative sense, or—which is originally connected with this—
instead of the complaints of an individual, sees here the
complaints of an entire people.   It is certainly true that such
plaints of a sick one, with the ring of bitter depair in them,
become rarer in the later portions of the Bible.   Only in its
earliest times had the true religion of the Old Testament to
contend so severely with such doubts.   At last it securely
obtained, by degrees (as the Psalter will presently show) even
on this side, a new and higher truth.   But we must not, therefore, misunderstand more ancient songs like this.

The most beautiful feature is rather that even in these earlier
times, when complaint and despondency still hold so unbroken
a reign, and the poet at first seems entirely to sink under the
burden,—there nevertheless readily occur to the faithful man,
along with the free outflow of his feelings, some considerations,

which at last by their counterpoise frequently bear him away to unexpected consolation, so that his unrest speedily subsides into joyous rest. For the good conscience, although not comprehending everything, can nevertheless turn with sad longing to Jahvé, beseeching, hoping, that He as the merciful One will not too severely chastise, but where grief and danger are extreme, there will earliest help. Then the calmer reflection may occur, that Jahvé must beforehand desire to preserve a faithful man, who on his recovery shall most mightily glorify His grace, and most actively further His kingdom. For Jahvé in general throughout furthers only goodness, and the rude malicious spirit of the light-minded He cannot suffer ever to triumph. If the poet through his earlier life does not feel himself deserted by such strivings and such hopes, his troubled mind may again be speedily brightened and he may rise with courage over grief as well as over the scorn of the malicious. Examples of such a hope, rising at last boldly above despair, are given in the following songs, which are certainly ancient, although it is difficult to recover historically the particular relations of the poet.

23-24. Psalms VI. XIII.

Long tormented and wearied by a severe illness, and by the scorn of malicious enemies, the poet cries, Ps. vi., for help to Jahvé,—feeling himself not indeed quite guiltless, and not refusing every chastisement from the Divine hand, but in the consciousness of the want of relation between the sufferings as punishments, and between his higher endeavours, begging for a mitigation of the sufferings, and for a passing over of the danger of death, and soon securely heping in the consciousness of being heard. This transition from despondent complaint to consolation and strength appears here very plainly in three strophés. First, the cry of anguish for help in the greatest distress, where Jahvé seems to tarry, vv. 2-4, then a renewed cry, already calmer, to Jahvé as the merciful One, from whom the poet hopes deliverance,—and this first, because in the lower world, at whose doors he stands, he can no longer render thanks to the redeeming God, and he wishes to live long that he may instruct the living, and God Himself must be pleased that His kingdom is furthered. Secondly, because in the present crisis or never, the Divine deliverance must come, for the redemption of one most violently persecuted by many fierce enemies, who would rejoice in the fall of one who is higher and nobler, vv. 5-8. But simply because the truth stands firm that Jahvé will satisfy not the fierce malicious joy, but the hope of the faithful in Him, there is a rapid turn in courageous outlook into the future with the feeling of strength received by prayer, vv. 9-11.

The strophés are manifestly very simple, each of three verses with six verse-members. But after ver. 6, a few members appear to be wanting, which would extend the song to four strophés. In fact the mention of the horror at the lower world, ver. 6, is too brief (comp. especially xxx. 10), and the transition thence to the description of the present state of sickness, vv. 7, 8, is too abrupt.

1.

2 Jahvé! not in Thine anger punish me,
    and not in wrath chastise me!
  Be gracious to me, Jahvé! for I wither—
    heal me, Jahvé! for my bones are deeply shaken;
  and my soul is violently moved;
    and Thou, Jahvé, how long— ?

2.

5 Return, Jahvé! deliver my soul,
    help me for Thy mercy's sake!
  for in death there is no thought of Thee;
    in the lower world—who sings praise to Thee?

3.

I am weary with my sighing,
    every night I make my couch to swim,
      in tears all my bed to flow :
consumed with grief is mine eye,
    grown old because of my oppressors.

4.

Depart from me, all evil-doers !
    for Jahvé has heard my loud weeping ;
Jahvé has heard my supplication,   10
    Jahvé will receive my prayer !
ashamed, violently agitated are all my enemies,
    they return, instantly ashamed.

Ver. 2. The stress lies on *not in Thy wrath ;* for generally, the poet does not refuse chastisement at God's hands. Only he could not endure the quite irresistible invasion of Divine punishment, so that he be completely prostrated, but prays that he may be mildly chastised, and in moderation, xxxviii. 2, Jer. x. 24.— Ver. 3. On אֲמַלֵּל, see § 157 b.—Ver. 5. The beginning of the new strophé is quite closely connected with the end of the preceding one. Already, for a very long time, the poet feels that God has been as if turned away from him. In grief he had asked; *how long* wilt Thou thus turn Thyself away without casting a friendly look upon me ? Now, while after some reflection, greater calm returns, the lowly prayer : *return,* looking on me again with a friendly eye ! not because of my desert, but of Thy grace ! The same rapid turn in the internal progress of the thought is seen, vv. 8, 9, at the end of the second and beginning of the third strophé.—Ver. 7. The בימעתי stands without copula at the beginning of the member, because its sense completes the preceding member.

If the song, Ps. xiii. is of the same poet, as is probable from the complete similarity of the language and of the thoughts, as well as of the external condition of the poet, it arose, after the preceding one, under circumstances of still greater misery. Already had the poet long complained without result under the same circumstances, conceiving a vain anguish. Most deeply bewailing himself, he had already often cried to Jahvé; and his present song is only a fresh short outcry for final help in the distress which has reached its acmé. In the background there lies too, in spite of the lament so woeful and grievous, that bursts forth with such violence, a deeper confidence, firmly grounded, as the result of earlier prayers. Whilst in extreme sufferings all feelings are strained and excited to the highest pitch, the whole song rapidly unfolds in three short strophés, —from the ventilation of longing and anguish, vv. 2-3, to the free outpouring of prayer for help in the crisis, vv. 2-5,—thence advancing, in recovered higher consciousness, suddenly to joyous confidence, ver. 6. Unquestionably still more intense and more beautiful than the preceding song, the once more victorious glance of joy into the future still purer and nobler. But the words, under the increasing exhaustion and the nearness of death, are still more concise, the strophes still shorter, and (see I., pp. 148 sqq.) quite like a lament, in three stages, becoming ever briefer, from five to four, from that to three verse-members in the strophé.

1.

2   How long, Jahvé, wilt Thou forget me for ever,
        how long conceal Thy countenance from me?
    how long shall I cast anxieties into my soul,
        trouble daily into my heart?
    how long my enemy rise over me?

2.

    O behold, hear me, Jahvé my God!
        give light to my eyes, that I sleep not in death,
5   that my enemy say not: " I have overcome him!"
        my oppressors rejoice not that I falter!

3.

But I—trust in Thy grace;
  glad be my heart of Thy help!
sing I to Jahvé, because He hath done well to me!

The עֵצוֹת, ver. 3, must according to this punctuation signify *plans*, as the LXX translate βουλαί. And since in that case the plans or counsels and resolves for deliverance cast into the soul,—the despondent one forming a number of them in his haste and anxiety—would be like a trouble planted in the heart, and by this explained, it must be self-intelligible that they are ever frustrated counsels, which cannot in their very rise succeed. But much more suitable would be the expression עֵצוֹת to understand according to *oddah* (comp. Ibn. Arabshâh's *Fâhik*, p. 198, 6 v. u.) *of the anxieties*, or most anxious cares. —The יוֹמָם stands here not indeed opposed to night, but as *day and night*, = each day and each night; *by day* alone may stand for *continually, daily*, just as *diu* in Lat. is connected with *dies*. So in Ezek. xxx. 16, Jer. vii. 25. The addition καὶ νυκτός in the Cod. Alex. is therefore incorrect.—Ver. 4. The poet feels himself near to death, the light of his eyes already broken, fearing that the next sleep which may overpower him, may be the sleep of death. How unfortunate that we cannot verify the history more accurately! That any man who bears a higher consciousness in a time when ill-wishers would falsely explain his outward fall or death,—desires not death, is indeed in itself a very innocent feeling. It can however only then predominate and oppress even the pious man, if the ancient fear of death is not yet overcome by better conceptions of the lower world.

25-27. PSALMS XXX., XLI., LXVI. 13-20.

The more nobly then sounds, after such plaintive songs, the song of thanksgiving after deliverance. And he who feels himself urged to pay a vow, or voluntarily to express his thanksgiving to Jahvé after a deliverance in which he has wondrously experienced His power and goodness, thinks more calmly upon all changes and fortunes, and may thankfully depict Divine providence, in their grander connexion. As he is now full of higher truths, serene, and strong in God, his inmost impulse is in the praise of Jahvé publicly to make known the experience and instruction of his life, and to exhort and move all, even the many who are troubled in mind and wretched, to the same high confidence in Jahvé's goodness, that he himself feels. Hence the songs of thanksgiving contain many general sayings, and the didactic element here appears almost with design; for every song of the kind shows how deliverance and repose not merely relieve, but also expand the heart.

Ps. xxx. is a specimen of such customary thanksgiving songs, sung in the Temple according to ver. 5. The kind of sufferings from which the poet is delivered, his own recollection of how he cried in danger to Jahvé, vv. 9-11, and the stamp of the language, lead us to suppose that the same poet whose complaints and agony were seen in the two preceding songs, sung this noble song after the deliverance; so striking is the coincidence of the whole. Again, in form this song is an example of thanksgiving songs. As joy expands the heart, so too does the thank-song extend itself in ever larger circles, and becomes, in a gradual advance from rest to excitement and warmth, more complete, more creative, closing with a grand contemplation. First, the impulse to thanksgiving and the short announcement, ver. 2; then, more definite praise -for the wondrous deliverance, and exhortation to all to praise Jahvé as the merciful One, as the poet has learned to praise him, vv. 3-6. But the poet dwelt not ever in this higher life, and so comes finally the completest summary of all his experiences. From out the blessed feeling of the present, he looks back upon the time before his suffering, and must confess to himself that so little has the suffering been for him without fruit, that he has come out of it rather stronger and more courageous, nearer to God, and with the resolve ever to praise Him. Suffering, therefore, has served for his purification and elevation. For suffering fell upon him, as he now feels, unexpectedly, in too great security, therefore the more keenly and crushingly. But so soon as he again sincerely turned to Jahvé, he was delivered, that he may now, in a higher recognition, for ever praise Him, vv. 7-13. Three strophés accordingly. Comp. I., pp. 152 sq.

1.

Praise I Thee, Jahvé, that Thou didst lift me up,   2
   and sufferedest not enemies to rejoice over me!

2.

Jahvé, Thou my God!
   to Thee I cried and Thou healedst me;
Jahvé, Thou deliveredst from hell my soul,
   didst call me into life from the depths of the grave.—
Play to Jahvé, ye his saints,   5
   and sing praises to His holy fame!
A moment indeed endures His anger, His favour a life-
     time;
   in the evening tears prevail, and towards morning,
     rejoicing.

3.

Yet I said in my security:
   "never shall I waver!"
—Jahvé, through Thy favour Thou hadst granted strength
     to my fortress:
   Thou didst conceal Thy countenance—I was shaken.
To Thee, Jahvé, I cry,
   and to Jahvé I make entreaty:

10   "what then profits my blood, my going into the pit?
     will dust praise Thee? will it proclaim Thy faithful-
       ness?
    hear, Jahvé, and be gracious to me,
     Jahvé, be my deliverer!"
  and my mourning Thou didst turn into dancing,
     didst loose my mourning garment—and didst gird me
      round with joy!
  that I may sing high praise to Thee, never silent,
     Jahvé my God, that I may thank Thee for ever!

Ver. 2. *Didst lift up*, did not suffer to sink into hell, as is further explained in ver. 4. But if *daly*, Sur. 7, 21, signifies the opposite, it must be remembered that with the *pail* דְּלִי anything may be drawn up as well as let down.—The *healing*, ver. 3, is certainly to be understood of healing from a deadly sickness, as the poet himself immediately explains further, ver. 4 and then ver. 10; though it is readily understood that God heals otherwise than a man.—Ver. 4. The *hell* or *pit* is, according to ancient habit, generally used here for the lower world. Dr. Hitzig gave in 1828 the correct explanation of שְׁאֹל.—Ver. 8. הר *mountain*, is like *rock*, a figure of firmness, of firm good fortune, as we might use *fortress*, comp. lxxvi. 5. (In Arabic poets *djamal* rather stands, so far as the moun-tain gives shade and refuge, *Hamâsa*, p. 413, 6.) But to this citadel of my happiness Thou hadst merely by Thy favour (not through my desert) lent strength. So soon, therefore, as Thou didst turn away Thy favour and Thy light in the sudden temptation, I became the more violently shaken and bowed down, I who had fancied that I could never tremble. The העמיד seems, where עז is spoken of, in like manner as in the phrase, Ps. viii. 3, susceptible of the meaning *found*, as if it were to *found strength for my mountain* or *defence*, as well as give it solid strength. But the idiom is nevertheless quite different here, and העמיד לְ is, according to 2 Chron.

xxxiii. 8, rather *cause that* something *should serve one, i.e.,* favour him with it, the phrase being taken from lending.— Ver. 9. The imperf. with following perf. ver. 12 : *I call—Thou hast turned, i.e.,* so soon as I call, or called, Thou hadst already, as in anticipation, turned to me, as xxxii. 5, 6, comp. § 357 *b*. For this reason the copula may be wanting, ver. 12, and is wanting even with the more emphasis, in order to bring out the very swift result, the coincidence of both actions.— Ver. 13. כָּבוֹד, here external nobleness and honour, which ever falls to the lot of the noble soul, streams back upon him, as it originally streamed forth from him, therefore praise, δόξα, comp. xxix. 1, 2, xcvi. 7, 8, cxlix. 5 ; *honores*, Hor. *Od.*, i., 26, 10.

On the superscription, ver. 1, comp. p. 55.

Thanksgiving songs, like this fine song, were presented by the individual,—whether he would thereby fulfil a definite vow or not,—in the Temple, with rich sacrifices, music and dancing, and along with the public assistance of a great sacrificial assembly.* Hence they are naturally of the most attractive and perfect poetry.

Ps. xli., correctly understood, gives indeed the example of a species of thanksgiving song from this period; but in other respects this song stands in a peculiar position in respect of its stamp and style. For certain modes of expression which it has in common with others, as ver. 3 with xxvii. 12, in themselves supply no necessary evidence of like origin. According to the relations described by it, it probably belongs to the same times of bitter domestic enmity with the preceding songs. Only such distracted times make a cry of vengeance like that of ver. 11 *b* explicable.

The poet, according to ver. 11, 12, certainly a mighty man of his time, had sunk down into a severe sickness. But what at that time depressed him still more deeply than those sufferings was the contemptuous treatment of pretended friends, who

---

* Comp. the *Alterth. des V. Isr.*, pp. 56 sqq., 2nd edition.

only watched for his death in order to destroy his house, who hypocritically visited him only to draw all kinds of malicious conclusions from looking upon and listening to the sick man, and then to take counsel against him outside, along with others of like disposition. *One* man in particular was most active in this, ver. 7. By such a private experience the poet had been doubly brought to feel during his sickness how unworthy and unmanly such treatment of a sufferer was. He was despised because of his sufferings, and persecuted all the more boldly as he could do little to help himself. He feels himself incapable of such villany, for he had formerly shown constant compassion towards sufferers. He now, delivered from sickness and the persecution of those pretended friends, at the moment when the deserved punishment had already overtaken them, more calmly reviews the past, and his inmost heart would offer itself in the song of thanksgiving. There presses upon him, therefore, along with the duty of thanks to God, in this moment pre-eminently *one* grand Divine truth, to which he finds himself urged to give clear expression in the song. In the opinion of the world, *he* is a prudent and fortunate man who raises himself by severity to the unfortunate. But in the deepest knowledge of our poet now obtained, he on the contrary is only to be commended as blessed, who is mild and gentle to the unfortunate, and may hope in Divine deliverance whether from sickness or from other sufferings ; whilst the man who is pitiless and mischievous ever prepares destruction for himself alone. Thus he briefly declares from the first the compassionate man to be happy, not without the retrospect which here forces itself upon him, of his own experience, since he desires at the same time to thank God for his deliverance from sickness, vv. 2-4. Then passing on to the confirmation of this from his own history, he recalls the counterpart to mind, how in deep distress he besought God for deliverance, vexed most terribly by treacherous friends, but disclosing all his distress to Jahvé in prayer full of confidence. He therefore here briefly

repeats the whole of the main contents of his prayer at that
time, which is now so vividly present to his mind, vv. 5-12;
and he concludes finally, ver. 13, with the rapid mention of
his deliverance from these dangers by the Divine grace, already
touched upon in the introduction. The whole song becomes
thus something like a mere arrangement and discrimination of
the various feelings which had been collected in the bosom of
the poet, so deeply moved and in so many ways. But the flow
of the song from the Divine primary thought now gained,
calms the storm of those manifold thoughts to such a degree,
that the language fulfils its course with evenness, in four
similar strophés, each of three verses and six verse-members,
while the words sound only in the first somewhat too full and
too excited.

The dark background in this song consists only in the fact
that we do not historically know how the recovered poet took
the recompense of which he here incidentally speaks. We may
then readily suppose the worst; but there are many ways in
which one may take recompense; and the noble mind which
the poet here generally reveals, does not permit us to suppose
he took an ignoble revenge. If he was—as is manifest—a
prince, the most various ways were open to him of taking also
a noble revenge. And in any case this song was not originally, like the preceding, a Temple song.

1.

Blessed he who considers the suffering!   2
   him on the day of calamity Jahvé delivers,
Jahvé preserves, animates him, highly praised in the
    land;
     to the greed of his foes wilt Thou not sacrifice
     him!
Jahvé supports him upon the bed of sickness;
   all his sick couch Thou hast made!

2.

5   I spoke myself: "Jahvé be gracious to me!
         heal my soul, for I have sinned against Thee!
       my enemies speak evil of me:
         ' when will he die and his name pass away?' "
       if he comes to visit me, his heart thinks evil,
         mischief he gathers to himself, and goes forth to
           tell it.

3.

       "Together whisper against me all my haters,
         against me devise they my ill:
       ' some mischief has broken forth in him;
         whereon he lies, thence he shall not rise again!' "
10   " yea, my table and allied friend, whom I trusted,
         has lifted the heel against me!

4.

       " But Thou, Jahvé, graciously raise me up,
         that I may requite them for this;
       and hereby I know that Thou favourest me,
         that my enemy may not triumph over me!"
       And—in my innocence Thou heldest me fast,
         didst cause me to stand before Thee for ever!

It might readily be supposed that at the end some verses
were wanting, since the conclusion is too hasty, the whole is
too unequal, perhaps too, a more definite word of thanksgiving
is expected. But this would be an error, since on closer
consideration all speaks rather in favour of the present form.
Nor can it by any means be asserted that the whole song was
spoken in too great haste, or with harsh and precipitate transition. It must necessarily, according to its final object, contain
thanksgiving to Jahvé; and therefore Jahvé is actually
immediately so addressed, although at first only briefly and in
quick transition, vv. 3, 4. But the last word, ver. 13,

sufficiently makes good the whole, because all the words from the second strophé onwards so clearly explain all that is necessary, that at length the brief thanksgiving for the actual preservation of the poet suffices. That the terrible enemies fell and were chastised, whilst the poet was saved (the exact particulars indeed cannot be historically substantiated), follows from the opposition, vv. 2-4, as well as from the conclusion of the penultimate words, vv. 11, 12, established by means of the final words, ver. 13. Probably a noble feeling deters the poet from further describing the retribution taken. Finally, if thanksgiving be the glorious mention of the great deeds of the benefactor, it is not wanting in this song (vv. 2-4, 13), although it is here again otherwise expressed than in Pss. xxx., xl. In the words, ver. 3 *b*, there suddenly comes out the excited feeling of the poet (as אַל shows), as he now correspondently to the contents of ver. 4 *b* now speaks merely from his own experience.

On אֲשֶׁר and the whole sentence ver. 9 *b*, comp. § 281 *c* and § 331 *c*, properly, *that will he not again endure*. The sense of the words is thus in itself correct, and at the same time consistently fits into the structure of the verse.

The repetition of longer words from earlier songs is a constant peculiarity of the poets of this age, xxx. 9-11, xl. 4-6, 8, 9; lxxxviii. 10-13, lxxvii. 4 sqq., B. Jer. xxxviii. 10-14.

Ps. lxvi. 13-20 is on the other hand again a pure Temple-song, but more of the character of an ordinary song of thanksgiving, offered by an individual along with the richest sacrifices, for personal deliverance. But we here append it because this is its most suitable position, considering its contents. Although, according to its pure language, and still more its contents, it certainly falls in the times of the first Temple; yet its easy perspicuous mode of presentation, and the elegance both of the language and of the verse-structure, shows that it belongs to these later times. We might almost suppose it was designed only as a

13 *

pattern song for all who brought rich thank-offerings into the Temple. But in the second of the three small strophés, the singer alludes too plainly to the words of his earlier vow to allow us to suppose any other origin than that of his own life-experiences.

It is readily perceptible that this piece is erroneously combined with vv. 1-12, which are quite different in contents and scope. What is similar is merely that that song, like Pss. lxv., lxvii., lxviii., is a species of thanksgiving-song; and this may be the cause of the present song being brought into this connexion. Originally it may have stood after Ps. lxv.

1.

I come into Thy house with sacrifices,
   pay Thee what I vowed;
what my lips uttered,
    what in my distress my mouth declared!
fat calves I bring to Thee, with the sweet savour
    of rams;
15   offer bullocks to Thee with goats! *

2.

Come, hear me relate, all ye fearers of God,
   What He did to my soul!
to Him I cried with open mouth,
   high praise upon my tongue:
" when I feel iniquity in my heart,
   the Lord will not hear."

3.

But God did hear,
   attended to my loud praying.
20   Blessed be God,
    who turned not away my prayer,
  nor His mercy from me!

Ver. 16, as xxii. 23, 24. Ver. 17 properly: *under my tongue,* because the thought or the word which remains long and copiously in the mouth, or very willingly or secretly is there retained, lies *under* the tongue like a concealed or inexhaustible treasure, x. 7, Job xx. 12, 13. If between ver. 17 and ver. 18 nothing is wanting (and this does not seem to be the case), we must assume the poet desired only here to repeat, from the entire contents of his earlier vow-songs, the *one* thought which he then expressed,—that he well knows God will not listen to his vow, if he does not express it with cleanest heart, with previous self-probation and self-cleansing. While he now recalls the more earnestly the hearing of his vow at that moment, this forms at the same time the easiest transition to the last strophé.

Comp. especially further the thanksgiving song, Jon. ii., see above I. pp. 155 sq.

28. PSALM XII.

But what are common sufferings and grief compared with those which the godly men of the time of deeper thought must have felt concerning the gradual and ever deepening ruir of the whole people ! And such griefs would have been the more heartrending, had not great prophets even in the kingdom of the Ten Tribes early risen up with energy to stay this corruption. Ps. xii. shows how mighty the prophetic word lifted up against the growing perversion of ambitious men, was in its influence also upon the entire people. The poet sees greater perversion always prevailing among men, as they drive out power and honour by hypocrisy and false speeches ; yea, encouraged by favourable results, even more secure, more daring and proud, found skill and art upon sin as standing at their command, scorning truth, and its defenders. The vast diffusion of these vices, and the experience that the number of the faithful and truthful is ever on the wane, most deeply grieves and troubles the poet's heart. Yet there spoke at that time great prophets promising restoration of the right and of divine judgment. The poet, then, here depicts in brief and

powerful words the existing corruption; and anxiously cries
for help to Jahvé against such danger, which threatens the
whole human race,—the madness of men who render homage
to a new and sensuous god.   But there occurs to him the
declaration,—which he had heard from a prophet, foretelling the
approach of Divine judgment,—resounding most vividly in his
soul, with a peculiar feeling of its truth, and giving him peace
and rest.   After the cry for help against these evils to God,
vv. 2, 3, the wrath of the poet rises, vv. 4, 5, against the
wickedness of such men.   At the point where the description
of it has touched its extreme,—its assumption against the
Divine supremacy itself,—that faithful and sure oracle occurs,
with the greater tranquillizing power, vv. 6-7; although at last
with this sure hope there is imperceptibly mingled something
again of the depressing view of the present, vv. 8-9.   The song
is certainly the oldest of this kind, and points to the earlier
times of Isaiah.   But to the great emotion of the poet
corresponds the rapid progress of the language in four quite
short strophés.

1.

2   Help, Jahvé! for the godly decrease,
     for faithfulness vanishes from among the sons of men,
   vanity do they speak among one another;
     with hypocritical lip—they speak with double heart.

2.

   Let Jahvé destroy all the hypocritical lips,
     the tongue which speaks proud things;
5   who say: " our tongue we confederate,
     our lips stand by us! who is lord of us?"

3.

   " Out of the oppression of the sufferers, out of the
     sighing of the helpless,
   I will now rise," saith Jahvé,
   " place in safety him that longs after it."

The sayings of Jahvé are pure sayings,
    silver purified in the glowing heat from earth, seven
    times smelted.

4.

Thou, O Jahvé, wilt protect them,
    from this generation wilt preserve him for ever !
Round about throng wicked men,
    as villany lifts itself among men.

On the *sing.* הסיד see § 278 *a.* In the second member,
when a *new* ground for this is adduced, and there is further
expatiation, אמונים is for that reason better taken as an
abstractum (§ 179 *b*) from the *sing.* אֵמוּן, Prov. xiii. 17, xiv. 5,
comp. Jer. vii. 28, Isa. lix. 14, 15. Otherwise Ps. xxxi. 24,
where it signifies *faithful people* by way of contrast, from the
sing. אָמוּן.—Because the cry for help passes over in its course
more into contemplation and description,—in the second appeal,
ver. 4, Jahvé is named only in the third person. How *proudly*
they speak is immediately described with more particularity in
ver. 5 : if not outwardly so clearly and shrilly, yet in their heart
fully so thinking and acting, they say they required not the
ancient and venerable God, because they had for themselves a
particular God, allied with them, powerful, and standing at
their command,—namely their tongue, or art of falsehood,
which they honour and adore as the highest power in life. It
has already procured for them many good things, and further
would procure, if they only remained true to it. Comp.
Hab. i. 11, 16 ; Job xii. 6 ; Phil. iii. 19. Accordingly, נַגְבִּיר
is best understood of the concluding a firm covenant (prop.
make fast, Lat. *pangere*), Dan. ix. 27. The following indeed
appears tolerable : our tongue *we praise* as our God (to make
great = praise, sing praise with the dative) LXX, μεγαλυνοῦμεν,
but neither does this Hiph. nor גבר generally thus occur, and
this is much less suitable to the sense.—That in ver. 6, an
earlier oracle, merely heard by the poet, resounds in his

memory, is plain from the whole connexion. The poet does not adduce it as his own oracle, nor so introduce it. Comp. lxii. 12. Were it such, it would necessarily occupy the middle place and be the life of the whole song, and the cry for help would not so predominate. But in ver. 7 the poet himself says how he regarded the oracle, namely as received, but true and certain, bright and clear, without alloy, like the purest silver. יָפִיחַ is a part, intrans. See on Prov. xiii. 18: *he who* לוֹ *after it* (salvation) *longs*,—which sufferers long for, as הֵפִיחַ לְ— breathe, pant *for* something, hastening towards it, longing, Hab. ii. 3. Quite otherwise with בְּ, Ps. x. 5. בַּעֲלִיל might be " with repetition, repeated" = seven times, from *alal*, Arab., But more suitably " in glow," from *ghalal*, properly be hot (thirsty) = *ghaly*, so that the signification " smelting-furnace " or " crucible" in the Targ. would not be without support. לָאָרֶץ is in regard to the earth, earthly parts, as לְ— in other instances refers a substantive placed in separation, to its adjective, Job xxxii. 6.—Ver. 8, *them* the good, and used after ver. 2, and ver. 6 c, rather *him*, the sufferer. *This generation,* the present corrupt one, Prov. xxx. 11-14. The generation is further described, ver. 9, while the thought recurs to the beginning. Wicked men must show themselves on all sides, as or so soon as (unpunished) villany, baseness (זֻלּוּת comp. Jer. xv. 19, the *Syr.,* Clem. *Rom. de virgin,* ii., 3, pp. 90, Beelen) arises among men—as it has actually now arisen.

But how the Prophets themselves could in these times suffer far more deeply than all others, is shown most expressively in

29-30. PSALMS LXII., XXXIX.

Songs of a very peculiar character, which, although of diverse contents, yet bear plain marks of derivation from the same poet. He was, it is obvious, a prophet, lxii. 12, and one of the great pillars of the true religion in strife with the dissolute men of his time. It is greatly to be deplored that, in the case of such distinguished and powerful songs, we can only

conjecture the occasion and the poet. But words like lxii.
10, 11, and all other indications, point to a prophet of the
kingdom of the Ten Tribes, such as we shall again find
immediately in Ps. xc.

In Ps. lxii. we see the poet in the very heat of contest with
light-minded slanderous fellow-citizens, who, supported by a
newly risen worldly power favourable to them (possibly a new
royal house in the kingdom of the Ten Tribes), seek to drag
him into the dust and to destroy him, because they cannot
endure his spiritual elevation and superiority. Already they
had long set upon him; and at last it seems that he must fall.
But in the poet, with his trust in God, there is such inward
strength and brightness, that he, anew provoked and
threatened, seeks before everything, in quiet submission to the
true Redeemer, and in the endeavour always to be clear in His
sight, rest and soothing. Yea, he is capable of addressing all
men in language of encouragement, explanation, consolation.
And hardly can the good conscience more calmly conquer; the
vanity of worldly power be more acutely recognized, the
exhortation only to trust the Eternal be more earnest, and even
the scorn against frivolity be more powerful and more noble
than in this song, whose vigorous style corresponds to the
noblest inspiration. Thus the poet is led at the beginning by
his good conscience to submission and hope in God, vv. 2-3;
and although he raises himself from this rest and serenity with
the greater violence against the light-minded, depicting their
inward perverseness, yet soon the higher restfulness and
softening returns, again composing all, vv. 4-8. And thus
the primary thought with which the first strophé hopefully
closed, again resounds at the end of the second; and with this
second the peculiar heart-concern of the poet may be entirely
brought to an end. The third, therefore, turns to external
relations, passing to exhortation and instruction, at last somewhat more marked again with emotion, vv. 9-13.

If, therefore, the first strophé remains perfectly quiet and

brief, as expression of blessed delight, the storm with which
the second begins extends the latter from two to five verses;
but the higher uniformity is again restored in the third, which
falls into the same measure of five verses. But where the
inward unrest appears in flashes, there the verse takes a more
restless, extended form, vv. 4, 5, 9, or is more strained,
vv. 12, 13.

1.

2   Only to God, peace, my soul!
    from Him comes my deliverance;
only He is my rock and my deliverance,
    He my fortress; I shall not greatly tremble!

2.

How long will ye assault a man, breaking him into
    ruin, all,
    like a crumbled wall,
    a barrier to be cast down?
5   From his height they devise only to cast him down,
    they, loving lies,
    blessing with mouth and cursing in heart!
But in God alone be still, my soul!
    for my hope is from Him;
He alone is my rock and my deliverance,
    He my fortress; I shall not be moved!
in God lies my help and honour,
    the rock of my strength, of my refuge, is in God.

3.

Trust in Him at all times, ye people,
    pour out before Him your heart:
    God have we for a refuge.   *
10   Children of men are but a breath, sons of heroes a lie:
    to measure with the balance,
    they are altogether of wind!
Trust not in unrighteousness, be not vain in robbery
    might, when it springs up—give no heed to it!

once has God spoken, twice did I hear :
the power be God's !—
And Thou, O Lord, hast grace :
for *Thou* requitest the man according to his deeds !

דומיה, ver. 2, is an adverb as in xxxix. 3, and stands here at the same time in the exclamation. On הותת, ver. 4, comp. *hatat, hathat, hathath,* Arab., *storm, assault.* As even the firmest fence or wall, continually thrust against, must at last fall, so do they rush upon the poet who mightily resists by his nobility and elevation—with the one object of thrusting him down from his height. Note, vv. 4, 5, 10, 11, the very long verse-member at the beginning, followed by one or two shorter ones. The *sing.* suff. in פִּיו, ver. 5, was only possible along with the plural, because here the language is indefinite : *people, one* : § 319 *a.* יִרְצוּ, etc., expresses a *state,* just as תִּרְצְחוּ, ver. 4.—When, as in ver. 10, sons of human beings* are plainly distinguishable from sons of men* or heroes, the former are the common inferiors, the latter the strong ones already preferred through their birth. Comp. xlix. 3, Ezek. xxxi. 14. But elsewhere in particular names this distinction does not appear, and even the latter name may stand quite generally, iv. 3. עָלָה, *go up,* where the balance is spoken. of, be measured, like lift actively = measure, Job vi. 2. Therefore literally : to be measured with a balance, or most exactly to measure, they are together *of breath* (Isa. xl. 17, xli. 24). Ver. 12 leads directly into the living laboratory of the prophetic spirit. Once, twice (Job xl. 5), the spirit plucks at him, ever more audibly whispering the truth in his ear. Finally, no resistance is longer possible, the heard word presses forth. Here it is not necessary that such truth should be in the naked sense quite new ; but in this application, in the new enigma of the time, it is new. But if to this truth, that upon no external power however increasing, is confidence

---

* *Mensch* and *mann.*

to be placed, or that the power is alone of God, the other is added, that God is also grace, or that he who honestly struggles towards Him may find in Him inner rest and serenity, ver. 13, the consolation and the soothing are indeed as complete as they can be.

Ps. xxxix. is incontestably the finest of all the elegies in the Psalter. The stamp of the language (comp. only *e.g.*, דּוּמִיָּה and the אַךְ, nowhere else so frequent) and tenderness of the feeling infer the same poet. But we see him here struggling not only with other dangers but with the horrors of a deadly sickness. This, in the mind of higher antiquity, was so singularly fearful, that the same hero who resists most boldly the assaults of men, may well blench before the danger of death. Comp. just previously Pss. vi. xiii. To the inner sufferings and anxieties of the poet there is now in addition the fear of laying himself open on his weak side by too free a burst of complaint, in the eyes of the many light-minded ones, who, turned away from Jahvé, willingly despise those who revere Him. They will readily explain these complaints and in a much worse sense than they are intended. To endure then in silence, and rather mutely bear the worst, than speak imprudently before light-minded men, was and is still the ruling maxim of the poet. But on the other side, the grief thus repressed becomes increasingly troubled, and demands the more stormy and unrestrained expression, the warmer, the more inflamed he has become through silence. Therefore—although resisting, and at bottom quietly resigned, and resolved to be patient, because he is bound to regard that suffering as a Divine dispensation for his awakening and chastisement (vv. 9-11), but nevertheless incapable of longer restraining in silence the tide of woe—the poet breaks at length forth into this brief comprehensive song, which powerfully expresses the inner strife of the two opposed feelings. The despair which at first breaks forth with violence is gradually resolved by higher considerations and consolations, until a sorrowful prayer, entreating the Divine compassion, has been reached, and the faint heart is thereby at least so far soothed as is possible, so long as death is deemed the greatest evil. The view that in God is the only hope, ver. 8, is here not so far made clear, that the poet could see how hope triumphs even over death itself. The song is hence developed in strophés that increase in restfulness, composure, brevity. First, in spite of the resolve of silence, the impetuous outbreak of despair at the violence of his grief, and the too brief, transitory life of men, vv. 2-7. Then, more calmly the reflection that nevertheless under all sufferings in God alone is hope, who alone can save; but yet again troubled by the consideration of the want of relation between the sufferings as Divine punishment to the sins of weak man, so that the strophé almost finishes again in equal despair, vv. 8-12. Finally, in perfect collectedness, the prayer, vv. 13, 14. The foundation of the verse-structure is formed as in the preceding song, by the deeply moved flow of language, at first only gathered into two verses. But as here, quite conversely to the previous instance, the storm of the language spends its violence from the very beginning, vv. 2, 3, three of such smallest strophés are at once closely rolled together, before a rest follows, then two, until at last only one remains. The whole thus bears the structure of an elegy, comp. I. pp. 148 sqq.

To the speeches of Job iii.—xxxi., this song bears a great and not accidental resemblance, and since the poet—according to the stamp of the language and the style of the verse—is different, either our poet has read the book of Job, or the poet of the book of Job was determined by the complaints of this song to attempt a higher solution. The latter is more probable, because the higher point of view of the book of Job is not yet found here, and the Psalm may be of the ninth or beginning of the eighth century.

1.

2 I thought : "let me take heed to my ways,
   not to sin with my tongue ;
  keep I for my mouth a bridle,
    so long as the impious man is still before me !"
 I was dumb in quietness, I kept silence from good ;
   but my grief became distressful.—
  Hot is my heart in my bosom,
   in my mind burns fire,
  I speak out with my tongue :
5 let me, Jahvé, know my end,
    and measure of my days, how great it is,
   that I may know how weak I am !—
  See, a span long hast Thou made my life,
    and my duration is as nothing before Thee ;
   every man is nothing but breath ! *
  as but a phantom each man walks ;
   but vainly do they busy themselves :
   he heaps up, knowing not who shall take it !

2.

  And now, what hope I, O Lord ?
   my tarrying—it depends on Thee !
  from all my transgressions deliver me,
   make me not the scorn of the fool !—
10 I am stricken dumb, opening not my mouth :
   for *Thou* hast done it !
  remove from me Thy rod,
   before the anger of Thy hand I pass away !
  with punishments for sin Thou chastisest one—
   and consumest like the moth his dearest things ;
  only breath is every man ! *

3.

Hear my prayer, Jahvé, and mark my complaint,
  be not silent at my tears !
for a guest am I with Thee,
  a foreigner like all my fathers ;
Look away from me, that I may behold clearly,
  before I go and—am no more !

What is adduced in vv. 2, 3 as a thought of the poet, was
ever his abiding principle, and becomes so here again, ver. 10;
but in the overflowing of grief he cannot here, at least in the
first strophé, hold it quite firmly. The perfects in the
beginning of ver. 2 must therefore be understood as purely
past time, as similarly Isa. xxxviii. 10. On the other hand,
דִּבַּרְתִּ, ver. 4 as נֶאֱלַמְתִּי, ver. 10, as present (§ 135 *b*). The corresponding proposition begins with an emphatic placing in the
front of the וּכְאֵבִי (§ 340 *a*). *I was silent from good*, good or
happiness that I lacked, not impetuously and loudly demanding
it ; but now I speak *with my tongue*, aloud, not merely in my
heart. The first outburst of despair, ver. 5, is truly very
strong, indeed almost mocking (sarcastic). That is then the
much-boasted life, wherein I only view unending griefs and a
certainly near end. No, rather would I at once learn from
Jahvé when the end of my short life is to be, in order to feel
the strange incomprehensible right, namely how frail and
pitiful I am as a man—although true to God. Comp. Job. vi.
8-10. More sorrowfully and mildly follow, vv. 6, 7, considerations on the brief human life generally in comparison
with the Divine. טְפָחוֹת is " some spans (prop. handbreadths)
long." For the notion of extension in space lies in the
accusative, that of the indefinite " some " in the absence
of the article with the plural, Isa. lxv. 20, *Gr. ar.* ii. p. 7.
Only altogether breath, as nothing because vain and quickly
passing away *stands* = is, *every* standing living *man*, for that
נִצָּב has further no significant emphasis at all, is clear from

ver. 12, where it is wanting. *Only in a figure,* properly phantom, *subsisting, i.e.,* appearing as a phantom (§ 299 *b*), so not for duration, because he is as little anything in himself as the shadow, and quickly like the shadow flees; similarly the vision, lxxiii. 20, Isa. xxix. 7, 8. Equally vain therefore is the endeavour and toil of man to obtain external goods, even if the fullest of bustle and commotion. In the last member, ver. 7, the singular recurs from the first, which might be enlarged, because of the general truth in the middle one, into the plural.—Ver. 8. Reflection. If it be thus with him, what is then eternal hope? It is only in God, who may save the poet from all *guilts,* for the troubles of sickness are also by this poet as by earlier ones, dimly felt to be guilty, or closely connected with sins, as Ps. xxxviii. But will he now again prefer to be quietly resigned, ver. 10? only the too great punishment to which one must succumb, may God remove, ver. 11 (comp. vi. 2), since life is so readily attacked in secret as by the canker of moths, and the dearest possession like a moth-eaten garment (Job xiii. 27) for ever falls asunder with transitory man,—so that in ver. 12 the despondency of the first strophé again threatens. חָמוּד like יְחִידָה xxii. 21. Most affecting in the last strophé, where first the set prayer follows, is the figure of man as a mere guest or sojourner with God upon the upper world. The sunny upper world is primarily the place of God, where His power, grace, and light are experienced. Why then will God, who is praised as the Good, send man, who yet cannot for ever rejoice in the upper world, before his time into the lower world? Why ever like a dread lord turn His strict eye upon him, leaving him not for a moment rest and respite (cxxiii. 2)? Job x. 20, 21. The words, ver. 14, are quite in the style of Job, comp. vii. 19, x. 20, xiv. 6.

31. PSALM XC.

Thus then did the ancient community feel in the ninth and the beginning of the eighth century, in spite of the influence of the great prophets in this time; already unhappy, far enough

sunk from the height of the old Mosaic and Davidic time,
serious contemplation, quiet recurrence to the eternal verities
must nevertheless have been stimulated by this influence
among the best of the time. And in Ps. xc. we see how a
poet equally serious and sublime, in a prayer designed for the
whole community, sought to lead even such depressing feelings
of a general discord and affliction in the right way.—Very long
and heavy sufferings had, according to vv. 13-16, visited the
people. Their weight and bitterness might sufficiently illus-
trate the truth, how little weak and frail man can do anything
against the Divine will manifesting itself in the course of
events. But instead of such a view leading necessarily to
gloom and despair, there lies in it, on the contrary, a grand
instruction. For if it be, first, true that man only by sepa-
rating himself from the Divine will, and as it were exciting the
Divine anger, falls into real sufferings; and secondly, that he,
the more and the longer he resists God, the weaker and frailer
must become : it does indeed rather follow that he must turn
the more intently and solely to God, and the knowledge of
Him; and in the very consciousness of his weakness, the more
zealously and wisely employ this brief life for this end; that in
the endeavour after God, the eternal, he may overcome the
fleeting and transient, and in spite of its extremely short duration, may live blessedly in Him. He only who thus regards
the time of sufferings, raising himself in and by them to a
higher calm, a complete resignation to God,—is able to pray to
God with success for the mitigation of his sufferings and for
invigoration. For he is already inwardly prepared for a new
life in God. To the purity and strength of this mode of
thought and feeling the poet here seeks to raise all, that they
may not earlier pray for the Divine grace than their inner life
is enlightened and glorified for it. In the first instance, therefore, the prayer wings its way out of the midst of these
contemplations to God as the unchangeable resource in all
times, the Eternal, before whom the races of brief-lived man

14

quickly pass away, vv. 1-6 (1, 2, 3-6). And if then the application of this is to be made to the present time, vv. 7-12, the suppliants must confess above all how *they* now need precisely that eternal succour and help the most. For they know very well that only sin could bring them into this condition, vv. 7, 8. Moreover, according to the teaching of history in the whole human race, the more passion and sin were developed in it, the more transitory and troublous did life become, vv. 9, 10. But for the very reason that the further the advance of human sin, the further also that of Divine wrath and human misery, they now perceive clearly that only the endeavour to become reflective and wise,—the more so as life is short, and the more earnestly to turn to God, can save man, vv. 11, 12. Only then in such a mood of mind, thus striving after the future, does the community pray at length in full faith and hope to Jahvé, their eternal resource, for blessing and grace after so severe and long sufferings, vv. 13-17. Thus there are three quite similar strophés,—the first bringing out the eternal and true ground of human endeavour; the second showing how this basis was lost and is again to be recovered; the third finally, the actual new elevation in faith to that position. Each strophé has six verses with thirteen verse-members; but the last is somewhat shorter, with five verses and eleven verse-members.

The song is characterized by an uncommon intensity and solemnity, fathoming the depths of Divinity; and is, besides, as a song, manifestly designed for a day of humiliation in the community, the first known to us in point of time, and in contents incomparably the noblest of its kind. Exactly as a solemn public hymn—for there can be no doubt it is this—it is throughout original and vigorous; and would on all grounds be rightly traceable to Moses, the man of God,—as the later collector names Moses, comp. Deut. xxxiii. 1 ; Ezr. iii. 2*—

---

* Comp also *Gesch des V Isr.,* ii., pp 319 sq.. 3rd edit.

did we only know more exactly the historical grounds which justified the collector in this assumption. At the end of the wandering in the desert, Moses may well have been seized by these more serious thoughts. And a man who had grown grey in great undertakings, standing at the end of his earthly career, is plainly the poet. The mention of the deep declining period of life, ver. 10, seems indeed to lead to an earlier century, since the narrative of Moses extends far over a hundred years; while it might be said that a poetic word from the same time speaks even more accurately than the later tradition. But what is here peculiarly decisive is the observation that so general and profound a feeling of human weakness and frailty of every kind, as expressed in this song, according to all indications, is only gradually formed and fixed. All certain tokens of the times under Moses and David do not lead to the possibility of such a song at so early a period. And the style of the prayer, ver. 13 *a*, is obviously borrowed from passages like Ps. vi. 4, 5. On the other hand, the whole contents of the song carry us to the time of the great prophets of the tenth or, at latest, of the eighth century; and from the eighth century proceeds also the song, Deut. xxxii., which bears a certain resemblance in language to this song, especially in the plural forms יְמוֹת, שְׁנוֹת, although I hold the Psalm to be the earlier, and rather as a sketch for Deut. xxxii. The composer of the superscription has therefore probably referred to the song of Moses, and placed it at the head of the collection, Pss. xc.—cv., for this reason only—that he found this solemn song, so worthy of Moses, distinguished in an older book. And this we may pursue a little further in the present day.

We saw above, pp. 160-172, 200 sqq., a few highly peculiar songs, which, according to all indications, belong to the kingdom of the Ten Tribes. We may make quite the same assumption in the case of this song as in the related one, Deut. xxxii. In that kingdom the transitoriness of all human things and the

14 *

necessity of deepest penitence might be recognized far earlier
than in Juda and be expressed by great prophets in such
public hymns.   If we now suppose that such songs as Ps. xc.,
Deut. xxxii. had been collected in a song-book designed for
the kingdom of the Ten Tribes, it may be readily understood
how they might be ascribed to Moses.   For as there were in
Jerusalem "songs of David" destined for the Temple, to
which similar ones were appended, so had they there, it is
certain, a collection destined for the like object, of "songs of
Moses," as the later Samaritans referred all sacred things to
Moses alone.

1.

1   Lord ! a Refuge wast Thou to us in every age !
Before mountains were born,
   before there circled earth and land,
  and from ever to evermore Thou art God.
Thou returnest man to dust,
   and sayest: "return, ye children of man !"
  (for a thousand years are in Thine eyes
   as yesterday when it passes,
  and a watch in the night) :
5   thus their races are a dream in the morning,
   like to grass that springs in the morning :
in the morning it blooms and sprouts,
   toward evening it fades and withers.

2.

For in Thy anger we are brought to naught,
   and in Thy wrath are shattered :
Thou hast placed our sins before Thee,
   our most secret things before the light of Thy glance.
All our days passed away indeed in Thy terror,
   quickly are our years gone like a sound,
10   the days of our life—comprise seventy years or scarce
    eighty years ;

also their fury is idle, empty,
> for hastily it is vanished and we—fly away.
Who knows the greatness of Thy anger,
> since Thy terror is like to Thy majesty?
to number our days therefore teach us,
> and to offer a wise heart!

3.

Return, O Jahvé! how long—?
> Have pity on Thy servants!
Refresh us speedily with Thy grace
> that joyously we may exult, so long as we live!
Make us glad as many days as thou hast bowed us down,　15
> as the years we have seen evil!
Make appear to Thy servants Thy deed,
> on high to their sons Thy glory!
So may thé mercy of the Lord our God come upon us!
> and our handiwork—O guard it for us,
> and our handiwork—O guard it!

Ver. 2. It appears that *circulate* חוֹלָל may stand poetically in general for "lie in the birth, in the origin," and it is hardly necessary to express חוֹלָל as a pure passive. To God as the second person תְּחוֹלָל in this connexion cannot be readily referred. אֵל must be predicative. Ver. 3 דַּכָּא as *fem. substant.* א_ for the more usual ה_, which mode of writing, here and there, might probably begin somewhat earlier, § 173 b. Num. xi. 20. שׁוּבוּ is plainly from the preceding תָּשֵׁב and from Gen. iii. 19.—Ver. 4. The figure is the more suitable if we consider how in the evening at the very moment when the previous day is passing away, when the space is leaving us, it seems shortest to us; like, again, a fleeting watch or a third part of the ensuing night, where justly a still shorter portion than a day is chosen, because in the still night all appears to move more slowly.—Were the זְרַמְתָּם, ver. 5, a word of action, *Thou didst stream them away,* and the reading throughout correct, the sense would be : if one observes an utterly vanishing human world, they appear as streamed away as by a flood from God, or rather like a fleeting vision which vanishes on awakening in the morning, and breaks up into nothing (see xxxix. 7, lxxiii. 20, Isa. xxix. 8). Into this double figure would then be pressed immediately as a third, that of the quickly fading grass, thus : *in the morning* already, early, soon (comp. ver. 14) *like the grass, that passes away,* חלף poetically = עבר, as the LXX render it by παρέρχεσθαι. But here the poet would feel that it was well to follow up the briefly expressed figure of the grass of the morning, and hence would thus continue : *in the morning* indeed *it blooms and—passes away* nevertheless, for already *towards evening* it fades and withers. For without doubt מולל is to be understood not of the cutting-off of the flowers, since the whole beauty of the comparison rests upon the fact that the flower still blooming in the morning dies unobserved, but certainly the same day through the heat of the sun, xxxvii. 2; Job xiv. 2; Isa. xxxvii. 27. Thus figure after figure would here most quickly press in, whereby the second בַּבְּקֶר would obtain a somewhat different reference ; and one must say that this very fulness and difficulty were peculiar to this Psalm.

The translation then would be :

> hast streamed them away, a dream they become,
> in the morning—like to the grass that passes away ;
> in the morning it blooms and passes away,
> towards evening it withers and is dried up.

But the figures would thus be too greatly involved in one another, and too obscure ; and חָלַף with its inchoative הֶחֱלִיף, Job xiv. 7, signifies where growth generally is spoken of, *drive after, newly swell.* Thus זְרַמְתָּם formed from a זֶרֶם (§ 257 *b*) might signify *their stream,* i.e., according to Nah. ii. 9, *their mass,* and as a word of multitude, be connected with the plural יִהְיוּ : but it is much easier to compare as זְרַמְתָּם with an

Aramaic *shrabat* (which the Pesch. here gives), and to explain as *their races.* But in that case the בבקר is better drawn to the first member, and the same is supplied at the end of the following one, since our poet does not shun, after ver. 17, the repetition of similar words. The best sense of the whole discourse is however only completed when we take the תָּשֵׁב, ver. 3 (§ 357 *b*) as introducing the antecedent sentence to vv. 5, 6, so that ver. 3 becomes merely an intermediate proposition.

Ver. 7. We need this recourse to Thee, *for—.* With the כֹּל ver. 9, the thought is generalized, which also lies in the whole connexion. If generally in the course of centuries the age of men has sunk so low; the greater human complications, strivings, passions became, the more wasting-away, the speedier death, the greater feeling of the reflex working of the anger of God upon the increasing unnaturalness. כִּלִּינוּ *thither we have,* standing at the goal, looking back at the end of the course, *let our years go like a sound* quickly arising and as quickly passing away; for the word הֶגֶה is so most correctly understood, as was observed in the *Beiträgen zur geschichte der ältesten auslegung,* I., p. 62.—Ver. 10 בָּהֶם is: *in them are =* they comprehend; for whatever is in a thing or a human being it embraces, comprehends, comp. ἐν αὐτῷ, John x. 11, and similarly is applied in the Arabic *py.*—The וְאִם בִּגְבֻרֹת seems to admit of the signification: *and if* the days are *with strength;* but the Pesch. has alone correctly *memachasan,* and *scarcely,* like *vix* from *vis,* μόλις, properly, with trouble. Then וְאִם must be understood as *sive.* It is to be regretted that the idiom is not elsewhere found: but the last in this connexion appears certainly to be the nearest and readiest; comp. also *bally,* with some *trouble, i.e., scarcely, Hamása,* p. 263, 7. רְהָב *the fury, the rage* of life is youth, the most energetic time, when man is full of the most impetuous projects and actions; but how many of them are attained? This raging noise is vain and empty, for if at the goal of life we look back, it has unexpectedly and hastily fled away (גו passed by), and we are already as good

as fled from fleeting life into the grave.—Ver. 11. יִרְאָה is
here throughout objective : the fear which any one diffuses by
his own means, fearfulness, *majesty* (Ez. i. 18), according to
the infinite measure of which in God His anger at sin and His
punishment is directed, so that if man would continue in further
sin against that majesty, still remaining infinitely high, the
farther would punishment proceed.   Thus *to number,* that we
wisely number our few days (Col. iv. 5), *therefore* teach such
things, and that we in consequence of this may offer to God as
the best sacrifice (Hos. xiv. 3, Ps. xl. 8) a heart of wisdom;
וְנָבִא continuation of לִמְנוֹת (§ 350 *b*).

Ver. 16 gives the *sing.* פָעֳלֶךָ the better reading, because
here manifestly the one great Divine deed is desired, the
Messianic, to which the prophets of the eighth century so often
point, Isa. xxviii. 21 ; xxix. 23 ; Hab. iii. 2.   But thus the
outcome of this song gives, by this significant and emphatic
indication of the Messianic hope, the most unmistakable hint
of its true period.

2.   NEW ELEVATION AT THE END OF THE EIGHTH CENTURY.

32-35.   PSALMS XLVI., XLVIII., LXXVI., LXXV.

And in fact, once more did at least the southern kingdom
rise, towards the end of the eighth century, to a higher flight,
—when Sanherib's army, just when it imagined it had conquered and destroyed Jerusalem, left Palestine, struck by a
deadly blow, and the Assyrian rule remained for a long time
broken.   The fall of so great a worldly power at so unexpected
a time, and in contrast to such slight external resources as
Juda possessed, was bound to awaken in every way joy and
rejoicing as well as profounder reflection.   Few times in
Israelitish history are there so striking at the moment, and so
influential in the result, as these.   For, in the first place, there
was again given, after a long period of misery, a grand token
of Divine deliverance, powerfully arresting the attention of all
men.   The old times of Moses and of David appeared to be

renewed,—that which was once only related in story being now actually beheld and experienced (xlviii. 9). Such a deliverance has indeed meaning and significance only for those who are striving on behalf of the truth to draw near to Jahvé, and could only in truth inspire and elevate Israel, in so far as it was the genuine Israel. Meanwhile, at that epoch, after the fall of Samaria, it was only Juda, and especially Jerusalem, before whose walls the Assyrian had already encamped, threatening the Temple, which had been wondrously delivered. Jerusalem and its Temple had been preserved as the firm impenetrable bulwark, before which the heathen's wild rage and lust of destruction suffered a rebound. Thus all the splendour of those times was reflected upon the holy city, the sacredness and inviolability of which was now apprehended in a much higher, sublimer manner than before. The recollection of loftier blessings, the eternity of the Divine salvation in the true community, and firm hope were connected more closely and more firmly with the picture of the city, holy through long ages, formed by great heroes and prophets, the fixity of which appeared immovable as the Divine energies. Out of these feelings error and blindness might no doubt be readily generated at a later time (comp. on lix. 12). However in that first period this view is pure and innocent, because still entirely drawn from the first prophetic inspiration.—But if on the other hand the experience of that period taught also in the most emphatic manner the transitoriness and the inward corruption of fancied power and of wild heathen feeling, there lay further in that experience the most serious exhortation to all light-minded kingdoms and men, to distinguish the true power from the false, and not to pass away in vanity and darkness. There was too, finally, the tranquil hope that at last all peoples of the earth, even the now estranged heathen peoples, would attain to true insight and reverence. The period then conceals a mass of higher truths in its bosom : and many as are the prophetic discourses which explain at this time such

teachings and hopes, there are also several poetical voices
which arise to glorify in nervous brevity and vividness the
life and aspiration of the time. Pss. xlvi. and xlviii., if not
from the same poet, yet originated and were sung almost at
the same period ; and they express the first stirrings of feeling
after the great event,—full of rapture, and of the joyous inspiration of the time, hovering about the immediate present, and
hastening on with light and bounding step. Pss. lxxvi. and
lxxv., certainly from the same poet, but as it appears, one
different from the former, speak on the other hand already
more from the distance, more in the style of a review, more
prophetically, and Ps. lxxv. is even predominantly prophetical.
But all these songs are beautiful, noble traces of a grand
period ; and Isaiah himself might almost be esteemed the poet
of Ps. xlvi., but that of Ps. xlviii., the pupil 'of Isaiah whom
we discover in the fragment, Isa. xxxiii.,—so much that in word
and spirit is in the highest degree related to him, do we find
here (comp. the *Propheten des Alten Bundes* i., pp. 293 sqq.,
Gesch. des V. Isr., iii., p. 632, 2nd edit.) But we must never
forget that the purely original inspiration belongs to the
Prophet, and songs of a period like the present are but an
echo of the much mightier and more original voices of the
Prophets.

In Ps. xlvi. there is the stirring of a joyous consciousness of
the protection and of the strength that is in God the Lord of all.
His power, the most raging peoples, like the stormy seas of the
world, must feel. He now from the holy tranquil seat of His
mild rule in Sion quells the storm of the earth and of the
peoples, and far and wide has changed war into peace. O
that all peoples, at last become wise, would turn to Him !
These very general contents are completed in three strophés,
while the fundamental thought, " God is to us in the stormiest
distress Salvation," wherewith the song begins, is gathered up
at the end of each strophé into a brief and powerful refrain.

Thus all three strophés contain the ever more widely developed confirmation of that primary truth. The first, vv. 2-4, brings out this truth in its most general form; the second, vv. 5-8, leads us nearer to Sion, which is peculiarly the soft and tranquil seat of God, far from earth's storms. Before it therefore all the raging of the wild fermenting elements vanishes, its citizens, even in the midst of the universal vacillation of all things, enjoy protection and hope. The third strophé, vv. 9-12, finally points, in admonition and encouragement, to the present clear illustration of God's great deliverance, and the destruction of worldly rage and clamour, and thus the conception is completed. In I., p. 191, it was remarked that this song as a true public hymn is so arranged that the whole community should fall into the refrain at the end of each strophé. Hence it follows of itself that it must be supplied in the present arrangement of the words after ver. 4, where it was omitted purely through a copyist's error. And as this refrain consists only of a most simple pair of members, just so each strophé only of three verses, or six verse-members.

1.

God is a refuge to us and strength,   2
    a help truly found in times of need.
Therefore we fear not if the earth shakes,
    if in the heart of the seas mountains tremble.
Though its floods roar, ferment,
    mountains tremble when it swells :   *
[*Jahvé of Hosts is with us,*
    a firm fortress for us Jakob's God!]   5

2.

A stream's brooks rejoice the city of God,
    the high and holy dwellings of the Highest;
God Himself is in her : she trembles not,
    help her will God, the morning draws near.

Peoples roared, kingdoms trembled,
  sounded His thunder, earth is dismayed :
Jahvé of Hosts is with us,
  a firm fortress for us Jakob's God !   *

3.

Come, behold the deeds of Jahvé,
  who did high wonders on the earth;
10   who stills wars even to the earth's end,
  breaks bow, and blunts spear, scorches chariot in the
    fire l
" Cease, and know that I am God,
  am high beneath clouds, high upon earth l "
Jahvé of Hosts is with us,
  a firm fortress for us Jakob's God !   *

Ver. 3. הָמִיר cannot possibly be here "change, alter,"
but in the original signification "move." LXX, suitably,
ταράσσεσθαι. The meaning "change" is derived from this,
although the Lat. *mutare* is not from *movere*. The connexion
of the fourth verse appears doubtful. As it would be foolish
to connect it immediately with the following thought, vv. 5 ff.,
it might at first be supposed that it was a direct continuation
of ver. 3, the infinitive with בְ (§ 350 b) passing into the
finite verb. The suffix י־ must in any case refer twice to the
sing. יָם sea, to be supplied in general from ver. 3, and גַּאֲוָה
denote its violence or excessive swelling in an earthquake.
Comp. Job xxxviii. 11; Ps. lxxxix. 10. Vv. 3 and 4 would
then be either connected with ver. 2, or we must assume that
after ver. 4 the refrain, vv. 8-12, had fallen away, and this
latter is indeed on other grounds thoroughly probable. But
against this is the point, that in this way the earthquake would
merely be further described, without necessity and without
purpose, ver. 3 being in that case fully sufficient, especially in
so short and fugitive a song. It is better therefore to take

the whole verse as in sharp opposition to the following
(§ 362 *l*) ; in other instances the opposition—especially in
brief poetic language,—often lies merely in the sharp contra-
position of thoughts and words, as cxix. 51, 61.—Ver. 5. As
he discourse now comes to Sion, it was readily suggested to
place in opposition to the clamour and raging of external
foreign powers just mentioned, the never-exhausted refreshment of the softly flowing, calmly recurring Sílóah, which is
elsewhere, about this time, used as a figure of the gentle,
peaceful, and yet ever refreshing rule of Jahvé in Sion,
Isa. viii. 6.   Eternally as the brooks of this stream refresh
Sion, so with Jahvé's protection.   He in time of need will very
soon ("towards the arrival of morning," *i.e.*, before a night
passes, comp. xc. 14, xlix. 15, cxliii. 8) help her.   If then, as
at that time, the whole earth is in uproar and dissolution at
the time of Divine judgments, ver. 7, there remains nevertheless for Sion Jahvé's protection, ver. 8.   On the connexion of
the קֹדֶשׁ, ver. 5, lxv. 5, comp. § 293 *c.*—In ver. 9, שֵׁמוֹת must
signify *stupenda*, the LXX, not incorrectly, τέρατα.   Quite
cognate also, according to the original root, is the Æthiopic
madem. emât.   The astounding deeds of God are the destruction of au enemy so mighty and well equipped as were the Assyrians, and the restoration of peace far and wide over the long
wearied and exhausted earth.   The *chariots* designate like the
horses, xx. 8, that which is un-Israelitish.—Ver. 11. Then
breaks out, on this prospect, indignation at the perverseness
of false power and arrogance into a brief exclamation of
strictly prophetic exhortation.   Ps. lxxv. further develops what
is here briefly sketched.

If Ps. xlvi. is thus of the most general contents, and so
comprises all the lofty feelings of the time that it might be
sung by the whole people even upon the battle-field, so, on the
other hand, Ps. xlviii., according to ver. 10, is quite properly
designed for a Temple-song, and has in view in the first

instance Jerusalem and the Temple mount alone.   For it
expresses, in thanksgiving to the Saviour of Sion, pre-eminently the joy at the high dignity and glory of the holy city,
and the firm hope that Jahvé will in future ever protect and
guide her, as she now shines, wondrously protected and preserved in spite of the destructive rage of the enemy.   With
the main thought that Jahvé has proclaimed himself in Sion,
and will further protect her, the song begins,—with this closes
each following strophé; and even in external particulars
this song bears the highest resemblance to the preceding.   It
likewise falls, in the course of its progress, into three
strophés: the first develops the most general features of the
thought, vv. 2-4; the second shows the dignity of Sion more
in detail from the latest history,—how that a multitude of
mighty allied kings were suddenly in the neighbourhood of
the holy place seized by a strange terror, and fell back, and
the ancient history of the overthrow of Pharaoh was repeated
in their case, for the defence of the holy place, vv. 5-9.   The
third turns finally to the jubilation and thanksgiving to God
for this, now loudly resounding in the Temple as throughout
the land and the whole earth.   He in this rare moment was
clearly recognized as the great Judge of human affairs, by
whose defence, in spite of all wicked and evil-minded men,
Sion now shines in greater stability and glory than ever, and
who shall be perpetually known and praised as the eternal
guide of Israel, vv. 10-15.

According to I., p. 154, the song retains the true
ancient form of a song of joy in the characteristic that its
three strophés are gradually prolonged, from three to five and
to six verses, or from seven to ten and to twelve verse-members,
but these almost throughout of the most elegant brevity.
But along with this there is also a manifest similarity with the
preceding in the construction with a refrain after each strophé,
in which the congregation is to join, although it is wanting
after ver. 4, and runs somewhat differently at the end.   But

this much is clear, that in it, quite similarly to the case on
p. 167, in the royal song, the *ever* was always to be repeated.

1.

Great is Jahvé and praiseworthy greatly   2
     in the city, the holy mount of our God.
Of beauteous elevation, delight of all the earth
     is the Sion's mount, the extremest North,
        fortress of the great king :
God has made himself in her castles
     known as a firm retreat !
[*God will preserve her for ever !*]

2.

For the kings, lo ! took counsel,   5
     drew on together ;
looking thither they were forthwith astonished,
     were thrown into confusion, thrilled with fear ;
Terror seized them there,
     Convulsion as of a woman in travail—
by a storm from the East
     which breaks in pieces Tarshish-ships.—
As we had heard, so we saw it
     in the city of Jahvé of hosts, the city of our God:
God will preserve her for ever !   *

3.

We think O God, of Thy grace,   10
     in the midst of thy Temple :
as Thy name God, so resounds Thy praise to the ends of
        the earth :
     of righteousness is Thy right hand full !
Sion's mount rejoices,
     Judah's daughters exult,
       because of Thy judgments !—
Go about Sion and circulate around her,
     count her towers ;

observe her wall, reckon her castles
—that ye may tell it to the coming age !
15   this is God, our God, for ever and ever :
he will guide us to eternity !

Ver. 3 is one of the signs of the way in which the fancy of
the poet looks upon Sion, in itself small and insignificant, with
ever higher splendour, because of its religious dignity (comp.
below on Ps. lxviii. 16, 17). It is termed here of *fair elevation,*
rising on high with gentle blessing as the seat of true religion,
the centre (Ezek. v. 5) and the *delight of the whole earth ;*
and it is placed as in *the extreme North, i.e.,* according to
primæval Asiatic conception in the inviolable distance and
sacredness of the extreme North, upon the mountains of God
that reach the clouds, as *the city of the great king,* of Jahvé, as
the heathen supposed the mountain of the gods was the seat of
all the gods.   Unquestionably the poet glances, in ירכתי צפון,
at the conceptions, again come into great currency through the
rule of the Assyrians, of the mountain of the gods in the extreme
North (Isa. xiv. 13).   But in sharp opposition to all Assyrian
belief he transfers this mountain to Jerusalem, and holds
it to be equivalent to Sion ; almost as we speak of *Olympus.*
Besides, the North, apart from the East, passed for sacred
with the Hebrew from primæval times, (Levit. i. 11), as indeed
originally all Southern Asiatic peoples looked to the North
as the seat of gods.   That the mere locality of Sion is intended
to be described by these words (comp. Williams, *The Holy City,*
p. 396) is a notion unworthy of the poet ; although we must
not overlook the fact that the exaggeration was the more
readily suggested because the Temple lay on the north-east end
of the ancient Jerusalem.—Vv. 5-8, a fugitive description, very
fine, corresponding to the haste and sudden turn in the action,
of the haughty, vain march of the kings (who were allied with
the Assyrians, Isa. xxxvi. 4-6) against Sion ; comp. Isa. x.
28-34.   In accordance with their design, they advance in good

order; but as soon as they are in the neighbourhood of Sion,
as they dare to lift their impious eyes toward the sanctuary,
they are affrighted by sudden panic and fear of death, as if a
fearful storm, shattering the strongest ships of Tarshish (the
Tarshish-ships), drove them back from the holiest place, which
they desired to profane. On הֲפָה־יִן, comp. § 341 *d* and
360 *b:* Thus was a great example of Divine judgment,—such
as was at that time told and heard only in ancient stories,
especially of Pharaoh,—seen and heard, and that in a new place,
in Sion, ver. 9, comp. Job xlii. 5.—Ver. 11. In correspondence
with the name, or the inner being of God which had long
been open to men's recognition, and therefore as high and
worthy as is His Name,—so highly now resounds His praise
everywhere, because it is now one of the rare earthly moments
when the inner being of God comes into manifestation
most clearly and most powerfully, so that all may recognize
His true splendour and glory, and may praise Him as His
Name deserves. May the freshness and inspiration of this
moment long last, and the recollection of this miracle—how
Sion, despite the rage of superior foes, already prepared for
destruction, was so well preserved and remains in all her
ancient splendour—never be effaced! And although—according to Isa. xxxiii. 18—the haughty Assyrian but a short time
before had the towers counted, as if he would seize and destroy
them all in a moment,—Sion now sees once for all how,
in spite of all this, there is not the least loss of its fortifications.
What splendour, what strength,—the wonder may be told to
the after-world!—For (ver. 15) *He who so wondrously guards*
Sion, *is God, our God, for ever; He will guide us* (here the
sentence cannot end) *into eternities,* LXX εἰς τοὺς αἰῶνας, if
עַלְמוֹת is read. The plur. is indeed עֲלָמִים, but the termi-
nation יוֹת (§ 174 *d*, 177 *d*) is not altogether unexpected. To
explain *"over death and after"* according to the Massôra
appears very feeling; but is suspicious as totally unprepared
for here.—Otherwise it might be supposed that the word here

15

(I. pp. 224 sq.), just as in xlvi. 1, is intended to have a musical
significance, and so stands in a subscription to this song.   But
(p. 35) such subscriptions are not proper to the Psalter, and,
in any case, something would be wanting here, if the word did
not belong to the verse.

As Ps. xlviii. is a kind of continuation of Ps. xlvi.—similarly
Ps. lxxvi. starts, as if connected with Ps. xlviii., from Sion as
the place from which God has mightily revealed Himself as
Judge.   But it directs our glance to the whole of Juda as the
seat of the purest kingdom of God upon earth.   For it is
applied predominantly to tranquil contemplation and instruction,
striving to hold fast the inner and permanent significance of the
great event.   In this Psalm the infinite power and glory of Jahvé
has been made manifest, before which even the most splendid
and well-equipped foe blenched, and also—a higher truth—
His holy justice, before which no impious man can stand,—
embracing the whole earth.   But thus must it be, thus must
Jahvé act : for his work must be finished, all men must finally
come to true understanding and humility.   As the poet, impelled
by these purely Messianic conceptions, would praise God, the
song of itself falls into four perfectly uniform strophés,—the
first and the last two being closely inter-dependent, but the
third stands side by side with the second as its supplement.
In the first he praises Jahvé generally as great in Sion, and as
the annihilator of the peoples that have pleasure in war, vv. 2-4.
In the second, he further celebrates the splendid power of
Jahvé, which surpasses all things, which even the mightiest
may not resist, vv. 5-7 ; and praises in the third, in correspondence with this on the other side, the high and holy justice
of Jahvé over all peoples, vv. 8-10.   Finally, he subjoins,
looking into the future, the inner, eternal basis of the Divine
activity among men,—namely, the necessity that in the end all,
even the most furious and the most enraged, should come to
the thankful acknowledgment of God.   O that all men alike
would do homage to Him, to Him who subdues the pride of

all kings! vv. 11-13. This close rises somewhat higher, and
with more vital energy, and is in fact the most beautiful, the
most powerful, and in significance the weightiest portion of the
whole. The four strophés are, in accordance with the
didactic spirit of the song, of a highly tranquil and uniform
tenor, each of three verses and six members.

1.

God makes Himself known in Juda,   2
  in Israel His Name is great.
For His tent was in Salem,
  and His resting-place in Sion ;
There He brake in pieces the flashes of the bow;
  shield and sword, and war !   *

2.

Splendid art Thou, more glorious   5.
  than the fortresses of robbery.
Bare of arms were the stout-hearted, slumbering their
                                    sleep,
  and all the men of might found not their hands ;
at Thy threatening, O Jakob's God,
  lie stunned both horse and chariot.

3.

Thou—awful art Thou,
  and who will stand before Thee when Thou art
                                 angry ?
Thou didst cause right to sound loudly from heaven,
  earth feared and—was silent ;
when God arose to judgment,   10
  to help all earth's sufferers.   *

4.

For the rage of man will praise Thee,
  to Thee the remainder of rage will do honour,

                                   15 *

Utter and pay vows to Jahvé your God!
    let all round about Him—offer homage to His
        majesty.
He mows down the spirit of the nobles,
    fearful He to the kings of the earth.

Ver. 3. A new poetic abbreviation from Jerusalem, the
verbal signification of which had become obscure in later
times, while the former signifies *peaceful*, place of peace,
which appeared to the poet the more suitable, because it was
precisely Jerusalem that was here to be described as the holy
place of Jahvé, before which war and rage must be hushed.
On ל for our *for*, see I. p. 173.—Ver. 5. הר *mountain* is here
plainly, from the addition *of robbery*, a *fortress* (like xxx. 8)
inhabited and adorned by tyrant-lords,—*e.g.*, with splendid
shields hung on the walls, HL. 4, 4; Ezek. xxvii. 10, 11;
Heeren's *Hist. Schriften*, Th. 2, p. 359. Firm and splendid as
may be these robber-holds, gleaming in the distance; mightier
and more splendid, though invisible, is Jahvé. This has even
now been confirmed, vv. 6, 7. For coming down from such
robber-holds and trusting in them as their God, the Assyrians
in proud array of arms fell upon Jerusalem. But the splendour
of their arms and their courage availed naught. Bare of their
arms the bravest lie in the sleep of death, having no longer at
their command their hands, once so menacingly lifted against
the sanctuary,—having, as it were, lost them, and not again
finding them (comp. cxxxvii. 5). With them lie also chariot
and horse (comp. xx. 8) motionless, as in the deepest sleep.
As in the second strophé the general thought, vv. 6, 7, was
illustrated from the last great experience, just so in the third,
vv. 9, 10.—Ver. 11 contains a very lofty conception. Jahvé
judges and punishes to this end alone, that the ungodly even
who are most raging and furious in their senselessness, may at
last come to the knowledge and therewith to the praise of
Jahvé. And although many may fall under punishment, at

least the remainder, instructed by such powerful experiences, will yet be saved; comp. lxviii. 30 sqq., B. Isa. xlv. 24. Thus more briefly and emphatically: the fury of men itself will praise thee, turning suddenly into its opposite, and as if against their will. According to this clear sense of the whole we are to read for תִּחְגֹּר after the LXX ἑορτάσει σοι, תָּחָגְּךָ, since out of תחגך if ך was written somewhat too short or read falsely, תחגר might readily arise. תִּחְגֹּר yields in itself only a highly inconvenient and strange, and in this connexion quite unsuitable sense. On בָּצַר, ver. 13, comp. Isa. xviii. 4, 5, from the same time, a very important coincidence of figures and thoughts. Also the use of the וְיֵן, ver. 9 (§ 359 c) is, according to B. Isa. xxxviii. 15, a thorough characteristic of the poets of that time.

If the preceding song was predominantly contemplative, the last, Ps. lxxv., is now quite prophetic in its style. For with the overthrow of the Assyrians all the evils and wants of the time were far from being removed. On the one hand arrogance and scorn were broken, yet on the other there was a fresh threatening of it, because in Israel itself there was much of baseness fermenting. Hence the prophets of this higher time, Jesaja, Mikha, in the midst of the rejoicing justly regard the fall of the Assyrians only as the first visible beginning of an universal judgment of God upon all peoples, and find in that very great event itself a support for the assurance that Jahvé will ever, even in the last confusions and storms, restore right, and give peace. By the truth of such prophetic discourses the poet feels himself so profoundly moved, that these thoughts are anew kindled within him, and re-echo in this song in most forcible and characteristic language (comp. Ps. xii. which originated, according to p. 198, in a similar manner). Whilst a prophet develops a series of thoughts, the poet, impressed by a single profound word, may further intensely feel its force, and express it in bold fashion; for the prophet must seek

Truth on a grand scale, while the lyric poet enters into the
intensity of particular great feelings. After in this way the
joy of that time, with the words and truths peculiarly appropriate
in this connexion, has in the beginning found expression, vv. 2-4,
he gives utterance most fully to the prophetic primary truth out
of his own heart and with his own stamp of language, vv. 5-9,
and concludes with the resolve of eternal praise to Jahvé,—a
similar prophetic diction once more powerfully resounding in
his mind, and not suffering itself to be suppressed, vv. 10, 11.
Thus there are three strophés ; but so constructed that the
intermediate one is made the most restful and most weighty,
the first and last sound only as prelude and epilogue.

1.

2   We sang praise to Thee, O God,
     we sang praise, and Thy Name is near ;
  Thy wondrous deeds were told.
" For I choose a fixed time ;
   I—I judge rightly ;
let earth and all her inhabitants tremble :
  I have set firmly their pillars."   *

2.

5   To the fools I speak : be not foolish !
    and to wicked men : lift not high the horn,
  lift not on high your horn,
    speak not with insolent neck !
for not from East and not from West,
    not from the desert, from the mountains :
but God will judge,
    casting this man down, lifting up that man !
But Jahvé holds a cup already,
    pours in of wine, foaming, of full mixture :
  —yea the dregs shall suck, drink
   all the ungodly of the earth.

3.

But I will ever praise,   10
    I will play to Jakob's God !
" And the horns of the wicked *all* do I cast down ;
    the horns of the righteous shall be exalted !"

Ver. 2 : *near is Thy name,* brought most near to us all, Thy
high being has made itself most sensible, as it can only be
manifest to man, comp. xlviii. 11 ; and immediately vv. 3, 4,
the poet now repeats what appears from the prophetic rejoicing
of that day peculiarly to belong to this place,—namely, how in
the fall of the Assyrians the eternal righteousness is revealed in
its activity and influence, inasmuch as God in this event puts
the truth before man that He judges *at the right time* and
allays the storms. On ver. 4 comp. xlvi. 3, 4, 7, the highest
mountains appear to be the eternally fixed pillars of the earth,
and firm as they are, in spite of apparent trembling,—so is the
righteousness and help of Jahvé unshakable and eternal.—
Vv. 7, 8. The *desert,* the *mountains* (מִדְבָּר in the *st. abs.* is
to be read with trustworthy copies and editions) must here
through some poetic variety correspond to the East and West.
It may be most safely assumed therefore that the barren desert
is that usually so called, that towards the South, especially
extending towards Egypt,—consequently the *South* is denoted.
But the fruitful *mountains,* according to the situation of
Palestine, designate those of Lebanon and Hermon, and therefore the *North* (comp. cxxxii. 6, Hag. i. 8, also similarly,
Ezek. vi. 14). But in this way the sentence is not completed.
Ver. 8 first contains the completion of the sense : not from
here or there, from Assyria, or Egypt, *e.g.,* comes the true judge,
so that one, if he came from one single side, might readily save
himself and flee ; but from heaven He comes, God Himself,
invisible, and surprising all, as irresistible judge. He has
already (ver. 9) made the beginning with punishment, for
many already are prostrate, stupefied by the wine of death

which Jahvé as the Host of all offers them as their proper
portion at the feast.   But this cup is full of intoxicating wine,
and *all* impious men shall be compelled to drain it.   Note
what emphasis here and in ver. 11, where the other figure,
begun in 5, 6, is completed, is laid upon the thought, that *all*
impious men must everywhere fall.   The words, ver. 9, give
certainly the foreshadowing of Jer. xxv.; and the change of
the *I* of the poet and the *I* of God, vv. 10, 11, is not more rapid
than in B. Isa. xlviii. 15.   Which *I* is meant in each place is
plain enough from the sense of the proposition in both
instances.

In point of time, the song of King Hizqia would be placed
in this connexion, which is explained in I. pp. 161 sqq.; but it
originated with an occasion remote from the otherwise lofty
thoughts stirred up by this period.

A more distant echo of the lofty inspiration of those times
may be however traced even in the rural thanksgiving song

36. Psalm lxv.

After the long drought and vain hopes of rain, an abundant
rainfall had refreshed the whole earth, ploughed land and
pasture and desert, and lifted up the standing corn which had
been quite parched by the drought, so that the richest harvest
might be looked forward to with the most joyous hope.

It is readily explicable, that universal rejoicing should arise
at this, and those who had earlier made their vows in the
Temple at Sion and prayed for rain, now should on the spot
pay those vows with thanks to Jahvé.   But the manner in
which the thought is carried out is peculiar and unusual.
According to vv. 6-9, this event fell in the period of great
movements of the people, and of a powerful convulsion of all
kingdoms and lands, in which the final conquest of the violent
and rude had taken place, and Jahvé had been proved to be
the true defence of Israel,—in short, in the times after the

great fall of the Assyrians. As Jahvé had now made Himself
known to the people amidst the disquiet and storms of the
kingdoms as the only great and almighty giver of peace, and
righteous director of the whole earth,—so at this moment in
nature. From nature as from history Jahvé is praised, and
His way of working in nature then only receives full light and
powerful meaning, when he is recognized in the higher spiritual
revelations of history. The greater and more glorious Jahvé
thus appears, the more humble must in justice the thanksgiving to Him in the Temple be; not confused and wild
jubilation, but dignified hymns of praise corresponding to the
sacredness of this spot, of those who ponder the infinite
greatness and goodness of God, as contrasted with their own
unworthiness. In such a sense the poet here becomes a worthy
interpreter of the noblest feelings of the people, assembled for
a solemn festival, and sings in its name and on its behalf a soft
and tender, very beautiful song. In the first strophé the
feelings of those who begin a worthy thanksgiving prayer are
expressed, along with an appeal to Jahvé, vv. 2-5. Then in
the second the universal praise of Jahvé, based on both nature
and history, resounds, vv. 6-9. In the third, finally and appropriately introduced, thanksgiving for the last, just experienced
benefit, with a delightful description of the joy and pleasure
everywhere being diffused by the refreshing rain, concludes the
poem, vv. 10-14.—On the evidence of the language, the song
falls probably in the beginning of the seventh century. The
style is somewhat forced and artificial, the progress in particulars no longer so easy and bounding, only raising itself to
a higher pitch at the end through the feeling of the present
high joy. But in other respects the song is extremely pregnant
in its contents and rich in thoughts. The most emphatic
brevity and depth is united with peculiar loveliness and tenderness; and we must not here forget that the priestly poetry of
which we have manifestly here a sample, may readily have an
archaic and harsh sound.

Each of the two first strophés moves in four lines and eight verse-members, these for the most part of the elegant mode of construction, but so that the concluding line in both assumes the long formation. But whilst the third strophé adopts five lines, with thirteen members, the whole is moulded (I. p. 154) as a genuine song of joy and thanksgiving. In other respects this song bears great resemblance partly to Ps. xlvi., partly to Ps. xlviii.

1.

2 To thee praise is due, O God, in Sion,
    and to Thee the vow is paid!
  Thou who hearest prayer,
    to Thee come all mortals!
  Sin oppresses me all too heavily:
    our faults—*Thou* will forget them!
5 blessing to him whom Thou choosest and adoptest
      in Thy courts to dwell;
    let us refresh ourselves at the delight of Thy house,
      at the Holiness of Thy temple!

2.

  Wondrously dost Thou vouchsafe grace to us, God
        of our salvation,
    hope of all earth's bounds, of the farthest sea!
  who with His power furnishes the mountains,
    girding Himself with might;
  softens the sea's roaring, waves' roaring,
    likewise noises of the peoples,
  that the farthest dwellers may fear thy wonders,
    sunrise and setting Thou fillest with rejoicing!

3.

10 Hast visited the earth, streaming over her,
    richly fructifying with a gush of God, full of
            water;
    their corn preparing, as Thou dost thus prepare her:

> her furrows soaking, washing down her clods,
>> under showers softening her,
>>> blessing her shoots.
> Hast crowned the year with Thy goodness,
>> and Thy steps dropped fat,
> the very pastures of the desert dropped,
>> and with rejoicing the hills are attired,
> the meadows are clothed with sheep,
>> and the valleys are covered with corn :
> they vie in exultation and—singing !

1. Ver. 2. On דְּמִיָּה as adverb : quietly, quietly resigned, see lxii. 2. But this would not readily suit in this place, and the expression is better with the LXX, דֹּמִיָּת being read, as *part.* from דמה *be like, fitting.*—Ver. 3. All mortals who come with thanks to Him who hears their vows, are simply all who lived at that time in Juda, great and small, for all without distinction solemnize this feast of thanksgiving. But it is self-intelligible that we are by this expression directed especially to the inhabitants of Jerusalem, as also the further words, ver. 5, compared with Ps. xv. 1 (pp. 84 sq.), still more closely suggest. But every community that approaches to the Holiest must before everything feel its unworthiness (עֲוֺנֹת דְּבָרֵי *matters of sin,* expresses, according to § 286 *b* taken generally "sinful things," related to and arising out of sin). Therefore it begins here, ver. 3, the closer address with this, and hopes only from the Divine grace forgiveness, ever highly sensible of the blessing by which it is permitted to enjoy in the Temple the delight of the Divine nearness. And this is the more expressive, because at that time the exile in the wider sense had already begun, and many, hindered by it, could not get to the festival at Jerusalem, Isa. xi. 11, 12 ; Ps. l., xxxiv. 2. The *sing.,* interchangeable with the *plur.,* when the congregation speaks of itself, is here and there so found in some later songs, xliv. 2 sqq., comp. lxxx. 15-20 ; although the connexion

is here more abrupt than in other places, and the LXX with some copies read the *plur.*

2. Ver. 6. ענה is closely connected with בְּ־ : listen with something, *i.e.*, listening, give or grant something, as cxviii. 5, cxliii. 1. On צֶדֶק, see on xxiv. 5. Note well how throughout, in songs of this period, the wide compass of Jahvé's power presents itself to the feeling of the inhabitants of the earth : Thou hope *of all ends* of the earth and *of the sea of the distant ones,* where at the end of the earth, on the ocean the furthest men do dwell. Comp. Isa. xi. 11, 12. Thus the first words of this strophé, ver. 6 *a,* allude to the rich blessing of which in the third only the poet further speaks. But the matter of further significance likewise brought out in ver. 6 *b,*—is alone by itself of sufficient importance to fill the whole following contents of this strophé, vv. 7-9. It is pre-eminently the sweetness and gentleness of the Divine power which is here brought out, conformably to the object of the song,—how He girds Himself with power and strength to make again fast the shaking mountains, and again compose the roaring waves, comp. lxxv. 4, Isa. xvii. 12. Yet on the other hand, there is mingled with this description at once a more serious element, in plain allusion to the great deliverance which Jerusalem had at that time found from the world-storm of the Assyrians. While God *girds* Himself like a hero of war *with omnipotence,* (גְּבוּרָה), *he furnishes mountains with his strength,* so that mountains which but now appeared to tremble not only again become firm, but may also afford protection to His people, with manifest allusion to the firmness of Sion, comp. Ps. cxxv. 1. Thus this forms the best transition to the *noises of the seas and of the peoples,* ver. 8, according to xlvi. 2, 3, 7 ; and there also follows, as is expressed retrospectively, ver. 9, that all must at once fear Him and yet rejoice. The מוֹצָאֵי בֹקֶר וָעֶרֶב is noteworthily expressed with brevity : in full it would run מוֹצָא בֹקֶר וּמְבֹא עֶרֶב, "uprise of the morning and setting of the evening." But because of the great

similarity of the morning and evening redness, by which the
two appear like brothers, the last is more briefly linked to the
first, מוֹצָא taking the dual (or plural).   A similar construction
is not infrequent in Arabic (comp. *Gr. Ar.* I., p. 156, note), and
especially the passages of the Qor'ân adduced in *Lehrb.* § 180 *a*,
also *djaban*, the month Ragáb, and the following *kamran*,
"the moon-brothers," *i.e.*, moon and sun (*Ibn-Khacan*, p. 57,
3, 200) and in Indian, as *sandhî,* in the dual, the morning and
evening rednesses, *Man.* 2, 69, 78, *pitarau*, "father and
mother," *parentes*, and other instances of the kind.   According
to the more ancient figure of עַרְבַּיִם the time of the setting of
the sun, and bordering upon this, צָהֳרַיִם *noon* in the wider
sense.

3. The last strophé depicts the last piece of prosperity in
two stages : ver. 12 returns to the beginning of ver. 10.
The פֶּלֶג is the second object both to תְּשֹׁקְקֶהָ and to תַּעְרְנָה
(§ 283 *b*).   In the following תָּכִין there is a play of thought
and of words.   *Thou preparest their, i.e.,* man's *corn*, as
necessary for men, which was about to be dried up and perish,
for the harvest, *because Thou dost thus prepare it, i.e.,* the
earth, namely as is described in detail ver. 11, § 280 *a*, 350 *a*.
The הֵכִין is throughout in this song equivalent to *furnish,
prepare, fit out*, both in ver. 7 and here twice in ver. 10.   But
here it gives rise to the play of words and thoughts that God
furnishes the crops which had become weak and sickly for the
later harvest, because He already *furnishes* the earth for them,
as expressed in ver. 11.—Ver. 12.   While the rain necessary
for the harvest, now at last falls (as latter rain) in a year which
at the beginning had great promise, and in the highest
abundance, God has, as it were, crowned the year with his
goodness.   And everywhere, whither this blessing of God had
come, or whither it is felt that God Himself has come with
blessing,—His steps drop with fatness, superfluity, even in the
unfruitful pastures of the desert (Job xxxviii. 26, 27) ; even
the flocks appear more joyous and more numerous.   The

plural of the reflexive יִתְרוֹעֲעוּ can scarcely be rendered more briefly than is above attempted.

3. The last times of the kingdom.

But notwithstanding these facts, the times—in what concerns the condition of the people and the existing kingdom—soon again become more perplexed, feeble, and unhappy. The elevation of the people above spoken of towards the end of the eighth century soon passed away. The prosperous rule of Hizqia was followed by the long melancholy period of Manasse, during which the people sank into that condition of deepest confusion, the beginnings and origins of which reached up to earlier times. For the more powerfully the nobler prophetic element of the ancient religion was by degrees aroused, and the deeper the influence of the great prophets of the eighth century,—especially in the elevation of the people under Hizqia—impressed itself on all relations, the more decisively did the inferior element which yet clave to the ancient religion, or in the course of time had been added to it, strive for dominance. The heathen nature, not yet fully vanquished, forced its way into the light with the more violence and menace, the less strong and enduring the kingdom became, and the more, by the invasion of foreign powers, heathenism was favoured in Palestine. There may, indeed, have come from the stranger, along with many evils, much that was good and useful in the lower things of life; but since frivolity and ignorance of higher truths sought at that time, mostly on the side of the innovators, to burst the old bonds,—so on the other side, among the conscientious and faithful the contradiction and opposition became more severe. A violent struggle is kindled, troubling the innermost relations of the kingdom and of the house, the parties stand in fierce and irreconcilable opposition, embitterment and hostility pervade everything, and the few faithful are often assailed by severe persecution. The party of the faithful does indeed attain an external reformation under

Josia, and Holy Scripture becomes from that time generally more known and read, and therein a firmer meeting ground for the faithful is established. But the division of parties becomes thereby for the moment only the more pronounced and irreconcilable; while in that very external reformation lay concealed the new temptation to be contented with the externals of the ancient religion, and to take shelter behind the appearance of piety, and people and kingdom, in the midst of these ceaseless destructive struggles, suffer incréasingly and approach their end.

As the whole life of the people now at last issues in this struggle, and the noblest endeavour of the spirit is narrowed down to it, the songs which are preserved from the beginning of the seventh century in ever greater number, must bear the strongest traces of it. The ancient restfulness and dignity disappear more and more, the pure loftiness of earlier untroubled times; even in song is depicted the strained and bitter state of feeling, the convulsion and irreconcilable alienation, the whole dark suffering of the period, and the stamp of the language tends to sharpness and violence. We see here many of the most faithful reverers of Jahvé and of the most undaunted prophets, through their inflexible resistance against the increasing wickedness and perversion of the time, thrown into a whirlpool of suffering. All sufferings and griefs of the time rush in a mass upon the few who had determined most sharply to oppose its crimes and blacknesses. And it is no wonder that under these sufferings,—especially among those faithful who have not yet achieved, like the poet of Pss. xvi., xlix., the eternal hope which vanquishes death itself,—the horror of despair should threaten, and the most grievous complaint should break forth. Nevertheless, faith is for the most part victorious, most nobly, and in the most beautiful form, in the songs sung possibly by a prophet; since in the prophet lived the higher, clearer consciousness, most immediately and most powerfully, which was the impulse of the faithful, Pss. lvi., lvii.

In several songs we see only the conflict in general,—the

warding-off, the revolt, the cry for help against evil, and the longing for better things, Pss. v., xxvi., xxviii. ; from others manifold dangers are apparent, deep sufferings and sore conflict, when exposed it might be to the biting scorn of foes, or to the dread of a deadly sickness, Pss. cxl.—cxlii., lv., xxxi., xxxv., xxxviii., lxxxviii. From the excess of grief and the too severely wounded feelings, there springs up here and there amidst the fierce division of parties a flash of imprecation, while distress, incapable of self-solution, turns back against its cruel author, lv. 16, 24, v. 11, xxix. 4, comp. xli. 11 *b*. But with chastising severity pure prophetic truth rises up against all such perversions in the most manifold ways, involuntarily flashing forth along with the prayer for help, Ps. lxiv., comp. above Ps. xii., as a thundering voice against wickedness, Pss. lii. l., as biting scorn and contempt for vice, Ps. lviii. And in spite of all provocations and distresses the higher repose and blessedness now and again obtains the pure and untroubled victory, Ps. xxxvi.—These songs are also to be recognized by the fact that here and there an echo of older words and verses is heard. We place here, following as far as possible the times and the poets, in the first place,

A. 37-39. Pss. cxl.—cxlii.,

a series of songs of such similar contents and of a stamp so uniform,* that it cannot be doubted they are of the same poet; again, such relations are brought to light in all of them that no real difficulty is to be seen why the same poet should not have composed them at brief intervals, as, moreover, in the succession of time these songs might very

---

* The figurative idioms of פַּח, the *noose*, cxl. 6, cxli. 9, cxlii. 4, very strongly distinguish this poet. This word is, with exception of 'Amôs and Hosea, very rare in old writers, including Jesaja, and is not frequent in such connexions until the later Psalm-poets and other writers. A similar note is the fact that all these three songs bear no trace of a retrospect of Jerusalem ; perhaps because the poet belonged to the kingdom of the Ten Tribes.—In other respects, the language of these songs is related to that of Pss. xvi., xvii., xlix. : but we cannot discern the same poet in these.

well follow one another according to the present order. This
presumed, the occasion of the songs, so far as we can learn
from themselves, was thus brought about. At a time when the
heads of the party of the faithful and conscientious are persecuted extremely, and their community broken up in the most
fearful manner (clxi. 5-7), the poet, as it appears a prince or
eminent warrior (cxlii. 8, at the end), would be also overthrown
by the multitude of the light-minded who had now come into
power. It is desired to bring him over to the ruling party,
and it is hoped that by suitable means this object may be readily
attained ; for probably the poet had not previously been the
very warmest and most strenuous adherent of the other party.
(clxi. 5.) It is therefore sought to terrify him by a threatening
accusation (cxl. 4, 13), or again to flatter him (cxli. 4) ; in
short, a variety of snares are laid in order to tempt him, or, if
this be impossible, to destroy him (cxl. 6, cxli. 9, 10, cxlii. 4).
But these very trials only excite the more powerfully the better
feeling of the poet, and instead of giving himself up to evil
seductions, he becomes only the more intensely conscious of
Divine truth, and turns the more hopefully to Jahvé. Yea, he
would rather take reproaches and chastisement for his earlier
lukewarmness and imperfection from the party of the faithful
to which he now purely inclines, than yield to the alluring
seduction (cxli. 5). And when, amidst such steadfastness, his
enemies at last treat him in the most dreadful manner, cast
him into close confinement, and there leave him to starve
(cxlii. 8) : his bosom, amidst the storm without, in the nearness
of death, though urgent and panting for deliverance, fails not
nor doubts of Jahvé. To observe this unfolding of the inner
mind of the poet in the progress of the action itself, affords
here a peculiar pleasure. For we have few songs so closely
attached to one another, which, like particular members of one
inseparable whole, reveal the individual stirrings of the noble
soul, pulsing on with the movements of an extraordinary time,
but in itself unchangeable.—It is difficult to ascertain more

16

exactly the time and the poet; but most probably the sense of the songs would belong, if not yet to the kingdom of the Ten Tribes, to the times of the rule of Manasse. The language also is devoid of any trace of an imitation of older songs.

Ps. cxl. Twice the persecuted one cries, as out of the deepest distress, to Jahvé, each time depicting those by whom he sees himself so mercilessly pursued; more fully, vv. 2-4, 5, 6; then first he begins in the two following small strophés to become conscious of the grounds of his confidence in God. Nevertheless, he is again so powerfully moved, in the midst of his address, by the thought of the life-danger which threatens him through such foes, vv. 7-9, 10-12, that at last, with a few brief powerful words expressive of up-looking to God, and not till then, he regains entire repose of heart, vv. 13, 14.—In consistency with the great disquiet of the moment, the stream of his language gushes forth in a somewhat long series of five hasty strophés, of which each carries six verse-members, and the last only is shorter.

1.

2   Set me free, Jahvé, from evil men,
           from rude men preserving me,
       who think evil in their heart,
           every day stir up wars,
       have sharpened tongues like serpents,
           conceal the dragon's venom on their lips! *

2.

5   Protect me, Jahvé, from the hands of the wicked man,
           preserving me from rude men,
       who meditate to overthrow my steps!—
       Proud men have hidden cord and nooses for me,
           stretched a net on the side of the track,
           laid snares for me. *

3.

I say to Jahvé: my God art Thou:
    take heed, Jahvé, of my loud supplication!
Jahvé the Lord is the strength of my salvation,
    covering for my head on the day of arming,
Grant not, Jahvé, the wishes of the wicked man,
    let not his scheme succeed that they conquer! *

4.

The poison of those encircling me—   10
    let them be covered with the perdition of their lips!
let coals be hurled upon them,
   let them fall into the fire,
     into pitfalls that they may not arise!
The slanderer shall not stand on the earth,
    the cruel man—evil hunts him to headlong ruin!

5.

I know that Jahvé will conduct the right of the sufferer,
    the affair of the helpless!
only righteous men will give thanks to Thy name,
    upright men dwell in quiet before Thee.

. Ver. 5. *To overthrow my steps,* that I, in the matter which I defend in my life, can no more stand upright and proceed. —With the beginning of the third small strophé, ver. 7, first plainly appears the great turn in the sense of the entire song. Nevertheless the poet can express the brief, cheerful *I know* with Job (xix. 25) only quite at the end, ver. 13. And since the words, vv. 7, 8, ·contain mere contemplation, after which then only at the end of the small strophé, ver. 9, the opening powerful cry to Jahvé for help from vv. 2, 5, recurs for the third time, to resolve itself at the beginning of the fourth strophé, vv. 10, 11, completely into malediction: the סַכּוֹתָה, ver. 8 *b,* is not well taken as the second person *perf.* as if it meant *Thou hast given a covering to my head,* but as a simple denominative (§ 165 c, 173 g). Were now ראשׁ in ver. 10, as in ver. 8, the head as seat of life which the punishment must affect, especially that which comes from above, the Divine, vii. 17: instead of it in the second member,—since in reflection on the great crime the excessively agitated language some-what changes,—the person himself would be named who is to be struck. But in accordance with the sense of vv. 10-12, 3-6, the crime of the foes consisted especially in false speeches, so that the poet says: with the *destruction* that comes from their own *lips* (evil speeches) *let them be covered,* that it may completely fall upon them and bow them down, כְּסָה connected according to § 283 b; and for this very reason the ראשׁ is better taken as *poison,* according to the figure of ver. 4. Further: the K'tîb יְמִיטוּ, יְכַסְּמוֹ (lv. 4) is certainly better, because the more general expression better suits the sense, while it is sufficient and perhaps milder to name the mere punishment. יַפְּלֵם, ver. 11, and יְצוּדֶנּוּ, ver. 12, would indeed, according to this Masoretic reading, be referable to Jahvé; but there יַפְּלֵם may be read; here, on all grounds רָע is better taken as subject, giving up the Masoretic accentuation. בַּל יָקוּמוּ expresses a state (§ 341 b). מַהֲמֹר seems to denote an earthquake, Sym. and Theed. βόθυνος, *hamar, Arab.,* is shake, shatter, from which figure (comp. lv. 16). מדחפה, ver. 12, appears to be expressed, prop. shock, ruin, LXX, καταφθορά. Both words are found only in this place. *Coals,* according to xi. 6, plainly, *fire,* according to Gen. xix. 24-28, so that it forms the transition to the pits, Gen. xiv. 10.—In ver. 14 b the leading thoughts of Pss. xxvii., xxiii., are again heard, but throughout in an independent manner.

Ps. cxli. Meanwhile the attempt must be made to seduce the poet, and entice from him some hasty word or promise; for after a short introduction, vv. 1, 2, from which it is clear that the song is sung towards evening, the main portion of this prayer dwells upon this strange subject, vv. 3-7. It appears that at the royal court the more that stress was laid upon the change of mind of our poet, and the more it was sought to draw him over to the ruling party of the light-minded,—the greater was the consideration he enjoyed amongst the faithful then so severely persecuted, not only as a man, but as a poet. But the more his poetic art was in request at the court, the more does he confirm himself in the prayer, in the resolve to resist all such enticements, and the more will he be on his guard, at a time when the faithful are most sorely persecuted, against allowing songs of pleasure to be heard at the court, according to the wish of the ruling party. Therefore he concludes at last with an echo of higher hepe from the preceding song, although all around him was gathering up to a yet much more threatening danger, vv. 8-10. The style of the strophés as in the preceding song, but altogether only four, the first moreover shorter.

1.

Jahvé, I call Thee, O hasten to me !   1
   hear how loudly I cry to Thee !
Let my prayer be presented as incense before Thee,
   the lifting of my hands as an evening sacrifice !

2.

O set, Jahvé, a guard before my mouth,
   keep the doors of my lips !
incline not my heart to evil things,
   to commit deeds in wickedness
   with men who practise evil ;
and let me not taste their dainties !

3.

Let the righteous smite me with love and chastise me ; 5
   oil of anointing mollify not my head ! for still—my
      prayer sounds amidst their evils !

their judges are hurled into the hands of the rock ;
  and should it be heard that my words are delightsome ?
As if one would cleave through and rend the earth,
  our bones were spread for the jaws of hell.

4.

But to Thee, O Jahvé, Lord ! are mine eyes ;
  on Thee I trust, pour not out my life !
preserve me from the nooses which are laid for me,
  from the power of the snares of the wicked !
Into their threads may impious men fall,
  while at the same time I—I escape !

The words, ver. 2, allude to the daily evening sacrifice in the
Temple, at the time of which individuals learned more and more
to offer their prayers, comp. the *Alterthümer*, p. 132 of the second
edit. The dainty bits with which the wicked entice, ver. 4, are
readily to be understood, comp. Prov. ix. 13-18.—Ver. 5 gives
quite sharply the contrast : rather to the righteous will I turn
and follow their advice ; and if they chasten and reprove me
severely because of my previous lukewarmness, nevertheless I
know that their rod is and remains love (Prov. xxvii. 6) ; חֶסֶד
second object (§ 283 *a*). Just so : the oil of the head, wherewith at other times the head is anointed for joy and comfort,—
let it not soften my head ! I will have at present nothing
luxurious, no comfort, that the wicked offer me ; יָנִי a voluntative, according to § 224 *b*, like יָשִׁי, lv. 16, from בוא =
יָנֹה, יוֹן be soft, actively,—press, cause something to yield, make
soft, xxxiii. 10, as in German, "*weich sein*," and "*weichen*"
are connected ; therefore also actively in Hiph., "mollify,"
LXX correctly following the sense, λιπανάτω. The cause
for mourning is : because the righteous are still ever suffering
so severely, therefore the poet during their calamities must
pray. וְ עוֹד *still* is it—*that*, is only somewhat more emphatic,
comp. Zech. viii. 20, Prov. xxiv. 27, § 348 *a*.—Ver. 6 must now

manifestly describe more in detail these calamities, as still
more ver. 7. Their judges, the mightiest, the heads of the
righteous sitting in judgment, are thrown into the power of the
rock. The יְדֵי *hands,* if indeed the language were of an
actual rock, might be understood as its *sides,* or clefts, but
even then in the actual sense we should have no clear thought.
In any case this word must be figurative, as is most clearly
shown by the corresponding passages, ver. 9, lxiii. 11. But if
then it were proposed to take the rock as real, as if the sense
were : they are horribly hurled down on the rock or from it,
and, as it were, so handed over to the power of the rock, that
they are dashed in pieces by it, this fearful mode of death
having actually occurred, 2 Chron. xxv. 12, comp. cxxxvii. 9,
Hos. x. 14 ; this would be difficult to conceive, both as regards
the words and the fact. But the rock itself may stand in many
figurative ways as the dry land, unfruitful land (Prov. xiii. 15,
Job xv. 34, comp. xxiv. 8). Then the *being thrown into the
hands of the rock* or *being given up entirely* to them, will
·signify simply the bitterest want, such as is described by
another figure, ver. 8. The mode of expression is then indeed
very peculiar ; but the present three songs present much in
general of this kind ; and in any case it is noteworthy that the
rock nowhere in them denotes, as in so many songs of similar
character, in Davidic fashion, refuge.—In the second member,
וְשָׁמְעוּ (§ 349 *b*) may very well refer, as a question, to the
future ; and,—whilst the poet asks whether, when the heads of
the righteous have so ignominiously perished, it should be
heard that he is singing pleasant songs at the luxurious court,
—he now actually does that for which he had desired the
strength in vv. 3, 4 ; he guards strenuously against profaning
as it were the voice of his song, and doing anything against
the faithful. But indeed the suffering of the friends to which
the poet will remain faithful is too terrible to allow of his not
alluding to it by a further harsh figure : and if, ver. 6 *a*, the
language were used of an actual dashing to pieces on the

rocks, it might be supposed that the poet included himself, in deep fellow-feeling, amongst the number of the already slain heads, exclaiming : we are already as if reduced to ruins, our bones are seen scattered on the ground as on a field of battle (Ps. liii. 6), given up to the jaws of death, as if they had been as pitilessly cut through, scattered and thrown about, as the ploughman cuts up the earth, and throws it about, 2 Chron. xxv. 12. This explanation appears not impossible in these certainly very compressed and abruptly uttered verses, and is suitable to Ps. liii. 6 ; nevertheless, the explanation of the living ones, ver. 7, better agrees with ver. 6 *a* and with the words themselves, as though they were so emaciated and dispirited by constant fear and fasting, that their bones stand far out and apart, as if their sufferings had pierced through them as terribly as the earth is ploughed through, sundering their body, and in this way giving them up to death. Comp. xxii. 15, 18, *Hamâsa*, 246, ver. 1 fr. *Fâkihat Chul.* pg. 13, 5 v. u. כְּמוֹפְלָח is : *like one who splits,* i.e., as if one splits.

But only the more convulsively does the poet tear himself away from all such melancholy pictures and thoughts of death, to turn back his hope, vv. 8-10, upon God alone, and conclude the song in consistency with its beginning, and thus nothing further follows but the most glorious echo of what is most beautiful from the preceding song. כִּי may as an interjection deny, like *imo, no! yet!* or *but!* Lam. iv. 15 ; Isa. ii. 6 ; viii. 23 ; xlviii. 2. The *sing.* suffix in מכמריו ver. 10, is most readily referred to פַּח, ver. 9, the threads of the noose, of the net.

Ps. cxlii. At a later time, under ever increasing oppression, new outburst of supplication, this time merely a most urgent cry for help at hand ; for the poet already sees himself forsaken by all men, languishing in lonely confinement ; the whole forming but *one* impression, breaking forth in three small strophés, each of six mostly very short verse-members.

While these three songs thus gradually become shorter, they are related to one another very similarly to the way in which Ps. vi. is related to Ps. xiii. See above, pp. 183 sqq.

1.

Loudly I to Jahvé cry,
> loudly I to Jahvé pray ;   2
pour forth before Him my sighs,
> tell my distress before Him,
while my spirit becomes faint :
> > yet *Thou* knowest my way, how snares are laid
> > > for me in the path that I walk !

2.

Though I look to the right hand and behold :   5
> I have none there who knows me ;
lost is my refuge,
> not one asks after my soul.
I cry to Thee, Jahvé !
> > I consider, Thou art my refuge, my portion in the
> > > land of the living.

3.

Observe my crying, for I am very miserable ;
> deliver me from the persecutors,
because they are too mighty for me ;
Let my soul escape from the prison,
> that I may praise Thy name,
the righteous wait upon me, that Thou shouldst do
> > me good !

The circumstances under which the poet hopes for a hearing, are, according to ver. 4, first his complete exhaustion, secondly the certainty that Jahvé knows his way, or as it is immediately explained, knows well how dangerous is his life-way through the craft of his foes. If in ver. 5, הַבֵּיט and רְאֵה were imperative, one does not see who would be suitably

addressed, since to suppose God here would be unseason-
able; in that case too לִימִינִי would be found; therefore better
(§ 328 *a*) as inf. abs. (in which case רָאֹה must be read) : *to look
to the right and see!* *i.e.*, though I never so earnestly—behold,
there is none who recognized me, who did not overlook and
despise me, none who as friend and advocate defended me in
need; for a friend, according to this, places himself as a
defender on the right side of the accused person (but the later
custom is different, Zech. iii. 1; Ps. cix. 6). On חֶלְקִי, ver. 6,
comp. xvi. 5 sqq.—הִכְתִּיר, ver. 8, is not properly surround, and
then lurk, wait (borrowed from the hunter or warrior, who on all
sides watchfully lurks for his prey), but from קרר, קתר = כתר,
as Piel, Job xxxvi. 2, and as here the LXX and Aq. rightly
translate. The poet was unquestionably a man of consideration,
whose fall or deliverance must be a sign of the time.

40-50. PSALMS LV., V., LXIV., LII., XXXVI.; LIV., LXI., LXIII., LVI.— LVIII.

The greatest probability presents itself, that all these songs
are of the same poet, as they, even in the present Psalter, with
the exception of v., xxxvi., stand all very near to one another
and form the main stock of the collection, Pss. lii.—lxiv. We
might most readily conjecture another poet possibly in Pss.
lvi. and lvii. alone, because their stamp is somewhat more
elevated, were not the other resemblances too great. We
view the poet, even if in very different situations, as nevertheless generally the same in position, feeling, and impulse.
Obviously he is a prophet; in Pss. lvi. and lvii. he allows
himself in his conflict with the world plainly to be recognized
as such; and as with the prophet the word and the truth is the
highest thing, so he fights in every instance especially against
the perverted tongue, lying and cunning. No earlier poet
speaks so constantly of the false *tongue*, v. 10; hi. 4, 6;
lv. 10, 22; lvii. 5; lxiii. 12; lxiv. 4, 9. Comp. similar
expressions only in xii. 3, 4; cxl. 4; lix. 8; xxxi. 19; cxx. 2, 3.

But his song rises with perfect purity to prophetic height and origin, whether it be only in passing over into urgent aspirations, xxxvi. 13 ; lxiv. 6-11, or with design throughout, Pss. lii., lviii. As prophet further, he best knows what the Divine work in the human race is, how it is known and advanced, lii. 8, 9 ; lviii. 11, 12 ; lxiv. 10, 11 ; and his most severe morality, which everywhere shines out, his sacred earnestness strikes the party of the light-minded and violent frequently with crushing blows, with the fiery glow of unceasing malediction, v. 11 ; lv. 16, 24 ; lii. 7, 8 ; lviii. 11, 12 ; lxiii. 10, 11. But such outbursts in these times are very readily pardonable in him in the character of a prophet.—As such, he once lived in the neighbourhood of the sacred place as its diligent visitor, and its delight and protective security is everywhere most vividly present to his eyes, v. 4, 8 ; lv. 14 ; lii. 10, 11 ; liv. 8 ; xxxvi. 9 ; lxi. 5 ; lxiii. 3. But while we see him in Pss. lv., v., lii., quite plainly, living in Jerusalem itself, rejoicing in the delights of the Temple,—according to Pss. lxi., lxiii., he is manifestly wandering in the distance, with mournful recollections of the Temple, and thus gives one of the first examples of the sorrows and struggles of the exiles. But certainly he went into exile long before the destruction of the Temple, and he may have sung under Josia and his immediate successor, since according to Pss. lxi., lxiii., Jerusalem was not yet destroyed,—to which the words, especially lv. 11,—comp. with Ps. lix. explained below, point. —Add to the above, that in particular features the stamp of the language admits of the conclusion that the author is the same. The phrase *in the shadow* or *in the covert of His wings*, is as frequent here, xxxvi. 8, lvii. 2, lxi. 5, lxiii. 8, as it is otherwise rare, xvii. 8 ; הלל *Pi.* and *Hipt.* very freely used lvi. 5, 11 ; lxiii. 6 ; lii. 3 ; lxiii. 12 ; lxiv. 11 ; שׁוֹרְרָי (see above on Ps. xxvii.) is nowhere so frequent as in these songs, and in like manner the plur. הַוּוֹת, with the exception of v. 10, lv. 12, lii. 4, lvii. 2, is only further found in xxxviii. 13

xci. 3, xciv. 20, a word whose singular, lii. 9, is likewise rare. עוֹלָה *wickedness* is found only in lviii., iii., lxiv., vii., חלק *smooth*, in the figurative sense, only in v. 10, lv. 22, xxxvi. 3, by the side of xii. 3, 4 ; the interchange of סוּר and רֶגֶשׁ, with the exception of the remoter resemblance, Ps. ii. 1, 2, only in lv. 15 ; lxiv. 3, whilst רגשׁ is generally rare in this signification.

Further, אוֹיֵב so shortly, *the enemy*, for *my enemy, my enemies*, usual elsewhere, recurs in lv. 4, lxi. 4, lxiv. 2, elsewhere only in vii. 6, Ex. xv. 9 (whence perhaps it is taken, as יִשְׁרֵי לֵב, xxxvi. 11, lxiv. 1, and other instances from Davidic songs), possibly about the same time, ii. 10, xliii. 3, xxxi. 7, and later cxliii. 3 ; lxxiv. 3, 10, 18. אַנְשֵׁי דָמִים וּמִרְמָה in like manner recurs, v. 7, lv. 24 (comp. the simpler דָמִים אַנְשֵׁי, xxvi. 9, lix. 3, thence repeated later, cxxxix. 19), דֹּבְרֵי כָזָב, v. 7, lviii. 4, the figure of the fat, xxxvi. 9, lxiii. 6, and other instances of the kind.

In the structure of the verse the recurrence of the last word to the first after intermediate sentences, is peculiar to this poet, lii. 11, lvii. 4. On the whole the poet's art tends decidedly to the structure of longer lines than in the preceding poet. And although in the times when the ·Temple had long been standing, poets speak ever more frequently of vows and their discharge, yet the manner in which this is done, liv. 8, lvi. 13, lxi. 6, 9, betray again the same hand. In this way these eleven songs plainly, according to all indications stand apart as songs of the same poet. If it is sought to compare therewith those partly similar elsewhere, as Pss. cxl.—cxlii., too much that is dissimilar will always be found. Yet probably the interpolated lines in Ps. xxvii. (pp. 176 sqq.), of the suppliant song of a devout man pursued by extreme party hatred, according to all signs, belong likewise to our poet.—We arrange them here on the assumption that those still referring to Jeruaalem are the earlier.

The long song, Ps. lv., leads us very deeply into the inner

contests and dangers of Jerusalem,* in the last century before its destruction. Among the whole people, high and low, continuous misunderstanding and endless schism, so that friend despises and betrays friend; a condition of things like that depicted by a prophet of those times in his manner, B. Mikha, vii. 1-6,† Peculiarly forcible is the schism of those who take a frivolous view of the ancient religion, or entirely give it up, who even shun not the base arts of dissimulation and of deceit, in order to injure the more serious, or utterly hunt them down. By such faithlessness and villany the poet now sees himself to be unexpectedly surrounded; and it admits no doubt, according to vv. 14-15, 21-22, that a friend, whom he had hitherto heartily trusted, had suddenly deceived him, shamefully slandered him, and thrown him into the most urgent danger. Already the persecutors took counsel how they might utterly destroy him and his following, ver. 10. Thus between the most fearful oppression from without and the most violent emotion at the unworthy treatment of his friend, and the brutishness of the people, he here cries for help to Jahvé, that he may recover inner repose and serenity in Him. The song shows predominantly the highest trouble and disquiet, somewhat soothed towards the end. But even when the language is more composed, there arises again unexpectedly the excitement, hard to be mastered, concerning the friend's unworthiness, vv. 20 sqq. Not till quite at the close does complete tranquillity set in. First, urgent entreaty to God for help from the threatening danger, which has so terrified the peaceful poet and in so deadly a manner, that he longs to be able to flee far away from the populous and as it were beleaguered city, into the desert, vv. 2-9 (2-4; 5-9). Then, on a closer view of the civil discord, and the villany of the light-minded, therewith connected,—the poet, keenly affected, cannot refrain,

---

* For by *the city*, ver. 10, certainly Jerusalem is to be understood, comp. § 277 *b.*

† Comp. on this prophet the *Jahrbb. der Bibl. Wiss.*, xi., p. 29.

in his violent passion, from desiring at Jahvé's hands, the annihilation and punishment of all evil counsels and deeds, vv. 10-16 (10-12; 13-16). Only after this outburst does he return more calmly to himself, and seeks and finds in entire trust in Jahvé, strength and repose, silencing his rising reflections on the unworthiness of his opponents, vv. 17-24 (17-20; 21-22; 23-24). Thus there are three long strophés of eight two-membered verses each, but so that the middle one is the most emotional, and hence (if no verse has been lost) broken off at the end as before a mighty spasm, and possibly shorter by a verse; the last is the longest.—The more detailed circumstances of the situation of this poet cannot unfortunately be now discovered; but that the song falls in times when even the great men were greatly degenerated through foreign conquest or ascendancy, is shown by vv. 13, 15.

1.

2 Observe, O God, my prayer,
    and hide Thyself not from my supplication!
  incline to me, listen to me
    —I am dizzy in my sighs and must complain!
  before the enemy's cries, before the oppression of the
            impious man,
    because they cast destruction upon me, and in wrath
            persecute me!

5 My heart turns in my bosom,
    and death's pains have fallen upon me;
  fear pierces me and trembling,
    that a shuddering covers me,
  and I think: would I had wings like the dove,
    that I might flee and—come to rest!
    —yea, far hence would I flee,
      would pass the night in the desert!—
  that I might hasten to a refuge for me
    from the rushing wind, from the storm!

2.

Bring to naught, O Lord, split asunder their tongues ! 10
   for violence and brawls I saw in the city ;
by day and night they surround it on its walls,
   and destruction and misery is in herself :
corruption is in her midst,   *not*
   and from her market departs oppression and deceit !—
For it is not a foe that scorns me, that I might bear it,
   my hater shows not pride against me, that I might
               conceal myself from him :
No, thou, a man as my equal,
   my friend and my acquaintance,
we took sweet counsel together,
   walked together into God's house in fellowship—
Death surprise them ! may they sink alive into hell !
   because wickedness is in their storehouse, their
               bosom.—

3.

I.—I will cry to God,
   and Jahvé will help me ;
evening and morning and at noon I groan and com-
               plain !
   (so He hears my voice,
redeems by salvation my life from the stress of battle,
   because they made war against me with many)
may God hear and bow them down Who is   20
             throned from of old,   *
   —them, who have no fidelity to their oath, and who
   fear not God !
He has laid his hand on his friends,
   has profaned his covenant :
smooth are the butter-lips of his mouth—and war his
               heart ;
   softer than oil are his words — and yet drawn
   swords !—

> Cast upon Jahvé thy care and *He* will care for Thee,
> will never suffer the righteous to totter!
> and Thou, O God, wilt plunge them into the pit of the
> grave ;
> the men of blood and deceit live not half their life ;
> but I—trust in Thee !

1. What is first briefly suggested by the second member of ver. 3, is further developed in vv. 5, 6. On the —â of emotion in אָחִימָה in the signification *I must*, see § 228 *a*. In the drawing of the fine picture, vv. 7-9, the sentence, ver. 8, is manifestly interpolated, or rather ver. 9 resumes the complete picture in the same style of language in order to complete it: as the dove flies before storm and tempest into its place of refuge, so might the poet flee before the storm of his foes. The last words from ver. 9 hence likewise point back to ver. 4, as they immediately prepare for the following, vv. 10 sqq., and it can be in nowise doubtful how the מִן is to be taken. מִפְלָט לִי is any place, which may serve as a place of deliverance to me ; but שׁכן, ver 7, may, standing alone, signify *come to rest*, lxviii. 19, Prov. vii. 11.

2. The second strophé begins and concludes with the urgent wish for the bringing to naught of the wicked, so that in the interval the causes are more calmly explained,—first with retrospect of the whole band of the light-minded, vv. 10-12, then especially with a glance at their leader, the faithless friend of the poet, vv. 13-15. And thus all the magnitude of the corruption, and the impossibility that such hardened sinners could improve, having presented themselves to the poet's mind, —at last, ver. 16, the agitation of his soul breaks forth irresistibly into the stormy wish, that all these faithless and horrible men may quickly vanish from the earth (as the old story told in Num. xvi. 32 sqq., comp. Isa. v. 14 ; Prov. i. 12), since indeed, as is more calmly added in ver. 24, it is contained in the laws of all creation that such reckless ones shorten their own life.

How the poet is surprised by this wish and this anticipation is shown also by the sudden transition thereto,—the more tranquil description which has been begun ver. 16, being broken off. The *tongue* in the first instance, ver. 10, the poet would see destroyed or split, namely the slanderous tongues of those who take evil counsel together; which, as is explained, ver. 11 *a*, is the more dangerous, because now to these internal sufferings of dissension and oppression the similar broils of the restless suburbans are added.

Were they good men, at least this external danger would warn them, but these are men who will take warning from nothing. The רֶגֶשׁ, ver. 15, in the signification of "tumult," would necessarily denote the mass of human beings thronging to the Temple; but the word manifestly corresponds here and lxiv. 3, to סוֹד; and we are to assume that the root signifies not merely *movement*, but also the running together and *assembling* (hence *mark*, feel), comp. *ragash*, Syr., and the LXX, Sym. on this passage. The reading יַשִּׁי according to the Q'rî is certainly more suitable; *delusion* came *over them*, for the notion of coming lies in עַל, and the two yield the simple notion *surprise them*. The nearest construction of verbs of deceiving with בְּ is in such cases designedly neglected. On יַשִּׁי as voluntative, comp. above, on cxli. 5, 6. The expression יְשִׁימוֹת must signify *desolations upon them!* which in this connexion where also after the conclusion of the following strophé, ver. 24, death must be spoken of, would be little suitable.—The words, ver. 11 *a*, are probably not to be understood of an actual siege, as in lix. 7, 15; such a circumstance would not be so cursorily mentioned; but of similar broils among the suburbans dwelling around the city (on its walls), whose dwelling place as outside the city is also distinguished in ver. 16, by *hamlet*, מָגוּר, and ver. 12 as רְחוֹב, *broad way* (Neh. viii. 16) from the interior of the city.*

---

* As מְגוּרָה, Hab. ii. 19, or as more original, מִמְּגֻרֹת, Joel i. 17 denotes also the *store-house* (from מגר = *gamar*, Arab., = גמל; shut together, collect),

3. After the poet's soul has thus taken an outward flight, the beginning of the third strophé shows how intensely and zealously he would on the other hand turn to Jahvé, seeking strength in Him alone. He draws hope specially from two reasons: (1) because the enemy attacks him with superior power, proud in his numbers, whilst God pities the helpless, ver. 19 (לִי מִקְּרָב) from a battle to me, *i.e.*, from a battle to which I am forced, as the following member explains); (2) because God never endures faithlessness so specially shameful as is that which the poet has experienced, so that he cannot avoid once more drawing the dreadful picture of it, almost forgetting the connexion of the song, vv. 20-22. But from this cause he tears himself from the sad picture with a pithy saying, and the more boldly resumes his hope,—although at last scarcely able to drive away the picture of the contrast, nevertheless trustful, vv. 23-24. The וַיִּשְׁמַע־פָּדָה, vv. 18, 19, is,—because of the great security with which the poet here suddenly contemplates beforehand the deliverance— expressed instead of וְשָׁמַע־יִפְדֶּה (§ 343 a): but on this very account these words are only as intermediate sentences, so that the regular strain recurs, ver. 20, in close connexion with ver. 18 a. Expression and turn of thought are very similar in our poet, lxiv. 8-11. The words, *they were against me with many* (attacked me, solitary, with many), are of similar sound to B. Jer. iv. 3.—Ver. 20. יֹשֵׁב with the LXX, read instead of וִישֵׁב, which admits of no reference here, comp. above on vii. 10. חֲלִיפוֹת, prop. *vicissitudines*, changes on both sides, reciprocities, can in this connexion be nothing else than reciprocal fidelity, sworn fidelity, or that of friendship, which

---

it may also be supposed that it is intended here to signify the same as that which is presently termed the *inward* part, namely the spirit, as the council chamber of thoughts. The word denotes indeed only the great corn-granaries, not the small, closely-shut chests; and the language here rather returns at the close of the strophé to its beginning, vv. 10 12 Yet it thus suits the nearest sense so well that I prefer it in a poet who has used a similar figure, lvi. 19. It must, too, be always considered that the poet might then allude to the expression of a song much used at that time.

rests upon reciprocal obligation and performance, comp. *jalofon,* Arab.; hence immediately, ver. 21, the profanation of the covenant is mentioned.—The יְרָב, ver. 23, without doubt a substantive like הֶרָב, vv. 19, 22 (§ 153 *a*), must, it appears, according to the whole figure, denote " burden," prop., that given, given to bear; since meanwhile it may be assumed ·that יהב = יאב, cxix. 131, the signification "longing" or "care" would still more readily follow, LXX μέριμναν, similarly *Targ.,* comp. xxii. 9; xxxvii. 5.

This great song is among those here collocated, certainly in many points of view of peculiar character both in contents and in structure and expression; and moreover stands so close to the others that we can assign it to no other poet. Hence we may most correctly suppose it to be the earliest of those pre-served to us, and that it fell in a period which was for the poet one somewhat different from that in which his next songs fall.

Ps. v. is with Ps. xxvi. the specimen of a Temple-song, such as at that time an individual possibly composed for himself; and shows, like Ps. xxvi., that even on the occasion of the visit to the Temple strong internal schisms were developed, whilst the few faithful stood over against the many vain ones who abstained from visiting the Temple, partly from indifference (for there was little external compulsion prevailing) and partly from an evil conscience. The poet, on the other hand, a diligent visitor of the Temple, begs in this morning-prayer (ver. 4), Divine strength on his difficult life-path, especially that he may not in the least exhibit a failing or a fall before those who lie in wait for him with evil intentions, and may give them no opportunity to rejoice in the overthrow of a fearer of Jahvé. To this main occasion of the prayer he does not come however until ver. 9; it is prepared and introduced by a general and urgent cry for a hearing, vv. 2-3, and more particularly by the observation,—how zealously and willingly the petitioner appears in the Temple under Divine grace,

17 *

relying upon Divine salvation and righteousness, whilst he who
shuns the light,—the wicked man for ever cast away from God's
presence,—must flee the spot whose sanctity destroys him,
vv. 4-7. First, in this blessed certainty the poet now again
prays,—since he is threatened round about by the cunning craft
and lying-in-wait of the impious men who seek to take him
with treacherous words,—for strength on his own behalf, and
that of all faithful men, in the certain hope that God will ever
deliver innocence, **vv. 8-13.** The distress of the faithful at
that time, and the shameless spirit of persecution of the vain
audacious adversaries, must already have been very great. In
pressing fear of this he who here prays in the Temple cannot
but beseech, at the beginning of the last strophé, ver. 11, with
quite special insistance, the Divine protection against it, and
its righteous Divine punishment, whilst he can only repose
in the hope of the just redress of all present human confusions.
Thus the inward unrest breaking forth with increasing violence
is in turn lighted up by the sun of eternal hope ; and his song
is shaped, after the brief introduction, into three equal strophés,
each of eight verse-members.

1.

2   Hear my words, Jahvé,
       give heed to my meditation !
    Bend to my loud complaint, my king and my God !
       for to Thee I pray.

2.

Jahvé ! early Thou hearest my voice,
    early I wait on Thee and look out ;
for not a God who loves wickedness art Thou,
    the wicked man is not Thy guest ;
fools shall never stand before Thine eyes,
    Thou hatest all evil-doers,
destroyest the speakers of lies ;
    the friend of blood and deceit Jähvé abhors.

But I—through Thy great mercy enter Thy house,
  doing homage at the holy Temple in Thy fear.
Jahvé! O lead me in Thy righteousness—because of
    them that lie in wait for me,
    O make smooth before me Thy way!
for there is nothing sincere in their mouth,
    since their heart is corruption;
  an open grave is their throat,
    for they keep a smooth tongue.

4.

Let them repay, O God, fall from their places,
    overthrow them in the multitude of their sins,
  because they rose up against Thee;
that all who trust in Thee may rejoice,
    for ever shout for joy, and Thou protectest them,
  and the friends of Thy name are mirthful in Thee,
because Thou, O Jahvé, blessest the righteous man,
  enduest him, as with the shield, with Thy favour.

חָגִיג, ver 2, as xxxix. 4.—Ver. 4, עָרַךְ, equip, prepare, without further object, is to present oneself in readiness, appear, like *apparere*, comp. with *parare; and spy* what Thou commandest, how I in following Thee may be saved (lix. 10).— Vv. 5-7 explains why the poet appears so willingly and hopefully in the Temple; because he knows that the God, whose nearness is here felt, loves not unrighteousness, affords no harbour and refuge with Himself for the wicked. (On גוּר, see § 282 *a*). Rather does he destroy for ever the impious who might dare to despise Him.—If, on the other hand, the poet, with a good conscience, appears with serenity and joy in the sanctuary, and this because he can there ever refresh and recreate himself in the contemplation of the Supreme, experiencing as a Divine gift of grace that he can use the words of ver. 8 in all innocence with new fervour before God: he is now truly able to express his deepest prayer for Divine strengthening with true faith, ver. 9 (with words quite similar to those in xxvii. 11). But here he feels himself irresistibly impelled further to explain, ver. 10, the interjected words, "because of those who lie in wait for me :" so little confidence is to be placed in their smooth words and false hearts, that a confiding spirit may readily fall into their dangerous snares as into open pits or graves—the like of which are frequently hewn out in rocks.—And the picture thus more nearly presented of these sins carries away the poet finally to such a degree that he prays the more energetically that they may be brought to naught, ver. 11, in order that all faithful ones, shielded by Jahvé, may rejoice in Him and in the manifested right, ver. 12. We must not overlook here as frequently elsewhere, the very usual passive after וֹ, § 347 *a*. Tranquillity comes with eternal truth, ver. 13; in such unsafe times the attire of Divine grace which covers the righteous is regarded above all as one of protection, and so compared with the shield. But this hope too is placed in dependence on ver. 12, in accordance with a peculiarity of our poet, which is plainly exhibited in several of his songs, at their conclusion, liv. 8, 9; lvi. 13, 14; lxiii. 12.—Further, that the חַסְדְּךָ, ver. 8, can only signify the Divine grace, and does not correspond to the יראתך *b*, is also confirmed by the favourite usage of our poet, comp. xxxvi. 6, 8, 11; lii. 3; lvii. 4, 11; lxi. 8. In this many poets follow him, but it is quite otherwise in the preceding, comp. especially cxli. 5.

To this Ps. lxiv. appears to be next related, where we see the poet still surrounded by similar circumstances. But this short song, which begins like a customary song of supplication, vv. 2-5, falls by a sudden turn into the prophetic vein, depicting the certain overthrow of the wicked and the final victory of the righteous, vv. 6-11. But the intermediate member, from the first to the second member, makes the contemplation that of the manner in which the wicked act, how they come to the ground through their own perversity and craft ; so that he who closely observes their actions may readily anticipate that the evil which they plan in order to destroy the innocent, must — in spite of their extreme foresight and prudence—fall back upon themselves, being cast upon them unexpectedly, and on that account the more fearfully and destructively, as from the hand of God. Fine description of this sudden turn of things against all conjectures of the wicked. One might be tempted, because of the resemblance of this Psalm and Ps. vii., to derive it from David, did not a closer comparison contradict this view.

The structure of the strophés is substantially the same as in the preceding song, only the third and last is somewhat shorter; there is no introduction.

1.

O hear, O God, me as I groan forth my cry,   2
    preserving my life from the fear of the enemy,
protecting me from the counsel of the ill-disposed,
    from the perjury of the evil-doers,
who like to the sword sharpen their tongues,
    bend as their bows bitter speech,
to shoot innocent men in the corners,   5
    to shoot them unexpectedly without fear.

2.

They fix on evil counsel,
    confer to hide nets,
" who will take heed of them ?" they think ;
they search through wicked deeds,
    are ready with most subtle enterprise—
and every mind and heart is deeply closed up :
then God shoots them with an arrow,
    their blows come unexpectedly !

3.

And overthrown, their tongue overreaches them,
    all their admirers flee away :

10   so do all men fear,
        proclaim God's deed
            and perceive His work.
     Rejoicing in Jahvé, the righteous man will trust Him;
        all the upright in heart will boast.

In open war, according to ver. 5, the enemies do not live,
but by slanders they would craftily overthrow the poet at a
convenient time; on יָרְחוּ § 350 b. — Vv. 6, 7. Striking
description of the extremely cunning, cautious manner with
which the wicked prepare their misdeed; they first closely
take counsel for the deed, thinking that no one (not even
God) will observe them (לָמוֹ, half indirectly spoken, § 338 a,
comp. lix. 8), and thus fix in secret a firm resolve. Yet again
they investigate the plan most closely before its execution, and
now they have made the most thorough examination and found
all safe. Now comes the solemn sacred moment of execution,
for which all wicked men wait, strained in silent expectation
and anxiety to the highest degree, as for the hour which shall
at last reward so much foresight and trouble (just as the bird-
catchers are silent in secret expectation when they have all
ready—Wilkinson's *Manners of the Ancient Egyptians,* Vol. III.,
pp. 45 sq.): but during the crisis there comes at the right
time Divine punishment, striking the keener and more destructive a blow, because it comes unexpectedly in the moment
when the wicked might believe they had now gained everything. The arrow which they secretly desire to cast against
others, vv. 4, 5, strikes themselves. Because prophetic fancy
foresees this issue as if accomplished, soon with תָּמְנוּ, ver. 7,
the *perf.* is introduced, and is continued until ver. 10; in
ver. 11 the usual style returns. חֵפֶשׂ מְחֻפָּשׂ inquired inquiry,
i.e., completed, therefore very close (as in Ex. xii. 9; Isa. xxviii.
16; Prov. xxx. 24; comp. § 313 c) as accusative of definition
(comp. Jer. xxvii. 8) dependent on תָּמְנוּ, which is not the
first person plural, but as in Lam. iii. 22, arose from תַּמּוּ; at

least this most readily suits the connexion, comp. § 83 *b*. Otherwise we must recognize here an interjected speech of the people " we are ready " ⋯ פְּתָאֹם, ver. 8, is, against the accents, to be taken with the second member. *Their tongue comes over them*, an additional proposition to the main verb, *he* or more indefinitely *they* (§ 319 *a*, comp. lxiii. 11) *are cast down so that the sin of their own tongue* (lying), wherewith they would destroy others, according to 4, 5,—comes upon them; comp. in words and sense similar and yet very dissimilar matter, cxl. 10, 11.

If the language in the previous songs often suddenly turned aside from the whole herd of the wicked to a single individual, as if the poet had such a ringleader of the others peculiarly in his eye, lv. 14, 21, 22, v. 9, lxiv. 9.—Ps. lii. contains nothing further than the bold, seriously threatening outburst of poetic indignation at the perversity of this individual who rules by slander and deceit, this proud man who has inherited riches for evil,—possibly a high placed potentate or servant of the state; for the purely prophetic commentary on this poetic lamentation is Isa. xxii. 16 sqq.; that the tyrant lived in Jerusalem is clear from the contrast, vv. 10, 11. The excited spirit of the poet dwells only on the contemplation and the castigation of this perversity; the tyrant speaks and acts as if the delivering grace of God had been lost in the world; and therefore the poet must now the more energetically appeal to Him that it may remain firm, so that the whole sense of the song already properly compresses itself into the first brief utterance of ver. 3. But then he more calmly explains the tyrant's perversities, and how in requital of them God on His side will severely chastise the fool for the destruction and warning of all, with which the language again gradually rises to a higher pitch, vv. 4-9 (4-6; 7-9); and finally adds, because he was certainly himself one of the many sacrifices of the folly of this tyrant, a few words of personal consolation and encouragement, vv. 10, 11.

The three strophés of this song also conform to the measure of eight verse-members; the last only is here more shortly broken off.

1.

3   Why boastest thou of evil, thou tyrant?
        the grace of God is abiding!—
    Thy tongue meditates destruction;
        like to a wetted knife, thou intriguer!
5   lovest evil more than good,
        lying more than to speak rightly,
    lovest all pernicious words,
        Thou deceitful tongue!

2.

So may God for ever root thee out,
    seize thee and carry thee away from the tent;
        root thee out of the living land;
    that beholding this, righteous men may be afraid,
        but laugh at him:
" Behold the man who makes not God his protection,
    and trusted in the fulness of his riches,
        was proud in his blind greed!"

3.

10   But I am like a green olive tree in the house of God,
        I trust in God's grace, ever, aye!
    will praise Thee for ever, that Thou didst work,
        and wait on Thy name, because it is dear,
        before the face of Thy saints!

That the ancient word גִּבּוֹר, *hero*, ver. 2, sank down just as גֶּבֶר, *man*, from its early high and noble signification,—gradually sank in these later times through the guilt of potentates, to the half scornful, half evil signification, in which also among us our ancient *hero* is sometimes used,—I have already observed on Prov. xxx. 1; Isa. xxii. 17.—The figure of the

sword, of the sharp knife, ver. 4, and similar ones in poets
of this time frequently describe the sharp hurtful speech of
slanderers, cxl. 4, lxiv. 4, lvii. 5, lviii. 5, lix. 8; on ver. 6 *b*
comp. cxx. 3. בַ, ver. 7, frequently is thus used for what is
reciprocal, for what is done or is to be done in compensation on
the other hand, Am. iv. 6; Job vii. 11. Now apparently the
tyrant lives in abiding prosperity, deeply rooted and blooming
like the soundest tree (Job v. 3); but God will wrench him
forth with higher power, though he were like the firmest tree,
so that he can remain nowhere in a tent, nowhere among the
living upon earth, comp. Isa. xxii. 17 sqq. But *the* tent which
the poet has here is his eye according to old poetic phraseology
(xxvii. 5, 6) is the Temple itself.—חִתַּח, or more strongly
expressed, חָתַף, is seize, lay violent hands upon. The nearer
does the comparison of the faithful man with the ever-green
olive tree lie, ver. 10. Thus does he look green and shines,
but not so greatly for and by himself, as in the congregation and
the Temple, prospering by God's blessing, and ever waiting upon
Him, xcii. 13, 14. But unquestionably such olive trees and
others stood near the old Temple, and were there most carefully
tended.—The phrase *workest,* ver. 11, actively, that is for man's
good, becomes gradually more frequent in this period in individual poets in this sharp, short acceptation, comp. xxii. 32;
xxxvii. 5. But the second member of ver. 11 recurs almost
identically, liv. 8, comp. also lxiii. 4, lxix. 17, is then further
developed, Jer. xxxiii. 11, and thence frequently in the latest
songs. Comp. below on cxviii. 1; cvi. 1; cvii 1, and finally
again, somewhat transformed, cxlvii. 1.

But that the same poet who with such crushing force, like a
prophet, rises in opposition to others, can in other moments
collect himself in the most tranquil contemplation and most
blessed experience, is shown by Ps. xxxvi.—a softer and more
inward song, with grand eternal thoughts. By his outburst
the poet manifestly seeks as an individual to console himself

under the prevailing corruption and danger, becoming the more intensely conscious of all the consolatory eternal truths. The progress of the song is hence here reversed. First the calm contemplation and description—yet concealing no truth— of completed wickedness, which might readily excite horror in the mind of the godly, vv. 2-5. Yet against their power and quest of pleasure there is the protection of Jahvé's infinite grace, unassailable and indestructible by the wicked. To this the poet, like all the faithful, flees, vv. 6-12; finally, the mind of the poet having become greatly elevated and cheered by this outburst, the brief and certain foresight of the fall of the ungodly, ver. 13.—According to ver. 9, the Temple was still standing, and the poet, according to ver. 12, did not yet live in exile, but he fears this as something readily possible, whilst he at present still recreates himself at the Temple, vv. 8, 9.

We have here again in our poet quite the same measure of the three strophés; and the last, here too as in the preceding song, tends to a more abrupt form; but a verse, as it were superfluous, is thrown from the powerful ebullition to which the language, at first tranquil, imperceptibly rises, and forms a kind of echoing outcry at the end, ver. 13.

1.

2　　The saying of sin is in the deep heart of the wicked,
　　　　fear of God is never before his eyes:
　　but it flatters him in his eyes
　　　　to find his misdeed, to hate;
　　his mouth's words are mischief and deceit,
　　　　he has ceased to have understanding, virtue;
5　　only mischief does he meditate upon his bed,
　　　　sets himself in ways which are not good, not con-
　　　　　　　　temning wickedness!

2.

Jahvé! to the heaven reaches Thy grace,
　　to the bright clouds Thy truth!

Thy righteousness is as the mountains of God,
  Thy judgments like the great sea :
men and beasts Thou helpest, Jahvé !
Yet how precious is Thy grace, O God !
    and sons of men—they flee to the shadow of Thy
           wings,
refresh themselves at the fulness of Thy house,
    and Thou waterest them with the stream of Thy
    delights.

3.

For with Thee is the spring of life ;   10
  in Thy light we see light !
Preserve Thy grace for them that know Thee,
  Thy righteousness for the upright in heart ;
let not the foot of pride touch me,
  nor the hand of wicked men persecute me !
There are fallen evil-doers,
  cast down, unable to rise !

The description, vv. 2-5, pierces very deeply into the nature of finished villany. In virtue of the law of sequence in the spiritual life, the feeling and impulse which ever anew leads the faithful man to the Divine, becoming for him ever a fresh oracle and unceasing counsellor to goodness, becomes perverted for the impious man into the opposite, into an impulse and oracle of sin. It is ever suggesting to him evil thoughts, pictures, plans, words. (Unquestionably לְבּוֹ is instead of לְבִּי the reading). No fear of God is before him, but *it seems* (בְּעֵינָיו opposite to עֵינָיו, ver. 2, comp. § 217 *f.*) *flattering*, he thinks it fine, it gives him self-complacency and conceit, *to find*, to invent and think out his own misdeed, so that he can be consequential in his sins,—whenever he deliberates and finds sin to carry out as the favourite material for him,—*to hate* instead of to love, to entertain universal hatred as the first and greatest sin,—an explanation of the preceding infinitive. The

two deeds, ver. 3 *b*, thus form a climax, as in ver. 4. But the
further explanation comes in vv. 4, 5—as he can only think,
speak, commit sin, because *he does not despise* evil in his heart,
because his most secret feeling finds joy in evil, and no longer
feels any horror of it. But again the second strophé is very
fine and full of feeling, ever rising in strength, vv. 6-12. Infinite
as the heaven, as unassailable and indestructible by men, is the
Divine grace,—exalted, infinite, inexhaustible as the highest
(God's) mountains and the ocean, His righteousness and His
judgments, and special punishments, lxviii. 16, Am. vii. 4.
That which passages like lii. 10, lxxxiv. 2 sqq., express of the
delight of the enjoyment of God at the sanctuary, rises here,
vv. 8, 9, to the purest illustration. Therefore in His presence,
in fellowship with Him, is genuine, imperishable strengthening
and refreshment, true life, pure light, as is very beautifully
expressed in vv. 8-10.—But the poet still feels that the pure
feeling of this pleasure, if it is to be quite safe and clear, must
be yet more deeply founded ; so that he expresses at the
beginning of the third strophé, ver. 10, the truth concerning
all human relations to God,—even without regard to a particular
holy spot,—in the most general and eternal way. And thereby
he first receives the right disposition to pray for that which is
now his nearest want, vv. 11, 12. It is clear from the word
house, ver. 9, *i.e.*, Temple, that this was not yet at that time
destroyed. The sacred modes of speech remain, it is true,
frequently in their inner sense, and the congregation never
entirely ceased ; but from ver. 12 it follows anew that that the
poet still lived in Kanáan. That the *foot*, ver. 12, of the conqueror or tyrant treading upon the vanquished may not pursue
the poet, violently separate him from the community : thus
does he most intensely pray. And as if he felt in the same
moment that he was heard, he cannot refrain, after a short pause
in the language, from further suddenly appending the joyous
picture of this answer to prayer, ver. 13, which presses with
overwhelming force upon his spirit. The *perf.*, ver. 13, as in our

poet above, lxiv. 7-10, and in all similar passages of prophetic vision, Ps. lxxxii. 14.

In Ps. liv. we further see the poet for the first time threatened by strangers, and condensing his feelings in a short song. After he has prayed for help from the strange persecutors, vv. 3-5, he becomes, after short reflection, again more collected and calm, full of secure hope in Jahvé; yea, he already promises for the deliverance joyously contemplated in his spirit, thanksgiving, vv. 6-9 (6-7, 8-9). The expressions are on the whole too general to enable us to ascertain the particular relations of the poet. But the danger of being violently carried away among strangers was already expressed clearly by the poet at the end of the two preceding songs.

There are here only two of the strophés of the proportion usual with our poet; and the first is too short by one member, probably because one has fallen away after ver. 4.

1.

O God, by Thy name, save me   3
  by Thy power directing me;
O God, hear my prayer,
  observe the words of my mouth;
for strangers stand against me,   5
  tyrants seek my soul,
not having God before their eyes!   *

2.

Lo, God is my helper,
  the Lord is a preserver of my life;
He will recompense evil to those that lie in wait for
                           me;
  through Thy faithfulness destroy them!
With free impulse will I sacrifice to Thee,
  will praise Thy name, Jahvé, how dear it is,
how it freed me from all trouble,
  mine eye was refreshed at the sight of my foes!

From ver. 5 peculiarly it is plain that the foes are rude strangers who rage the more fearfully against a weak Israelite the less they know and fear the God of Israel. The poet, in his review of the ancient great deliverance of Jahvé, wishes, on the other hand, merely that Jahvé's name, or His strength—extolled, as being revealed from ancient times onwards,—and what is connected therewith, His promised faithfulness, may now work for deliverance, and he may be able to praise it. The *perf.*, ver. 9, is plainly, as always in such cases, like the *fut. exact.* Very similarly lvi. 13, 14 (lxi. 6); *it*, Thy name and glory, Thy majesty.

In Ps. lxi. the poet prays,—from a far distant land, in deep exhaustion and danger—for strength and help, vv. 2, 3; but he immediately collects himself again in hearty confidence in the might of *that* God,—already experienced at an earlier time,—in whose Temple he would ever sojourn, that Temple where he hopes once more to be able to render the thanksgiving for deliverance here celebrated, vv. 4-6. In conclusion, good wishes for the king, to whom probably a great part of the true Israel is attached, vv. 7-9.—The song has manifestly again the fundamental form of most songs of this poet; in the middle of the three strophés, however, there is wanting after ver. 5, as is plainly recognizable, a whole line. The first remains a mere preface.

Historically, the wish on behalf of the king is noteworthy. It is repeated in the following song, in like manner at the end, lxiii. 12, but there more briefly: and in this we have a sign of the later date of that song. Who this king of Israel is, to whom the poet, in the midst of a foreign land, adheres, with such glowing reverence, is indeed difficult to say: but King Josia is here very readily suggested.

1.

O hear, O God, my entreaty,
    observe my prayer!

from the end of the earth I cry unto Thee,
  in my heart's weakness :
to a rock, for me too high, Thou wilt lead me !

2.

Thou wert indeed a refuge for me,
  a mighty tower from foes ;
would that I might take shelter in Thy tent for ever,
  flee to the protection of Thy wings !   *
[*might praise Thee in the Temple*]
  because Thou, O God, didst hear my vows,
didst give me the heritage of the fearers of Thy
    name !

3.

Thou will add to the king's days new ones,
  make his years like everlasting times ;
let him reign for ever before God,
  appoint mercy and truth to protect him !
So will I make music to Thy name for ever,
  that daily I may pay my vow !

Ver. 3. The difficulty which he cannot overcome presents itself to him like a rock too high for him, which must nevertheless be surmounted.—Between vv. 5 and 6 a verse appears to have fallen out, possibly of this sense : and there in the Temple would that I might sing praise to Thee and thank Thee *because Thou*, listening to my vow, didst give me (liv. 8, 9) the inheritance of those fearing Thy name, *i.e.*, the dwelling in the holy land, which indeed is the privilege, the portion of the faithful, and which is intended under another name in cxxv. 3.—Ver. 8 *Before God*, in the upper world, lvi. 14, especially in the neighbourhood of the sanctuary ; so that God ever looks graciously upon him, and suffers him to live. *So*, ver. 9, in this hope, the poet will continually praise God as the deliverer, in order, as he wishes, that he may pay

18

the vows he has often made, by untiring praise after his deliverance. Comp. lxiii. 3, 5.

Ps. lxiii. A fresh and more woful, in part a sharper outburst of this longing in new life-dangers. The song is formed (I., p. 152) evidently like an elegy, with strophés of decreasing length; but as the poet would bring to mind less complaints than Divine hope, and would strengthen himself in it,—pure longing rises, intense and strong, but measured and gentle, seeking *the* God whose glory the poet had ever beheld in the Temple, in sublimity not to be forgotten, the memory of whom had ever given him the most blessed moments, vv. 2-7. Then, since his heart thus again most boldly revels in Divine thoughts and pictures, he expresses more freely and serenely his eternal hope, unable to suppress a glance at his wicked persecutors, who are deserving of the greatest punishment, vv. 8-11. And yet his song becomes at last more gentle, at least in a further word of love and of glowing wish on the king's behalf, whom the same ungodly men strive to slander or to destroy, ver. 12.

1.

2　　O God! my God art Thou, I seek Thee:
　　　　for Thee my soul thirsts,
　　　　for Thee my body longs
　　　　in the land dry and parched, without water.
　　　So have I beheld Thee in the sanctuary,
　　　　viewing Thy might and glory;
　　　for " better is Thy favour than life"
　　　　was the praise of my lips to Thee.
5　　*So* I bless Thee as long as I live,
　　　　lift in Thy name my hands;
　　　like as on fat and fulness my soul is refreshed,
　　　　and my mouth with joyous lips sings praise,
　　　when I remember Thee on my couch,
　　　　in night-watches think of Thee!

2.

Thou wert verily a help to me,
 and in the shadow of Thy wings I rejoice;
my soul clave to Thee:
 Thy right hand holds me fast.—
But they—for destruction seek my soul:　　　　10
 let them go into the depths of the earth!
let them be given over to the hands of the sword,
 be they the portion of jackals!—

3.

But let the king rejoice in God!
 let every one who swears by him boast
 that the mouth of the liars is stopped!

The first and longest strophé is not merely very gentle
and beautiful, but also closely knit together. The fundamental thought that Jahvé is his God, of whom the poet
will rightly assure himself, seeking Him and longing after
Him, ver. 2, is confirmed in two ways. *Thus*, that is, as his
God, the poet has earlier beheld him in the splendour of the
Temple, and in holy devotion has recognized and praised His
majesty and grace, vv. 3, 4; and even *thus*, as his God, he
blesses Him ever and feels in lonely serious recollection of
Him the highest joy, vv. 5-7, כִּי, as lxi. 9, only here somewhat differently applied. The לִרְאוֹת, ver. 3, is thus explanatory, *to see*, *i.e.*, so that I saw, seeing, as also elsewhere at
times this לְ with the *inf.* introduces an explanatory subordinate action; and ver. 4 must briefly interject the words of
the high joy at that time experienced, יְשַׁבְּחוּנְךָ, as *imperf.
praet.* The mention of the dry land, ver. 2, belongs merely
to the whole image, by which the poet in distress and forsaken-
ness is presented as one thirsting in the desert: far more in
detail the danger is quite otherwise described, vv. 10 sqq.—In
God therefore the poet feels himself as earlier, so now always
completely secure, as in vv. 8, 9 finely appears from his clear

18 *

consciousness. But his bloodthirsty foes are of other mind than God; and the poet can only leave them to the Divine vengeance and punishment, in the recollection of how often before tyrants in like manner, overtaken by sudden punishment, came to a shameful end, vv. 10, 11. The powerful picture of the *deepest earth*, ver. 10 b, is substantially the same as that expressed by our poet, lv. 16, in a yet more ebullient style; yet there follow immediately, ver. 12, only pictures of the battle-field. *The portion of jackals*, becoming the prey of jackals, like fallen warriors on the battle-field. But *the king*, ver. 12, against whom these rude foes have evil will, as against the poet and all Israel. will abide; and every one who is faithful to this king, and therefore swears by him (Gen. xlii. 15, 16) who now must patiently listen to calumny against his beloved person, may boast that the liars must at length be silent! In what these lying speeches about the king consisted, it is now difficult for us to say. Probably the light-minded said the king would not long be able to hold out against his severe Assyrian, Chaldee, or Egyptian foes, and desired that he might not; and in the foreign land where the poet now was, such language might the more freely be heard.

As the two preceding songs are closely connected together, and probably fall in the time of the departure into exile,—so again, Pss. lvi. and lvii., where we see the poet in the midst of the heathen, as is specially clear from lvi. 8 (where "peoples" are for that reason mentioned) lvii. 6, 12 (where a judgment upon the whole earth is therefore desired), and lvii. 5, 10; comp. lix. 8. He lived in the midst of exile among still greater dangers,—which his very loyalty to Jahvé or his confidence, prophetically certain and loudly expressed, of deliverance through Jahvé increased—among suspicious and bloodthirsty foes, who misunderstand and disturb the agency of the prophet. For already in struggle with the heathen world the prophetic vein has been in full life within him, and now throbs in stronger pulses. The greater the irritation and menace the more nobly and powerfully does Divine confidence in the struggle proceed from his bosom. Yea, the hidden deep glow of the pure Messianic hope breaks forth in the outburst of his words, often with absolute unrestraint, in a blazing fire (lvi. 9 ; lvii. 6, 12; comp. lviii. 10-12). These two songs are among the finest in the whole Psalter.

In Ps. lvi. the poet, long threatened by severe dangers, strains after consolation and hope in the memory of his higher blessings and endeavours ; and it costs him a struggle, not too difficult, to obtain consolation and invigoration in the prophetic calling. Immediately, in the first short strophé, this comes with the cry of supplication, vv. 2-5, and although in the further outburst of his feelings the consideration of the dangers recurs, here first eliciting indignation at such horrors from his distressed soul, vv. 6-9, yet much more nobly does comfort return, soothing his excitement, so that at last, in the increasing presentiment of certain deliverance, he renders inspired thanksgiving, vv. 10-14.—Thus there are three similar strophés, so that the twofold representation, compressed in the first, is unfolded and further arranged in the two following. That is the simple art of this song : but the short strophés become more ebullient ; and whilst the two first stream forth in four verses with nine members, the last is expanded to five verses, with—in some instances—very agitated members, to the number of eleven.

1.

Be gracious to me, O God ! for men snatch at me,   2
    continually warriors oppress me ;
my lyers-in-wait snort continually,
    for many proudly war against me.—
On the day that I feared,
    I flee, trusting to Thee,
through God I praise His word,   5
    in God I trust without fear ;
what shall mortals do to me ?

2.

Continually they wrest my words,
  ill-disposed to me is all that they think :
they stir, lie in wait; they watch my heels
  as if they sought after my life.
According to their wickedness weigh out to them,
  and anger overturn peoples, O God !
the breaths of my sighs Thou countest ;
  —kept in Thy bottle are my tears,
yea, in Thy account-book.

3.

10   But my enemies shall turn back on the day that I call !
  this I know, God is mine !
through God I praise the word ;
  through Jahvé I praise the word ;
in God I trust without fear ;
  what shall mortals do to me ?—
I owe Thee, O God, my vows :
  I will pay thanks to Thee,
that Thou hast freed my life from death,
  yea, my foot from overthrow,
that I may freely walk before God—in the light of life !

1. רַבִּים, ver. 3, as lv. 19.—Ver. 4, יוֹם in the st. const.
(286 *i*, 332 *d*) here and lxxxviii. 2, in the briefer style of the
poets of this time; also the חֲלֹוא vv. 9, 14 is of peculiar
brevity.—Ver. 5 shows the prophetic element. The highest
element in the prophet is that he through God, in God's mind
and strength, and thus by God impelled and inspired, praises
the word of God, or His eternal promise of salvation in the
right way, and thereby warns all mortals, or,—as was peculiarly
necessary at that time among his companions in suffering,—
consoles them (comp. cxxx. 5). Because this Divine word eternally endures through the whole history with a force independent

of the prophet and of all individual men, it may subsequently,
ver. 11, be named absolutely, דָּבָר, "the word," almost
ὁ λόγος. Comp. Prov. xiii. 13 ; xvi. 20. If the poet departs
not from this and from his praise, he may fearlessly meet all
mortals ; he may refuse to tremble in the presence of threats or
dangers from men, as is here so powerfully expressed.

2. *They vex* indeed the poet most deeply by wresting his
prophetic *words and deeds,* and persecuting him as a prophet,
and who would not be carried away by indignation at this in
the first moment ? Thus the second strophé begins, vv. 6-9.
They stir, ver. 7, the fire of contention and of persecution,
cxl. 5, *lie in wait* in secret to see whether this fire is kindled,
comp. lxiv. 6, 7 ; and though they do not openly urge on my
destruction, yet they *haunt my steps,* as if *they lay in wait for
my soul,* are like to my deadly enemies. The הֵמָּה, ver. 7,
laying a fresh emphasis on the subject, appears because of the
following strong comparison ; for the כַּאֲשֶׁר is *as though,* and
hence is connected (§ 355 *b*) with the *perf.,* because it expresses
the equivalent of *as if.* Hence then breaks through irresistibly in this place, ver. 8, for the first time the might of
prophetic indignation : according to *unrighteousness repay to
them, O God !* (For פַּלֵּט as " deliverance," xxxii. 7, will not
suit here, nor as imperative, " deliver," but it appears = פַּלֵּס
a frequent word in poets of this age, lviii. 1 ; ט may stand for
ס from a copyist's mistake, or probably from change of sound ;
עַל thus expresses the measure, as iu lxix. 28.) This indignation further increases immediately to its Messianic height ; *in
wrath cast down peoples !* comp. lvii. 6, 12. But it is as if the
poet himself observed that his word could not remain in this
most violent ebullition, so that before the end of the strophés,
as if exculpating himself before God for this, ver. 9 points to
the endless sighs which he had already consumed, and which,
as he exclaims with renewed sighs, he hopes he had not spent in
vain before God. Thus his word here becomes a half obscure
sighing, dissolved in nameless grief, scarce indicating, as in

allusive words, how infinitely he has already sighed in his urgent prayer. נד, the "being driven hither and thither," is here probably not the mere flight, the wandering about of an exile, which corresponds too little to the following "tears;" but is to be understood inwardly of the violent unrest, the complaint and cries of misery, comp. lv. 3, Jer. xxxi. 18; frequently the poet has thus complained in the highest grief, how great the measure of his sufferings is, yea, God knows, who has *counted* his sighs; and suddenly he adds,—carried away by sorrow through this recollection of the tears shed with indefinite frequency,—that he well knows that none of them is forgotten with God, that they do not all run away, dissolved into nothing, but would be taken up by Jahvé as into the great bottle in which He, as the Righteous One, keeps the tears of all the innocent until the right time, as he has marked all the deeds of man in his book (lxix. 29; cxxxix. 16). The figure of the bottle, נאד, thus lay at hand if only in נד the tears were indicated. But we must not overlook the fact that at the same time a play of words mingles with the play of thoughts, and excuses this rare and bold figure. In German it may be thus represented: my *schluchzen*—thy *schlauch;* or, as this is not pointed enough, in the way adopted in the translation above (*hauche—schlauche*). And yet the poet, before he entirely concludes, must also complete the other figure of counting, so that he further suddenly adds, *yea, they are placed* to be noted at the right time in the book of numbers (reckoning-book), lxxxvii. 6. But we read instead of the unsuitable imperative שִׂימָה *lege!* rather שִׂימָה (§ 149 *f.*) Comp. also *Gesch. des V. Isr.,* III., p. 756, of the second edition.

3. Ver. 10. *Yet* at the crisis, if the highest danger threatens me, my enemies will rebound, as soon as I cry: אָז; thus at the same time adversative like *doch,* from *denn* (dann) *auch,* as in lxix. 5; Lat. *at,* comp. Sanskr. *atha* (§ 354 *a*). On *before God,* ver. 14, comp. that more definitely said in vi. 6; xli. 13.

In Ps. lvii., fresh irritation and menace, fresh complaint. But from the very beginning more resigned and trustful, the result gained in the preceding song of higher joyousness and certainty here from the first stirs in the poet's mind, and so also in the end leads to the serenest hope and boldest self-encouragement. The whole song so overflows with blessed exaltation and inspiration, that the recollection of present dangers but feebly breaks in during its course, passing away immediately in the Divine certainty which beams over all. When in this way from the first beginning and cry, the inspiration, speedily glorifying the picture of the present, has once reached the highest point in the wish for a universal Divine judgment upon all peoples, vv. 2-6 : it rises for the second time from the recurring picture of the present,—readily and through tranquil hope, to the same height vv. 7-12 ; so that the whole presentation exhausts itself in two similar strophés. Both conclude with the same primary thought, the last hope ; in the same way in the preceding Psalm the same highest thought, tranquillizing, glorifying, twice recurred, vv. 4-5, 11-12.

In one word, it is the Messianic hope,—which at the time of our poet must have been already all-powerful among prophetically minded men,—that here becomes—as the conclusion and the fresh firm ground of all conceptions—a recurrent verse, 6, 12. The style of the congregational song accordingly passes before the mind of our poet. See I., pp. 199 sq.

And probably he feels as if this hope must become the leading thought of all pious men, as it is his own ; and thereby all fear and anxiety in presence of the dread experiences of the present is to be overcome. Thus the very structure of the strophés here is formed afresh by our poet. The song breaks into two strophés only, each, with inclusion of the recurrent verse, of fourteen verse-members.

1.

Be gracious to me, O God, be gracious to me,   2
    for to Thee my soul fleeth,

into the shadow of Thy wings I flee,
    till the danger be past !
I cry to God the Highest,
    the God Who doeth good to me,
to send from heaven and help me,
    reproaching him who snorteth at me.   *
    God send His mercy and His truth !
Among lions I live, tarry among greedy men,
    among sons of men whose teeth are spears and
      arrows,
    and whose tongue is a sharp sword :
Lift Thyself high above the heavens, O God,
    over the whole earth high Thy glory !

2.

They have placed a net for my steps :
    their soul bends down !
have digged before me a grave
    —and fall themselves therein !   *
Firm is my heart, O God, firm is my heart ;
    let me sing and play !
wake up, my noble part, up, Thou harp, zither,
    let me wake up the dawn !
10   let me praise Thee among the peoples, Lord,
    play to Thee among nations,
how, high unto heaven is Thy mercy,
    to the very clouds Thy faithfulness !
Lift Thyself high above the heavens, O God,
    over the whole earth high Thy glory !

1. The גָּמַר, ver. 3, is indeed properly finish, come to an end
without an object, vii. 10 ; but from that very signification of
finishing arises that of ready action, conduct towards persons
(good or evil), in which it is then ordinarily more softly
expressed as גָּמַל and is independent. Here however it appears
in the above harsher expression, said with עַל of God who

ordains concerning man,—loads him especially with benefits,
xiii. 6; ciii. 10; cxvi. 7; cxix. 17; cxlii. 8,—in the latter
sense very well explained by גָּמַר בְּעַד *do for* any one, cxxxviii. 8.
On יִשְׁלַח, ver. 4, which in any case (§ 347 *a b*) must depend on
ver. 3, we might compare xviii. 17: but as the figures would
then be too mixed, it is better taken along with the last
member, where by repetition its meaning is only completed.
The חֵרֵף is however (§ 341 *b*) used in constant explanation of
the subordinate action contemporaneous with the main action:
holding reviled, i.e., violently thrust back as they deserve.

This strong figure is,—as *him who snorts for me* shows,—
borrowed from wild beasts, whose snorting attack must be in
time resisted with the right word. While then this figure of
the lion openly appears in ver. 5, repeated in ver. 7 (for the
lion *bends himself* in vain in the pit-nets laid deep under the
earth), one may say it is introduced as the figure here generally
most closely suggested to the poet through the whole song
(comp. again lviii. 7). But our poet is wont to interweave the
most different figures with one another (lvi. 9; lviii. 7-9); so
also here vv. 4, 5. The לֹהֵם = *laham*, Arab., לחם, related also
on the other side to לִעֵט, Gen. xxv. 30, be *greedy* (eat), yields
a new word for lion: but who these greedy lions are, is explained
in the second member: men with consuming greed and sharp
tongue, acting and speaking horribly, lii. 4.—On ver. 6, comp.
vii. 7-9, which passage passed before the poet's mind, only
that here the outlook of the poet in Messianic hope is
infinitely extended.

2. Also on ver. 7, comp. vii. 16. The representation of the
danger which has all but seized upon the poet, turns at the
end with נָפְלוּ into the opposite, the fall of the adversaries
(§ 223 *b*) being looked upon as certain, and so desired in
prayer from God; as this quickly returning confidence is then
further suddenly explained, vv. 8 sqq. But for this very reason,
according to the connexion of the whole discourse and its
members, נַפְשָׁם must be read for נַפְשִׁי, while the LXX read

כִּפְפוּ, *they bound me,* which however, just as כָּפַף, *my soul bound-down,* would here express too much.—My *noble part,* ver. 9, my spirit, the noblest thing in man, likewise after vii. 6. In וְכָבוֹד הַגֶּבֶל the article belongs, because it is rather externally added in the address, also to the second nomen. The words, ver. 11, are echoed here as from the same poet, from xxxvi. 6 : but the poet places them here, in accordance with his custom, only as dependent on ver. 10, and has in this ver. 10, as generally one of the first imitations of Davidic songs, Ps. xviii. 50 in his eye.—From ver. 9, it is clear that the poet was wont to sing much; as he at an earlier time sang much in prosperity, so he encourages himself now, when the joyous song was silenced, to sing in future again with equal serenity. And since he now speaks in the evening or in the night, as soon as possible in the still early morning he will thus cheerfully sing, *waking* as it were the *dawn* in his anticipatory zeal. The words from ver. 8 forwards to the conclusion are so readily separable into a short special prayer, that they are verbally repeated in Ps. cviii. 2-6.

But with the purest prophetic boldness and severity the poet finally rises in those circumstances, in another moment, Ps. lviii., against unjust judges, certainly heathen ones, since he names them in heathen fashion, though with bitter scorn in his own sense,—*Gods,* ver. 2. It suffices not to the poet to express his anger and imprecations on the perverse behaviour of these mighty judges merely in the first way. Rather does he proceed with his views into the midst of the secret forge of their thoughts and purposes, and when he has thus ascertained and set them forth in their naked and irredeemable wickedness, the wish and the anticipation of the Messianic overthrow of those hardened ones in the midst of their power, and the deliverance of sufferers, can no longer be restrained, and then comes with the greater force. As if he desired to summon the judges only to self-defence, he calls to them at first with taunting words, asking whether they who would be gods and as such be honoured, actually judged men and the earth righteously,—they the double-minded, unjust ones, who so bitterly destroyed everything by their actions : what is to be thought of them ? vv. 2, 3. And since no answer and defence is heard, because it is impossible in the presence of the strict questioner who knows the inward life,—the questioner must himself in their stead, after the pause, answer, as if in explanation, with a sharp, severe, but just estimate and description of these completely corrupt and hardened, hopeless offenders, vv. 4-6. Thus despatching them, he now turns in prophetic prayer to God as the Destroyer of all evil, vv. 7-9, and with the prophetic forecast of the future towards those who are past deliverance, vv. 10-12.

Our poet is thoroughly original in this artistic manner of casting unobserved, bitter satire upon the mighty ones of the earth, and of operating by means of the only too deeply merited Divine anger ; but he finds a worthy imitator later in the poet of Ps. lxxxii. And as in such sharp artistic representations a tranquil tenor from the first, and a correct distribution of all the larger shadows is the most necessary thing, he knows here completely how to adapt himself to the new style of such a satirical song. Four brief slender strophés in the most uniform style, with all the inward glow which at each step breaks forth. The first is even somewhat shorter than the others.

1.

Do ye then truly speak righteousness, ye gods,   2
   judge with equity the sons of men ;
and yet do wickedness in your heart,
   weigh out upon earth the iniquity of your hands ?—

2.

Estranged are the wicked from their mother's womb,
   gone astray from the bosom they who speak lies !

5   They have poison like to the poison of serpents,
     like deaf viper which stops her ear,
which listens not to the voice of the charmer,
     of the most skilful of magicians !

3.

O God, destroy their teeth in their mouth,
     tear out the teeth of the lions, O Jahvé !
let them stretch their arrows as if they were blunt,
     let them flow away as water vanishing,
like wax which is about to dissolve,
     a woman's untimely birth which has not beheld the
                                 sun !

4.

10   • Before your thorns observe it,
     He will burn up the bushes, whether green or dry.
The righteous man rejoices that he saw vengeance,
     washing his steps in the blood of the ungodly :
that it may be said : " the righteous man hath never-
                         theless fruit,
nevertheless there are Gods judging on the earth."

1. For אֵלֶם, ver. 2, which yields no sense at all as "dumbness,"
we must unquestionably read אֵלִם ; it may be said that the
whole Psalm imperatively demands this ; for without this the
true irony and thereby the life of the song is destroyed. The
rulers and judges allow themselves, especially among the
heathen, to be revered as gods, or lower deities, and would
pass for such. The poet, too, would very willingly allow them
to pass for such (at least in the sense which such words may
bear when used of man, comp. Ex. xxi. 6; xxii. 7, and Ps.
ii. 7; lxxxix. 28) if they did but actually show themselves like
gods on the earth toward men ; accordingly he appeals to
these earth-gods—whether they did really show themselves in
a Divine aspect? Comp. lxxxii. 1-7. Provisionally he allows

them according to common opinion to pass for gods, and asks whether they are so actually, and deserved to remain so ?—they who have only wickedness in their thoughts, and instead of right weigh out with unjust balance only the iniquity performed by their own hands. The opposition must not be overlooked : *children of men, earth.*

2. Vv. 4-6. The poet himself answers, since those addressed cannot defend themselves,—unwillingly indeed, yet at the same time indicating the reason, already anticipated, of their silence, and rising to a higher point, their wickedness. The reason of all this lies, in fact, in their finished malice. For when this has reached its highest degree, it appears unalterably bound up with the person as he is, firmly rooted in him ; it has become his nature and his impulse. For even in sin as a disposition and impulse there is constancy and logical sequence, from the smallest and most secret beginning to the highest degree and indefinitely,—so far as the life of the individual admits of this. And if a completely impious man is seen, you there discover as little a visible beginning of his wicked disposition as an end—unless with the exception of death. As he is now once for all, so does all, from his birth, appear to have co-operated to form him, and as he through a dim, dark night appears to be from the earliest moment estranged and aberrant from the Divine life (li. 7), he is for the present and future indifferent in the midst of his wickedness to reflection and exhortation. He is like a poisonous serpent, which its tamer the magician thinks to be tame, but which nevertheless suddenly, as if it had in vain been sought to fetter it by arts and charms, again spits forth its venom, and which then stops as it were its ear against the most clever magician, at the very moment when the magician would most seek to lead it according to his art, by magic spells.*

---

* That the art of serpent-taming and the magic connected with it is of high antiquity, especially in Egypt, and thence spread into surrounding lands, admits no doubt. Comp. the *Gesch. des V. Isr*, ii., pp. 90 sq., 249 sq. of the 3rd edit.; and

As in the Bible frequently only this natural side of sin is brought out in strong, apparently too severe, but nevertheless true and apt figures (Isa. vi. 9, 10) : so also here appears uniquely the element of hardening and incapacity for amendment in the finished sinner, because this truth simply— at the view of the ungodly, impenetrable to every exhortation, refusing to defend themselves,—so strongly comes out, that the poet himself must reluctantly and mournfully doubt whether they could ever be cured. But that the poet, on the other side, conceives of the ungodly as fallen not merely by dark necessity or nature, but also through their own guilt, is self-intelligible, and comes out immediately, ver. 7.

3. But again in the two last strophés the figures are very severe, on account of the great bitterness between the two parties, when the greatest guilt incontestably lay with him here named the "ungodly." If the reading, vv. 8, 9, were quite correct, of the four members the first and third would mutually correspond. May they pass away in and by themselves, as water vanishes, without trace, as wax gradually melts in the fire. (This sense of שבלול according to the LXX is more suitable than that of a snail, which seems to wear itself away by the streaming forth of its moisture as it crawls). The second and fourth member on the other hand would depict how they pass away, rejected as unserviceable and useless, as blunt arrows which are uselessly shot away (comp. xlvi. 10, properly *let one stretch his arrows, i.e.,* the arrows may be shot *as if they were blunt*), or as unripe births, which are quickly cast aside again, probably here and Eccl. vii. 6, thus expressed after Job iii. 16. But we must not mistake that a much better connexion both of these five

---

from later times Jer. viii. 17; Eccl. x. 11 ; Sir. xii. 13 ; Clem. *Hom.* iii. 36 ; Plato's *Rep.*, ii. 2 ; *Journal of the R. As. Soc. of Lond.*, vii., pp. 109 f. ; Seetzen's *Reisen*, iii., p. 446 ; Fletcher's *Narrative of Travel in Mesopotamia*, ii., p. 293 f.; Layard's *Discoveries*, p. 257; Onomandy's *Altes und Neues aus den Landern des Ostens*, i., pp. 59-63 ; N. Davis' *Carthage and her Remains*, pp. 425 f.

members as well as for the progress of the thoughts in the whole strophé arises if the second member of ver. 8 is joined to the first (as is done in the translation above). The interchange of the *sing.* with the *plur.* is then only such as frequently is found. On the connexion of נִפֵּל, however, see § 176 *b*.

4. Ver. 10. The ungodly are confused and sharp as thorns and thorn-bushes (Nah. i. 10): thorns may keenly prick and defend themselves, but *before your thorns observe it,* quickly therefore and unexpectedly, *will He* (God) carry away in the storm *the thorn-bushes* (the whole nest of the ungodly), *green and dry* (חרוי from חרר), be they dry or soft and fresh as you will (comp. § 360 *a*); for to the storm of Divine anger all must give way. The אָמֵר is thus better attached to the second member; according to the accents it should be connected with the preceding word (§ 291 *b*); but in the first member the word is superfluous, in the second only in its right place. But in the picture of the tempest שָׂעֵר is nevertheless here, where thorn-bushes are spoken of, far from appropriate. If, on the other hand, יִשְׂעָר be read, this may signify a *burning* or *burning up,* which far better agrees with all sides of this grandly executed picture, and is recommended also by the language about contemporaneous with our poet of Nah. i. 10, in the same figure. Comp. further the *Jahrbb. der Bibl. Wiss.,* v., p. 172. Bloody revenge is, ver. 11, in fact merely mentioned according to the general experience of the fearful wars of those times; in any other way retribution did not at that epoch usually come. But the great and main matter is indeed only that at last the true gods must ever again be recognized, ver. 12, with which purely Messianic truth the song most fitly recurs to its beginning. And that the language in the whole of the last strophé turns back in boldest address to the same man whom its first word, vv. 2, 3, had struck, but now in quite another manner, and seriously enough, is shown by the beautiful completion of the whole.

19

51. Psalm lix.,

which stands in the midst of the main body of the songs just explained, has also in style and stamp much that is common with them and Pss. cxl.—cxlii. (comp. ver. 8 with lii. 4 and the places there noted; נגר, ver. 4 with cxl. 3; lvi. 7, and other instances), although the similarity of the representation, vv. 7, 15, to lv. 11 *b* is not so great that there could be reason for the assumption that this song falls in the time of the same siege of Jerusalem in which perhaps Ps. lv. arose. But the poet is probably another, since the language in other particulars has important deviations, and the peculiar situation of the poet is manifestly of that kind that he stands over against the besiegers here described as prince or king.

For the poet is in the city beleaguered by heathen peoples, vv. 6, 15, who scoff at Jahvé (ver. 8), who at the same time in rude arrogance, relying on groundless accusations, seek after his life. Already they have for several days more closely blockaded the city, in the night time especially holding stricter watch and thinking of attack and conquest, by day dispersing for plunder (comp. Isa. xv. 1; xxi. 4).

In the few moments of such a morning, when they have for a short time retired, the poet's anxiety pours itself forth and is relieved in a hymn to Jahvé; and the danger was manifestly no slight one, so urgent and importunate is the poet's cry for help to God. There is finally but *one* thought which can illuminate and give repose to his spirit, but *one* hope in which he can fortify himself and rise to even firmer confidence in God, that is, the Messianic conception,—how the fire dwelling within him at that time, since the Assyrian days, pp. 216 sqq., might readily arise in Jerusalem and especially in the mind of a king of Israel under such circumstances. Is this rude heathen people by which the king is thus harassed in the holy city, rather an individual people, accidentally at present so mighty, rushing against it, and against the whole status of a kingdom of God upon earth ? And must not the kingdom of God over all the Gentiles finally begin? Must not all who rise up against it end like the Assyrians before Jerusalem's walls? And the more the poet, manifestly a king in Jerusalem, is conscious how insolent and perverted the speeches and thoughts of those rude foes are, with the greater inspiration does he behold in Jahvé the eternal protector of Sion and of Israel, and the higher flame of hope is soon kindled from the fire of those ideas. And thus the song, beginning with an anxious cry for help, turns aside to prophetic anticipation and sarcastic portrayal of the terrible annulment of the hostile beginning which must at last ensue, and to joyous confidence in Jahvé. This progress is exhibited in three stages, whence flow three strophés of the song—at first a lively cry for help, description of wickedness, but also hope in Jahvé from this very fact, vv. 2-6 (2, 3, 4, 5, 6). Then, after a short reflection, the complete picture of the near danger presses forward, yet immediately in contrast with it still more powerfully the picture of Jahvé's dignity and grace, so that confidence in God here having risen to the highest pitch is menacingly directed against the foe, especially when his insolent God-denying speeches are noted, vv. 7-11 (7, 8, 9-11). But there then finally rises the hope, the wish and the prayer of the poet before God to the highest pitch, so that he exclaims : would that those rude warriors, safe from their present excursions, might again rush upon the city; their dreaded return must be their grave, so as finally to quiet their greed for destruction at this city ! But this thought becoming too powerful, he fills the measure of the whole third strophé independently in such wise, that the glorious hope which the king has now apprehended,—after the outpouring of these thoughts before God,—with a confidence never before experienced, can only be expressed in a shorter concluding strophé. Thus there arise three strophés, each of five verses and eleven members, with a closing strophé; and the two oppositions compressed in the second, separate in the two following, as the structure of Ps. lvi. (pp. 276 sqq.) quite similarly shows.

If it is asked what siege of Jerusalem is here meant, it is plain, from ver. 12, that the song may have been written a considerable time after the deliverance of Jerusalem from the Assyrian dominion; for the wondrous deliverance of the holy city (comp. above Ps. xlvi. sqq.) passes before the poet's mind in a higher picture, and he wishes that the like may again occur; as generally the later writers from the Assyrian period frequently regard in the boldest manner and with the most swelling hopes the threatening of a powerful enemy of the holy city, Zech. xiv.; Jer. xxvi. 7 sqq.; Rev. xx. 9. Then too the opposition between Israel and the Gentiles is brought to an acmé; and we see here for the first time the greatest bitterness developed. Accordingly we might think of the first Chaldean siege, 2 Kings xxiii. 33; xxiv. 1, 2; but the description of the Chaldeans which at that time Habaqquq gave, departs greatly from the picture here sketched of the besiegers, vv. 7, 15, and in other respects there is no indication leading us to that period. As the besiegers are here manifestly distinguished as rude nomad peoples, who give up the siege by day to plunder in the vicinity, but return towards evening like howling, greedy dogs: the Scythians are most readily suggested, who in Josia's reign overran Palestine as far as Egypt.* In this view, what is known otherwise of the pious Josia very well suits him as the author of the song; and another song, which in all probability is referable to him, we shall presently find in Ps. xxviii. Indeed the very preservation of these two songs, poetically not greatly distinct from one another, is most readily explained in the theory of this pious king's authorship.

1.

2　　Deliver me from my enemies, my God,
　　　　protecting me before my adversaries;

---

* Comp. *Gesch. des V. Isr.*, III., pp. 689 sqq.

free me from evil-doers,
    and from men of blood help Thou me!
For lo, they lie in wait against my life,
    insolent ones stir against me—
    without my guilt and my offence, O Jahve!
without cause they run and array themselves: 5.
    rouse Thyself, on my behalf, and behold!—
But Thou Jahve, God of Hosts, God of Israel,
    awaken to punish all the peoples,
    spare not any of the sinful robbers! *

2.

May they return towards evening,
    howl as dogs and surround the city!
lo, they will boast with loud mouth,
      swords upon their lips,
    for " who will hear it ? "
But Thou, Jahvé, wilt laugh at them,
    Thou wilt scorn all peoples!
my strength! on Thee will I wait!   10
    for God is my fortress;
my God will grant me His grace,
    God will give me to prevail over those that lie in wait
                        for me!

3.

Slay them not, that my people may not forget it,
    let them stagger through Thy strength and overthrow
          them, Thou our shield, O Lord!
the sin of their mouth, the speech of their lips—
    O let them be taken in their pride,
    and for the perjury and the lies which they speak!
Consume in wrath, consume, that they pass away,
    that men may know God rules in Jacob to the earth's
                  ends! *

15　And may they return toward evening,
　　　howl as dogs and surround the city !
　　they will stagger at the meal,
　　　satisfy themselves forsooth and—remain !

4.

But I will sing Thy strength,
　　And rejoice every morning in Thy grace,
　　that Thou wert to me a fortress,
　　　and refuge on the day of my distress,
　　my strength, to Thee let me pray ;
　　　for God is my fortress, my gracious God !

1. On לֹא פְשָׁעִי comp. §§ 286 *g*, 320 *c*. The וְאַתָּה, ver. 6, is as ver. 9, and in a like manner further on, ver. 17 oppositional,—the poet now for the first time, on the approaching close of the strophé and of its conception, lifting himself as it were above himself and all the immediate present with its immediate distress and taking refuge in the Messianic ideas, and thus with altogether new fervour turning entirely to God, and immediately demanding, in more general terms, a judgment upon all the heathen. The connexion בֹּגְדֵי אָוֶן is like הַבְלֵי שָׁוְא, xxxi. 7.

2. The second strophé plainly moves in three main thoughts : may they, like dogs, greedily snapping, return to the siege, when they will renew their insolent scoffing speeches against Jahvé, Israel, and the king, hoping God will not hear and punish them, vv. 7, 8 : yet Jahvé will in calm dignity despise them (ver. 9 from ii. 4) as also the poet calmly relies upon Him and His victory, vv. 9-11. Yea, so boldly and securely does he, strengthened by this hope, look forward to the certain overthrow of the enemy, so certain is it in itself to him that villany, the more audacious and insolent it is, the more shamelessly in its blindness it assails the holiest, the more fearful and memorable will be its fall, that he

3. forthwith at the beginning of the third strophé, vv. 12-16, as if in righteous indignation at the impious speeches of the enemy, demands a *decision*, wishing that the enemy might not hold off, might not suddenly fall in the desert far from Jerusalem, unseen by the people of Jerusalem, but in their giddiness assail the sanctuary, and then in their extreme impiety, in the last crisis, perish for ever; partly to punish their pride, partly that thereby in view of the holy city a great and ever memorable token of the Divine power and retribution may be given, for Israel and for all peoples (as formerly at the time of the Assyrian attack on Jerusalem and its king, now alas! again forgotten by many faint-hearted unbelieving Jews themselves). Therefore, may God not slay them before they come again, but cause them to reel (נוּעַ) in the giddiness and drunkenness of pride, and suffer them so to come on and so overthrow them, like the giants in the attempt to storm Olympus. For he who is dizzy with passion becomes through his dizziness, as by irresistible Divine power, still more drunken and blinded till he reaches the edge of the precipice, comp. lxxv. 8, 9. That which, ver. 12, broke forth with such surprising swiftness, becomes, vv. 13, 14, milder and more tranquil, although always very agitated, and is further explained : " the sin of their mouth, their lips' word,"—that which concerns these already well-known impious speeches, " *so may they* in their own (thus manifested) pride be taken," the וְ in וְיִלָּכְדוּ (§ 347 a). That the pride is especially expressed in speeches is explained by the following, " perjury and lies." Thus then the inspired language towards the end of the strophé, ver. 15, once more comprises that demand from ver. 7 more shortly and sharply : *may they but return !* but it may here also immediately add, ver. 16 : *they will stagger to eat,* i.e., come on, staggering, to their greed; but to quiet it for ever ; *forsooth they will satisfy themselves* (get sated at the meal of this Divine punishment, utterly drain the cup of reeling) and *remain*, be no longer able to stir in death, like one excessively drunk. But the poet would not have been

able to speak so clearly of the holy place had he not been able to hope for the present renewal of the example of the Assyrians; the type is perhaps Isa. xxix. 1-9, and a similar prophecy is much later, B. Zakh. xii. 2.

4. Ver. 17, "every morning," as to-day in the morning, agrees with vv. 7, 15. In accordance with עֻזִּי and חַסְדִּי, ver. 18, we expect also in vv. 10 and 11 the same reading, especially as the sense of both words is fixed by ver. 17. Nevertheless the present text has vv. 10, 11, עֻזּוֹ and הַסְדּוֹ, and strangely would only restore the Q'ri in ver. 11 חסדי. The pronoun of the third person, according to vv. 6 and 12, was bound to be referred to Israel, because generally in this song Israel and the Gentiles are very sharply opposed, and the poet finds comfort in the fact that he belongs to Israel. But such a reference is not here so ready at hand; and in ver. 10 at least the old translators have the first person, while in ver. 11 the third, apart from the Q'ri, is substantiated by all original evidence. Perhaps, then, in ver. 11, הַסְדּוֹ is correct, and אֱלֹהַי to be read after ver. 2. If the connexion of the קֶדֶם is taken as in xxi. 4, the full sense of ver. 11 is obviously improved, and a verbal repetition between vv. 10, 11 and ver. 18 is not to be supplied.—It is clear enough that neither vv. 7, 15, nor vv. 10, 11, 18, are intended to form a refrain in the artistic sense (I., pp. 198 sq.). The repetitions which this poet, more than any other, favours, are rather explained simply from the ideas of the strophé.

This song, Ps. lix. is thus unusual in its contents, as belonging to those times, because it does not, in the first place, like many of the above, refer to the confused internal condition of the people at that time. The large fragment, Ps. x. 2-11, would well belong to this place; but this will be better explained below.—But the sense of the sufferings of those times takes a quite peculiar form when as

B. 52, 53. PSALMS XXVI. AND XXVIII.

show, a special and rare suffering, *e.g.*, a desolating malady came upon them all. That these two songs which are still separated only by Ps. xxvii., explained on p. 176, have much that is alike, and originated in a rare occurrence is plain ; and this occasion may be seen clearly to appear from xxvi. 9; xxviii. 3. A severe calamity, sweeping away many human beings, must have come upon the land, perhaps a pest, in short a general suffering, wherein, according to the sense of all antiquity, men viewed a punishment doomed upon the whole people, while the ancient horror of premature death increased the alarm to such an extent as was further described above, pp. 181 sqq. But as the feeling of such Divine punishment can only become most fearful to him who is already consciously unhappy and inwardly corrupt, and as it actually carries him off most speedily,—these songs spoken in the asylum of the Temple teach how the man who is free from the consciousness of guilt need not, even under such sufferings, despond, under this heavy burden need not bow down without feeling and without hope; for out of the midst of universal despondency and perplexity, we here see the faithful who had been earlier tried become conscious of their indefeasible hope in Jahvé. As high as these faithful ones are conscious of elevation above the great mass of the frivolous and impious and over their fear and horror,—so high is the comfort they obtain in believing prayer amidst fresh dangers that surprise all. We see here again, as in Ps. v., clearly the wide rent which at that time separated the few faithful who zealously visited the Temple from the great mass ever sinking lower,—a rent which in the course of time could not continue without alienation, easily attended by danger. For some found their token and their union in the Temple and its visitation, others in its neglect. Already these songs stand on the boundary whence the tenacious maintenance of separation may readily on the one side degenerate into spiritual pride, a danger which we meanwhile do not see realized in the innocent words of this Psalm. But we see clearly that which, under the predo-

minant idea of natural troubles, remains for the noble consciousness to do.* Not indeed from the same poet (for the
stamp of the language and conceptions is to be distinguished
in the two) but yet certainly from the same time, the two songs
originated, and in this way. The more beautiful, the more
intense is Ps. xxvi.

In the poet of this song there is expressed with freedom
and force the noble indignation against the opinion that he,
like any other, must be carried away by the national calamity.
Conscious of his innocence and inward strength, not shunning
strict trial before God, would that he might long time and
ever freshly as now be cheered at the sweet place of the
sanctuary. He prays in prevailing hope to the Jahvé who
knows him, to judge him whether he deserves such punishment,
and gradually softens, in modest request to Jahvé, ever
faithfully honoured, his first indignation into most tranquil
hope. Hence three unequal strophés ; the more agitated at the
beginning, betraying indignation and hope, ver. 1,—further, the
more tranquil recovery of the consciousness of his relation to
God and the world with renewed prayer, vv. 2-10, and along
with this abiding hope, vv. 11, 12; the long intermediate
strophé falls of itself into three smaller, of three calm verses
each. The song is manifestly a Temple-song, but one of no
ordinary kind, and not one to be sung immediately at the
sacrifice. It is best taken as the preparatory song for the
sacrifice, occasioned by the peculiar great commotion and disquiet among the people above mentioned.

1.

1   Judge me, O Jahvé !
         for I—in my innocence I lived,
         and in Jahvé I trusted without wavering !

---

* Comp. on this and particularly on Ps. xxvi., further the *Jahrbb. der Bibl.
Wiss*, ix., p. 169.

2*a*.

O prove, Jahvé, and try me,
    search through my loins and my heart!
for thy grace is before mine eyes,
    and I choose my way in Thy truth;
I sat not ever with idle folk,
    into the house of hypocrites I come not.

2*b*.

I hate every company of evil-doers,   5
    with ungodly men I sit not together;
in innocence I wash my hands,
    to circle round about Thy altar, Jahvé,
singing praise with the loudest thanks,
    and telling all Thy wonders!

2*c*.

Jahvé! I love Thy house's refuge,
    the place of the dwelling of Thy glory:
carry not away with sinners my soul,
    nor my life with shedders of blood,
in whose hands are deeds of shame,   10
    and whose right hand is full of bribery!

3.

But I—in my innocence I live:
    redeem and be gracious to me!
on even ground stands my foot:
    in holy choirs I bless Jahvé.

Ver. 3: for I know well that I may, in fidelity to Thee, firmly hepe in Thy grace and faithfulness, comp. ver. 11. *Concealed ones*, ver. 4; false people, hypocrites. *Surround* the altar, vv. 6, 7, according to ancient custom—the sacrificer circling round the altar with singing and thanksgiving during the sacred function. Comp. the *Mégha-dúta* çl. 56, and Wilson's

observation thereon. That the poet actually sung this whole
song at the sanctuary, and performed in presence of the sacrifice all the customary sacred usages amidst the rest of the
assembled mass of praying and singing worshippers, is clear
also from the last words, ver. 12 *b*, comp. with lxviii. 27. But
for this very reason he might desire to join in the others that
were in use, as is clear from ver. 7, comp. xl. 6. But for
this is required the true preparation in the spirit; and since
the poet alludes to this, ver. 6 *a*, וָאֶסְבְּכָה is best understood
according to § 347 *a*. All this under the assumption that the
song is designed to serve for something more than mere preparation for the solemn ceremony. Thus as an earnest self-
probation before the sacred function, and on so serious an
occasion, the poet does not speak too highly of himself, and it
would be unjust to reproach him with self-righteousness. He
is only as sincere and at the same time supported by a good
conscience, as calm in God as David in Ps. xviii. 20-27.

Ps. xxviii. contains the same main prayer. ver. 3, but in far
more threatening danger for him who prays, already near to
death, ver. 1, and in much greater excitement against the party
of the light-minded who persecute the poet. Yet the more
violent this outburst of complaint, the more cheering is the
addition, vv. 6-9, which joyously thanks Jahvé as the deliverer,
concluding with noble prayer and hope. This was certainly
added by the poet a short time after the passing by of the
danger (as xxxi. 20-25). According to ver. 8, comp. lxxxiv. 10,
a king must be the poet; for ver. 8 contains no mere prayer
or a wish for the king, but the experience of his deliverance,
which in this connexion presents itself entirely as a personal
experience. The incomplete and abrupt suggestiveness of this
song is thus best explained. And in fact the same Josia
whom we supposed to be the author of Ps. lix., may the more
certainly be here assumed as the poet, the more clearly vv. 7, 8
and lix. 10, 11, 12, 17, 18 correspond to one another.

1.

To Thee, O Jahvé, I call,   1
  my rock, be not silent before me,
that I may not, if thou art silent before me, be like
              to those sunk into the grave !
hear my loud supplication, whilst I cry to Thee,
  lift my hand to Thy holy chamber !

2.

Take me not away with ungodly men and with evil-
                     doers,
  who speak peace with their neighbours—having
              evil in the heart !
give them according to their desert, according to the
             wickedness of their deeds,
  according to their handiwork give to them,
    repay their deeds to them !

3.

Because they heed not the deeds of Jahvé and His
                 handiwork,   5
  let Him destroy them and build them not !

Blessed be Jahvé,
  that He has heard my loud supplication !
Jahvé is my strength and my shield,
  on Him my heart trusts and I am saved ;
and my heart rejoiced, with many a song will I praise
              Him !
O Jahvé, who is strength to them,
  and rock of deliverance of His Anointed,
help Thy people, give blessing to Thine heritage,
  and tend them, and bear them for ever !

How the expression, ver. 2 *b*, points locally to the position of the king and the Temple, is remarked in the *Gesch. des V. Isr.*, III., pp. 342 sq., of the 3rd edit.

The וְרָעָה, ver. 3, introduces an additional proposition (§ 341 *a*). But by ver. 5 the violent prayer against the enemies is significantly founded in reason, and it is explained that the poet does not merely follow his own humour and vengeance. Jeremiah's book, as well as Ps. lxix. 23.29, may be compared, and it may be borne in mind that history itself most terribly suggested the inner corruption of the state and the blinding of parties through the violent destruction of the whole kingdom, proving the impossible duration of such conditions impossible.

The מְשִׁירִי, ver. 7, as *of my song,* is nevertheless best here taken as a modest expression instead of the pure accusation.— The first member, ver. 8, is very abrupt; but no one can be thought of under " them" except the Israelites generally who, considered as a people, ever are vividly present to the mind of the king as his counterpart; just so he says again, ver. 9, " them" for "us." We see that the poet stands between Jahvé and the people, comp. iii. 9; and quite the same impression is made on the whole by the poet of Ps. lix.

We connect with Ps. xxviii. one standing not merely in local neighbourhood to it,

54. PSALM XXXI.,

which indeed proceeded out of similar perplexities to those above explained, Pss. lv., v., lii., but again reveals a quite peculiar situation of its poet. The poet, amidst incessant dangers, especially slanders, ver. 19, and threats of violent death, ver. 14, forsaken and scorned of all, completely exhausted and powerless, feels himself near to death. But strengthened by the experience of earlier times and by confirmed faith, he makes supplication in the midst of the deepest sufferings, full of confidence to Jahvé, placing his spirit in His

hands (vv. 6, 16). And so accustomed is he to this pure
resignation, that he, in the first strophé, begs only that he
may again be conscious and certain of it, vv. 2-7, in order then
in the second to pour forth with fulness of detail his complaint
and anguish, vv. 8-13; but again in the third finally to abide
alone by hope and prayer, vv. 14-19. By this intense spirit of
resignation the song is peculiarly distinguished, and quite as
one would expect from one of the most pious sufferers of the
Old Testament. However, the poet can only have written it
down in its present form after the most threatening danger
had passed by and the pleasure of deliverance was tasted,—
from good recollection, but with free not distressful repro-
duction. For in two small strophés he has, vv. 20-25, added
the expression of joy at the deliverance, thanksgiving and
praise to Jahvé for this and for so many others, and the cheerful
exhortation to all to true faith and perseverance. And thus
the whole appears to be a monument of the feelings of the
poet in the sufferings and the deliverance of an extraordinary
time (comp. just previously Ps. xxviii.).

Each of the three strophés of the main song has six verses
with thirteen members; each of those of the supplementary
song, shorter by a half, has three verses with seven members,
so that the two might be gathered into a large strophé of the
same measure.

There can be no great doubt of the derivation of this song
from the prophet Jéremjá. The stamp of the language is the
same; the whole first half of ver. 14 recurs in these rare words,
Jer. xx. 10. The figure of the worn-out vessel, ver. 13, after
Hos. viii. 8, is only found in Jer. xxii. 28, xlviii. 38. Ver. 11
sounds like Jer. xx. 18. The mood also agrees with this; the
peculiarity of Jéremjá's spirit shines out; and occasions for
this song were not wanting in the life of the elegiacally gentle
Jéremjá, who was strong in weakness. Even this connexion
of complaint and hope, the quick transition from suffering to
consolation, is in this style, in the description of his personal

features, peculiar to Jéremjá. The poet reveals himself as a
prophet who is pre-eminently persecuted for his word's sake,
vv. 19, 21.

1.

2   To Thee, Jahvé, I cleave; let me not for ever blush with
                            shame
      through the rightness of Thy grace deliver me!
bend to me Thine ear, free me speedily,
      be to me for a rock of defence,
   for a strong place, to help me!
But Thou art my rock and refuge :
      and for Thy name's sake Thou wilt lead me and guide,
5   draw me out of the net that they have hidden for me,
      because Thou art my place of protection.
Into Thy hand I commend my spirit,
      Thou art my Redeemer, Jahvé, faithful God!
Thou hatest those who wait on vain idols,
      but I trust in Jahvé.

2.

Let me rejoice and be glad in Thy favour,
      as Thou hast seen my suffering,
        known in distresses my soul,
and not given me up to the hand of the enemy,
      placed my foot at large!
10   Be gracious to me, Jahvé! for I am in distress,
      wasted in grief is my eye, my soul and body.
For care makes my life to pass away, and my years sighs,
      my strength is sunk in my suffering, and my bones
             wasted because of all the oppressions;
I was a scoff even to my neighbours greatly, and to my
             acquaintances a fear,
      they who see me without flee from me!
forgotten like a dead man to every heart,
      valued as a broken vessel.

3.

Truly I heard the report of many, horror round about,
   as they together took counsel together against me,
   devised to take my soul.
But *I*—trust in Thee, Jahvé,   15
   thinking that *Thou* art my God!
in Thy hand are my times;
   deliver me from the enemies' hand, from my perse-
     cutors!
let Thy glance shine upon Thy servant,
   help me through Thy grace!
Jahvé! let me not be ashamed, crying to Thee;
   let ungodly men be ashamed, be silent for the pit!
may lips of lies be silent,
   which speak insolently against the righteous—in
                  pride and contempt!

1.

How great is Thy goodness, which Thou hast stored up
                for Thy fearers,   20
   hast shown to those praying to Thee
clearly before the children of men;
protectest them in the shelter of Thy countenance from
                man's noises,
   hidest them in a hut from the brawl of tongues!—
Blessed be **Jahvé**, that He has wondrously shown His
                grace to me
   in the distress of oppression!

2.

I thought indeed in my anguish, "I am destroyed
              before Thine eyes:"
   but thou didst hear my loud supplication, when I
             complained to Thee.

O love Jahvé, all His pious ones!
the faithful Jahvé ever preserves
and requites sufficiently those who indulge pride.
25   be strong and let your heart take courage
all ye who wait for Jahvé!

Vv. 2, 3, cry; vv. 4, 5, justification of it through faith and experience, so that the first strophé, vv. 6, 7, concludes with the most hearty hope towards Jahvé as the true God and Redeemer.—Ver. 7, שְׂנֵאתָ, according to the LXX, necessary because of the opposition, comp. in like manner v. 6. הֶבֶל for *idols* is a favourite expression of Jéremjá's; but the whole phrase recurs only in Jona ii. 9.—Yet now in the second strophé the complaint breaks forth from the very beginning, ver. 8, the more freely, and the אֲשֶׁר is best taken (because here the language is used of the manner of the gracious deliverance) according to § 333 a. " Wideness," ver. 9, comp. iv. 2.   And yet more strongly in ver. 10 the cry for help is raised because of great sufferings, more definitely, vv. 11-13, because of life-danger along with infinite sorrow and scorn. The מִכֹּל צֹרְרַי, ver. 12, seems to be better taken in conjunction with the preceding verse (as the Pesch. does) because it is only superflous and troublesome in ver. 12, even destroying the sense (for not merely because of the many foes is any one so generally scorned) and the structure of the members; with this agrees the fact that the poet certainly, according to vi. 8, speaks in the language of ver. 11, and the same construction here furthers the connexion of ver. 11.—Thus the supplicator, in the beginning of the last strophé, ver. 14, can not keep back that which is most distressful in the present: but only the more purely recurs at the end, vv. 15-19, the believing prayer.

Ver. 21. רֶכֶם is *rodjes*, Arab., comp. רֶשַׁע *trouble, disquiet*, LXX correctly ταραχή, with which also the following member best agrees.   Ver. 22. בְּעִיר מָצוֹר must, taking עִיר as " city,"

signify the poet had been harassed and set free in a strong
city (see on lx. 11), accordingly in Jerusalem, as we know from
Jéremjá; and in fact this occurs of itself to the unprejudiced
reader, according to lx. 11. But this long song falls nevertheless certainly in a time still anterior to the destruction of
Jerusalem, which is nowhere indicated in it; for that period it
is at the close too cheerful in tone. Again, the statement
above would be here quite too cold and prosaical. Therefore
עִיר here = צִיר be *anguish*, as Jer. xv. 8.—Ver. 25 after
xxxii. 11, xxvii. 14; as ver. 17 *a* after Num. vi. 25.

We insert here

55. Psalm lxxxviii.,

partly because, according to its contents, it is suitably placed
here, although it probably belongs to the first half of the
seventh century; partly because, so far as we can see, it stands
alone with reference to its authorship, although it bears much
resemblance to the songs to be explained below, Ps. xxxv. sqq.
on the one hand, and Ps. lxxvii. on the other. It is in
character an ordinary song of sickness, like a further development of Ps. vi.; it is only unique in the fact that of enemies
whom the sick man has no mention whatever is made. The
poet was still young, ver. 16, and had long struggled with the
most deadly sickness, had undergone all the most grievous
sufferings, and so lost all friends, had become an abhorrence to
all men, and as weak and frail as if he had long been among
the dead. The song is a long, languishing outburst of this
mournful, almost disconsolate temper, which seeks but to
excite pity and compassion by dread description of sufferings
and renewal of more cheerful songs that had earlier escaped
him. After a short introduction, vv. 2, 3, follows at once in
great detail the description of his sufferings, vv. 4-8. But the
fact that the sufferer merely through these sufferings had ever
lost all friends among man, determines him to most woeful
supplication to the Lord of Death and Life; and to the

20 *

reflection that he had, at an earlier day, sought to awaken the
Divine compassion by sweet song, vv. 9-13. Thus the poet in
extremity of suffering is carried away once more in a strain of
lugubrious prayer, all but utterly succumbing in the renewed
thought of the greatness of his sufferings and the approach of
death, vv. 14-19. Each of the three strophés which are here
formed after the brief prelude, has accordingly a compass of
twelve members, and those, as usual with the majority of poets,
of uniform short structure.

1.

2   O Jahvé, God of my salvation,
      when by day I call, in the night before Thee:
   let my prayer come before Thee,
      O bend Thine ear to my complaining !

2.

   For satiate with evils is my soul,
      and away to the pit tends my life,
5   I am esteemed as one sunk into the grave,
      become as a powerless man,
   among the dead is my couch,
      like to the slain, who rest in the grave,
   on whom Thou no more thinkest,
      since they are separated from Thy hand.
   Hast brought me into the deepest tomb,
      into darknesses, into shallows;
   on me Thy glowing heat came down,
      Thou hast caused all thy waves to come down.   *

3.

   Hast removed my trusted friends from me,
      made me an abhorrence to them,
      shut me in and without outlet !
10   Mine eye wastes with grief:
      I call, Jahvé, to Thee each day,
      spreading out my hands to Thee :

"Dost Thou then wonders to the dead,
    or do shadows stand, giving praise to Thee?
is then Thy grace told of in the grave,
    and Thy faithfulness in destruction?
are Thy wonders known in the darkness,
    Thy righteousness in the land of oblivion?"

4.

But I—to Thee, O Jahvé, complain,
    and in the morning my prayer is beforehand.
Why dost Thou reject, Jahvé, my soul,   15
    concealest Thy countenance from me?
wretched am I and departing from my youth,
    I bear Thy terrors, I must pass away;
Thy glowing heats have gone over me,
    Thy terrors destroy—destroyed me
surrounded me as floods daily,
    encircled me together!
Hast removed lover and friend from me,
    my trusted ones are—the place of darkness!

Ver. 2. The צעקתי is necessarily understood also before
נגדך; but the whole second member is by means of the יום
connected according to § 332 d, only a relative sentence to
the first, for that following the address is first seen in ver. 3.
What was last said in ver. 4, how the poet feels himself near
to hell or the dark lower world, or as if he were already among
the dead, is further described in vv. 5-7. A *powerless* man =
dead man, shadow; the וְהֵמָּה, ver. 6, introduces a static
proposition, as it has to be explained why God no longer has
any thought for the dead; for all that is living stands immediately in God's hand, Job xii. 10, not so the dead, violently
separated from the upper world, and from the light, and in so
far as if withdrawn from the hand of God, Ps. vi. 6; Jon. ii.
5, 7. More generally then is expressed in ver. 8 the sense of

most severe and most burning sufferings; עֲנִיתָ is derived either from עָנָה work (prop. trouble, *ana*, Syr., comp. Koh.) : suffer to be busy, set in activity, *appoint*, despatch, or better and here more appropriately from ענה in the physical sense be lowly, *fall*, come down (*ana = nazal*, Qam.) : *sink*, cause to fall, LXX ἐπήγαγες; to the עלי in the beginning refer thus uniformly both members; comp. on the figure, xlii. 8; xxxviii. 2, 3.—If with the recollection of his general forsaken condition as a further consequence of the long sickness, a new strophé here, ver. 9, begins, this is just as in Job xix. 13; as the poet had certainly the Book of Job in its original form generally before his mind. *Shut in without outlet*, simply because all fled from him, he was limited to his forsaken desert spot; the figurative signification of one encompassed on all sides by calamity, Job iii. 23, xix. 8, does not suit this connexion. Thus did the poet cry with tearful eye long time for aid, seeking to move God's compassion by the cheerful recollection of the actual thanksgiving after his deliverance.—Vv. 11-13 is a development from earlier songs, comp. on the sense, vi. 6.

From the new beginning, ver. 14, it is clear that this is a morning song, like ver. 44, and still more like lvii. 9; the transition and ver. 16 like xl. 18, lxix. 14, 30, cix. 21, 22. אָפוּנָה, ver. 16, from פִין = פנה, *affan*, Arab., faint away, turn dizzy, lose consciousness. The voluntative seems to denote: I shall faint, a dizziness seizes me; the LXX ἐξηπορήθην, and frequently the LXX thus render the otherwise voluntative formation by the aorist, certainly not without reason, § 233 *a*, but not altogether suitably. On צִמַּתְּתוּנִי, comp. § 120 *a*.— Ver. 19 closes with the most mournful turn: whilst all human living acquaintances have forsaken the poet, the dead have become his new intimates—the Orcus, comp. v. 7; Job xvii. 3, 4, may be present to the poet's mind.

C. 56. PSALM L.

There sounds indeed mightily even in these last times of the ancient kingdom, even in song, once more the eternal prophetic truth addressed to the whole people, and it seeks in serious language to remove the great dangers which threaten from within. This is shown by Ps. l., which may fall in the times of Josia. Since, that is to say, through King Josia's improvements the external reverence of Jahvé had been greatly increased, and was more strictly maintained from the court downwards, there arose a new evil. Side by side with the older evil of indifference prevailing in general among the people towards higher things, and the inclination to superstition, there sprung up hypocrisy in religion,—cunning men, under the cloak of external reverence and close acquaintance with the religion of Jahvé, the more securely practising their manifold impiety. Again, according to vv. 1, 23, the tranquillity of the kingdom must have been sorely troubled from without, as we know that Josia's reign was much disturbed by storms from external quarters. The better times which were expected from King Josia's new constitution of the kingdom refused to come, and Divine grace and help seemed to be as distant as possible. Through all this the kingdom was now threatened by extreme danger. The sense of misery mutely weighed upon the people, without any clear light on the true mode of deliverance (vv. 15, 23). A morose spirit, discontented with God and the world, had gained possession of the majority, whilst the hypocrites alluded to above fancied they would be able to live on quite securely in their practices. But a poet, who in the consciousness of the eternal Divine truth has deeply penetrated this condition of things, is so powerfully convinced that it cannot continue, that he already views in spirit in the most vivid manner the Divine judgment upon their perversities; and as he in a moment of devotion has seen this drama clearly within his own mind, and has plainly heard the voice of the strict judge—so now the appearance and indignation of the Supreme God is vividly renewed with detailed and powerful description. Both the manner of the appearance and that of the language are closely connected and reciprocally correspond. For already the former must provisionally but definitely leave it to be anticipated who will speak, and how.

Here, however, there is nothing more important to be noted than that the style in which God is here conceived as speaking is borrowed from the custom of a king speaking in the assembled council. I have shown in the *History* that the people Israel once had its high assemblies, when the king addressed the assembled states of his kingdom: a diet in the kingdom of Juda, when the words of this prophetic poetic address could be heard, was of course not to be thought of; but only the more clearly does it stand before our poet-prophet's spirit how God must now speak to His solemnly assembled people when he appears, and how he was heard with his divinely enlightened but pre-eminently also divinely-judging word. The true God cannot appear, and for this purpose, in His own community without the bright light of His word scattering gloom and darkness of all kinds, as it becomes mighty among men; and here, too, this bright glad light of His word is not wanting. But since the address of the Supreme Judge must in this instance still further sound, denouncing grave sins, and threatening the last penalty, the poet could not here otherwise conceive God and represent Him than as Him from out of Sion, indeed, but as God of the whole world, cursing wrathfully, with all-subduing, all-ordering power, in desolating storm and fire, summoning heaven and earth as witnesses to His judgment on Israel,— Jahvé speaking amidst loud thunder, whom Israel, covenanted to Him, but now become unfaithful, must hear before all peoples in assembled congregation, as the strict Judge, vv. 1-6. The address thus introduced, turns justly first to the great mass,—the multitude that errs more through sloth and superstition than intentional wickedness, who are firmly admonished, with apt irony, that not by sacrifices senselessly offered amidst dull grief, which God does not require, but by the recognition of the Divine benefits, in a new life, assurance of Divine grace and joy may be obtained, vv. 7-15. But then it flames up in indignation against the hypocrite or intentional wrong-doer in particular, vv. 16-21; and finally returns with a few words of benevolent intent, but serious menace, to exhortation to the whole people, vv. 22, 23. The thoughts in the whole song are as noble and profound as those in the greatest prophets; and although the poet without doubt speaks according to prophetic patterns, yet the whole disposition is peculiar to him, and in particular points the execution is of an unusual character.—That Sion still at that time was flourishing, entirely uninjured, is clear from the description, ver. 2, to which there is allusion later, Lam. ii. 15; but other-wise the language and the elegant metrical structure does not point to earlier times than King Josia. As the poet here gave rather a prophetic forecast and address than a song, the ordi-nary structure of the strophés cannot be here applicable. But a correspondent measure is here retained, the main portion of the address being built up of three small strophés, each of three verses, and accordingly both the description of the appearing God at the beginning, and the second, or the more severe portion of the address, consists each of six verses, while the after-address admits of the greater brevity. Thus here too, the poetic sense, well articulating the whole, prevails.

> The God of Gods, Jahvé, spake and called the earth   1
>   from sunrise to sunset.
> From out of Sion, crown of beauty,
>   beamed forth God,
> (let our God come and not be silent !)
>   Before Him devouring fire,
>   and about Him there was a great tempest.
> He calls to heaven above
>   and to the earth that He would judge His people :
> " assemble my saints before me,   5
>   who concluded my covenant with sacrifices !"

and the heavens announced His right,
  that God Himself now judges :

1.

" Hear my people that I may speak,
    Israel, that I may exhort thee ;
  God, thy God am I !
Not for thy sacrifices do I punish thee,
    since before me are ever thy gifts ;
will take no bullock from thy house,
    nor he-goat from thy folds !

10   All wild beasts of the forest are indeed mine,
        great beasts on a thousand mountains
    I know all mountain-birds,
        and the brood of the field is not strange to me ;
    should I hunger, I would not tell it thee :
        mine is indeed the world and its fulness !

Do I eat the flesh of bulls,
    drink blood of goats ?
sacrifice thou to God thanksgiving
    and pay to the Highest thy vows
15   and then call on me in the day of distress :
        and I will deliver thee and thou shalt honour me !"

2.

And to the wicked spake God :
    " How darest thou enumerate my doctrines,
      take my covenant on thy lips,
for thou hatest correction,
    hast cast my word behind thee,
seest thou a thief, willingly thou goest with him,
    and with adulterers hast thy portion,
didst loose thy mouth with wickedness,
    causest thy tongue to weave deceit,

sitting speakest against thy brother, 20
   against thy mother's son **pourest** out abuse ?—
This didst thou—and I was silent;
   thoughtest surely I were as Thou :
I will punish thee, and produce it against thee !"

3.

" Observe this, ye who forget God,
   that I tear not asunder without deliverance !
He who sacrifices thanksgiving will honour me;
   and he who walks carefully—
him will I cause to enjoy God's salvation !"

Vv. 1-6. The simple narration or the *perf.* predominates, because the poet has actually, before he thus writes, the scene in his mind. Of course, the prophet in the moment of consecration, can only be met by the thought in a concrete solid picture, which lays the more powerful hold on the imagination, the more it is undivided and concrete. For the development in particulars and the orderly description does not appear until afterwards, with the wish to fix and pursue the picture; but whilst the poet or prophet would now in particular set forth that which he beheld in concrete form, he necessarily turns back in thought to that moment, and may narrate in the *perf.* what he has beheld. But the personal wish for fulfilment may well be pressed forward, since in truth in the external sense nothing has yet been actually accomplished; and it is quite as if the poet heard with the words ver. 3 *a*, the deep-hearted exclamations with which the saints long for the Divine appearance and accompany its arrival.—The figure itself of the approaching God is indeed current at an earlier date, Ex. xix., and at a nearer time of the judging God, Mic. i. 2; Hab. iii.; but in the particular delineation there is much here that is new. First, the whole description of the God summoning the assembled world to judgment (highest God; incon-

testably the poet thinks of אל in the *st. const.*) briefly set
forth, ver. 1, then the description of this again more tran-
quilly and in more detail begun and completed, vv. 2-6. From
His sanctuary, from out the beloved Sion the highest God, the
God of Israel arises, calling heaven and earth as witnesses
(Isa. i. 2; Deut. xxxii. 1) to the contest against His own
people, who must at His behest, summoned by mighty angels
or by the heralds of the assembly and the court, immediately
appear, as it must be shown whether they who are honourably
termed "the saints of Jahvé," who have entered into holy
covenant and plight with Him (according to the idea of the
true congregation, Ex. xix.—xxiv.) whether these are still
actually what they ought to be, and may boast to have kept
the covenant, ver. 5. After these preparations the judgment
begins in presence of the assembled people, whilst the
thunders announce the Divine right, or the fact that God has
to speak in judgment, and what He has to say—that is, that
God *Himself* (הוא § 314 *a*) judges, and speaks in the following
way.

Now the first and at once serious word is directed, ver. 7,
as the general summons of the Lord to hear His word, to
the whole congregation thus assembled. But while the
discourse first applies to the great multitude who err chiefly
through superstition and dulness of mind, it betakes itself
presently to subtle scorn, as the last weapon against this, and
even lowers itself, with profound humanness, to the ideas of
the people, vv. 8, 9, 12; but only the more readily to refute
all that is erroneous, and cause the Divine truth the more
freely to shine through, vv. 10, 11; and straightway with the
beginning of the last small strophé, vv. 13, 14, to express the
more briefly the truth in all its aspects. *If I hungered* is,
ver. 12, only assumed as a pure possibility; but at last, ver. 13,
this is also removed, and error having been thus chastised by
irony, the highest truth may be stated in contrast with the
more striking force, vv. 14, 15. The first and most necessary

thing is in every moment and under all circumstances to be
conscious of the indestructibility of spiritual blessings or of
Divine benefits, and to remain in the temper of one serenely
and hopefully praising and thanking God; and thus instead of
thinking, in dull indolence and unconsciousness, after a
calamity, of external means of warding it off, *e.g.*, the
bringing of guilt-offerings,—rather to offer the purely spiritual,
conscious sacrifice of thanksgiving and of the external
beginning of an oft-praised new life (Hos. xiv. 3; Mic. vi.
6-8). Only he who stands in this higher condition is fit and
prepared for Divine salvation, and will not fear God as the
Author of penalty, but reverence and honour Him as the
wondrous Deliverer.

As the king in the throne-speech breaking off, turns to a
part of the assembly of the kingdoms, *e.g.*, to the great men in
particular, so here, vv. 16-21, God turns to the proud scribes and
lawyers, here termed *ungodly*; and here the character of the
address changes forthwith to that of the gravest reproof, so
that he demands of them what title they have to boast of their
knowledge of law and their fidelity in religion, although they
(with וְאַתָּה, ver. 17, begins the counter-series of static preposi-
tions) do the very opposite to all this.

Domestic crime, ver. 18, crafty invention, and devising of
evil in evil company, ver. 19, and in good company, at all
events calumny of the most intimate acquaintance or relative,
ver. 20, are examples of accomplished villany on all sides
(דֹּפִי properly thrust, blow, hence calumny = גדף, root
strengthened in the beginning); and the fact that this
remained without punishment for a time, has only strengthened
the ungodly man in the error that God is as weak as he is, but
now he is to learn the truth. The strangely-appearing connexion of the *inf. const.* הֱיוֹת with its *verb. fin.* is explained if
we reflect that the speech of the ungodly man demands indeed
the *inf. abs.* ("*certainly* God *is* as I," therefore הָיֹה יִהְיֶה);
but because here this speech was indirectly interpolated, *i.e.*,

was more closely connected with the main sentence, the *inf. abs.* became fluxive, *i.e.*, passed into the *inf. const.*, for this is in truth the general distinction of the infinitives, § 240 *c.*

But the language must finally turn back to the general ; and that in vv. 22-23 the whole people is again addressed, is clear from ver. 23, comp. vv. 14, 15. The שׂוּם is according to the brief usage of some poets of this time, *note* (B. Jes. xli. 20) : but observe that דרך is quite indefinite, and does not take the form דַּרְכּוֹ, since the whole mode of expression in this song is that of elegance, I., p. 27.

And shortly, the whole higher teaching of that century is brought by a poet who shows great affinity to the poet of Ps. xxvi., into proverbial poetry in

57. Psalm i.,

a very simple, didactic song, with solid brevity and florid style,—embracing many elements, a song of pointed power and incisive effect. The general character of the contents and the position of this song at the head of the Psalter, makes it highly probable that it was from the first composed with the object of furnishing a suitable introduction to an (older, smaller) collection of Psalms ; as moreover it comprises the germ of many songs and perfectly denotes the temper in which an old poet may have first selected and collated Psalms, and in which he desires the collection to be read. The whole only one lengthy strophé in six verses, but in the middle dividing into its two halves.

> Blessed the man who never went in the counsel of the
> > ungodly,
> > nor trod the sinner's path,
> > > nor sat in the society of the scorners ;
> > but has pleasure in Jahvé's doctrine,
> > > on His doctrine meditates day and night :

he is like a tree planted by water-brooks,
  which brings forth its fruit in season, and whose leaf
                                              withers not :
    and all that he doeth, succeeds.—
Not thus are the ungodly,
  but like chaff, which the wind drives away.
Therefore ungodly men shall not stand in the judgment,   5
  sinners in the congregation of the just:
for Jahvé knows the way of the righteous,
  but the ungodly man's way disappears.

The felicitations of the faithful, according to his nature and
his fruit, vv. 1-3, are followed more briefly by the description of
the misery of the ungodly and of the eternal foundation and
duration of those contrasted human fates in God, vv. 4-6. The
first half is the most elaborate and the clearest. The picture
of the faithful man, ver. 1, negatively depicted as complete
alienation from evil both in disposition (counsel) and in deed,
as well as in company and fellowship. He who thinks evil is
already a רָשָׁע, one led astray by passion; he who does the
counselled evil is a חַטָּא sinner; he who is even so greatly
inured to the suppression of a good conscience, that he despises
and perverts in company the good, is a לֵץ, scorner, and
persons of the kind are wont to hold together that they may
the more uninterruptedly, by themselves, gain strength in evil
thoughts, xxvi. 4, 5. The affirmative description follows,
ver. 2, suiting a time in which the written law first came truly
into force, and formed a barrier against many dangers, comp.
Jos. i. 8, with all the other Deuteronomic matter. The consequence or fruit of such a life is described, ver. 3 : וְהָיָה "*so
will it be* ever in strength and fulness, like the most happily
planted and most delightfully flourishing tree" (Jer. xvii. 7, 8
is repeated and further developed from this passage), all his
undertakings visibly succeed.—But since the ungodly are in
themselves nothingless and insipid, without contents and con-

sistency, without force and duration, ver. 4, they cannot stand
their ground and remain in the congregation, if once Divine
judgment and the hour of trial arrives. They may indeed
appear for a time prosperous and enduring, and at present the
ungodly and the faithful live so together, but when the
purification and strict trial comes, the time of decision, they
will not abide in the community of the righteous, since the act
of separation and punishment of the evil ever, even although
now invisibly, comes on, or since God knows very well the two
different modes of life (ver. 6, comp. vii. 10) and treats each
according to its desert, so that,—which is here the main matter
and the object of the discourse,—the way of the ungodly perishes
for ever, leads never to blessedness and well-being. The
conclusion, vv. 5, 6, is thus quite prophetical, indeed Messianic,
describing what is ever valid, and therefore ever to be hoped
and to be expected in the course of the world ; only that at
that time the hope of a Divine judgment was firmer and more
concrete.

Again, in those times proverbial poetry, as is shown in I., pp.
60 sqq., was uncommonly active in amalgamating the ancient
eternal truths of genuine religion with the experiences and
informations of later times ; and already proverbial poetry had
begun to mingle itself with lyric poetry. We possess now of
this mixed species in the Psalter the two grand pieces,

58, 59. Psalms ix., x., xxxvii.,

which, according to all signs, belong not only to the same time,
but also to the same poets. They are the two oldest alphabetic
songs preserved, as both their spirit and very independent contents and their art teaches. The alphabet proceeds in them first
with a small strophé of four lines, which conveniently here, according to I., pp. 202, 3, presents itself as the earliest mode. But
each, because it appeared in this wide extension too long, falls
into four greater divisions, just as the twenty-two letters readily

admit of being distributed into four sections, ו—א, ד—ז,
ת—ץ , ף—ל. In other respects we must immediately give a
particular explanation of the two fragments.

That Pss. ix. and x. might readily be somewhat more strongly
separated, follows from what has just been said. But that they
originally were connected is not less clear from many proofs,
specially from the peculiar resemblance of the language between
ix. 1-21 and x. 1, 12-18 (comp. לעתות בצרה, ix. 10, x. 1 ; אנוש
ix. 20, 21, x. 18 ; דך ix. 10, x. 18, elsewhere only lxxiv. 21).
Further, Ps. ix. is not complete in itself: ix. 20 is further
taken up, x. 12-18. We see now in the whole song (somewhat
as in lxxxv. 2-8) thanksgiving and prayer pouring forth ; whilst
at first pure thanksgiving for a last great deliverance and
revelation of gracious Divine operation is heard, ix. 2-11, but
then in this glad look upon the near past, thought of the more
troubled present and the prayer for help mingles, ix. 12-21 ;
and after this distress of the present has been depicted in
detailed complaint, x. 1-11, finally with the greater urgency
the prayer for speedy help and restoration of right recurs,
x. 12-18. These four uniform strophés appear to have been
designed by the poet for so many alternate song-strophés in
the Temple ; for the *I*, in which he often here speaks, cannot
designate an individual person in the people, but only the
whole people as an assembled congregation,—as Israel.

But the description of the contempt and pride, of the craft
and villany of the enemy, x. 2-11, is separated by a different
and severer language, and greater coherence, significantly from
the other parts, and may be interpolated only by the last poet
from an older song, which belongs in its whole style to the
first half of the seventh century, or to the period of Ps. lv.,
when general anarchy prevailed, and the right of the crafty and
the stronger prevailed, comp. above, pp. 253 sq., on Ps. lv. sqq.
In the proper verses of the last poet we discern also the arrangement or the beginning of an alphabetic order of verses, of four

members each. From 1-3, from 6-12, from 19-22, this order
of twenty-two letters is quite .plain (only in ix. 20 ק occurs
instead of כ), and the looser broken bond of the succession
of thoughts, the limitation of the immediate sense to four
members, which is visible throughout, except in x. 2-11, sub-
stantiates sufficiently the purpose of this order : but before the
completion of this art the poet must have been interrupted ; for
that the alphabetic pieces are not the borrowed ones, is shown
also by this, that x. 12-18 are linked to x. 2-11, and draw their
material from them, נָאֵץ, ver. 13, from ver. 3, תדרש, ver. 13,
15, from ver. 4, and particularly הלכח, ver. 14, from vv. 8, 10.
In this way it might also come about that the fourth section,
x. 12-18, is left somewhat shorter than it should be according
to the rest of the arrangement; but more probably there are
wanting only now before x. 12, the verses for צ.

At the time of the last poet the external condition of the
people, as is obvious from his indications, was the following. A great and rare example of Divine retribution,
nearly affecting Israel, in the case of a mighty kingdom
of the world of that time, had appeared in history. As
we now learn from the whole tenor of this song, and especially from the words ix. 15, that Jerusalem at that time
was not yet destroyed, we may understand by that mighty
kingdom, over whose overthrow the song at the beginning
rejoices, not the Chaldean but only the Assyrian, which completely passed away with the destruction of Nineve about
606 B.C. ; and the great cities, for the utter destruction of which
the song, ix. 7, thanks God, are above all those out of which
Nineve itself was composed, as well as the others thick in its
vicinity. But partly Juda itself was at that time overrun and
subjugated by Gentiles (the Egyptians), whence the wish,
x. 16, is explained ; partly the light-minded prevailed again
there, and this explains why the poet interweaves the large
piece, x. 2-11.

1.*

All my heart praises **Jahvé**, Thee, 2
   I tell all Thy wonders,
let me rejoice in Thee and make merry,
   make music to Thy name, O Highest,
Because of the conquest of my foes,
   who stumble and pass away before Thee;
because thou didst carry out my judgment and my
     cause,
   didst sit on the throne as just judge!
Didst threaten peoples, didst destroy the ungodly,
   didst blot out their name for ever, aye;
   the foes became utterly an everlasting wreck,
   and the cities which Thou didst destroy,—their,
       their memory passed away:
but **Jahvé** is throned for ever,
   has for judgment erected **His** throne;
and *He* will judge the world justly,
   decide equitably upon peoples,
Giver of protection to the bowed down will be
          Jahvé 10
   a protection for times of sultry distress,
   and they who know Thy name trust Thee,
    because Thou didst not forsake Thy seekers,
         Jahvé!

2.

Highly celebrate Jahvé, who inhabits Sion,
   makes known among the people His deeds;
   because He who avenges blood, remembered them,
   forgot not the complaint of sufferers:
In grace, Jahvé! see my suffering from my haters,
   thou who raisedst me from the gates of death,
   that I may tell Thy whole praise, 15

* The translation is conformed to the alphabetic arrangement, as in the German.—*Tr.*

in the daughter of Sion's gates may leap for joy
   at Thy deliverance!
Justly the Heathen sank into the pit which they made,
  in the net that they hid, their foot was taken;
  Jahvé made Himself known, carried out judgment,
   wicked men entangled themselves in their own
   handiwork,[1] *
Know the ungodly shall return to hell,
  the heathen all, the God-forgetters;
for not for ever will He forget the helpless,
  the hope of the sufferer shall not perish for ever!
20 Up, Jahvé! let not mortal man scorn,
   let the peoples be clearly judged before Thee!
  prepare, Jahvé, for them a terror,
   let the peoples feel they are mortal! *

3.

1 Meaning what, O Jahvé, stand'st Thou afar,
  with veiled eye for times of sultry distress?
in the pride of the ungodly sufferers burn,
  be they taken by intrigues who devised them;
the wicked man speaks praise to the lust of his soul,
  and greedily forsakes, despises Jahvé.

The wicked man according to his haughtiness, "no
   punishment,
  "no God is there"—are all his thoughts.
5 victorious are his ways at all times,
  Thy judgments are too high, too far for him,
all his foes,—he snorts at them,
in his heart thinking, "never shall I waver
  in any time, I who am without ill!"

Of perjury his mouth is full, of treachery and deceit,
  mischief, destruction his tongue conceals;

---

[1] Here for once the fuller musical notice is retained, comp. I., p. 232.

he sits in the ambush of the villages,
   in corners he murders the innocent ;
his eyes spy out the feeble ;
   in the corner he lurks as the lion in the thicket !

Lurks to seize a sufferer,
   seizes the sufferer, drawing him into his net ;
quietly he stoops, bows down,—   10
   and into his claws fall the feeble,
while he thinks in his heart, " God has forgotten it,
   concealed His countenance, never beholding it !"

4.

Up, Jahvé ! God, raise Thy hand,
   forget not the sufferers !
why does the wicked man forget God,
   thinking in his heart, Thou didst not punish ?—
Verily Thou didst see it ! because mischief and trouble
                    Thou dost behold
     into Thy hand to mark them ;
To Thee the feeble commits it :
   the orphan *Thou* didst ever help.
Wilt break that arm of the wicked,   15
   the evil man—seeking his wickedness shall find it
                    no more !
Jahvé is king, ever, aye,
   the heathen passed away from his land !
To (*Zu*) Thee has pierced the longing of the sufferers,
                   Jahvé !
   Thou wilt raise up their heart, open Thine ear,
to judge the orphan and bowed down,
   that earthly men may not further resist !

Vv. 2-11 are just ten verses, according to the Massôra for
א—ו : but the strophé is now wanting for ה, since ver. 7
begins too early with ה, and would be a transposition of the

verse against the sense. But it is possible that in ver. 8 it originally ran הֶן יהוה, *let Jahvé see* . . . for ויהוה.

1. ix. 7. תָּם is immediately united with a predicate, thus in the sense: become wholly, utterly something, comp. § 298 *b*, *Gr. ar.* II., p. 159; for without difficulty הָאוֹיב is connected with the *plur.* of the verb (comp. for the interchange of *sing.* and *pl.* § 317 *b*). According to this connexion one is indeed tempted to take עָרִים, not as cities but as = צָרִים (comp. § 58 *b*): but that this is not necessary is said above, and נָתַשׁ better suits for cities. The emphatic הֵמָּה ־ם § 311 *a*, finds its opposition immediately, ver. 8, in Jahvé, as remote in Israel, whose immediate overthrow had at that time been long expected.—The close of the first part, vv. 10, 11, alludes to a prayer lying in the background, for וִיהִי! must be understood according to § 347 *a*. בַּצָּרָה is the withholding of rain, *sultriness* and dryness which often lasts so long, comp. שְׁנַת בַּצֹּרֶת, Jer. xvii. 9; xiv. 1.

2. In the second part there is a twofold transition from thanksgiving to prayer, vv. 12, 13 to 14, 15, and vv. 16, 17 to 18-21: through recollection of what has been experienced, prayer and hope for the future is prepared. For חָנְנֵנִי some copies read, perhaps more correctly, חַנְנֵנִי, as derived from חָנַן; the doubled נ is thus at least more readily explained. The נוֹקֵשׁ, ver. 17, might be taken as part. Qal from נקשׁ = יקשׁ, so that either רָשָׁע would be subject: for his own work the enemy lays snares (1 Sam. xxviii. 9), or that Jahvé would be subject: by his own work He snares, takes him. But, to pass over other difficulties, here the *perf.* only suits according to the whole connexion, vv. 16, 17, in opposition to vv. 18-21. It must therefore be *perf.* Nif. § 140 *a*; comp. on the sense, Prov. xxix. 5. מוֹרָה־, ver. 21, appears a worse mode of writing for מוֹרָא, something at which one is shocked, which again awakens the thought of God and His fear, Deut. iv. 34. Further, from the word-play on the *gates* of hell and those of Sion, vv. 14, 15, it may be most plainly

recognized that the song was designed for a festival, to be sung in the Temple at Jerusalem.

3. In the description of the oppression of the tyrant, x. 2-11, the true ground of the conduct of the wicked man, his contempt of Jahvé and of Divine right, is first brought out, vv. 3-6, then further his impious speech, ver. 7, and behaviour is characterized, vv. 8-11, so that the discourse in vv. 8-11 recurs to ver. 2. הִלֵּל עַל, ver. 3, is: he expresses not praise concerning Jahvé, as was seemly, but concerning his own pleasure, comp. Hab. i. 11-16. That which stands at the end of the first and in the beginning of the second member, ver. 4, must contain the thoughts of the wicked man; " He resents not (comp. ver. 13), indeed, there is no God ;" for if the living, operative, all-punishing God be taken away, it is equivalent to taking away any true God. But he is tempted, according to ver. 5, to such deeds and thoughts, by the fact that *his ways* at all times appear *to be victorious* (הֵחִיל, formed after עָשָׂה חַיִל, Num. xxiv. 18), he sins so long without interruption, and the Divine judgments hitherto are too high (concealed in heaven) and distant, and he has not yet felt them; comp. Job xxii. 12 sqq., so that he thinks never to come to harm, never to waver. The word, misapprehended from the Q'rî, to be read probably חֶלְכָּאִים, ver. 10, *sing.* חֶלְכָּה, vv. 8, 14, is formed like חָפְשִׁי, only according to § 164 *c*, with the more Aram. adjective-ending *ae* for *î*; from יְחֶלֶה *weakness*, properly darkness, to be confused before the eyes, comp. *hâlakh* and *hâkhal*, Arab., which also *Qâm.,* p. 1354, holds to be related ; Aq. Sym., aptly, ἀσθενεῖς ; *halakh* is *grey, grizzled,* of the scapegoat, *Hamâsa,* p. 443, 6, or *dim, dark, Ibn.-'Arabshâh's Fakih.* p. 207, 2, and elsewhere.—Ver. 9. סֻכָּה may be read without suffix, according to Job xxxviii. 40, and since in ver. 10 the יָשֹׁחוּ, according to the above passage in Job, plainly continues the figure of the beast of prey (as also עֲצוּמָיו denotes, " the two strong ones," the claws, comp. עֲצַלְתָּיִם, § 180 *a*), וְדָכָה (according to the K'*tib*) is

also to be understood of the self-compression, or stooping of him who lies in wait.

4. The beginning, ver. 12, with ק, is observable as in ix. 20. —Ver. 14. *Give into the hand*, place, mark there, so that it may never be forgotten, ever to see before oneself, according to the figure B. Isa. xlix. 16.—Ver. 16 shows plainly how it was wished that the Canaan, overrun by the heathen (and heathen lords), might be purged from them; and the *perf.* is certainly to be understood according to § 223 *b*.—The last words, ver. 18, may be either thus connected according to the accentuation: " *that* (still dependent on the preceding ל, § 350 *b*) he (the wicked man, ver. 15) may not still further frighten men out of the land, hunt the unhappy Israelites by terror out of Canaan," but in that case a more correspondent word would be used instead of אנוש, which recalls ix. 21,—possibly עניים; or rather thus : that *not still further may men of the earth, earthly ones, strive against* (ערץ *eradd*, Arab., Isa. xlvii. 12, hence also be in fear, from reluctance, dread) the Divine will.

The interwoven piece, x. 2-11 (to which also ver. 1 might belong), has quite another structure of verses, since here manifestly three verses are found in each case united. One would like to know to what kind of poetry this piece originally belonged; for an original song the language in it winds off too slowly. Earlier it was simply a fragment of a longer discourse of the kind of which we find an example in Hab. ii. 6 sqq., but immediately designed to obtain a Divine answer to this long and yearning prayer, like to that which follows with vv. 9 sqq. in the far more briefly constructed Ps. lxxxv.

Ps. xxxvii. is one of the best alphabetic songs in warmth of contents and inner connexion (so far as an alphabetic song can have this). An aged, much experienced poet and teacher gives here to the disciple golden sayings with a view to engrave the truth that, since wrong and wickedness are ever in the end their own punishment, the apparent momentary good fortune of the wicked is not to be envied, but in rest and resignation the salvation of Jahvé, inwardly secure, is to be expected. In that time this doctrine was clearly illustrated in fact by the history of so many overthrows of unjust kingdoms and so many falls of tyrants, and is brought forward here with the higher confidence of a teacher blessed by such insight and experiences. And it may be truly said that the poet, who in the preceding song expressed the true joy and the true prayer for the congregation on a festive occasion, now seizes in this place artistic means to stamp by a properly proverbial poem the truth,—the more necessary under the intense disquiet and doubts of that period, that men must not allow themselves to be deceived by the prosperity of unrighteousness.

The arrangement of the series of proverbs expounded p. 320 also answers to this highest object. The four sections are quite correspondently divided into a twofold series of 6 and 5 (= 22) letters; but at the head of each of these four sections the language starts from the unrighteous, in order to come by contrast to that which it is the duty of the pious to do. Further, the contents of this piece are indeed too diverse from the preceding to permit us to find very many similar expressions in the two; yet such are not wanting, as x. 15 *a* and xxxvii. 17 *a*; x. 15 *b* and xxxvii. 36 *b*.

1.

Ah, be not jealous of mis-doers,   1
      envy not them who practise vice;
   for like the grass they quickly fade,
      pass away like the green herb.
By doing well trust in God;
      then dwell in the land and feed securely
   and have thy pleasure in Jahvé,
      and may He give thee thy heart's wishes!
Destiny leave to Jahvé,   5
      trust in Him, and *He* will bring about,

will make sun-bright thy right
    and thy cause like the noon-beam !
Even wait for Jahvé, calmly given up to Him,
    and be not jealous of the prosperity of many,
because of those who do wickedness.
Flee anger, cease from wrath,
    and be not jealous—only to sin ;
for mis-doers are destroyed,
    and those who wait for God — they are heirs
                    of the land.
10   Give heed awhile : the wicked is gone,
    thou lookest for his place : he is away !
but sufferers become heirs of the land,
    delight in the rich salvation.

2.

Hard gnasheth the wicked man with his teeth,
    meditating evil to the pious ;
but the Lord laugheth at him,
    certain that His day is coming.
Is the sword of the wicked also sharpened, their bow
                    bent,
    to fell sufferers, helpless ones, to slay those who
                  walk uprightly :
15   but their sword enters their own heart,
    their bows are broken asunder.
Judge better a little for the godly man,
    than the baggage of many wicked ;
for the arm of the wicked is broken,
    but the righteous Jahvé supports.
Known to the Lord are blameless lives,
    and eternal shall their heritage be ;
in misfortune they are not put to shame,
    and are sated in time of hunger.

Light-minded men do disappear, 20
 and Jahvé's foes are like the pomp of the meadows,
  passed away in the smoke, passed away !

3.

Moving about, borrowing, the wicked pay not;
 the godly presents and gives;
for they whom *He* blesses become heirs of the land,
 they whom *He* cùrses, are destroyed.
None but Jahvé places the man's steps securely
 and has pleasure in his way;
if he falls, he is not prostrated,
 for Jahvé takes his hand.
Oh, whether young I was, or old I am : 25
 never saw I the godly forsaken and his seed
                seeking bread;
he makes presents every day and lends,
 and blessed must his seed be.
Plighted to duty avoid thou evil:
 so dwellest thou for ever firm;
for Jahvé loveth right
 and forsakes not His beloved.
Reprobates are overthrown for ever,
 the seed of the wicked is destroyed;
righteous men become heirs of the land
 and dwell ever therein.
Still doth the mouth of the righteous meditate
                wisdom, 30
 and his tongue speaks right;
the instruction of his God is in his heart :
 his steps shall not waver !

4.

The wicked spying out, strives
 and seeks to slay the righteous;
but Jahvé leaves him not in his hand,
 rejects him not, when he is judged.

Unfailing in hope keep Jahvé's way :
  and He will exalt thee, to inherit the land,
    shalt joyfully behold the destruction of the wicked.

35   Verily, I saw the profligate great and fearful,
        spreading himself out like a green shoot :
      but he passed away—and was gone ;
        I sought him—not to be found.
  Well mark the honest, upright man,
      how the man of peace has posterity :
    but evil-doers are together overthrown,
        the posterity of the wicked is destroyed.
  Towards (*Zu*) Jahvé is the strong hope of the godly,
      from Him their victory in time of need ;

40   Jahvé supports, delivers them,
        delivers from the wicked, helps them, because
            they trust in Him.

Ver. 3 *b* plainly from vv. 9, 11, 22, 34, especially vv. 27, 29 sqq.;
Jer. xxv. 5, xxxv. 15 and § 347 *b*.—Ver. 28. Before לְעוֹלָם
the verse must plainly begin with עׄ, so that the first word has
been dropped out. One might suppose עֹשֵׂי טוֹב ; more readily,
according to the LXX, אֱוִלִים, so that then נשמדו, according
to ver. 38, is to be read for נשמרו.--Ver. 35 *b*. The LXX
read quite unsuitably כְּאֶרֶז הַלְּבָנֹן ὡς τὰς κέδρους τοῦ Λιβάνου.—
Observe, in other respects, how artistically this poet composes
his fine song out of more ancient flowers of poetry, especially
a book of Solomonic sayings, the book of Job and older
Psalms, comp. ver. 1 with Prov. xxiv. 19; ver. 4 with Job
xxvii. 10; ver. 5 with Ps. xxii. 9, 32; ver. 6 with Job xi. 17;
vv. 10, 36 with Job viii. 18; ver. 13 with Ps. ii. 4; ver. 18
with Prov. xii. 10; ver. 23 with Prov. xx. 24; ver. 34 with Ps.
xci. 8, &c. אחרית, ver. 37, perhaps taken somewhat more
sensuously than Prov. xxiii. 18, xxiv. 14, 20. Yet this
dependence of the poet on such patterns proves nothing
against his age as determined above, as it is seen in other
writers of the same period as in Jéremjá.

And finally the Messianic hope, which had long become so
mighty and so fixed, remains unaltered in those times as

60. PSALM LXXII.

shows. For this song was without question composed on the
occasion of the accession of a new ruler: for the king's son
(ver. 1) had,—this much is clear from the song—performed as
yet no deeds of his own, and all that is said of him is wish
and anticipation. If now the appearance of any new ruler
afresh and mightily awakens the eternal hope, so peculiarly
that of a young ruler, who gives much promise; and a poet
here seizes on such an occasion, in the finest manner, the hopes
which the time caused to germinate. About those times into
which this song introduces us, the Messianic hopes had long
been kindled: they were according to their nature necessarily
immature until they were finally fulfilled; and if they were
hitherto unfulfilled in any king of David's house, they might
arise afresh with every new one, especially if he were young
and uncorrupted; for they went far beyond the individuals
with whom they might possibly be connected. In this spirit
then the poet here sees in the first instance that all salvation
must come by means of inward improvement and strength, and
righteousness in highest purity, and with full decisive force
must proceed from the king, in order to guard the people from
corruption and vanity of mind. In this sense he further
sees that if in this way true insight, strength, and power
are diffused from within, at first in a narrow space, rule and
power may then readily of themselves pass into the external
sphere, not by means of the subjugating sword, but through
pure spiritual ascendency; strangers streaming in astonishment to that quarter where they see extraordinary prosperity
prevailing, and allowing themselves to be taught and directed
by *the* king whose distinction is true insight and practical
goodness, vv. 8-15. And thus, on the concurrence of this
inner and outer salvation, the highest conceivable prosperity

may arise on earth, and the earth itself, as if made young and new again, may bear the fruit of the purest weal for men who no longer pollute it, vv. 16, 17. (For the poetry gives the experience that the rudeness of the earth of human formation gives way, again anticipating only that which is higher and more spiritual.) But the higher this portion of the hopes of the poet is, the more clearly does he see that the fulfilment of such great things lies beyond the power of a common man, and even of a king. Therefore all his hopes take the form of a wish to God, with the prayer that he will thus strengthen the king. The whole song is directed not immediately to the king, but to God as, moreover, doubtless the poet cannot be understood to speak on the question whether what he anticipates is fulfilled at once and in the person of the same king who offered him the occasion for the song; for he speaks,—even where he discourses on the suggestion of individual men,—not so much of those, as of eternal thoughts or hopes. Here peculiarly predominates the pure and lofty Messianic hope, and this has its eternal strength. But how much of this, and when it is to be fulfilled in history, is quite another question.

But the poet has certainly not expressed the substance of such hopes for the first time : the way is already plainly smooth for him, and long before him great prophets had discoursed in a similar strain, after their manner. The Davidic kingdom was at that time greatly lessened, impoverished, and decayed ; the world-dominion was lost, and was to be regained after another fashion. And this leads to the inference that the king cannot be Salomo,* but a later successor of David, perhaps Josia, or if possible, one still later. For the language and much of presentation is also too light and fugitive for an older poet, it is too artificially polished and elaborated, and frequently it only further develops older thoughts and pictures or merely

---

* The short observation in the superscription of this song, " Salômo's," can only express a later conjecture ; but perhaps the last collector found this song in a collection of Salomonic songs in the sense explained in Vol. I., p 236.

repeats them. The poet of Ps. lxxxix. has, meantime, already read this song and partly imitated it; and that the king was a king of Israel and successor of David's may be gathered from the fact that it is here hoped his kingdom will extend from the people Israel (עַמְּךָ), vv. 1-7, over the whole circuit of the ancient Davidic kingdom, yea, if possible over the heathen peoples, vv. 8-15. *Who* the king was can now be stated with as little positiveness as the name of the poet; but nothing would be more perverse than were we to think of a foreign (heathen) king, on the ground that the song belongs thoroughly to later times. On the contrary, the picture of the boundaries to be desired, vv. 8, 9, and not merely so, but also every other sign in the song points to a Davidic king; and that Israel had not to learn the prayer on behalf of the king, ver. 15, for the first time (as would be erroneously inferred from Jer. xxix. 7; Ez. vi. 10) from foreigners, is partly understood of itself, and partly it may be proved from Pss. lxi. 7; lxiii. 12; Lam. iv. 20.

The structure of the strophés here manifestly proceeds by four verses and nine members, whilst the last concludes more abruptly with seven members. But the two first times two of those strophés are plainly blended into one larger strophé; but before ver. 5, according to all indications, a two-membered verse has been lost.

1.

God! give Thy judgments to the king,   1
   Thy righteousness to the king's son,
in equity to judge Thy people
   and Thy poor according to the right;
that mountains may bring welfare to the people
   and hills by righteousness!
Suffering folk let Him judge,
   let Him help poor children of men,
     break in pieces oppressors!

* * * *

* * * *

5 That men may fear Thee so long as the sun stands,
  in the sight of the moon, eternal times!
Like rain let it trickle on the shorn pastures,
  like showers of rain, the satiation of the earth;
let the righteous man flourish in His days,
  be there much of welfare, till the moon is no more.

2.

And let Him rule from sea to sea,
  and from the stream to the earth's ends;
The Adversaries shall bow before Him,
  and His enemies lick dust;
10 kings of Tarschisch and the Isles offer presents,
  Schebá's and Saba's kings present thanks,
and all the kings do Him homage,
  the peoples all serve Him!
Because He delivers the suppliant and helpless,
  the sufferer, who is without saviour,
spares the needy and poor,
  and saves the souls of the helpless,
—from oppression and severity He relieves their soul,
  and precious appears to Him their blood—
15 that reviving he may give him of the gold of Schebá,
  and for him pray unceasingly,
daily bless Him!

3.

Be there superfluity of corn in the land on the mountain
           tops!
  Its fruit o'ertop like the Lebanon,
  and the people of the city blossom like herb of the earth!
let His name be for ever,
  so long as the sun stands, may His name increase;

and may they bless themselves through Him—
all peoples happily praise Him !

According to the language, all is here the expression of
wishes; each strophé begins with the jussive, and it cannot be
once said in the progress of it that the jussive is resolved into
the more tranquil description of an anticipated and desired
future, as would be possible according to § 350 a.   On יָדִין,
ver. 2, and יוֹשִׁיעַ, ver. 4, comp. § 224 b.

1. Ver. 3. Comp. lxxxv. 12 ; Zach. vi. 12 ; נָשָׂא rare in this
sense for עָשָׂה, according to another figure, Ez. xvii. 18.—But
correctly as the poet makes righteousness his starting point as
the first and last thing to be expected from royal government,
and the foundation of all other welfare, as touched upon, ver. 3,
correctly as he brings out the truth that they chiefly to whom
good must come are the most depressed in the kingdom and
the most dependent on others ; it is nevertheless unmistakable
that the connexion of the language according to the present
arrangement of words is entirely broken off after ver. 4.   For
the close of the great strophé, ver. 7, corresponds,—in desig-
nating prosperity as the last fruit of righteousness,—plainly
enough to the close of the first half, vv. 3, 4 ; the requirement
of the fear of God, in ver. 5, appears however here so entirely
detached, that the second half cannot possibly begin with it.
Equally obscure is it to what the figure of the rain which
freshly revives the shorn pastures, and lifts them up, ver. 6, is
intended to refer.   On these grounds we infer with certainty,
quite apart from the broken structure of the strophés, that a
two-membered verse must have fallen out before ver. 5 ; and
little as we presume to be able entirely to restore it with the
words of the poet, we may nevertheless, according to all indications, justly suppose that it ran somewhat as follows :

> God ! strengthen with Thy right the king,
>   and arm him with Thy salvation,
>   that men may fear Thee, etc.

22

For the view that in ver. 5 the king is addressed, most roughly mars not only the whole connexion and the tenor of the song, but also the life of the old true religion. It is however perfectly true that the fear of God in general in the life of a people is purified and increased the more plainly that all men see that the righteousness demanded by God is no vain and fruitless thing, and conversely, doubt and denial of God are increased if the people see unrighteousness too long prevailing, as is expressed so strongly especially in Ps. lxxiii. In this way the clear ground-word to ver. 6 appears, namely, *the Divine right and salvation,* if it was named again before ver. 5 on the new beginning of the address; and the figure of the richly refreshing rain is there similar to the passage in 2 Sam. xxiii. 4, in the like connexion.—To describe eternity by comparison with the unchangeably shining heavenly bodies, ever returning in their path, as our poet loves to do, is in the Old Testament very rare (though lying so near at hand), and is only found further in lxxxix. 30, 37, 38, from imitation of this Ps., comp. *Anquetil Zend Av. T. I.,* pp. clxxvi. sq. Only such passages as Job xiv. 12; Deut. xi. 21, form the transition to this. These modes of expression are in fact too greatly borrowed from astrology to admit of their having been earlier favoured in the people of Israel. For other particulars, comp. above, pp. 112, 167.

2. Ver. 8. From the South-east or the Arabian Sea to the North-west on the Great Sea, and again from the North-east or the Euphrates to the South-west, where Canaan ends in deserts without fixed boundaries, Canaan therefore in its widest extent, as David and Solomon had scarcely ruled it in its entirety, Exod. xxiii. 31, Gen. xv. 18; in the first instance from Zach. ix. 10. From the lands without the Davidic territory, ver. 10, homages are only expected of the same kind and for the same services as in Isa. xviii., lx., ii. 2-4; but that also the most bitter *enemies,* even the *adversaries* (*unholde*)—on צִיִּים, comp. § 146 *f.* note—*i.e.,* the most savage men, must

finally come to recognize him, is here, as above, Ps. lxxvi.
11-13, the main matter ; and the phrase *lick dust* signifies also,
according to Mikha vii. 17, in these later times nothing but to
lie on the ground.—But now, as in the second half, vv. 12-15,
only righteousness is named as the reason impelling strangers
to such acts of homage—whose magic power, once become
great, will extend itself even over the nearest bounds of the
kingdom—the language recurs to its first starting-point, so
that it then in a. short after-word, vv. 16, 17, may the more
suddenly come quite to an end. Ver. 12, וְאֵין is a static proposition to describe the עָנִי, § 341 *a*; the whole verse almost
literally from Job. xxix. 12. After ver. 14 has been interjected,
in order to depict the greatness of the love and activity of
this king, in ver. 15 comes the completion of vv. 12, 13 and
the true close of the whole conception ; the *sing.* also recurs
for that reason as at the beginning, vv. 12, 13. On וִיהִי,
comp. § 347 *a*. Similar large connexion of sentences, xlix.
8-10, which passage is present to the mind of this poet.

3. Ver. 16. Even to the tops of the mountains may the
land produce the richest fruits, and the fruit of the bulky thick
corn on all mountains be moved and rustle in the wind (beautiful to behold and hear) as now takes place only in the fruitful
parts of the Libanon (Hos. xiv. 7). פס be dispersed,
divided, hence partly spread out, as here the substantive, and
partly pass away, take away, as the verb, xii. 2. In this sense
only the luxuriance of the growth of the corn, and of the
people would be here finally alluded to ; but the image in the
second member would be of little significance. Since the language at the end manifestly comprises further in all brevity the
most important matter, the intermediate member is better thus
understood : (רָעַשׁ from רָאַשׁ) *like to the Libanon his*, the king's
fruit, his posterity, as Ps. xxi. 11. In such unusual figures
this song is rich. The *city* is Jerusalem, just as in the
passages adduced above, p. 252.

WILLIAMS AND NORGATE'S PUBLICATIONS.

Works already published in the THEOLOGICAL TRANSLATION FUND
LIBRARY.

Baur (F. C.).—Church History of the First Three Centuries.
Translated from the Third German Edition. Edited by the Rev. ALLAN
MENZIES 2 vols. 8vo. cloth, 21s.

Baur (F. C.).—Paul, the Apostle of Jesus Christ: his Life and Work,
his Epistles and Doctrine. A Contribution to a Critical History of Primitive
Christianity. Translated from the Second Edition, edited by Dr. E. ZETLER,
by Rev. A. MENZIES. 2 vols. 8vo. cloth, 21s.

Hausrath.—History of the New Testament Times.—The Time of
Jesus. By Dr. A. HAUSRATH, Professor of Theology, Heidelberg. Translated,
with the Author's sanction, from the Third German Edition, by the Rev.
C. T. POYNTING and the Rev. P. QUENZER. 2 vols. 8vo. cloth, 21s.

Zeller, (Dr. E.).—The Contents and Origin of the Acts of the
Apostles Critically Investigated. Preceded by Dr. FR. OVERBECK'S
Introduction to the Acts of the Apostles from De Wette's Handbook.
Translated by JOSEPH DARE. 2 vols. 8vo. 21s.

Pfleiderer.—Paulinism: A Contribution to the History of Primitive
Christian Theology. By Prof. O. PFLEIDERER, of Jena. Translated by
E. PETERS. 2 vols. 8vo. cloth 21s.

Keim's History of Jesus of Nazara, Considered in its Connection
with the National Life of Israel, and related in detail. Translated by
A. RANSOM. Vols. I. to IV. 8vo. cloth, 10s 6d each.

Ewald's Commentary on the Prophets of the Old Testament.
Translated by the Rev. J. FREDERICK SMITH. Vols. I. to IV. 8vo. cloth,
10s 6d each.

Kuenen (Dr. A.).—The Religion of Israel to the Fall of the Jewish
State. By Dr. A. KUENEN, Professor of Theology at the University,
Leyden. Translated from the Dutch by A. H. MAY. 3 vols. 8vo. price
31s 6d.

Bleek's Lectures on the Apocalypse. Edited by the Rev. Dr. S.
DAVIDSON. 8vo. cloth, 10s 6d.

Ewald's Commentary on the Poetical Books of the Old Testament.
Part I. The Psalms, translated by the Rev. E. JOHNSON, M.A. (in 2 vols.)
Vol. I. 8vo. cloth, 10s 6d.

> Subscribers to the Theological Translation Fund Library receive these
> works for 7s, instead of 10s 6d per volume.

Shortly :

A Short Protestant Commentary on the New Testament; including
Introductions to the Books, by Lipsius, Holsten, Lang, Pfleiderer, Holtzmann,
Hilgenfeld, and others. Translated by the Rev. F. H. JONES, of Oldham.

G. NORMAN AND SON, PRINTERS, 29, MAIDEN LANE, COVENT GARDEN, LONDON.

Lightning Source UK Ltd.
Milton Keynes UK
UKHW011021271218
334506UK00012B/861/P

HARDPRESS.NET
HOME OF HARD-TO-FIND BOOKS

North Atlantic Coast Fisheries Tribunal of Arbitration
by Permanent Court of Arbitration